Scenic *Driving*

OREGON

By
Tom Barr

FALCON®
Falcon® Publishing, Inc.
Helena, Montana

A FALCON GUIDE

Falcon® is continually expanding its list of recreational guidebooks. All books include detailed descriptions, accurate maps, and all information necessary for enjoyable trips. You can order extra copies of this book and get information and prices for other Falcon® guidebooks by writing Falcon®, P.O. Box 1718, Helena, MT 59624 or calling toll-free 1-800-582-2665. Also, please ask for a free copy of our current catalog.

©1993 by Falcon® Publishing, Inc.
Helena, Montana
10 9 8 7 6 5

Printed in the United States of America

Front cover photo: Highway 101 Crook Point, Pistol River State Park by Greg Vaughan.
Back cover photo: St. John's Bridge over the Willamette River, by Larry Geddis.
All other black-and-white photos by author. Inside color photos by Larry Geddis.

Library of Congress Cataloging-in-Publication Data

Barr, Tom.
   Scenic driving Oregon / by Tom Barr.
     p. cm.
   Rev. ed. of: Oregon scenic drives. c1993
   "A Falcon guide."
   ISBN 1-56044-440-1 (pbk.)
   1. Oregon—Tours.   2. Automobile travel—Oregon—Guidebooks.
I. Barr, Tom. Oregon scenic drives. II. Title.
F874.3B37 1996
917.9504'43—dc20   96-33019
                                                            CIP

♻ Text pages printed on recycled paper

CAUTION

Outdoor recreation activities are by their very nature potentially hazardous. All participants in such activities must assume the responsibility for their own actions and safety. The information contained in this guidebook cannot replace sound judgment and good decision–making skills, which help reduce risk exposure, nor does the scope of this book allow for disclosure of all the potential hazards and risks involved in such activities.

Learn as much as possible about the outdoor recreation activities you participate in, prepare for the unexpected, and be safe and cautious. The reward will be a safer and more enjoyable experience.

The Hood River meanders through this section of the Hood River Valley, with Mount Hood, Oregon's highest mountain, in the background.—Oregon Department of Transportation photo

ACKNOWLEDGMENTS

Scenic Driving Oregon is not the work of a single person but of many. Without them the book would never have been written.

First and foremost are the people at Falcon Press who saw the need for interpreting Oregon's beauty and making it accessible to everyone with a family car. My thanks to assistant publisher Chris Cauble for giving me the opportunity to travel Oregon, write, and photograph its many splendors. Guidebook editors Malcolm Bates and Randall Green have my sincere appreciation for guiding the project through the production process and adding their professionalism to my manuscript.

My thanks as well to the staffs of Oregon's many chambers of commerce, visitor information centers, and regional tourism offices who shared their scenic drives with me, answered my many questions, and were always prompt in providing additional information. I found the same ready assistance from State and National Park Service, U.S. Forest Service, and Bureau of Land Management personnel.

Finally, this project would not have been possible without the support and encouragement of friends and family. Bill Palmroth, my lifelong friend, has always been there where I needed him whether its with a bed for the night as I moved from place to place, or by providing information on scenic drives, forests, and wildlife.

My wife Carole has always believed in me, even when I've lost faith in myself. She was rewarded with the tedious task of proofing my manuscript, checking spelling, names, and addresses. She has also given me David and Vicky, who added their support and understanding. This book is for all of you.

CONTENTS

Bridge over the Crooked River Gorge, seen on Drive 31, the Madras-Prineville Loop.

MAP LEGEND

Scenic Drive (paved)	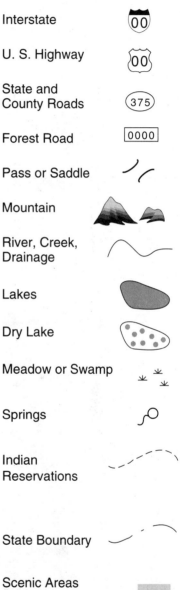	Interstate	
Scenic Drive (gravel)		U. S. Highway	
Interstate		State and County Roads	
Paved Roads			
Unpaved Roads		Forest Road	
Points of Interest		Pass or Saddle	
Hiking Trail		Mountain	
Overlook		River, Creek, Drainage	
Mine			
Ski Area		Lakes	
Wayside		Dry Lake	
Building		Meadow or Swamp	
Campground			
State Park		Springs	

Byway Location

OREGON

Indian Reservations

State Boundary

Scale of Miles

0   5   10   15

MILES

Scenic Areas Recreation Areas, National Monuments

LOCATOR MAP

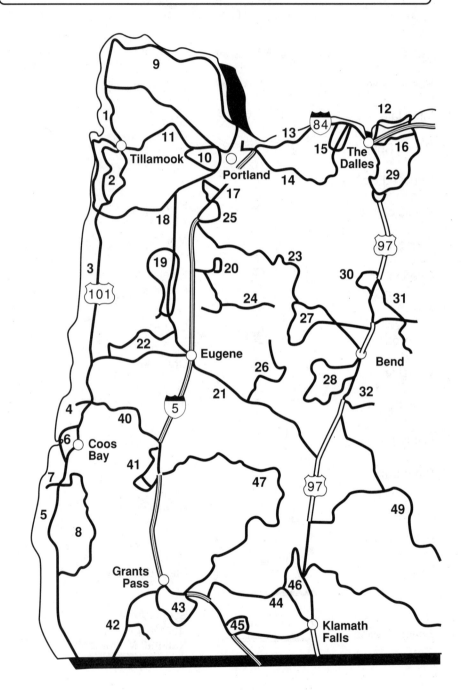

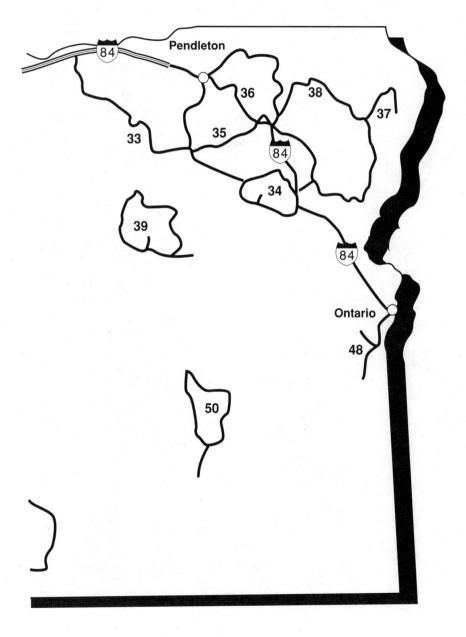

Salt Creek Falls, Drive 21, Eugene-Willamette Pass

INTRODUCTION

On travel posters, Oregon is often depicted as an isolated image of towering mountains surrounded by lush forests and rushing streams. That is but one image, for in Oregon you will find a coastline with some of the earth's most spectacular scenery, the magnificent Columbia River Gorge, deserts filled with sagebrush, unspoiled wilderness, fertile farmlands, vineyards, and orchards.

This is land created by uplifting and volcanism, sculptured by ice, and refined by water and wind. The Cascade Mountains extend north to south, forming a giant natural wall that divides the state and dictates its climate by trapping moisture-laden clouds from the Pacific Ocean. West of the mountains lie verdant valleys, lush forests, and rich farmlands.

East of the Cascades, the landscape turns to high desert, scattered forests of Ponderosa pine, grasslands and cattle ranches, and deep canyons. The Blue Mountains stand isolated and soar into the sky from flat plains. In the northeast corner, the Wallowa Mountains contain some of the state's most magnificent scenery and are often compared to the Swiss Alps.

In Oregon, nature has created a diverse landscape and climate ranging from rain forests to arid desert. Nature's violence has moved and uplifted mountain ranges, cut deep gorges, created Fort Rock, Crater Lake and Newberry Crater, and left as reminders of its awesome power unusual geologic formations like Hole-In-The-Ground, Crack-In-The-Ground, Abert Rim and Winter Ridge.

Criss-crossing the land are rivers celebrated in history and legend. The Columbia, which forms the northern border, was the river of exploration. Oregon Trail immigrants farmed the rich lands along the Willamette, and made it the river of settlement. Others, such as the Snake, Rogue, Umpqua, and Deschutes have acquired reputations for their breathtaking scenery, fishing, and white water rafting.

The land and water provide habitats for a vast array of wildlife. Forests and mountains are home to deer, elk, bear, cougar, and raccoons. Beaver and otter inhabit river banks, and along marshes and seashore you'll see thousands of ducks and geese, plus great blue herons, several species of cranes, woodpeckers, and bald and golden eagles.

Forests of Douglas-fir, ponderosa and lodgepole pine blanket mountain ranges and tower over oaks, alders, vine, and big leaf maples. Myrtlewoods stand in clusters near the coastline. In the Columbia River Gorge, the Kalmiopsis Wilderness, and Southern Oregon's Table Rocks, you will find plants that grow only in these protected spots.

Land and water have attracted people to Oregon since the dawn of man. The first inhabitants crossed the Bering Land Bridge, traveled down the Pacific shoreline to the Oregon beaches where they subsisted on the bounty of land and ocean. Centuries later the shoreline was explored by Sir Francis Drake, Captain James Cook, and other seafarers. Lewis and Clark, trappers,

1

From Sea Lion Caves on the Central Oregon Coast, Drive 3, you have an outstanding view of Heceta Head Lighthouse.

and mountain men followed the Columbia River to the sea. In the 1840s, pioneers by the thousands endured the hardships of the Oregon Trail to claim the rich lands of the Willamette Valley. They were followed by miners, merchants, ranchers, and timber men. Their legacy lives on in tales of lost gold mines and lost wagon trains, in sprawling ranches, historic districts, towns, and cities.

Scenic Driving Oregon invites you to explore Oregon's magnificent scenery and to discover its history. The fifty drives take you from the rock-bound coast to the high desert, into the Columbia River Gorge, through rugged canyons, and to secluded mountain lakes.

They cover the Oregon Coast from the Washington to California borders and include several short drives to exceptionally scenic bays, harbors, and state parks. You can discover the Columbia River Gorge on a historic highway that is considered an engineering masterpiece, travel by several waterfalls, or see views from the gorge's rim as you follow a segment of the Oregon Trail.

Several drives cross portions of the Oregon Trail. With *Scenic Driving Oregon* as your guide, you can follow the trail from the eastern border to its terminus at Oregon City, see the original ruts along Interstate 84 and stay in campgrounds where wagon trains camped.

Other drives take you to gold rush towns, museums, and historic sites. You can also select drives into the high Cascades, through lava beds, around mountain peaks, by wildlife refuges, and into national forests, parks, and monuments. En route you'll find roadside waterfalls, cascading streams, scenic overlooks, botanical gardens, mountain lakes, and desert reservoirs.

Along these drives you'll find attractions for children, outstanding camp-grounds, fishing streams, spots for board sailing, hand gliding, and whale watching. With *Scenic Driving Oregon*, you can take a romantic stroll on a black sand beach by a chalky white cliff, or watch blazing sunsets and winter storms in the shadow of an historic lighthouse. Other drives will guide you to trailheads leading into the Three Sisters Wilderness, to the rim of Crater Lake, inside Newberry Crater, and to the beautiful headwaters of the Metolius River. If you're adventurous, you can take a jet boat ride through the Wild and Scenic Rogue River, or a cliff-hugging dirt road into the heart of Hell's Canyon to the rim of the deepest gorge in the continental United States.

Most of these drives were created by local chambers of commerce and regional tourism divisions. With three exceptions, all are paved: The Bandon-Powers-Gold Beach Loop and the Oregon Trail Route through the Columbia River Gorge each contain approximately ten miles of gravel and are normally passable with a family car; the twenty-four miles from Imnaha to Hat Point is often rough and should not be attempted with a low clearance vehicle. Since unpaved surfaces change with the season, and some paved roads are closed in winter, check road conditions before you depart for these areas.

While *Scenic Driving Oregon* provides a comprehensive introduction to the state's scenery, it is by no means all-inclusive. To cover all of Oregon's scenic roads would fill another book, and require a four-wheel drive or heavy duty vehicle since many mountain and desert roads are rough and unpaved.

The drives that are included here range from 3 to 270 miles in length. Some are perfect for an afternoon getaway or a weekend side trip. Or you may wish to include several as part of an extended vacation. Regardless of which drives you select, you'll find them a rewarding experience.

HOW TO USE THIS BOOK

Scenic Driving Oregon describes fifty highways and backroads throughout the state. Each drive description is complemented with a map, photos, and additional informative text.

Each map shows the route, campgrounds, special features such as historic sites, recreation areas, connecting roads, and nearby towns.

Each written description is divided into ten categories. Most are self-explanatory, but the following information may help you get the most from each description:

General description provides a quick summary of the length, location, and scenic features of the drive.

Special attractions are prominent, interesting activities and features found along the route. Additional attractions are included in the description. Some activities, such as fishing and hunting, require permits or licenses that must be obtained locally.

Location gives the area of the state in which the drive is located.

Drive route names and numbers includes the specific highway names and numbers on which the drive travels.

Travel season notes if the specific route is open all year or closed seasonally. Some highways are closed to automobiles in winter due to snow but are open for snowshoeing, cross-country skiing, and snowmobiling. Opening and closing dates are approximate and subject to regional weather variations. Always check local conditions.

Camping includes listings of all state park, state forest, national forest, national park, and Bureau of Land Management campgrounds along the route.

Services lists communities with at least a restaurant, groceries, lodging, phone, and gasoline.

Nearby attractions are major attractions or activities found within fifty miles of the scenic drive.

For more information lists names, addresses, and telephone numbers of chambers of commerce, national forest and park service and other organizations that provide detailed information on the drive and its attractions.

The drive provides detailed traveler information, along with interesting regional history, geology, and natural history. Attractions are presented in the order a traveler encounters them when driving the route in the described direction. If you travel the route from the opposite direction, simply refer to the end of the drive descriptions first.

Haystack Rock at Cannon Beach is a refuge for wildlife and one of the most photographed sites on the northern Oregon coast, Drive 1.

1 NORTHERN OREGON COAST

General description: A 110-mile drive on a paved highway along the northern Oregon Coast through resorts, picturesque oceanside communities, and forests.

Special attractions: Historic sites, spectacular scenery, outstanding seafood, Seaside, Cannon Beach, Haystack Rock, fifteen state parks and waysides, lighthouses, whale and storm watching in season, camping, and fishing.

Location: Oregon Coast from Astoria to Lincoln City.

Highway: U.S. Highway 101.

Travel season: All year. Frost and snow are rare. Winter mornings bring heavy fog.

Camping: Five state park campgrounds. Three Forest Service campgrounds, plus numerous private RV parks.

Services: Full services are available at major cities along the route.

Nearby attractions: Washington's Long Beach Peninsula, Lower Columbia River, Lewis and Clark National Wildlife Refuge, Camp 18 Logging Museum.

For more information: Astoria/Warrenton Chamber of Commerce, 111 W. Marine Dr., P.O. Box 176, Astoria, OR 97103, (503) 325-6311, (800) 535-3637; Seaside Chamber of Commerce/Visitors Bureau, 7 N. Roosevelt, P.O. Box 7, Seaside, OR 97138, (503) 738-6391, (800) 444-6740 (USA); Cannon Beach Chamber of Commerce, 2nd and Spruce, P.O. Box 64, Cannon Beach, OR 97110, (503) 436-2623; Nehalem Bay Area Chamber of Commerce, 8th and Tohl St., Box 159, Nehalem, OR 97131, (503) 368-5100; Rockaway Beach Chamber of Commerce, 103 South 1st St., P.O. Box 198, Rockaway Beach, OR 97136, (503) 355-8108, (800) 331-5928 (USA); Tillamook Chamber of Commerce, 3705 Highway 101 N., Tillamook, OR 97141, (503) 842-7525; Lincoln City Visitors and Convention Bureau, 801 S.W. Highway 101, No. 1, Lincoln City, OR 97367, (541) 994-8378, (800) 452-2151 (USA).

The drive: On the northern Oregon coast, U.S. Highway 101 starts as a joint highway with U.S. Highway 26 in downtown Astoria at the Megler-Astoria Bridge. Continuing south, it is framed by forest on the east while offering intermittent views of coastline and small communities on the west. South of Seaside the highways divide as U.S. Highway 26 extends east to Portland. U.S. Highway 101 continues south, skirts Tillamook Head, weaves by Arch Cape and Cape Falcon, and curves along the shores of Nehalem and Tillamook Bays. After turning inland for twenty-four miles, it returns to the coast near Neskowin, then travels through forest on the final few miles to Lincoln City.

Allow more time than you think you'll need; leisurely travel is virtually a necessity. The scenery is spectacular. Traffic is usually heavy, even on weekdays, and the narrow, two-lane road has an abundance of curves.

Travelers will find mild temperatures throughout the year. Summer days

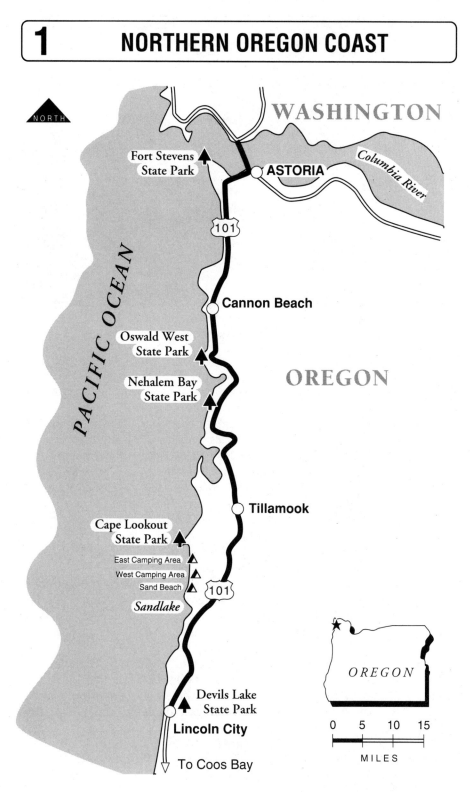

U.S. Highway 101 hugs the cliff sides of the northern coast's Cape Falcon, offering panoramic views of the Pacific Ocean coastline.

are usually in the sixty-to-seventy-degree range. While winter days also reach into the sixties, sun is limited. December and January bring heavy rains and foggy mornings. The calmest weather usually comes in autumn.

Astoria is the oldest American settlement west of the Rocky Mountains. Established in 1811 by John Jacob Astor as a fur trading post, it has evolved into a bustling seaport of 10,000 people. At Coxcomb Hill overlooking the city, coast, Columbia River, and mountains—the area's history—spirals around 128-foot-high Astoria Column. You can see dozens of Victorian homes on residential drives and step into an 1890s parlor at the restored Flavel House, built by a sea captain and converted into a museum. The Columbia Maritime Museum, six blocks east of the bridge on U.S. Highway 30, interprets a rich seafaring history with ship models, fishing equipment, a submarine conning tower, and historic photos.

Although the coast appears ageless, the section between the Columbia River and Tillamook Head is an infant in terms of geologic time. Astoria's mud and sandstone base was deposited about twenty million years ago. Sand dunes extended to near Tillamook head until the 1930s when European bunch grass and shrubs were planted to halt their progress.

Crossing Young's Bay, three miles south of town, U.S. Highway 101 intersects roads leading west to Warrenton and Fort Stevens State Park, and east to Fort Clatsop National Memorial. Warrenton is a center for deep-sea fishing and charter boats and also has moorage and other facilities for private crafts.

Fort Stevens dates to the Civil War. It was the only fortification in the Continental United States fired on by the Japanese in World War II. The spot where the shells landed is marked near the access road. Restored Civil War earthworks, original World War II gun batteries, a memorial rose garden, and museum can be toured. Near the shoreline parking area and campground, surf washes against the rusting ribs of the Peter Iredale—Oregon's most visible ship wreck. From the campground, with its 213 full hook-ups, 130 electrical, and 262 tent sites, you can explore the beach, hike to a small lake, and fish the surf.

At Fort Clatsop, children enjoy exploring a replica of the log fort that served as the 1805-06 winter quarters for Lewis and Clark's Corps of Discovery. A marked nature trail leads through a rain forest to a landing on the Lewis and Clark River where several replicas of Indian canoes are displayed.

Seaside, at mile 17, has been a popular resort for more than 100 years. You can learn about Pacific Ocean sea life at an aquarium and see a replica of the salt cairn where Lewis and Clark's expedition boiled sea water to make salt.

Ecola State Park, four miles south, marks the southernmost point explored by Lewis and Clark. There is a good chance of seeing deer roaming the grounds, and sea lions and birds on off-shore rookeries. The scenery can be enjoyed from six miles of sandy beaches surrounded by steep cliffs and offshore rocks, and on trails through a forest and atop Tillamook Head. A hike-in camp is situated on Indian Creek.

As you approach Cannon Beach, watch for a replica of a ship's cannon west of the highway. From the roadside, you'll also see Haystack Rock rising from the shore as a black bullet-shaped dome. At 235 feet, it is the world's third largest free-standing monolith, a protected bird sanctuary, and among the coast's most photographed sites. The beach connecting the rock to the south part of town is often filled with kite flyers, sunbathers, beach tricycles and sand castle builders.

During the next thirty miles, U.S. Highway 101 passes nine parks and waysides, crosses four rivers, and meanders through five beach-front towns. You can view the spectacular rocks, headlands, and open beaches from atop roadside viewpoints or at park shorelines. Depending on the site, you can explore sea caves, search for agates, stroll a secluded beach, hike into forested mountains, launch your boat, or ride a horse. Fishermen have a choice of casting into surf or stream from a jetty, beach, or boat. The rewards are usually superb catches of Silver and Chinook salmon, cutthroat trout, and steelhead. At low tide, you also can gather clams and catch crabs. Several roadside villages feature an abundance of antique and craft shops, galleries, and restaurants.

Oswald West State Park, four miles south of Cannon Beach, features thirty-six primitive campsites set in a rain forest of massive spruce and cedar trees. In the park you can hike a segment of the Oregon Coast Trail and take a short walk to the tip of Cape Falcon.

Continuing south, a series of jagged mountain peaks dominate the eastern horizon. Many are former volcanoes that erupted under the ocean. The most prominent, Neahkahnie Mountain, erupted about 20,000 years ago and may have been an offshore island.

At Nehalem, the route jogs inland around the secluded bay. Nehalem Bay State Park, on the south shore, caters to horsemen and bikers with equestrian trails, camps and corrals; a 1.5-mile bike trail, and a sixty-site hiker/biker camp. Along with 291 electrical hook-up sites there is a meeting hall and a fly-in camp.

Rockaway Beach, five miles south, stretches along the highway in a string of weathered, but well maintained hotels. It is a popular weekend retreat for those who wish to kick back and look out at vast expanses of waist-high beach grass, sandy shorelines, and arched offshore rocks.

From Garibaldi, five miles south, the route skirts the eastern shore of Tillamook Bay and touches the western tip of the Tillamook State Forest. A huge cement smokestack serves as sole reminder of Garibaldi's past as a bustling mill town.

Cheese has made Tillamook world famous. The factory on U.S. Highway 101, features historical exhibits, gift shop, and cafe. A full-scale replica of the commercial sailing ship Morning Star—the first chartered vessel in the Oregon Territory—is displayed at the chamber of commerce. The chamber shares the factory parking lot and has detailed information on local sightseeing, camping, and outdoor recreation. Downtown, the Pioneer Museum, housed in a former courthouse, is known for its natural history displays.

At Tillamook, you have a choice of either staying on U.S. Highway 101, which jogs inland for twenty-four miles before continuing along the ocean at Pacific City, or enjoying the magnificent scenery of the thirty-eight-mile Three Capes Scenic Loop through Capes Meares, Lookout, and Kiwanda. One state park campground with fifty-three hookups and 197 tent sites and three forest service campgrounds featuring 141 sites are situated along the loop.

On U.S. Highway 101, you'll pass two blimp hangers built during World War II. At 1,038 feet wide and 190 feet high, they are the world's largest wooden structures. This section also provides access to Trask River salmon, steelhead, and trout fishing. Two short trails take you from the roadside to 266-foot-high Munson Falls, the highest falls in the Coast Range.

A paved forest service road near the community of Hebo winds up the forested slopes and past a scenic lake to the summit of 3,154-foot Mount Hebo. The area offers outstanding views of forest and ocean, plus hiking, fishing, and nature study of rare silver spot butterflies and wild flowers. You can also camp in sixteen forest service sites in Hebo Lake Campground, which has toilets and drinking water.

From Pacific City, U.S. Highway 101 crosses the small inlet of Nestucca Bay then opens onto vistas of serene beaches and headlands as it continues through the family resort area of Neskowin. Near Neskowin you enter the western edge of the Siuslaw National Forest. Short roads branch from the highway to Cascade Summit, Nature Conservancy, and Harts Cove Trail.

Cascade Head Experimental Forest, one mile south of Neskowin, is situated in a scenic rain forest. At 1,770 feet, Cascade Head is the coast's highest headland. More than 230 birds and fifty-six species of mammals have been sighted in the ten square miles of Sitka spruce and cliff-top meadow.

10

North of Lincoln City, U.S. Highway 101 intersects Highway 18, which crosses the Coast Range to McMinnville, Newberg, and Salem. A short scenic side trip begins at East Devil's Lake Road, skirts the five-mile-long lake and ends in Lincoln City. Devil's Lake State Park offers fishing, boating, and picnicking. Thirty-two full-hookup camp and sixty-eight tent sites, plus a hiker/biker camp are on a shoreline surrounded by thick pine forest.

Lincoln City sits about a mile south of the 45th Parallel, equal distance between the Equator and the North Pole. Entering town, you'll cross the D River. At less than one mile long, it is the world's shortest river. Easy access to surf fishing, championship kite flying competitions, and a variety of antique, craft and art galleries make Lincoln City a favorite vacation and week-end getaway destination all year.

2 THREE CAPES SCENIC LOOP

General description: A thirty-eight-mile signed drive on a paved highway along bays, wildlife refuges, and three scenic capes.

Special attractions: Historic sites, spectacular coastal scenery, three state parks, Sand Dunes Recreation Area, lighthouses, wildlife, Octopus Tree, Oregon Islands National Wildlife Refuge, Three Arch Rocks National Bird and Sea Lion Refuge, hang gliding, sailboarding, fishing, hiking, camping.

Location: Oregon Coast between Tillamook and Pacific City.

Highway: Three Capes Scenic Loop Highway.

Travel season: All year. Winter storms can cause hazards from falling trees, blinding rain. If the day is foggy, delay your trip for you'll miss the most spectacular scenery.

Camping: One state park campground. Three forest service campgrounds, plus several private RV parks.

Services: Full services at Tillamook. Limited services at Oceanside, Netarts, Sandlake and Pacific City.

Nearby attractions: Munson Creek Falls, Mount Hebo recreation area, Trask River, Oregon North Coast and Central Coast Scenic drives, Depoe Bay, Newport.

For more information: Tillamook Chamber of Commerce, 3705 Highway 101 N., Tillamook, OR 97141, (503) 842-7525; Cape Lookout State Park, 13000 Whiskey Creek Road W., Tillamook, OR 97141, (503) 842-4981.

The drive: The drive starts in downtown Tillamook at the junction of U.S. Highway 101 and 3rd Street. Following Three Capes Scenic Loop signs west, travelers skirt scenic Tillamook Bay and Bayocean Spit, then take Cape Meares Loop Road through a mixed forest to the cape summit. Descending to near sea level at Oceanside the route curves around Netarts Bay and through old-growth forest to Cape Lookout. Taking Cape Lookout Road south through Sandlake's dunes, it passes the entrance to the vari-colored sandstone cliffs of Cape Kiwanda State Park then finishes with ocean views as it passes through Pacific City.

During summer, travelers will enjoy balmy, pleasant days in the sixties and seventies. Although winter days also reach into the sixties, fog and rain often obscure the scenery. Most of the 100 inches of rain the area receives falls between November and March.

The name Tillamook was derived from an Indian word meaning "Land of many waters." Several rivers meander through Tillamook County and empty into the ocean near the city. They offer good clamming, crabbing, fishing, bird watching, hunting, sailboarding, and hang gliding.

Tillamook County Pioneer Museum, on 2nd Street, one block east of U.S. Highway 101 and 3rd Avenue, occupies the former courthouse. It contains one of the state's best exhibits of natural history. Gun collections, Native American artifacts, a stagecoach, pioneer home, antique toys, and a full-sized forest fire lookout station are also displayed.

The cheese that has made the county world famous can be sampled at the Tillamook County Creamery Association factory, two miles north on U.S. Highway 101. The creamery shares a parking lot with the Tillamook Chamber of Commerce and a full-sized replica of the first chartered ship in the Oregon Territory.

Leaving Tillamook, the route passes a marina, RV park, and public boat launch. Staying at water level, the highway winds around oak-covered cliffs and Tillamook Bay where morning haze often evokes serenity as it cloaks land and water in various shades of blue. Low scrub-brush-covered headlands enclose the bay on the north and small islands protect the entrance.

Watch for birds as you turn south on Bayocean Road, for 250 species have been sighted in this area. From 1920 to 1950, Bayocean Spit, which separates Tillamook Bay from the Pacific Ocean, was the site of a resort community. Over the years it was washed into the sea by shifting sands, water, and winds. The spit offers a wide, sandy beach, and a jumble of driftwood washed ashore by tides. It also has a boat launch and good jetty fishing.

After two miles, the route turns inland and begins a short climb through a thick forest to Cape Meares State Park. The park extends from the summit to the shoreline several hundred feet below. It includes 138 acres of old-growth Sitka spruce and western hemlock, sandy beaches, and vertical sea cliffs. The cliffs and forest provide nesting areas for tufted puffins, pelagic cormorants, and pigeon guillemots. The area is protected as Cape Meares National Wildlife Refuge. Both Cape Meares and Cape Lookout are composed of basalt from volcanoes that erupted about fifteen to twenty million years ago.

You may see some of the wildlife on a short section of the Oregon Coast Hiking Trail that cuts through the woods near the parking lot, and along the cliffs edge. It also winds by the Octopus Tree, which is an easy 100-yard walk from the parking area. This giant Sitka spruce was once featured in Ripley's Believe It or Not. The tree has a base circumference of about fifty feet. Six candelabra limbs about twelve feet around extend thirty feet horizontally from the main trunk and then turn upward. The candelabra branching and

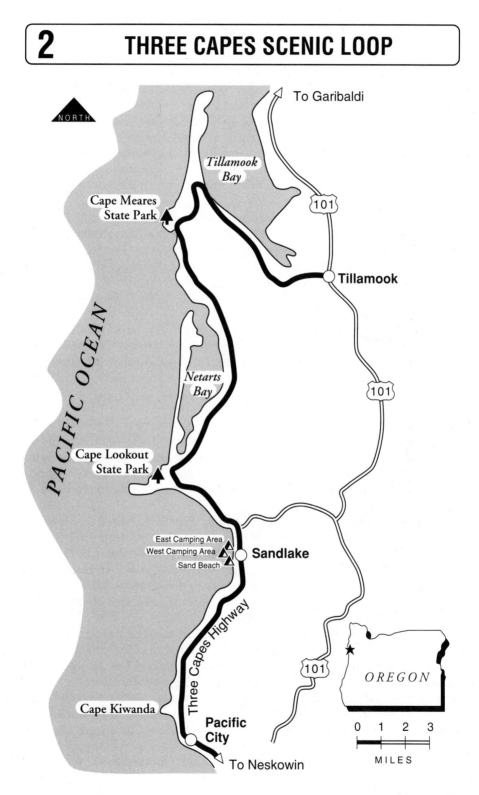

To Garibaldi

Tillamook Bay

NORTH

101

Cape Meares State Park

Tillamook

PACIFIC OCEAN

Netarts Bay

101

Cape Lookout State Park

East Camping Area
West Camping Area
Sand Beach

Sandlake

Three Capes Highway

Cape Kiwanda

Pacific City

To Neskowin

101

OREGON

0 1 2 3

MILES

unusual size were formed by strong coastal winds and abundant rain. Hikes into the cool, moist rain forest are often rewarded with displays of sunlight filtered through fog.

Walk west from the parking lot on a paved path and you'll see the giant lens of Cape Meares Lighthouse seemingly suspended in space. The path extends to the base of the lighthouse on a ledge below. Built in the 1880s, it is inactive but open to visitors from May to September. The one-ton, hand-ground lens was manufactured in Paris, shipped around Cape Horn, and lowered onto the 200-foot cliff with a special hand-operated crane made of local spruce trees. Despite all the planning and preparations, a legend persisted for a number of years that the lighthouse was built on the wrong cliff.

From the lighthouse cliff, you have a spectacular view of the Pacific Ocean below, crashing waves, sheer cliffs, sandy beaches, and the off-shore rocks and reefs of the Oregon Islands National Wildlife Refuge. The refuge is part of a network of 1,400 offshore promontories along 300 miles of the Oregon Coast that provide breeding and resting areas for seabirds and marine mammals. Because the wildlife is easily disturbed, the refuge is closed to public use.

A trail, protected by cyclone fencing, stays within inches of the cliffs edge as it leads east from the lighthouse into the forest along a small lake and down to the shore lined with sea caves that are filled with driftwood. The lake attracts boaters and water skiers. Surf fishermen, sailboarders, picnickers, and agate hunters congregate on the shoreline.

A few miles south of the park, the highway descends to superb near-sea level scenery at Oceanside, which offers excellent beachcombing, hang gliding, and surf fishing. The coast's largest concentration of tufted puffins gathers offshore on the Three Arch Rocks National Bird and Sea Lion Refuge. About 75,000 common murres, pigeon guillemots, storm-petrels, cormorants, and gulls nest on virtually every available ledge. Look for sea lions on the lower rocks.

About three miles south, the route winds around Netarts Bay affording magnificent views of rugged, black off-shore rocks. Netarts, a prime clamming, crabbing, and surf fishing area, provides ocean access with the only boat ramp along this section. The nearby Whiskey Creek Fish Hatchery is operated by Oregon State University and annually raises 100,000 spring Chinook salmon. Although information and viewing facilities are still in the development stages, visitors are welcome.

From Netarts, the highway traverses through five miles of mixed forest to Cape Lookout State Park where rugged cliffs, sandy beaches, and unspoiled Netart's estuary come together. The 1,974-acre park, set in a coastal rain forest of Douglas fir, western hemlock, red alder, and Sitka spruce, serves swimmers, sand castle builders, and fishermen who cast into the surf for perch and other bottom fish. More than 150 species of birds have been sighted, and thousands of California Murres nest here. Seventeen miles of trails meander through the forest and along the shore. A brochure identifies plants and trees on the 2.5-mile Cape Trail, which takes you through the

Cape Meares Lighthouse on the Three Capes Scenic Loop was built in the 1880s and perches on a ledge overlooking the Pacific Ocean.

The Three Capes Scenic Loop overlooks numerous offshore rocks that are refuges for a variety of wildlife.

woodlands to the tip of the basaltic cape.

Geologists have concluded that the Cape is a remnant of several ancient lava flows. Some parts are solid rock and appear to have cooled on dry land. Other sections contain rounded or billowing rocks called pillow basalts, which were formed under water.

The promontory is pocked with small coves on its north flank while the south face rises as a sheer precipice from the sea. From the tip, you can see Tillamook Head forty-two miles north and Cape Foulweather thirty-nine miles south, with capes Falcon, Meares, and Cascade Head in between. Some of the fifty-three full hook-ups and 197 tent sites offer beach-front views. Other facilities include a hiker/biker area, group camp, day-use and picnic grounds.

Five miles south of Cape Lookout, the route enters a tip of the Siuslaw National Forest, then quickly leaves the tree-lined corridor. Dunes flank the highway, and sand drifts across the road. Dune buggy and all-terrain vehicle tracks criss-cross the five-square-mile Sand Dunes Recreation Area. You're likely to see kites and hang gliders soaring above and brightly-colored sailboards in Sand Lake and eight other recommended sailboarding sites. The lake is frequented by trout, salmon, and steelhead fishermen. Near the beach, East and West camping areas are open all year and contain a total of 140 sites. Sand Beach is near the highway and has 101 sites and a dump station; but the campground closes in winter. The campgrounds are operated by the forest service.

Briefly, the highway turns inland and back to forest as it winds south to Cape Kiwanda. Photographers from around the world have been challenged

to capture on film the brilliant red and yellow sandstone cliffs and spectacular wave action. Hang glider enthusiasts launch from the huge dunes, which
extend from its eastern slope into the pine forest. On the south side, short
trails lead around the summit and down to tide pools at the base of steep,
wave-washed cliffs. Like Cannon Beach, Cape Kiwanda has a Haystack
Rock, which rises dramatically out of the surf a few hundred yards off shore.
Without the rock to protect it from the pounding of the ocean, Cape
Kiwanda's soft cliffs would already have been ground into sand.

Cape Kiwanda has been the local dory-launching site since the 1920s. It
is the only spot on the Pacific Coast where these picturesque fishing boats
launch into the surf. The open-topped, double-ended boats can usually be
seen on any calm day between Memorial and Labor days, trolling for chinook
and silver salmon or working the reefs around Haystack Rock for bottom fish.
Cape Kiwanda's waters and shorelines also yield clams and crabs.

At Bob Straub Wayside, walk over it and see picturesque Nestucca Spit
separating the bay from the ocean where the route reaches Pacific City. You
can park in front of a sand dune. In this fishing village without wharfs, docks,
or piers, virtually everyone owns a dory. Some are available for charters. On
one-day trips, you may land chinook and silver salmon, or ling cod, bass, red
snapper, and other bottom fish. The town also offers good opportunities for
whale watching, clamming, crabbing, sailboarding, and seeing wintering
geese.

A mile east of Pacific City the route concludes as it reaches a junction with
U.S. Highway 101.

3   CENTRAL OREGON COAST

General description: A 123-mile drive along the Central Oregon Coast
shoreline and sand dunes, affording spectacular views from water level and
ridgetops.

Special attractions: Depoe Bay, Cape Foulweather, lighthouses, Newport,
Darlingtonia Wayside, Oregon Dunes National Recreation Area, Sea Lion
Caves.

Location: Central Oregon Coast between Lincoln City and Coos Bay.

Drive route number: U.S. Highway 101.

Travel season: All year.

Camping: Four state park campgrounds with full hookups, and two with
electricity; Nineteen forest service campgrounds with fire pits, picnic tables
and either flush or vault toilets. Some with water. Numerous private RV
parks.

Services: Full services at Tillamook, Newport, Waldport, Florence, Reedsport,
North Bend, Coos Bay. Limited services at Depoe Bay, Yachats, Winchester
Bay, Gardiner.

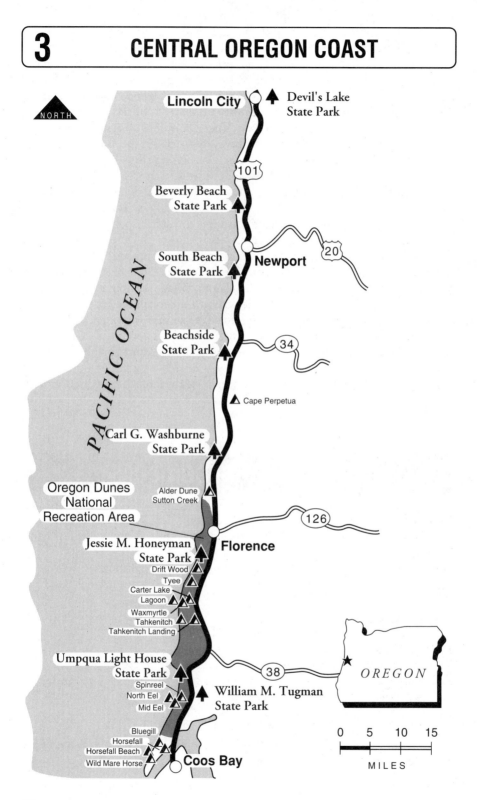

NORTH

Lincoln City

Devil's Lake
State Park

101

Beverly Beach
State Park

South Beach
State Park

Newport

20

PACIFIC OCEAN

Beachside
State Park

34

Cape Perpetua

Carl G. Washburne
State Park

Oregon Dunes
National
Recreation Area

Alder Dune
Sutton Creek

126

Jessie M. Honeyman
State Park

Florence

Drift Wood

Tyee

Carter Lake

Lagoon

Waxmyrtle

Tahkenitch

Tahkenitch Landing

Umpqua Light House
State Park

38

OREGON

Spinreel

North Eel

Mid Eel

William M. Tugman
State Park

Bluegill

Horsefall

Horsefall Beach

Wild Mare Horse

Coos Bay

0   5   10   15

MILES

Nearby attractions: Oregon North Coast and South Coast scenic drives, Three Capes Scenic Loop.

For more information: Lincoln City Visitors and Convention Bureau, 801 S.W. Highway 101, No. 1, Lincoln City, OR 97367, (541) 994-8378, (800) 452-2151 (USA). Depoe Bay Chamber of Commerce, 630 Highway 101, P.O. Box 21, Depoe Bay, OR 97341, (541) 765-2889. Greater Newport Chamber of Commerce, 555 S.W. Coast Highway, Newport, OR 97365, (541) 265-8801, (800) 262-7844 (USA). Waldport Chamber of Commerce and Visitors Center, 620 N.W. Spring St., P.O. Box 669, Waldport, OR 97394, (541) 563-2133; Yachats Area Chamber of Commerce, 441 Highway 101, P.O. Box 728, Yachats, OR 97498, (541) 547-3530. Florence Area Chamber of Commerce, 270 Highway 101, P.O. Box 26000, Florence, OR 97439, (541) 997-3128. North Bend Information Center, 1380 Sherman, North Bend, OR 97459, (541) 756-4613.

The drive: U.S. Highway 101 stays close to the ocean on the 123 miles between Lincoln City and Coos Bay. It begins with water level rocky coves and bays, then ascends Cape Foulweather and descends from Otter Crest to scenic beaches, and thick brushy hills. South of Waldport, it follows the base of hills, makes a steep ascent over Cape Perpetua, sweeps down to rugged shorelines and runs through the heart of the Oregon Dunes National Recreation Area.

Weather is usually mild with spring days in the fifties and summer days averaging sixty to seventy degrees. Although winter days can also reach the sixties, temperatures average in the low fifties. Fall is the most dependable season for calm, warm weather.

At Lincoln City, you'll find seven miles of beach, the greatest number of hotel rooms between San Francisco and Portland, and numerous shops specializing in coastal crafts and recreation equipment. "D" River Wayside, downtown, overlooks the world's shortest river, which is less than a mile long. Scenic Devils Lake State Park, nearby, includes campgrounds with thirty-two full hook-ups and sixty-eight tent sites.

Siletz Bay, seven miles south on U.S. Highway 101, contains high-yield crab beds, and is known for its salmon and steelhead fishing. Gleneden Beach Wayside, on the bay's south shore and across the highway from deluxe Salishan Resort and golf course, is a convenient beach access. Fogarty Creek State Park, a mile further, offers a sandy creek for wading, shorelines for ocean fishing, and 184 picnic units.

At Boiler Bay Wayside, three miles south, you can see the rusting remains of a ship's boiler which exploded in 1910. The bay is a designated marine garden, and a good spot for watching migrating whales and winter storms.

You cross a classic concrete arched bridge at Depoe Bay where the world's smallest harbor encompasses six square acres and shelters a picturesque fishing and charter fleet. When waves rush through a crevice in the rocky basalt coastline, a spouting horn, near the bridge, produces spectacular geysers of sea water. Migrating whales are often sighted near the shoreline.

For a short and exceptionally scenic side trip along Otter Crest, leave U.S.

Florence Marina, on the Central Oregon Coast, borders a picturesque historic district offering restaurants and boutiques.

Highway 101 at Rocky Creek Wayside and continue to Cape Foulweather. The cape is a jumble of volcanic rocks, some of which erupted under water and others on dry land. It emerged above sea level with the rising of the Coast Range island—around twenty million years ago. It was discovered and named by Captain James Cook in 1778.

From the visitor center, 453 feet above the rocky shore, you have a commanding view of tiny hilltop villages and miles of coastline. With binoculars, you may also see cormorants, sea lions, and other wildlife on off-shore rocks and reefs. Devil's Punchbowl State Park, on the loop, features a marine garden, a beach and a rock formation where sea water boils and churns at high tide.

The portion of U.S. Highway 101 that bypasses the loop meanders through forested highlands to Beverly Beach State Park. The park has a sandy shoreline and marine fossils impregnated in rocks. A campground with 152 tent, seventy-five improved and fifty-two full service hookups, plus primitive and group camps is situated in a forest of Douglas fir overlooking the beach.

About five miles south, Yaquina Head Lighthouse was built in 1873 and is still operating. From its headland, which is the last remnant of a volcano, you can see a variety of shorebirds on the cliffs and rocks and during migrations, glimpse whales in the waters below.

At Newport, two miles south, U.S. Highway 101 passes a junction with U.S. Highway 20, which links the coast to Philomath, Corvallis, and Albany. Wide shorelines have made Newport a year-round playground for surfers, scuba divers, fishermen, clam, and dungeness crab gatherers. Agate collectors comb beaches for the semi-precious stones uncovered by waves.

Several attractions are situated on or near U.S. Highway 101 in Newport. Yaquina Bay State Park's lighthouse, built in 1891, is Oregon's last example of a combined keeper's quarters and lighthouse tower. It opens for tours in summer and winter weekends and exhibits 1800s furnishings. Old Town bayfront encompasses commercial and charter fishing docks, an undersea gardens, and a wax museum. South of the bay, the Mark O. Hatfield Marine Science Center showcases a variety of marine life and has special handling pools for children. At the Oregon Coast Aquarium next door, visitors can view sea life and demonstrations on the twenty-nine-acre site landscaped with native flora. The nearby South Beach State Park provides 254 electrical campsites and contains a variety of coastal plant species.

The fifteen miles between Newport and Waldport offer access to sandy beaches, rocky shorelines, and fishing from trails at Seal Rock State Park and Driftwood Beach Wayside. North of Waldport, U.S. Highway 101 crosses Alsea Bay and a junction with Oregon Highway 34, which extends east through the coast range to Philomath.

The bay and Walport area are favorites of surf and freshwater fishermen, as trout, salmon, bay and razor clams are caught here. On the bay's south end, exhibits at Alsea Bay Interpretive Center depict the history of transportation and the coastal highway system. At Beachside State Park Campground, four miles south of Waldport, thirty-one electrical and fifty tent sites are scattered along the shoreline.

On the thirty-five mile section south to Florence, the highway cuts through some of the central coast's best scenery. It enters the Siuslaw National Forest, passes thirteen state parks and waysides, and five forest service campgrounds with a total of 243 sites.

The picturesque village of Yachats, eight miles south of Waldport, sits on an ancient beachline and is a favorite weekend retreat, renowned for spring-summer smelt runs, beaches for rockhounding, and rocky promontories offering dramatic views of churning surf. The name is a Native American word, meaning "at the foot of the mountain" and refers to nearby Cape Perpetua. Atop the 803-foot cape, also named by Captain Cook, you'll find a visitor center and several trails. They lead through some of Oregon's largest spruce trees to a thirty-seven-site forest service campground, and Devil's Churn, where tides rush through a shoreline channel and to outstanding views of the rocky coastline.

By contrast, Neptune State Park is about a mile south of the cape and displays a forest of wind-swept trees. Elk often wander into Carl G. Washburne State Park, a few miles further south, where fifty-eight full hook-ups, two tent and six primitive sites are situated close to tide pools.

Sea Lion Caves, a mile south, is one of the world's largest sea caves and the only mainland home of the Stellar sea lion. For a small admission, you can watch them sunning themselves on the rocky bluffs and take an elevator 208 feet down to their cavern, which is twelve stories high and as long as a football field. From the cavern's natural window, you have an outstanding view of Heceta Head Lighthouse, sitting on a bluff across a forested bay.

Darlingtonia State Wayside, five miles north of Florence is named after a carnivorous plant. A 0.5-mile trail meanders through bogs of the insect eating plants, which are also called cobra lilies.

In north Florence, U.S. Highway 101 junctions with Oregon Highway 126, a two-lane highly scenic route to Eugene. A turn west at the junction, takes you to the one-mile-long Siletz River Estuary Scenic drive and to the ocean beach, or south to Florence's Old Town waterfront. Its former factories and commercial businesses house many small arts and crafts shops and a variety of restaurants.

Florence is the northern gateway to the Oregon Dunes National Recreation Area, which stretches south forty-seven miles along the coast. The dunes were once sedimentary rock, which was eroded away by waves. Some are moving north from six to eighteen feet per year, burying trees and filling small lakes that were created when the sand dammed small stream beds. About half of the 14,000 acres of dunes—some over 500 feet high—are open to off-road vehicles. While dune buggy driving, hiking, and horseback riding are popular, the area is also a favorite of sailboarders, flower lovers, fishermen, and shellfish collectors. Cutthroat trout, salmon, and steelhead inhabit rivers; and trout, bass, catfish, bluegill, and perch are found in local lakes.

Jessie M. Honeyman State Park, three miles south of Florence, is known for its wild rhododendrons and magnificent white dunes that slope down to several freshwater lakes. Facilities include an outdoor theater, boat ramps, bathhouses, sixty-six full hook-ups, and seventy-five electrical and 240 tent sites.

At Oregon Dunes Overlook, midway between Florence and Reedsport, your view encompasses miles of pine forest, dunes, and the ocean. For a closer look at the landscape, take the hiking trail through the wildlife habitats: forest, grassland, beach, marsh, and dunes. Seven forest service campgrounds provide 264 sites. Trails from the campgrounds meander through the dunes to beaches and scenic viewpoints and border small lakes that are open for fishing.

At Reedsport, U.S. Highway 101 meets Oregon Highway 38. It parallels the Umpqua River east to the historic community of Scottsburg, then joins Interstate 5 near Drain. Dean Creek Elk Viewing Area, about seven miles east of the junction, contains a resident herd of Roosevelt Elk, which can be seen from the roadside. The Oregon Dunes National Recreation Area headquarters is located on U.S. Highway 101 in Reedsport and offers a twenty- minute film on the dunes, plus information on varied recreational opportunities including dune buggy rides, tours, hikes, beachcombing, camping, and fishing.

Winchester Bay, four miles south, houses one of Oregon's largest sport fishing charter fleets at Salmon Harbor. The Umpqua and Smith rivers, which form the bay, are reliable springtime bass fisheries. From mid-February to mid-May, operators also offer whale-watching trips.

Umpqua Lighthouse State Park, near an operating lighthouse, has twenty-two full hookups and forty-two tent sites by a forest, small lake, and sand dunes.

Oregon Dunes National Recreation Area stretches forty-seven miles along the Central Oregon Coast.

Three forest service campgrounds, south of the park, offer 115 sites. William A. Tugman State Park, near Lakeside contains 115 electrical sites.

From Lakeside, on the shores of Ten Mile Lake, the route continues south through six miles of forest and dunes. Four forest service campgrounds at the southern dune area boundary, provide 135 sites surrounded by sand dunes.

The drive concludes by crossing Coos Bay over the McCullough Memorial Bridge and entering North Bend. At 5,305 feet long, it is the longest coastal bridge. Its distinctive architectural and decorative features include a 1,709-foot cantilever truss main span flanked by a series of 170- to 265-foot concrete arches.

4 WINCHESTER BAY, SALMON HARBOR

General description: A three-mile drive around Salmon Harbor to a historic lighthouse overlooking dunes and the ocean.

Special attractions: Picturesque harbor, charter fishing, Umpqua Lighthouse and whale watching station, historic coast guard buildings, Oregon Dunes National Recreation Area, Umpqua River jetty, beaches, state park with lake, beachcombing, and camping.

Location: West of Winchester Bay.

Drive route name and number: Salmon Harbor Drive, Umpqua Lighthouse Road, Old U.S. Highway 101.

Travel season: All year. January and March are prime months for watching migrating whales.

Camping: One state park campground with full hookups and two Douglas

Lake Marie, in Umpqua Lighthouse State Park, offers a relaxing setting for picnicking, swimming, and walks along the shoreline.

County campgrounds with hookups.

Services: Full services at Winchester Bay, Reedsport.

Nearby attractions: Oregon Dunes National Recreation Area, Oregon Central Coast Scenic Drive, Lower Umpqua River Scenic Drive, Southern Oregon Coast Scenic Drive. Charleston Harbor/Seven Devils Loop drive.

For more information: Lower Umpqua Chamber of Commerce, U.S. Highway 101 and Highway 38, P.O. Box 11, Reedsport, OR 97467, (541) 271-3495, (800) 247-2155 (Oregon).

The drive: This short drive starts at U.S. Highway 101 in the community of Winchester Bay, heads west to Salmon Harbor, circles the base of a jetty, and climbs a short hill to Umpqua Lighthouse and whale watching station. Turning east it passes through a forested park, by a small lake, and takes Old U.S. Highway 101 back to the main highway.

Travelers can usually expect mild weather with spring days in the fifties and summer days averaging sixty to seventy degrees. While winters also reach the sixties, days average in the mid-fifties. Fall is the most dependable season for calm, warm weather.

Leaving U.S. Highway 101, the drive heads west on 8th Street for one long block to Salmon Harbor. At the waterfront, 8th street ends at Salmon Harbor Drive. As the road curves south around the harbor, it affords changing views

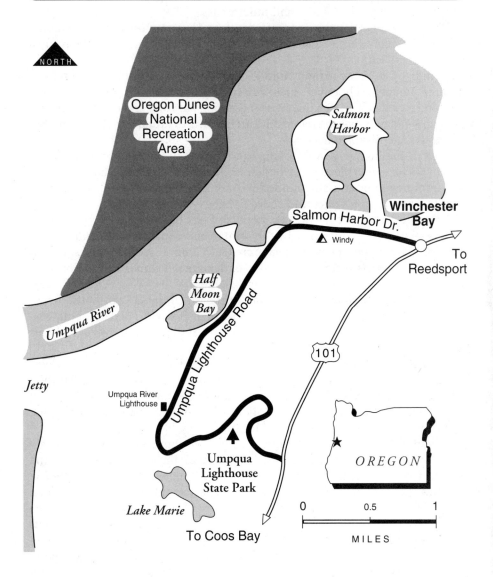

NORTH

Oregon Dunes National Recreation Area

Salmon Harbor

Salmon Harbor Dr. **Winchester Bay**

▲ Windy

Half Moon Bay

Umpqua Lighthouse Road

Umpqua River

To Reedsport

101

Jetty

Umpqua River Lighthouse ■

Umpqua Lighthouse State Park

Lake Marie

To Coos Bay

OREGON

0   0.5   1

MILES

of the boat basin and virtually unlimited angles for photographing private and commercial fishing boats of all shapes and sizes.

The harbor is home to the Oregon Coast's largest sport fishing fleet and provides transient and long-term moorage for 1,260 craft. Two launch ramps are capable of launching ten boats simultaneously. Salmon Harbor Basin County Park, on the western shore, provides boat launching, fishing, picnicking and a playground. Tackle and gift shops crowd the shorelines and you can drop a crab net and bottom fish from the pier.

Record catches of trophy-sized salmon are taken annually from the Pacific beyond the river bar. The Umpqua and Smith rivers, which meet here and form the bay, produce winter steelhead, white sturgeon, striped bass, and large numbers of shad and small mouth bass.

Turning west at the base of forested hills and layers of rock, the road passes a wayside memorial dedicated to the port's men and women who have lost their lives at sea.

Windy Cove Campground, at mile one, sits at the base of a forested ridge. It offers twenty-eight paved sites with full-service hookups, including cable TV, and four electric sites. An adjacent section has forty trailer sites with full hookups and twenty-nine tents. Both areas feature caretakers, restrooms, hot showers, and disabled access.

Across the highway, a flat, long sandbar has become a children's playground. The centerpiece is a wooden frontier fort with a stockade guarded by an old cannon and surrounded by monkey bars and play fields. It's a terrific spot for kite flyers and shore fishing.

Like the rest of the harbor, the sand spit has been shaped by prevailing winds that blow sand north in the winter and south during summer. At Salmon Harbor, summer winds have created a long crescent shaped sand spit that extends from the northern section of the Oregon Dunes Recreation Area around the mouth to provide a natural shelter.

Turning south, you pass a jetty and turn onto Umpqua Lighthouse Road. The jetty is known for collecting large piles of drift wood, good crabbing, and superb fishing for ling cod, cabezon, greenling, sea bass, and several varieties of perch.

At 0.6 mile south of the turn-off, you reach Umpqua River U.S. Coast Guard Station and Coast Visitor Center. Built in 1939, the administration office and barracks served as an important U.S. Coast Guard facility until 1971. In addition to visitor information, they contain displays interpreting the history of coastal shipping and logging.

About 100 yards south, Umpqua River Lighthouse overlooks a whale watching station, Oregon Dunes Recreation Area, the river's mouth, and the Pacific Ocean. Built in 1892 and still operating, it replaced an 1857 lighthouse that was the first in the Oregon Territory. The current sixty-seven-foot-high conical tower is listed on the National Register of Historic Places and contains a two-ton, ten-foot-high lens with about 1,000 prisms, which were hand-cut in Paris. The twelve separate beams shining from the 165-foot lighthouse can be seen for at least nineteen miles. Even with the lighthouse, the Umpqua River bar was the site of at least thirty-two shipwrecks between 1808 and 1956. Tours are conducted on special occasions.

The whale watching station, across the street, has information boards on whale migrations and sightings, and provides a sweeping view of the dunes, seashore, and jetty. In November of each year, California gray whales migrate down the Oregon Coast from the Arctic to Mexico where they give birth to calves. They return from February through May.

During the last seven days of the year Winchester Bay hosts an annual whale watching week. If you plan to watch whales, a promontory makes the

Umpqua River Lighthouse. Winchester Bay, Salmon Harbor, Umpqua Lighthouse State Park Drive.

best vantage point. Whales are easier to spot early in the morning when the sea has fewer whitecaps. In the off-season, the station is a prime spot for watching blazing sunsets.

Trails lead from the station over expanses of sand dunes to the beach. Beach explorers are rewarded with driftwood, agates, sand dollars, an occasional Japanese fishing float, and tide pools teeming with tiny sea life.

Turning east, you enter a pine forest and Umpqua Lighthouse State Park. The 450-acre-park touches the mouth of the bay and includes 500-foot sand dunes. Lake Marie, at the roadside, is a delightful stop where you can swim and row a boat on a tiny lake surrounded by trees. A 1.3-mile trail circles the lake. The campground by the north shore has forty-one tent and twenty-two full-hookup sites with showers and laundry facilities.

Continuing east to Old U.S. Highway 101, you conclude the drive by turning south and rejoining the main highway near a viewpoint overlooking the Umpqua River.

5 SOUTHERN OREGON COAST

General description: A 107-mile drive along the Southern Oregon Coast, with its magnificent beaches and forested hills.

Special attractions: Bandon waterfront and cheese factory, West Coast Game Park, Cape Blanco, prehistoric gardens, Battle Rock, Cape Sebastian, Rogue River, rugged coastline parks, storm and whale watching.

Location: Southern Oregon Coast between Coos Bay and the California border.

Drive route number: U.S. Highway 101.

Travel season: All year. Winter storms are major attractions. January and March are prime months for watching migrating whales.

Camping: Four state park campgrounds with full hookups and two with electricity, plus private RV parks.

Services: Full services at Coos Bay, Bandon, Gold Beach, Brookings. Limited services at Langlois, Port Orford, Wedderburn, Pistol River.

Nearby attractions: Oregon Dunes National Recreation Area, Golden and Silver Falls State Park, Oregon Central Coast Scenic Drive, Charleston Harbor/Seven Devils Loop Drive, Bandon Scenic Ocean Views Drive, Powers/Rogue River/Gold Beach Scenic Loop, California Redwoods, Smith River Scenic Byway.

For more information: Bay Area Chamber of Commerce, 50 E. Central, P.O. Box 210, Coos Bay, OR 97420, (541) 269-0215, (800) 824-8486 (USA). Bandon Chamber of Commerce, 350 S.E. 2nd St., P.O. Box 1515, Bandon, OR 97411, (541) 347-9616. Port Orford Chamber of Commerce, P.O. Box 637, Port Orford, OR 97465, (541) 332-8055. Gold Beach Chamber of Commerce, 1225 S. Ellensburg, No. 3, Gold Beach, OR 97444, (541) 247-7526, (800) 525-2334 (USA). Brookings-Harbor Chamber of Commerce, 16330 Lower Harbor

The Southern Oregon Coast is characterized by secluded coves, rugged headlands, and magnificent oceanside parks.

Rd., P.O. Box 940, South Harbor, Brookings, OR 97415, (541) 469-3181.

The drive: South of Coos Bay, U.S. Highway 101 parallels Isthmus Slough for a few miles then cuts southwest over wooded hills to Bandon. Traversing flat and rolling hills, it moves inland through thick forest, flanks mountains and descends along magnificent shorelines to Gold Beach. Climbing Cape Sebastian's western slopes, the scenery reaches its zenith in a series of state parks with spectacular views of deep ravines, offshore rocks, and inlets. The south coast is the heart of myrtlewood country. At roadside shops and factories, you can watch craftsmen shape the distinctive hardwood, carving out dishes, jewelry, and figurines.

The south coast enjoys Oregon's mildest climate. Near the California border, summer-like weather is common early in the year as winter days rise into the seventies and eighties. Summer temperatures climb to over ninety degrees. Most of the annual seventy to ninety inches of rain falls between November and April. Frost is rare, and snow is virtually unknown. The mild weather produces Christmas camellias, flowering plums and daffodils in January, and magnolia, azaleas, and rhododendron displays in late winter. Look for palm trees, eucalyptus, and towering redwoods near the California border.

Coos Bay is the world's largest lumber shipping port and the largest natural harbor between San Francisco and Puget Sound. On or near U.S. Highway 101, you can visit the Coos County Historical Museum, the Marshfield Sun

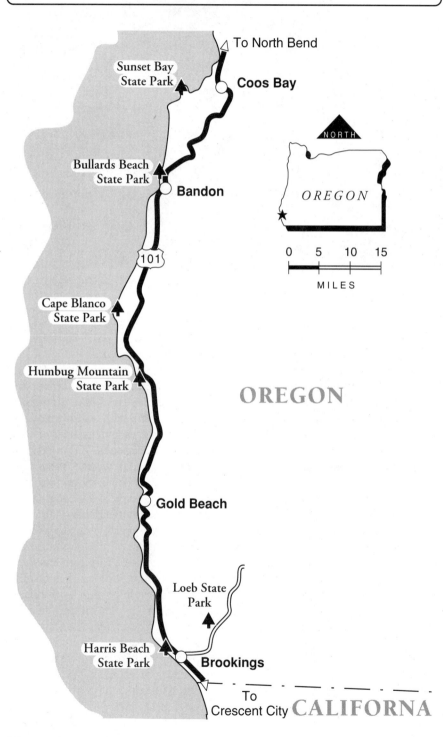

To North Bend

Sunset Bay
State Park

Coos Bay

Bullards Beach
State Park

Bandon

101

Cape Blanco
State Park

Humbug Mountain
State Park

NORTH

OREGON

0   5   10   15

MILES

OREGON

Gold Beach

Loeb State
Park

Harris Beach
State Park

Brookings

To
Crescent City CALIFORNA

printing museum, and tour a Coast Guard cutter at a roadside dock. Local industries offer tours of mills and myrtlewood factories.

The forty-mile Charleston Harbor/Seven Devils Scenic Loop is accessible by traveling west from either North Bend or Coos Bay. It offers the superb coastal scenery of Sunset Bay, Shore Acres and Cape Arago state parks and the 4,400-acre South Slough Estuarine Sanctuary. Bastendorff Beach County Park offers eighty campsites, and Sunset Bay has twenty-nine full hookups, thirty-four electrical and seventy-five tent sites.

Between Coos Bay and Bandon, U.S. Highway 101 meanders through a series of low hills, which were formed forty to fifty million years ago when sands and mud was deposited in near the shore. They contain coal that was mined in the early 1900s. Although all traces of mining have virtually disappeared, coal seams still remain, along with possibly oil and natural gas. Five miles south of Coos Bay, U.S. Highway 101 intersects with Oregon Highway 42, a scenic but slow route through Coquille, Myrtle Point, and Coast Range forests to Interstate 5 near Roseburg. After two miles of angling southwest through the Coos County Forest on U.S. Highway 101, a turn west onto Seven Devil's Road takes you to a sandy beach at Seven Devil's Wayside.

At Bullards Beach State Park, four miles south, photo and informational displays in the restored Coquille Lighthouse highlight coastal shipwrecks. The 1,266-acre park spreads over several miles of shoreline and impressive sand dunes, and contains ninety-two full hook-ups and 100 electrical campsites. A 1.5-mile hiking path, and seven miles of horse trails invite exploration of several expansive beaches and impressive sand dunes.

Cheese, cranberries, and winter storms have brought fame to Bandon, which is also called Bandon-By-The-Sea. The factory and gift shop on U.S. Highway 101 offers delectable free samplings. Old Town, at the waterfront, is the departure point for delightful sternwheeler cruises of the Coquille River and the five-mile Bandon Ocean Scenic Views drive that heads west past the Coquille River Museum to spectacular natural rock pillars.

Between Bandon and Port Orford, twenty-six miles south, you will travel inland by Ocean Spray's cranberry bogs, dairy and sheep farms, over rolling plains, and through fir forests. The coast, seen in glimpses, lies two to six miles west. Diversified recreation includes a wild game park where children can pet and feed some of its 400 exotic animals, sailboarding at Floras Lake, and quiet walks along secluded beaches at Paradise Point State Park. From July through October, rare brown pelicans feed along the Elk River. The nearby Sixes River and the Elk are both productive trout, salmon, and steelhead streams.

At the community of Sixes, take a side road west to Hughes House and Cape Blanco Lighthouse. Built in 1898, the two-story, eleven-room Victorian home was part of a 2,000-acre ranch. The 1878 lighthouse still operates and is the most westerly lighthouse in the contiguous forty-eight states. From adjacent Cape Blanco State Park, you have sweeping views of rocks and beaches. The campground has fifty-eight electrical sites, and a three-mile trail winding down to chalky white cliffs and a black sand beach.

At Port Orford, four miles south, you are in the nation's westernmost incorporated city. In 1851, it became the south coast's first settlement when a blockhouse was built to protect homesteaders from hostile Native Americans following a skirmish at the ocean front monolith of Battle Rock. Today, Battle Rock City Park is a short stroll from the highway and a picture-perfect setting for picnics, sunbathing, and swimming. Sweeping views of the southern coastline await visitors who walk to the top of the often photographed rock.

The geologic history of the south coast is dramatically different from the northern and central shoreline. Rocks on the south coast are much older, having been laid down as sediments about 100 to 200 million years ago. Afterwards, the oceanic crust shifted and they were twisted, crystallized, and thrust up against the Coast Range.

South of Port Orford, the highway climbs through a lush Douglas fir rain forest and follows a thin stream along the north base and eastern edge of Humbug Mountain, a gravel conglomerate deposited over a 100 million years ago. A steep, three-mile path to the 1,756-foot peak starts at the highway near Humbug Mountain State Park and rewards the hearty with a panoramic view that extends into California. At Humbug Mountain State Park, your options include picnicking and camping in a virgin forest, strolling a sandy beach, and spending the night in one of thirty full hookup and seventy-eight tent campsites. Short trails take you to nearby trout streams and an unusual black sand beach.

The rain forest aura continues through Prehistoric Gardens, twelve miles south of the park, near Humbug Mountain's base. Life-sized dinosaur replicas peeking through lush vegetation delight children, and there's a gift shop and restaurant for adults.

Near Gold Beach, the highway crosses the mouth of the Rogue River. The river has a legendary reputation for outstanding salmon and steelhead fishing. Its headwaters begin about 200 miles east in the Cascade Mountains near Crater Lake. Jet boat excursions into the Rogue's Coast Range canyons are available from several operators. Most feature either a thirty-two-mile run east to Agness, or a 104-mile-round trip that takes you into the Wild and Scenic section and through whitewater rapids. Some trips deliver the mail to families and businesses along the shore, and all feature narratives covering history and wildlife. North and south river bank roads offer a scenic sidetrip to Agness and with views of the river from ridgetops.

Gold Beach, one mile south, takes its name from placer gold deposits found at the Rogue's mouth during the 1880s. Today, the county seat attracts whale, sea lion, bird, and storm watchers. Look for palm trees along the highway, and agates and a variety of salt and fresh water fishing.

South of Gold Beach the drive climaxes in a thick rain forest and series of spectacular capes, and parks that have been called the earth's finest shoreline scenery. At Cape Sebastian, 700 feet above sea level, wild azaleas and rhododendrons brighten spring landscapes along a two-mile segment of the Oregon Coast Trail. Pistol River State Park is a sailboarder's and sightseer's delight with a sandy beach where you can hike over sand dunes while enjoying magnificent cliffs and offshore rocks.

At Boardman State Park, ten miles of the Oregon Coast Trail extends along remote beaches and cliff sides overlooking magnificent arches, sea stacks, and off-shore monoliths. Rainbow Rock, south of the park, displays colorful bands of chert, which formed in deep water on the ocean floor. Harris Beach State Park features thirty-four full hook-up, fifty-three electrical and sixty-nine tent campsites above a spacious beach with trails winding down to shorelines and tide pools. The panoramic view extends into California, and encompasses huge off-shore monoliths, beach rock formations, and Goat Island, Oregon's largest coastal island. Goat Island is a bird refuge, and most of the off-shore rocks and reefs are part of the Oregon Islands National Wildlife Refuge. During this segment you'll also cross Thomas Creek Bridge. At 300 feet above water level, it is the highest coastal span north of San Francisco.

Brookings, five miles north of the California border, is a fresh and salt water fishing hot spot. At Azalea State Park, on the highway, in late spring and fall several varieties of azaleas bloom on thirty-six acres. The community of Harbor, separated from Brookings by the Chetco River, has the only lily research station in the United States. Ninety-five percent of the world's commercial Easter lilies are grown between Brookings in the thirteen miles south to Smith River, California.

The Chetco River is an outstanding trout, steelhead, and cutthroat fishing stream. Loeb State Park is ten miles northeast of Brookings on the river's north bank and features outstanding wild flower displays and fifty-three electrical sites near a myrtlewood grove. A one-mile nature trail winds through a virgin stand of Coastal redwoods, some of which are more than 500 years old.

About four miles south of Brookings, the nation's largest Monterey cypress sits along U.S. Highway 101 in front of the Chetco Valley Museum. A mile south, Winchuck Wayside offers access to the Winchuck River, and one last spot to watch birds and beachcomb the Oregon shoreline.

From the border, U.S. Highway 101 continues south twenty-one miles to Crescent City. You can reenter Oregon by taking U.S. Highway 199 north to Jedediah Smith Redwoods State Park, Oregon Caves National Monument, and on to Grants Pass.

33

General description: A forty-mile drive through Charleston Harbor, into three magnificent coastal parks and an estuary.

Special attractions: Charleston Harbor, Sunsct Bay, Shore Acres, and Cape Arago state parks, South Slough National Estuarine Reserve, formal gardens, storm, whale, and wildlife watching.

Location: Southern Oregon Coast west of Coos Bay and north of Bandon.

Drive route names: Cape Arago Highway, Seven Devils Road.

Travel season: All year. Prime whale watching periods are mid-December through mid-January and mid-March to mid-April. February is usually the best month for crashing surf and magnificent waves.

Camping: One county park with full hookups and one state park campground with full hookups and electrical sites. Two small hiker/biker camps, plus private RV parks.

Services: Full services at Coos Bay and Charleston.

Nearby attractions: Golden and Silver Falls state parks, Oregon Dunes National Recreation Area, Oregon Central Coast Scenic Drive, Bandon Scenic Ocean Views Drive, Bandon/Rogue River/Gold Beach Scenic Loop.

For more information: Bay Area Chamber of Commerce, 50 E. Central, P.O. Box 210, Coos Bay, OR 97420, (541) 269-0215, (800) 824-8486 (USA). Charleston Information Center, P.O. Box 5735, Boat Basin Drive & Cape Arago Highway, Charleston, OR 97420, (541) 888-2311, (800)824-8486.

The drive: The route can be driven by taking either the ocean beach exits at North Bend and Coos Bay and traveling west to Cape Arago Highway, or by turning onto Seven Devil's Road thirteen miles north of Bandon and following the itinerary in reverse.

From North Bend/Coos Bay, the route travels south along the bay to Charleston Harbor, descends to the shoreline at Bastindorff Beach and Sunset Bay, then climbs a bluff for sweeping overlooks at Shore Acres and Cape Arago state parks. Backtracking four miles, it heads south to South Slough Estuary and two state park waysides, then ends at a junction with U.S. Highway 101, about thirteen miles north of Bandon.

Travelers can expect warm summer days in the seventies and eighties and winters in the sixties to seventies. November through February brings heavy rains and gale force winter storms with spectacular waves.

From the Coos County Museum and Information Center in North Bend, the drive heads west for several blocks on Virginia Street. Turning south, it enters Coos Bay and proceeds west through the Empire District. At the waterfront, the highway stays along the shoreline for the six miles south to Charleston. This section is a local favorite for clamming, crabbing, and perch and salmon fishing.

Crossing the bridge to Charleston, you'll see a picturesque small boat basin filled with commercial and pleasure craft. The town is the heart of local

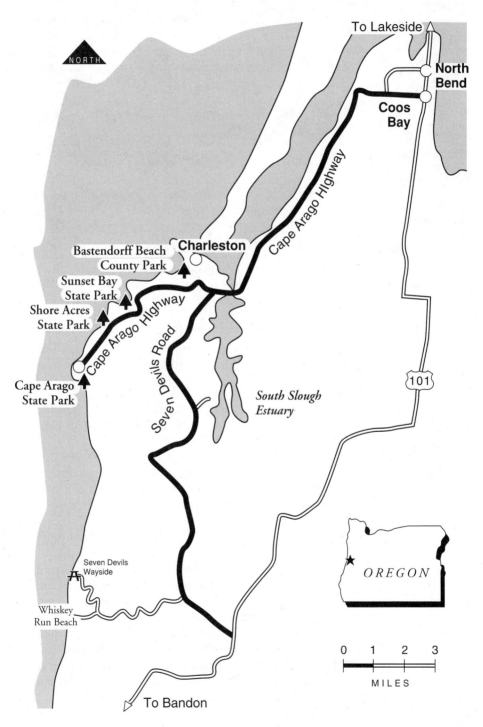

To Lakeside

North Bend

Coos Bay

Cape Arago Highway

Bastendorff Beach County Park

Charleston

Sunset Bay State Park

Shore Acres State Park

Cape Arago Highway

Seven Devils Road

Cape Arago State Park

South Slough Estuary

101

Seven Devils Wayside

Whiskey Run Beach

To Bandon

NORTH

OREGON

0 1 2 3

MILES

Shore Acres State Park features a formal garden and a glass-enclosed observatory for watching waves crash against shoreline rocks.

commercial and sport fishing, and you may wish to take time to explore its oyster farms, tide pools, fresh fish markets, shops, and boutiques. Charter services, marine suppliers, and boat ramp facilities are available. At the docks, you can catch crab and fish for surf perch and smelt, herring, and tomcod, or dig for razor clams on the flats at low tide.

A mile south of town, turn west onto Coos Ed Road. South Jetty is at the base of a small hill and offers a large parking area, and a short walk to the base of a wave eroded sea cliff.

Bastindorff Beach County Park, at the jetty's south end, is a great spot for walking dogs, building beach fires, playing in the surf, and watching sunsets. Cast your line in the ocean, and you may land kelp greenling, ling cod, and starry flounder. The twenty-five tent and fifty-six RV sites overlook rugged headlands and lush marsh grass.

Returning to the main highway, you enter a thick forest of coastal pine, spruce, alder, maple, and hemlock.

At Sunset Bay State Park, one mile south, two high headlands form a natural frame for a white sand beach. They also protect the camp and picnic grounds, situated in a forested ravine, from strong winds. While you may find kelp and other flotsam in the parking lot after a storm, the absence of undertows and currents make Sunset Bay one of Oregon's safest swimming, small boating, and kayaking areas. A three-mile section of the Oregon Coast Trail begins at the parking lot. It goes over cliffs near a cormorant rookery, down to the shore, up to Shore Acres, across Simpson Beach, and ends on a cliff top three miles south at Cape Arago.

A huge picnic area provides a magnificent view of the bay. Short trails lead into the dense forest, across three foot bridges over a small stream, and to a promontory viewpoint. The twenty-nine full hook-up, thirty-four electrical campsites, and hiker/biker camp border an old-growth forest with a lush undergrowth of ferns and lupine. Deer and raccoon sometimes wander into the park, and, in season, blackberries, huckleberries, thimble berries, and salmon berries are free for the picking. Porcupines and bobcats prowl the woods but are seldom seen.

The highway is part of the Oregon Coast bicycle route and you'll need to watch for bicyclists on the narrow section to Shore Acres. Midway between the two parks, a viewpoint overlooks a meadow of sea grasses, spectacular headlands, and Cape Arago Lighthouse to the north. Built in 1866, it sits on an island three miles west of Charleston. It is still active and not open to the public. A barrier-free trail starts at the viewpoint, passes through the meadow near the cormorant rookery, and ends at Shore Acres State Park.

In the early 1900s, Shore Acres was the centerpiece of an estate that included Sunset Bay and Cape Arago. It was owned by timber magnate Louis Simpson, whose pride and joy was his formal garden. Ship captains often brought him exotic flowers from around the world. New varieties of rhododendrons, azaleas, and other flowering shrubs were planted at Shore Acres years before they appeared in American nurseries.

Today, Shore Acres draws visitors in equal numbers to see the restored gardens and to watch waves crash against the sandstone cliffs.

A tall spruce and pine forest forms a natural amphitheater for the 7.5-acre garden and an original caretaker's cottage. As an American Rose Society test site, the garden features a variety of roses, plus several species of hydrangeas, fuchsias, and wisterias. Snowball bushes, several kinds of roses and other flowers bloom during winter.

An adjacent oriental garden and some of Simpson's original pampas grass, bamboo, cypress, and palm trees surround a circular pond. The pond is fed by a stream from nearby coastal hills and flows over a cliff to empty into the ocean. Plaques identify water hawthorne, floating heart, oriental cherry, and other plants.

The gardens are used as an open-air theater for concerts, receptions, and other events. Each month several marriages take place at the caretaker's cottage. Protected from westerly winds by tall hedges, the gardens also offer the best picnic spots. Paved paths descend to a sandy, secluded cove at Simpson's Beach, and wind along cliffs to a glass observation building.

From late November through February, the shoreline is the setting for some of nature's most spectacular shows. Breakers surge into sandstone cliffs, spread in giant 100-foot fans, collapse, and are pulled out to the ocean as churning waves of creamy, milk-white water. On calm days, the shoreline is an endless succession of curves, coves, headlands, and beaches that appears to extend to Cape Arago lighthouse. Rocks north of the glassed storm-watching shelter exhibit distinctive layers of sediment and stand broken and tilted like ships bows poised before sinking. Deposited some forty to fifty million years ago as a series of thick sands and muds, they are prime examples of the power of nature and the relentless pounding of the sea.

At Simpson Reef Viewpoint, near the entrance to Cape Arago, thirty to forty sea lions or seals are often seen on the off-shore rocks of Oregon Islands National Wildlife Refuge. Since the wildlife is easily disturbed, the refuge is closed to public use.

Cape Arago's parking lot is one of the coast's best whale-watching sites. Each year thousands of gray whales migrate by here on a 6,000-mile journey from Alaska to Mexico and back.

The cape was recorded by early explorers. A plaque in the south cove commemorates a possible anchoring in 1579 by Sir Francis Drake. Captain James Cook sighted it in 1778 and named it Cape Gregory. Later it was renamed to honor a 1800s French physicist and geographer.

From the parking lot, a serpentine trail winds down the triangular shaped headland to two beaches. With the natural amphitheater of tall cliffs as a backdrop, you can enjoy a beach bonfire, beachcombing, sunbathing, and wading in the water. You'll need a licence to surf fish, and a permit if you plan to collect sea urchins, crabs, abalone, clams, mussels, and other invertebrates. Picnic tables and benches are situated on ledges along the trail, and a small hiker/biker camp is nestled in the forest near the park entrance.

Leaving Cape Arago, the route backtracks five miles, then turns south on Seven Devil's Road. The highway curves through four miles of thick pine forest and clear cuts to South Slough Estuary's visitor center.

During the last ice age, sea level in this area dropped about 300 feet, as water froze into thick sheets. About 10,000 years ago, when the ice melted, it flooded the Millicoma River's mouth and created Coos Bay. South Slough is a southern extension of the bay, which is Oregon's second largest estuary. Here fresh and salt water meet, and the plant and wildlife of both intermingle. Uplands provide shelter for raccoons, bobcats, and bald eagles, and beaver's build dams along the wetlands. The estuary provides a nursery for sole, flounder, salmon, crab, and a stopover for vultures, great blue herons, and mergansers. As the home of the nation's first estuarine reserve, South Slough preserves more than 4,400 acres of salt marsh, tide flats, open water and upland forest.

From the hilltop visitor center, the panorama encompasses the various habitats between forest and water. Several trails offer splendid views as they meander through majestic Sitka spruce stands and wildflower meadows to the water's edge for closer looks at old logging railroad pilings, beaver dams, and islands.

Bring your canoe and you can spend the day paddling through scenic Winchester and Sengstacken arms. Before departing, check weather and tides, make sure you have at least one approved floatation device for each passenger, and obtain a free route map from the visitor center. The canoe launch is situated off a side road, one mile south of the visitor center.

A mile beyond the canoe launch, Seven Devils Road bends east. South of the curve a short side road branches west to Whiskey Run Beach and Seven Devils Wayside. Nearby, twenty-five wind turbines provide energy for a wind-powered farm.

Shore Acres State Park's formal garden is often used for concerts and weddings.

Jedediah Smith camped at Whiskey Run in 1828. A gold rush in 1851 led to the establishment of a camp that lasted about two years. Its seemingly endless sandy shoreline is perfect for beachcombing, clam digging, and agate hunting.

The drive concludes 1.5 miles south of the Whiskey Run turnoff, where Seven Devils Road reaches a junction with U.S. Highway 101.

7 BANDON, OCEAN SCENIC LOOP

General description: A five-mile drive along the Bandon waterfront and a coastline of spectacular seascapes and monoliths.

Special attractions: Bandon Waterfront, Bandon Historical Museum, South Jetty, Elephant Rock, Face Rock, Devil's Kitchen, Bradley Lake, views of lighthouse, sailboarding, fishing, beachcombing, wildlife, and storm and whale watching.

Location: Southern Oregon Coast west and south of Bandon.

Drive route names: First Street, Jetty Road, Ocean Drive, llth Street, Beach Loop Drive, Seabird Drive.

Travel season: All-year. Winter storms are major attractions in January and February.

Camping: One state park campground one mile north of drive with full hookups and electrical sites, plus commercial RV parks.

Services: All services at Bandon.

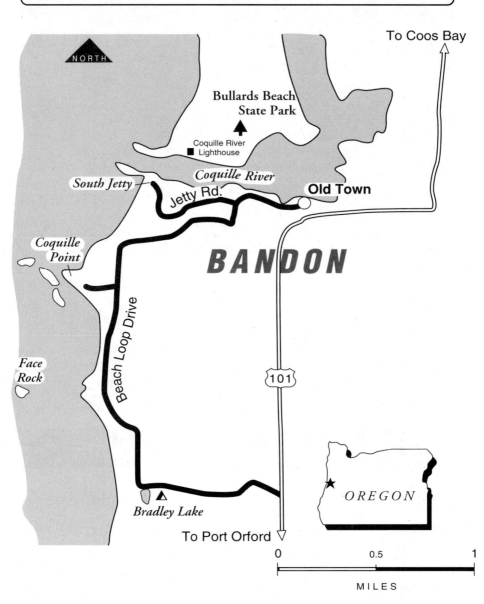

Nearby attractions: Charleston Harbor-Seven Devils Scenic Drive, Oregon Dunes National Recreation Area, Oregon Central Coast Scenic Drive, Bandon/Rogue River/Gold Beach Scenic Loop.

For more information: Bandon Chamber of Commerce, 300 S.E. 2nd St., P.O. Box 1515, Bandon, OR 97411, (541) 347-9616.

The drive: Starting from Bandon's Old Town waterfront, the drive travels southwest to the multi-use South Jetty, offering good views of the Coquille River, Bandon Bar, and a lighthouse across the river. Climbing a small hill, it passes several cliff-top viewing areas that provide beach access and spectacular offshore rock formations. A fresh-water lake enclosed by a sand dune can be reached on a short walk near the southern end of the drive. The shoreline and favorable winds have made Coquille River Bay and the beaches favorite sailboarding areas.

Summer temperatures climb to the seventies and low eighties, and summer-like days in early spring are not uncommon. Early autumn is the most dependable season for warm, calm weather. Temperatures average in the mid-fifties and low sixties during winter. Storm watching has become such a major winter activity that Bandon has proclaimed itself the storm watching capital of the world. The Bandon Storm Watchers Society offers informational programs on weather, ship wrecks, oceanography, and other subjects.

At the turn of the century, Bandon was a bustling seaport serving sailing ships, riverboats, and sternwheelers. In September 1936, the town was virtually destroyed in seven hours as a devastating fire leveled all but fifteen of the estimated 500 buildings.

Sternwheeler Rose, docked at the waterfront in Old Town, recalls a bit of 1800s river travel with guided cruises of the Coquille River. You can also fish and throw a crab net from the docks at the small picturesque boat basin and stroll the short boardwalk. If you're looking for local arts and crafts, you may wish to plan a couple of extra hours browsing Old Town's many shops. They feature local paintings, weaving, leather, silversmithing, stained glass, woodworking, and pottery. The section is also notable for its antique shops, restaurants, and stores specializing in local candies, and cranberry and cheese products.

From the waterfront, you'll see Coquille River Lighthouse, perched on the north jetty across the river. Built in 1896, it was the last of eight lighthouses constructed on the coast and one of the few ever hit by a ship. Decommissioned in 1939, it displays historic photos.

To visit the lighthouse travel north one mile, and turn west on Bullards Beach State Park Road. The park offers ninety-two full hookup and 100 electrical sites, hiker/biker and horse camps. A 1.5-mile hiking and seven-mile horse trail will take you along the ocean beach and river banks.

From Old Town, begin the scenic drive by traveling west on First Street by canneries, and waterfront buildings. About two blocks west of Old Town, a U.S. Coast Guard station building, constructed in 1939 and decommissioned in 1946, houses the Bandon/Coquille River Historical Museum. Exhibits cover local maritime operations and shipwrecks and include a natural history room and several thousand Native American artifacts.

As the route turns west onto Jetty Road, it passes a pond that attracts pelicans, egrets, herons, and shorebirds. The Coquille River meets the sea at the usually treacherous Bandon Bar off the south jetty, affording one of the best spots for watching breakers crash against rocks. Be careful where you

The short drive along the Pacific at Bandon overlooks some of the southern Oregon coast's most impressive off-shore monoliths.

park. During winter storms, waves toss driftwood like matchsticks and cover the parking lot with snow white foam.

The jetty area has some of the best local clam beds and fine surf fishing for perch, kelp greenling, ling cod, starry flounder, and smelt. You're also likely to see kites fluttering from the beach. The wide sandy shoreline, which continues south 0.5 mile to Elephant Rock, is one of the coast's most scenic beaches. Walkers may be rewarded with a variety of agates, jasper, and serpentine. At low tide look for shells, sand dollars, petrified wood, and fossilized scallops. Whales are often sighted from the jetty where the view also includes the lighthouse and Tupper Rock, a traditional Native American sacred site.

Back on the main loop, the route climbs a small hill and turns west onto Beach Loop Drive. Coquille Point, 0.8 mile south, overlooks Elephant Rock. Like all of the off-shore reefs and seastacks, Elephant Rock was once part of the shoreline. As the ocean eroded away soft sands and soil, the rocks became separated from the mainland.

They are part of the Oregon Islands National Wildlife Refuge and closed to public access. In summer, you'll see murres, puffins, and pelicans. Winter brings migrating whales and the spectacle of waves crashing through the elephant's eye. Stairs connect the viewpoint to the beach where harbor and elephant seals congregate and there are also tide pools and caves to explore. In this section, it's against the law to touch the seals and collect tide pool life.

From Elephant Rock, you can hike south along the beach to Face Rock. If you go, watch for sneaker waves which come unexpectedly and are capable of moving large logs.

Face Rock and Bandon Ocean State Park, 0.7 mile south, overlook one of the largest and strangest displays of offshore rocks to be seen anywhere along the Oregon Coast. According to a local legend, the Face Rock is a Native American maiden who was turned to stone by an evil spirit. Surrounding rocks are her dog, cat, and kittens. Nearby, magnificent stone pillars rise out of the ocean. You can descend to the beach by stairs and hike south about fourteen miles on a wide sandy beach. Several small streams empty into the ocean along the way. The shoreline is pocked with tide pools and often yields semi-precious agates, petrified wood and drift wood.

The route continues south, providing good views of the ocean and passes a stable that rents horses for beach and lake rides. Despite its name, Devil's Kitchen offers a safe beach for children to play in the water and a picnic area protected from wind by huge headlands. A small stream runs near the picnic area, which is framed both north and south by magnificent offshore seastacks. The rock formations are particularly striking when silhouetted by a flaming sunset. While waiting for the sun to work its magic, you can keep warm with a beach fire made from the usually plentiful supply of driftwood.

During the next mile, the route traverses forest and scrub brush and passes three entrances to Bandon State Park. The day-use areas feature numerous picnic tables looking out at off-shore monoliths. Beaches are popular with sunbathers and horseback riders. Motorized vehicles are allowed south of the third exit. Although you can hike several miles south along the shoreline, the scenery does not offer the spectacular rocks seen along the coast near town.

At a curve where the route turns east, a large parking area signals access to unsigned Bradley Lake. From the parking area, a short walk on a wooded trail and up and down a large sand dune will take you to its shores. The fresh-water pond, enclosed by dunes, is a favorite local swimming, sunbathing, and stocked rainbow trout fishing hole. Although there are no facilities at the site, a nearby commercial campground in a refreshing pine grove contains forty sites, twenty of which have electricity.

Six-tenths mile east, the drive concludes at a junction with U.S. Highway 101. You can return to Bandon city center and Old Town by traveling three miles north on U.S. Highway 101.

8 BANDON, ROGUE RIVER, GOLD BEACH SCENIC LOOP

General description: A 114-mile drive, including eleven miles of gravel through southern Oregon's Coquille River Valley, over the spine of the Coast Range mountains and along the Rogue River.

Special attractions: Bandon, Victorian homes, Coos County Logging Museum, Siskiyou National Forest, Powers Pioneer House museum, Wild and Scenic Illinois and Rogue rivers, wildlife observation, waterfalls, camping, hunting, outstanding mountain and river views.

Location: Southern Oregon between Bandon, Coquille, Agness and Gold Beach.

Drive route names and numbers: State Highway 42 South, State Highway

42, County Highway 242, Forest Service Road 33.

Travel season: Although the route is open all year, travel is best between June and September.

Camping: One state park campground with full hookups and electrical sites; Six U.S. Forest Service campgrounds with picnic tables, fire pits, vault or flush toilet, some with water. Several county and private RV parks.

Services: Full services at Bandon, Coquille, Myrtle Point, Gold Beach. Limited services at Powers, Agness.

Nearby attractions: Rogue River Wilderness, Wild and Scenic Rogue River, Oregon Dunes National Recreation Area, Oregon Central Coast scenic drive, Charleston Harbor/Seven Devils Loop drive, Bandon Scenic Ocean Views drive, California redwoods, Smith River scenic byway.

For more information: Bandon Chamber of Commerce, 300 S.E. 2nd St., P.O. Box 1515, Bandon, OR 97411, (541) 347-9616. Coquille Chamber of Commerce, 119 N. Birch, Coquille, OR 97423, (541) 396-3414. Gold Beach Chamber of Commerce, 1225 S. Ellensburg, No. 3, Gold Beach, OR 97444, (503) 247-7526, (800) 525-2334 (USA). Myrtle Point Chamber of Commerce, 424 5th St., P.O. Box 265, Myrtle Point, OR 97458, (541) 572-2626. Powers Chamber of Commerce, P.O. Box 92, Powers, OR 97466. Siskiyou National Forest-Powers Ranger District, Powers, OR 97466, (541) 439-3011.

The drive: At Bandon and Gold Beach, the drive begins at sea level and reaches an elevation of about 2,290 feet north of Agness. From Bandon, it proceeds east on Oregon Highway 42 South along the Coquille River eighteen miles to Coquille, then follows Highway 42 through Myrtle Point. Turning south on County Highway 242, it traverses a wide, flat, wooded valley. Near Powers, the Coquille River meanders in and away from the route offering a spectacular deep roadside canyon. Climbing into the Coast Range, it follows Forest Service Road 33 to Agness and along the Rogue River canyon's rim to Gold Beach.

Winter days with temperatures in the seventies and eighties are common on the south coast. Summer temperatures climb to over ninety degrees. Inland, at Agness and Powers, weather is slightly warmer. Frost is rare and snow is virtually unknown on the coast. Snow in the Coast Range usually melts quickly.

Highway 42 South begins in north Bandon at a junction with U.S. Highway 101. Bullards Beach State Park, west of the junction, offers ninety-two full hookups and 100 electrical campsites overlooking the beach. At Bandon Fish Hatchery, one mile east, you can picnic on lawns along Geiger Creek and see large schools of fingerlings and adult salmon.

From the hatchery, Highway 42 South crosses the southern end of the Coos basin. Underneath the ravine-like fold are thousands of feet of sand and mudstone that may have been deposited in a shallow bay some forty-five million years ago. They contain thick deposits of coal, some of which were mined early in the century.

The mines have disappeared and been replaced by flocks of sheep and cattle, rustic barns and farm houses, rolling hills, and stands of isolated oaks

BANDON, ROGUE RIVER, GOLD BEACH SCENIC LOOP

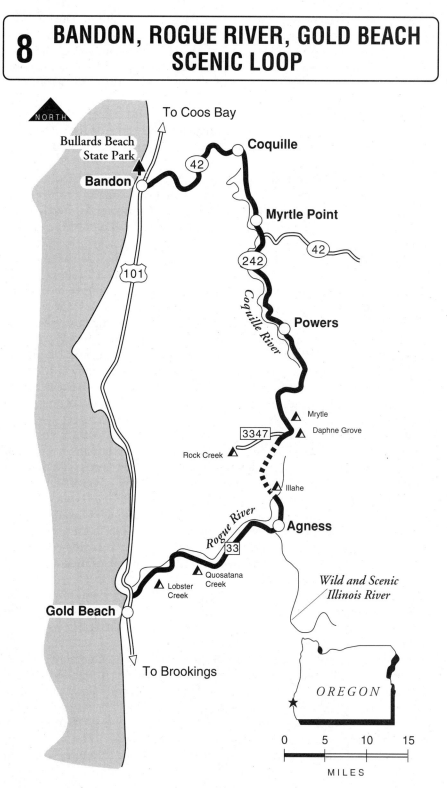

To Coos Bay

Bullards Beach
State Park

Bandon

NORTH

42

Coquille

Myrtle Point

242

42

101

Powers

Coquille River

▲ Mrytle

3347

▲ Daphne Grove

Rock Creek ▲

▲ Illahe

Rogue River

Agness

33

▲ Quosatana
Creek

▲ Lobster
Creek

Gold Beach

*Wild and Scenic
Illinois River*

To Brookings

OREGON

★

0   5   10   15

MILES

that share the landscape with the narrow, placid Coquille River. During July, wild sweet peas add splashes of purple and white along the roadside.

Boat ramps at Riverton and Sturdivant Riverfront Park near Coquille offer access to the river for boating, canoeing, and fishing for fall chinook and coho salmon, stripped bass, American shad, winter steelhead, and sea run cut-throat. Sturdivant also has moorage docks.

About four miles east, you'll enter the first of the route's several myrtlewood groves. The trees, which grow to 100 feet tall and can live for 300 years, provide raw materials for a thriving cottage industry that produces an assortment of souvenirs.

Coquille, three miles east, features some of the area's best preserved Victorian Homes. As Highway 42 follows the flood plane of the Coquille River nine miles southeast to Myrtle Point, you'll pass more myrtlewood groves, and crumpled lava and sandstone that were once part of the Pacific Ocean floor.

As you enter town, one block west of the highway you'll see a dark gray onion-domed building. It was modeled after Utah's Mormon Tabernacle and built in 1910 by the Church of the Latter Day Saints. As the Coos County Logging Museum, it now displays collections of blacksmith tools, various saws, and high climbing gear. Several of Myrtle Point's Queen Anne-styled homes and commercial buildings date from the 1860s to 1910.

Three miles east of Myrtle Point, the route turns south on County Highway 242. The pastoral landscape is rimmed by thick forest east and south of the highway and the lazy Coquille River and fields of cattle on the west. A coffee pot-shaped sawmill burner evokes a bit of nostalgia and hints of the area's once booming timber economy.

After a few miles, mountain slopes come down to the roadway, and the highway becomes a series of curves and starts a gentle climb. At Coquille Myrtle Grove State Park, ten miles south of the junction, thick oak, maples, and myrtle trees close off sunlight for a dense ground cover of ferns and provide a cool respite for picnickers on the Coquille River banks. In dry summers, the river is only a few feet wide, shallow enough to wade across, and so still that shoreline trees are reflected in its waters. On the six miles to Powers, the river becomes a thin blue ribbon in a deep roadside canyon as the highway passes under a canopy of trees, by a jumble of meadows, and through a dense fir forest.

If you're planning on hiking, camping, and wildlife observation, stop at the Powers Ranger Station for trail maps, campground locations, and information on road conditions. It also issues bird and animal check lists as well as fact sheets on black bear and other wildlife.

The Wagner House in Powers is a 1.5-story hand-hewn cabin built in 1872. It is Coos County's oldest preserved building, and inside you can see original family furnishings and historic artifacts. At Powers County Park, you'll find tennis courts, basketball hoops, a baseball field, and a large pond for swimming, canoeing, boating, and stocked rainbow trout fishing. The campground features thirty tent/RV sites with hookups.

From Powers, the route follows the south fork of the Coquille River into the jumbled and twisted mountains. Some 200 million years ago these mountains were sediment on the Pacific Ocean floor. When the oceanic crust slid out from under them, they were scraped off the ocean flood, jammed against the land mass, heated, crystallized, bent and uplifted.

After about four miles, the road enters the 1.09-million-acre Siskiyou National Forest. This section is a mixture of predominately Douglas fir, with myrtlewood, alders, maples, and oaks in valleys, and a lush undergrowth of ferns, blackberries, willows, and manzanita. You may see black-tailed deer and Roosevelt elk along the highway. Black bear, river otters, and raccoon are common along with great blue herons and red-tailed hawks. The forest is also a habitat for cougars, bobcats, and great horned owls.

Elk Creek Falls, two miles south of the boundary, drops from a cliff near the highway. A one-mile trail winds past the falls and through a stand of old-growth timber to the Big Tree picnic area that contains the world's largest Port Orford cedar tree.

During the next ten miles, the road winds through a rugged, narrow canyon, around ridges, and by two forest service campgrounds. Myrtle and Daphne groves each have five sites.

At Eden Valley and Glendale Junction, you leave Highway 219 and continue southwest on Forest Service Road 33. Forest Service Road 3347, near the junction, heads southwest about a mile to seven tent sites at Rock Creek Campground. Nearby, Azalea Lake Trail offers a moderate to steep 1.2-mile hike to the lake and several unimproved campsites along the shore.

The pavement ends at a summit overlooking a seemingly endless ocean of fir trees which fill valleys, hills and mountains in every direction. Logging truck traffic comes from several side roads, and you will want to proceed carefully on the somewhat narrow 10.7 miles of gravel downgrade. Foster Bar Campground about four miles south is a day-use area that serves primarily Rogue River hikers and rafters. It has restrooms but no drinking water. Illahe Campground is near the gravel's southern end and features twenty-two tent sites. Near the campground, the forty-mile Rogue River Trail begins and extends east forty miles through the Rogue River Wilderness to Graves Creek.

Back on pavement, you pass a small resort and continue south 2.5 miles to Agness on the banks of the Rogue River. The resort has campground and cabin rentals, restaurant and lounge, gas and oil, fishing supplies, groceries, a liquor store, and post office.

As you cross the bridge, look east and you'll see the wild and scenic section of the Rogue River and the western edge of the 36,000-acre Rogue River Wilderness. A forty-mile stretch of the river bisects the wilderness, which is accessible only by boat and two trails.

This section is one of the few where mail is delivered by boat. The route, which took days when deliveries started in 1895, now takes only a few hours. Fishermen and vacationers have been passengers since 1926.

A lodge on the south bank is a Rogue River mail boat lunch stop. Established in 1903, it offers a main lodge with the atmosphere of an inn, plus several rustic cabins and a store stocked with groceries, gas, propane, bait and tackle. Next door, Agness R.V. Park features eighty-four full hookup sites on 1,000 feet of river frontage.

Cougar Lake Resort is a mile west and caters to hunters and fishermen. The Rogue has a legendary reputation as a premier salmon, steelhead and trout stream, and the area is also known for its deer, elk, bear, and grouse hunting.

A mile west of the resort the Wild and Scenic Illinois River empties into the Rogue. From a viewpoint on the west end of the bridge, you can photograph the streams as they come together. Continuing west on the edge of a ridge, several pullouts offer spectacular views of the sheer cliffs, deep blue river, forested banks, and sand bars. Occasionally mail and jet boats filled with sightseers, streak up the river, around curves, and disappear into the wilderness.

Intermittent views of the canyon are broken by stands of maples, oak, Douglas fir, alder, and cedar. After 12.5 miles, the road descends to river level at Quosatana Creek Campground. A favorite of fishermen, it provides fish cleaning and trailer dump stations, boat ramp, and forty-three tent sites near the river bank. Walking the short barrier-free trail through the myrtlewood grove is a great way to loosen up while enjoying the cool pine-scented forest and shaded river.

The route exits the Siskiyou National Forest under a tunnel of tree limbs then continues through a wooded corridor to U.S. Highway 101. Lobster Campground is about four miles west of Quosatana Creek and has seven tent trailer sites, a boat ramp, and restrooms.

The Rogue River Bridge, on U.S. Highway 101 at the exit, has been designated a National Historic Civil Engineering Landmark. Built in 1931 and designed by Oregon's premier bridge builder, Conde B. McCullough, its decorative features include Egyptian obelisks, Gothic arches, and repeated use of supporting arches.

9 PORTLAND, COLUMBIA RIVER, ASTORIA

General description: A 198-mile drive through northwestern Oregon along the Columbia River, along the northern Oregon coast, and through the Tillamook State Forests.

Special attractions: Willamette River, Sauvie Island, Columbia River, Astoria, Fort Stevens, Fort Clatsop, Clatsop and Tillamook state forests, wildlife, sailboarding.

Location: Northwestern Oregon between Portland and Astoria.

Drive route numbers: U.S. Highway 30, U.S. Highway 26/101, U.S. Highway 26.

Travel season: All year. Winter can bring extremely icy conditions but rarely closes the highways.

Camping: One state park with full hookups and electrical sites; One state park with primitive sites. Several city and county campgrounds and RV parks.

Services: All services at Portland, St. Helens, Rainier, Astoria, Seaside. Limited services at Scappoose, Columbia City and Clatskanie.

Nearby attractions: Columbia River Gorge, Oregon City, Fort Vancouver National Historic Site, Mount St. Helens, Cannon Beach, Northern Oregon Coast drive, Washington County Scenic Loop.

For more information: Portland/Oregon Visitors Association, 26 S.W. Salmon, Portland, OR 97204, (503) 222-2223, (800) 962-3700; St. Helens-Scappoose Chamber of Commerce, 1934 Columbia Blvd., P.O. Box 1036, St. Helens, OR 97051, (503) 397-0685. Astoria/Warrenton Chamber of Commerce, 111 W. Marine Dr., P.O. Box 176, Astoria, OR 97103, (503) 325-6311, (800) 875-9807; Seaside Chamber of Commerce/Visitors Bureau, 7 N. Roosevelt, P.O. Box 7, Seaside, OR 97138, (503) 738-6391, (800) 444-6740 (USA).

The drive: Leaving Portland the route follows the trail of Lewis and Clark north along the Willamette and Columbia rivers to Rainier. En route, it passes through several small towns, two to twelve miles apart and scenery that varies from intermittent views of the Columbia, its river traffic, tiny islands and the verdant Washington shoreline to patches of marshland, and mixed forests of Douglas fir, western hemlock, and willows. Fossils found in rocks along this section indicate that thirty to thirty-five million years ago, this was part of the continental shelf. At Rainier, the Columbia bends around a promontory and U.S. Highway 30 cuts inland and through the forested Coast Range. After returning to the Columbia near Astoria, the drive takes U.S. Highway 101/26 south along the Oregon Coast for nineteen miles. It returns to Portland by following U.S. Highway 26 through Tillamook State Forest and Washington County farmlands.

Summer temperatures range from the upper fifties to mid-eighties and drop to the forties and mid-fifties in winter. Spring brings warm sunny days in the sixties and seventies. Autumn is the most dependable season for warm, calm weather. While these routes seldom close, fog and surface or "black" ice are hazards in winter.

As the drive leaves Portland, it offers good views of the Willamette River, and the Port of Portland's docks filled with loading equipment and products awaiting export.

The Willamette empties into the Columbia a few miles north at Sauvie Island. Both rivers figured prominently in the settlement of the Pacific Northwest. The Columbia, which begins in British Columbia and flows about 2,000 miles through Washington and Oregon to Astoria, attracted fur trappers and explorers seeking the "Great River of the West." Oregon Trail emigrants came west, attracted by the rich farmlands along the Willamette's banks.

Idyllic Sauvie Island, Accessible by a short bridge across Multnomah Channel, is the world's largest freshwater island and a favorite spot to buy fresh fruits and vegetables from roadside stands and fish sloughs and ponds for catfish, crappie, and perch. Each year more than 250 species of birds live

The Caples House Museum, at Columbia City, is one of several historic sites on the Portland, Columbia River, Astoria drive.

or pass through the island. At Bybee Howell Territorial Park, two miles north of the bridge, split-rail fences enclose a pioneer orchard and an 1880s home.

At Scappoose, eight miles north, a two-story candle and a totem pole stand out among buildings lining the highway. J.J. Collins Marine Park, accessible by boat, is a wildlife area with a few tent campsites. Airport Park, inside the city limits, has RV sites and electrical hookups. North of town, a two-lane county road links Scappoose with the settlements of Pittsburg and Vernonia, twenty and twenty-six miles west.

St. Helens, at twenty-eight miles, offers three marinas and the 1800s buildings of the Riverfront National Historic District. The Georgian Revival-styled Columbia County Courthouse, built of black basalt, is the district's centerpiece and one of the best places to see Washington's Mount St. Helens. Departures for Sand Island, Oregon's only designated marine park, leave from a boat dock behind the courthouse. On the island, you'll find seven campsites, nature trails to waterfowl areas, and a beach.

The Columbia River is almost a mile wide as it flows past Columbia City, where you can watch large freighters mingle with pleasure boats at Ruth Rose Richardson River Front Park and take a path down to the water's edge. The Caples House Museum, across the street, was built in 1870 and is divided into

50

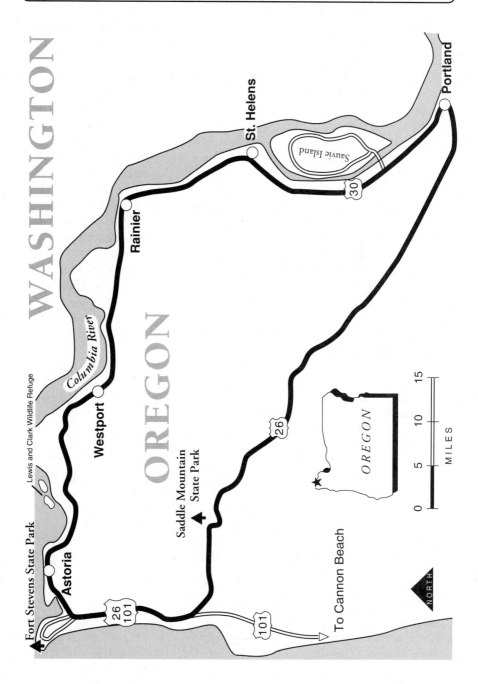

period parlors, doctor's offices, kitchens, and family rooms furnished with antiques.

En route to the recently closed Trojan Nuclear Power Plant, the highway crosses Deer Island, named by Lewis and Clark, and traverses open fields, a mixed forest and rocky bluffs. They were formed between eleven and twenty-five million years ago when lava from northeastern Oregon volcanos flowed into the area.

The scenery changes to marshlands, open fields, and a corridor of Douglas fir as the drive heads five miles north to Rainier. In the port city, Riverfront Park and Prescott Beach afford free access to the Columbia shoreline, and great views of river traffic. Lewis and Clark Bridge provides a giant arched frame behind the town and links Oregon with Longview, Washington.

Beyond Rainier, U.S. Highway 30 cuts across a plain, away from the river, through rock cliffs and by two Mount St. Helens viewpoints. At Clatskanie, deer and elk sometimes venture out of the forest and into town. You can fish for trout, salmon, and steelhead within the city limits and sailboard at nearby Jones Beach. The Flippin House, a few blocks south of the highway, is a National Historic Site, built by a logger in the 1880s, and patterned after a castle. It is furnished with antiques.

Leaving the Clatskanie Valley, the highway bisects meadows filled with sheep, Christmas tree farms, and stands of cottonwoods that are harvested and used in paper making.

At Westport for a change of pace and a small toll, you can take a ferry on a twenty-five-minute round trip to Washington's Puget Island where you may see deer, seal, and eagles.

The road climbs into the thick woodlands of Clatsop State Forest and the Coast Range, where posted speeds slow to thirty and forty miles per hour before reaching a high point of 656 feet. Bradley State Park, on the eastern slopes, is a day-use area with picnic tables and scenic views of mountains and river. Deer and elk frequent the area.

West of the mountains, the Columbia River sand bars and islands reappear and are visible for the rest of the way into Astoria. Twenty of the islands comprise the 35,000-acre Lewis and Clark National Wildlife Refuge, which is accessible only by boat. The refuge is a resting area for swans, geese, and ducks.

Approaching Astoria, you'll see the Astoria-Megler Bridge spanning the Columbia. At 4.1 miles long, it is the world's longest continuous truss span bridge. On foggy days, its easy to understand why early seafarers missed the mouth of the river, which was finally discovered by Captain Robert Gray on May 11, 1792, and named after his ship.

The Columbia River Maritime Museum and Heritage Center Museum, on U.S. Highway 30, and nearby Astoria Column interpret various aspects of the area's colorful history. From the 125- foot-column's observation tower, you have a superb view of the city, Pacific Ocean, Columbia River, and Washington and Oregon forests.

U.S. Highway 30 ends at the Astoria Bridge. The drive proceeds south on U.S. Highway 101/U.S. Highway 26, passing a junction with Oregon High-

The wreck of the Peter Iredale rests on the beach at Fort Stevens State Park and can be seen on either the Portland, Columbia River, Astoria or Northern Oregon Coast drives.

way 202, a scenic mountain route leading east to Jewell and Mist. Crossing Youngs Bay, it enters the Warrenton/Hammond Recreation Area, the north coast's major center for deep sea fishing charters.

Two miles further, signs direct you three miles east to Fort Clatsop National Memorial, the site of Lewis and Clark's 1805-06 winter encampment. It rests in a dense forest of Douglas fir and hemlock and contains a reconstructed log fort, marked nature trail, and a canoe landing on the Lewis and Clark River.

Fort Stevens, seven miles west of U.S. Highway 101/U.S. Highway 26, guarded the Pacific Coast from the Civil War through World War II, when it became the only U.S. mainland installation fired upon by the Japanese. At the 3,700-acre state park you can fish two lakes and the ocean for bass, perch, and stocked trout, and tour concrete batteries, guns, and a memorial garden with 170 species of roses. Nine miles of hiking and biking trails meander through a forest of shore pine to the beach and a campground with 213 full hookups, 130 electrical, and 262 tent sites.

Continuing south, the main highway passes fields of European bunch grass—planted during the 1930s to arrest spreading sand dunes—woodlands, Del Rey Beach, and the resort communities of Gearhart and Seaside.

South of Seaside the highways divide, and the drive takes U.S. Highway 26 to Portland. The land grows older as you continue east. Sandstones near the ocean were formed about fifteen to twenty million years ago while interior sands and basalts were laid down about forty to fifty million years ago. Along U.S. Highway 26, called the Sunset Highway, attractions are few and services are limited. The highway honors the Oregon National Guard's 41st Infantry Division, which is known as the Sunset Division.

The world's largest Sitka spruce tree stands two miles east of the junction at a roadside rest area. It is fifty-two feet six inches in circumference, 216 feet high, and has a crown spread of ninety-three feet.

The Necanicum River parallels the highway as you travel through a spruce corridor and at mile 10 pass a junction with Oregon Highway 53 which leads fourteen miles south to Wheeler.

Saddle Mountain State Park, one mile beyond the junction, has restrooms, picnic grounds and nine primitive campsites. A seven-mile, steep, narrow paved road twists through a thick forest to a trailhead parking lot. The six-mile round-trip hike to the top is strenuous. From the 3,283-foot summit—the highest point in Oregon's northern Coast Range—on clear days, the view can extend from Nehalem Bay to Mount Hood and north to Washington's Mount St. Helens, Mount Adams, and Mount Rainier. Saddle Mountain, known for its spring wildflower displays, also exhibits prime examples of pillow basalts, which were formed under water some fifty-five million years ago.

Camp 18, at eighteen miles, is a beautiful lodge-style restaurant made from local stone and logs that were hand peeled with draw knives. An outdoor logging museum exhibits 1900s steam donkeys and locomotives, rigging poles, and high wheel skidders.

A continuous sea of Douglas and noble fir, Sitka spruce and western red cedar frames the highway as it climbs into the Coast Range and through the Clatsop and Tillamook state forests. Between 1933 and 1945, several forest fires burned a total of 355,000 acres of the Tillamook Forest. The area has been replanted through aerial seeding. Cresting at 1,642 feet, it affords horizon-wide views of valleys, hillsides, and mountain slopes covered with waves of fir trees. A county road at twenty- two miles extends north to Jewel where elk, deer, and waterfowl congregate near the highway.

Sunset Springs Rest Area, a few miles east, includes a history of the Tillamook Burn, picnic tables, and rest rooms. Dairy farms, meadows, apple and nut orchards provide the scenery from the Washington County line to Beaverton's industrial parks and shopping malls. Portland's west hills, a string of small volcanos three miles east of Beaverton, were active as recently as three to five million years ago. Hilly Washington Park borders U.S. Highway 26 and brings the drive to a perfect end by offering a magnificent view of the city, with Mount Hood serving as a dramatic backdrop. The beautiful park's attractions include the Portland Zoo, World Forestry Center, an arboretum, rose test gardens and a Japanese garden.

10 WASHINGTON COUNTY LOOP

General description: A seventy-five-mile signed loop on paved highways through northwestern Oregon's Washington County farmlands, orchards, and wine country.

Special attractions: Vineyards, museums, historic sites, orchards, farmlands, scenic vistas, Hagg Lake Recreation Area.

Location: Northwestern Oregon nine miles west of Portland.

Drive route names and numbers: Oregon Highway 99 West; Beef Bend Road; Oregon Highways 210 and 217; U.S. Highway 26; Old Scotch Church, Glenco roads, Oregon highways 6, 8, and 47; Gaston, Laurelwood, and Scholls Ferry roads.

Travel season: All year.

Camping: There are no campgrounds along the route or in Washington County.

Services: All services in Tigard, Beaverton, and Forest Grove.

Nearby attractions: Columbia River Gorge, Oregon City historic sites, Champoeg State Park, Fort Vancouver National Historic Site, Washington Park Zoo, World Forestry Center, Portland/Columbia River/Astoria Scenic Drive. 99 West Scenic Drive.

For more information: Washington County Visitors Association, 5075 SW Griffith Dr., Suite 120, Beaverton, OR 97005, (503) 644-5555, (800) 537-3149 (USA).

The drive: The loop starts in the business and residential areas of Tigard, then heads north to U.S. Highway 26, which is a good place to start the drive if you wish to avoid the congestion of the first few miles. Turning west, it bisects business parks and farmlands, briefly touches the edge of a forest, then moves south through vineyards to Forest Grove. After circling scenic Hagg Lake, it concludes by traveling east through farms and fruit and nut orchards.

Washington County lies on a bed of basalt lava, which represents the westernmost end of the Columbia Plateau. The lava flowed out of eastern Oregon and down the Columbia River about twenty million years ago. After the last ice age, the area was buried in flood waters that deposited sand, gravel, and topsoil.

The rich land and six months of frost-free weather are conducive to growing a variety of fruits, vegetables, and commercial crops. An assortment of farms, roadside stands, and vineyards along the drive offer seasonal produce and wine tastings. The Washington County Visitors Association publishes a tour brochure that lists addresses, telephone numbers, and the products of each market.

Summer days in the high seventies to mid-eighties are ideal for driving. Spring and fall days average in the high sixties. While temperatures dip to an average of thirty-three degrees in January, they climb into the fifties during February and March.

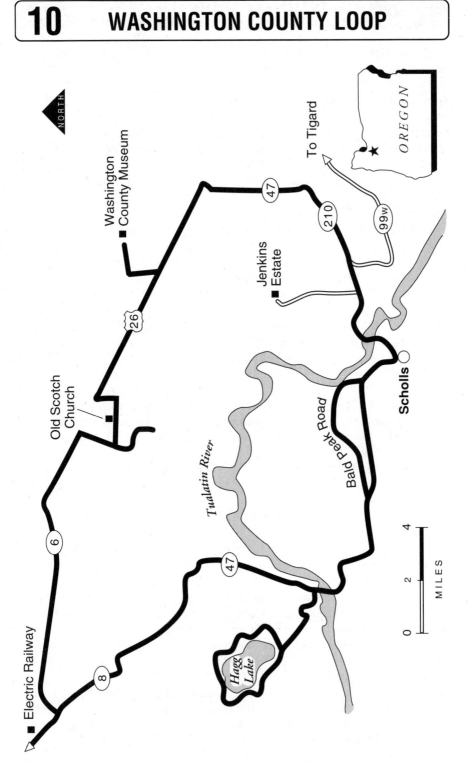

In Tigard, the drive starts by following Highway 99 West 3.5 miles west, turns north on Beef Bend Road, passing through two miles of a residential area, apple orchards, and Christmas tree farms and ends at Oregon Highway 210. A turn west on Highway 210 takes you to Ponzi Vineyards—one mile from the junction—where you can sample award-winning pinots, chardonnays, and dry white reislings.

The route turns east on Highway 210, bisecting pastoral farms with cement-block barns, and pastures enclosed with white wooden fences. At Washington Square, the area's largest shopping center, the drive turns north on Highway 217, passing business parks, commercial centers, motels, and Beaverton Town Center Mall before entering a greenway. Four miles north, it turns west at the Astoria/Tillamook exit onto U.S. Highway 26.

U.S. Highway 26 is also called The Sunset Highway. The name honors Oregon's 41st Infantry Division, which saw extensive combat in both world wars. To reach Portland Community College's Rock Creek campus turn north on 185th Street, then east on Springville Road. The Washington County Museum on campus displays an extensive collection of photographic equipment, thematic exhibits on the history of Washington County from Indians to high technology, and 16,000 historic photographs.

Rejoining U.S. Highway 26, the drive continues west through grass and grain fields to Jackson School Road. A turn south and then west puts you on Old Scotch Road, where the Tualatin Plains Presbyterian Church has served local residents since 1878. The white wooden building with an unusual eight-sided steeple is the county's most photographed site. Joe Meek, mountain man and first U.S. Marshall of the Oregon Territory, is buried in the church cemetery along with his family and other pioneers.

Peterson Farm Apple Country, about one mile west and south on Glenco Road, raises fifty varieties of apples, pears, and cherries. You can picnic in the farm's orchard and sample cider from July through December.

Following Glenco Road north to U.S. Highway 26, the drive continues west to Oregon Highway 6. After seven miles of brushy rolling hills, broken by wheat fields, it passes a junction with Oregon Highway 8 and winds northwest through thick stands of Douglas fir. Gales Creek, known for its large steelhead, cascades over moss-covered rocks along the roadside.

The Oregon Electric Railway Museum, five miles northwest of the junction, is tucked away in the forest on the creek's banks. At the museum, you can see double-decker trolleys from England, open cars from Australia, electric locomotives, and an interurban car. The admission includes the museum, trolley barn tours, and unlimited trolley rides through woods and fields to a picnic area by a mountain stream.

Returning to the junction, the drive follows Highway 8 south through berry fields, oak-covered hillsides, and picturesque farms with aging barns and herds of dairy cattle. Several wineries along this segment offer public tastings and feature pinot noirs, gerwurztraminer, rieslings, and specialties.

At Tualatin Valley Winery, you can sample and purchase chardonnay and others in a tasting room or picnic area overlooking a magnificent eighty-five-acre vineyard and the Tualatin Valley. Shafer Vineyard Cellars offers

The Oregon Electric Railway Museum, northwest of Forest Grove, features vintage cars and equipment from England, Australia, and the United States.

sauvignon blanc and others in a tasting room or large oak-shaded picnic area with a gazebo. The Gales Creek Valley spreads below, and on Sundays during July and August you can listen to jazz concerts. Laurel Ridge Winery is one of a few Oregon vintners making sparkling wines by the traditional French method. Vineyard plantings include semillon and sylvaner.

Forest Grove, ten miles south of the junction, was named for its white oak and fir forests that shade virtually every street. Old College Hall, on the Pacific University campus in downtown, is the oldest educational building in use west of the Rocky Mountains. Inside you'll find a magnificent reception room and a museum with oriental and pioneer relics. The Valley Art Association, close to campus, exhibits and sells Northwest pottery, jewelry, and paintings.

South of Forest Grove, Highway 47 becomes Scoggins Road. After two miles, a turn west on Dilly Road will take you to Montinore Winery. A Victorian mansion, a drive lined with oak trees, and rolling hills covered with grapes create a relaxing setting for sampling Müller-Thurgua, sauvignon, and chenin blanc.

The loop's scenic highlight lies two miles south at Scoggins Valley Park and Henry Hagg Lake. An eleven-mile scenic drive circles the 1,113-acre man-made lake, situated in a dense forest at the base of the Coast Range. In summer the water is covered with boaters, water skiers, and fishermen angling for rainbow trout, perch, and largemouth and smallmouth bass. You can also enjoy numerous picnic sites, fifteen miles of hiking trails to shorelines and surrounding forest, observation decks for viewing elk, deer, eagles and osprey, and an elevator-equipped fishing dock that floats on the lake.

South of the lake entrance, the drive crosses the Tualatin River, which bends in a great curve through the center of the county and turns east onto Gaston, Springhill, and Laurelview roads. In this six-mile stretch you'll pass farmlands, fruit and nut orchards, and turn north onto Bald Peak Road. At the summit of the small hill, which is the County's highest point, Bald Peak State Park's picnic tables and lawns offer a panorama of the Cascades, Coast Range, and Willamette Valley.

This region produces ninety-five percent of the nation's filberts. You'll see some of the groves along with stands of walnuts, and apple and cherry orchards as the remaining five miles of the loop returns to Highway 210 (SW Scholls Ferry Road) and another crossing of the Tualatin River.

At Smith Berry Barn and Boutique in the crossroads of Scholls, you can pick raspberries and purchase jams, nuts, and hand-crafted gifts. A few miles east, Oregon Heritage Farm offers samplings of fresh cider, plus apples, vegetables, and nuts in season.

Turning onto Tile Flat Road, the drive heads north three miles over a series of roller coaster, grass-covered hills to Jenkins Estate. The hunting lodge-styled main house is a National Historic Site. Paths wind through the sixty-eight acres of forest, lawns, flower and rock gardens. Wild rhododendrons start the displays in spring, and formal gardens bloom throughout the summer. Although the home is only open by appointment, you can stroll through the gardens from 9 a.m. to 4 p.m. Monday through Friday.

To and from the estate, you'll pass Cooper Mountain Vineyards. The seventy-five-acre vineyard was homesteaded in 1865 and is situated on an extinct volcano. Tastings of pinot noir, chardonnay, and pinot gris are offered on weekends.

After passing Scholls Ferry Farm—where you can buy Oregon-grown products—and Ponzi Vineyards, the drive concludes at Beef Bend Road.

11 WILSON RIVER, OREGON COAST, WILLAMETTE VALLEY

General description: A 194-mile loop on paved roads through northwestern Oregon's Tillamook State Forest, Coast Range, northern coast, and the Willamette Valley.

Special attractions: Historic Tillamook Burn, scenic Wilson River, vineyards, mountain and ocean scenery, dairylands, historic sites.

Location: Northwestern Oregon between Forest Grove, the Oregon Coast and Tigard.

Drive route names and numbers: Oregon Highway 8, Oregon Highway 6 (Wilson River Highway), Three Capes Scenic Loop Road, U.S. Highway 101, Oregon Highway 18, Oregon Highway 99 West.

Travel season: All year. During summer dry periods, smoking is prohibited on Tillamook State Forest trail hikes.

Camping: Six state forest and four National Forest Service campgrounds with picnic tables, fire rings, flush or vault toilets. Some have drinking water. Two state parks, one with full hookups, standard and hiker/biker campsites; one with hiker/biker sites.

Services: All services in Forest Grove, Tillamook, Lincoln City, McMinnville, Tigard. Limited services in Pacific City, Sheridan.

Nearby attractions: Columbia River Gorge, Washington Park Zoo, World Forestry Center, Portland/Columbia River/Astoria Scenic Drive, Depoe Bay, Cannon Beach, Newport, Washington County Scenic Loop, 99 East and West Scenic Drives.

For more information: Forest Grove Chamber of Commerce, 2417 Pacific Ave., Forest Grove, OR 97116, (503) 357-3006. Washington County Visitors Association, 5075 SW Griffith Dr., Suite 120, Beaverton, OR 97005, (503) 644-5555, (800) 537-3149 (USA). Oregon Department of Forestry, Forest Grove District, 801 Gales Creek Rd., Forest Grove, OR 97116-1199, (503) 357-2191. Tillamook Chamber of Commerce, 3705 Highway 101 N., Tillamook, OR 97141, (503) 842-7525. Lincoln City Visitors and Convention Bureau, 801 S.W. Highway 101, No. 1, P.O. Box 109, Lincoln City, OR 97367, (541) 994-2164, (800) 452-2151 (USA). West Valley Chamber of Commerce, 147 W. Main, P.O. Box 98, Sheridan, OR 97378, (503) 843-4964. McMinnville Chamber of Commerce, 417 N. Adams, McMinnville, OR 97128, (503) 472-6196. Newberg Area Chamber of Commerce, 115 N. Washington, Newberg, OR 97132, (503) 538-2014. Tigard Chamber of Commerce, 12420 S.W. Main St., Tigard, OR 97223, (503) 639-1656.

The drive: Portland travelers can join the loop by taking the Sunset Highway (U.S. Highway 26) west about twenty- five miles to a junction with Highway 6. From Forest Grove, the drive follows Highway 8 ten miles northwest to Highway 6, then travels through the Tillamook National Forest and over the peaks of the Coast Range. Although the area was devastated by a series of fires between 1939 and 1950, it has been replanted and exhibits a mature forest of noble fir, Sitka spruce and western red cedar, dominated by seventy-five-foot Douglas firs. After following the Wilson River to Tillamook, sightseers can choose between traveling south on U.S. Highway 101, which jogs inland through a forested corridor, or taking the Three Capes Scenic Loop. The return on Oregon highways 18 and 99 stays on relatively low, flat land as it mixes forest at the beginning with Willamette Valley farmlands near the end. Traffic is generally light on Highway 6. Highways 18 and 99 West are major connecting routes to the coast. Traffic is moderate during week-days and heavy on weekends.

Inland summer days range in the high seventies to mid-eighties. Spring and fall average in the high sixties. Although temperatures average in the low thirties in January, they range in the fifties during February and March. On the coast, summer days are usually in the sixty- to seventy-degree range and winter days fall in the mid-fifties, and the calmest weather comes in autumn.

From Forest Grove, the drive follows Oregon Highway 8 northwest through stands of oak trees, picturesque farms, and several vineyards that

11 WILSON RIVER, OREGON COAST, WILLAMETTE VALLEY

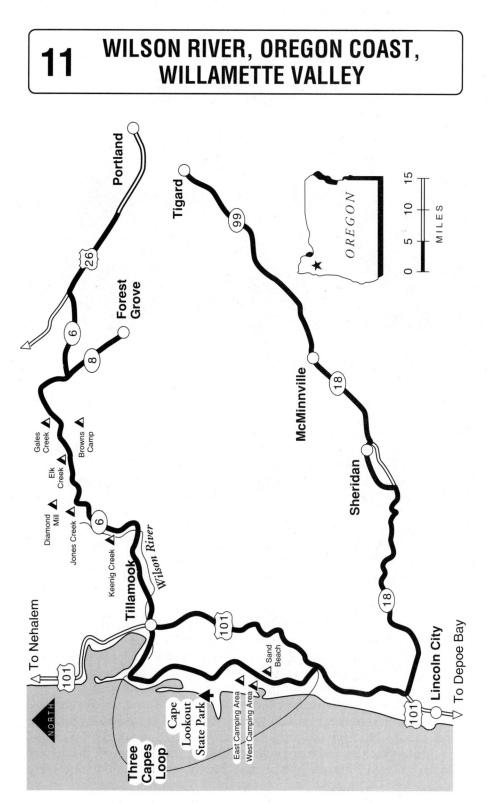

Portland

Tigard

99

OREGON

★

15
10
5
0
MILES

26

Forest Grove

6

8

McMinnville

18

Gales Creek

Browns Camp

Elk Creek

Sheridan

Diamond Mill

6

Jones Creek

Keenig Creek

Wilson River

Tillamook

To Nehalem

101

18

NORTH

101

Sand Beach

Cape Lookout State Park

East Camping Area

West Camping Area

Lincoln City

To Depoe Bay

101

Three Capes Loop

61

Tillamook National Forest and the scenic Wilson River share the roadside as Oregon Highway 6 meanders through the Coast Range.

offer tastings at selected hours. Turning west onto Oregon Highway 6, Gales Creek riffles along the roadway lined with giant Douglas firs. The Oregon Electric Railway Museum Trolley Park, four miles west of the junction, features a car barn filled with rolling stock and train rides through the forest to a picnic area by a stream.

Less than a mile beyond the park, you enter the eastern boundary of the 364,000-acre Tillamook State Forest and begin a five-mile ascent to the Coast Range summit of 1,556 feet. Gales Creek Forest Park, north of the highway, offers thirty-two shaded sites. Rogers Camp at the summit provides a parking area for hikers and motorcyclists. An easy two-mile trail along a wooded stream with a beaver colony, an old railroad grade, and logging roads link it with Gales Creek Park. Another easy hike takes an elk trail two miles south to Camp Brown, which has fifteen campsites and is a staging area for horseback riders and motorcyclists.

The forest fire of 1933, the infamous Tillamook Burn, started four miles north of the summit and raged through the Coast Range with a force that uprooted and twisted off trees and cracked cliffs with the intense heat. Ash and cinders fell on Tillamook, forty miles away and had to be shoveled off the streets. Later fires brought the total burned to 355,000 acres.

The Wilson River, a rushing torrent in springtime and a lazy, sluggish stream during summer, begins near the summit and meanders in and away from the roadside for the rest of the drive to Tillamook. The layers of sedimentary rock, interspersed with basalt lava, which you'll see in the river canyon's rugged cliffs, are part of an ancient ocean floor. About thirty-five million years ago, a tectonic plate shifted, slid under another plate and jacked it up, raising the ocean floor above sea level and creating the Coast Range mountains.

The endless waves of hills, valleys, and peaks covered with dark blue-green trees, are havens for deer, elk, and the seldom-seen black bear and mountain lion. All are fair game for hunters.

A few miles west of the summit, a side road leads north about a mile to fifteen campsites situated near the base of Kings Mountain and at the confluence of Elk Creek and the Wilson River. Several hikes start at Elk Creek Campground and wind around the mountain, by waterfalls, and wild flower displays, and to the 3,226-foot summit. The hikes range from easy to difficult and cover from two to nine miles.

Continuing west, the highway passes side roads extending one to two miles north to twenty sites at Diamond Mill Campground, thirty at Jones Creek, and Keenig Creek, with twenty. Two area stores offer bait, gas, and groceries, serving not only picnickers but whitewater rafters, steelhead, and sea-run cutthroat trout fishermen.

Foothills of moss-covered oaks signal the beginning of Tillamook County's dairylands. The road's final fifteen miles, passes several boat ramps as it follows the shallow river channel through farmlands into Tillamook.

Tillamook County Pioneer Museum, on the corner of Highway 6 and 2nd Street, occupies a former courthouse and contains one of the state's best natural history exhibits. Highway 6 ends one block west of the museum at an intersection with U.S. Highway 101. Two miles north of the junction at the Tillamook County Creamery Association factory, you can sample the cheese that has made the town internationally famous.

The thirty-eight-mile Three Capes Scenic Loop starts at the intersection of Highway 6 and U.S. Highway 101. It features magnificent coastal scenery, several off-shore wildlife refuges, a sand dune area, and full hookup camping at Cape Lookout State Park. Three Forest Service campgrounds offer a total of 241 sites.

At Tillamook, U.S. Highway 101 jogs inland and away from the ocean for twenty-one miles before continuing along the shoreline at Pacific City. Along this section is a World War II blimp hanger, which has been converted to an aircraft museum, and is one of the world's largest wooden structures. The area is also the gateway to the Trask River's salmon, steelhead, and trout fishing, plus backroads and trails to Hebo Mountain summit (elevation 3,154 feet), which offers lake fishing and a sixteen-site forest service campground. Two short trails start at the highway and end at 266-foot Munson Creek Falls, the highest of the Coast Range waterfalls.

From Pacific City where the three capes loop ends, U.S. Highway 101 heads south through the family resort area of Neskowin and over Cascade Head. Three miles north of Lincoln City, the drive turns east onto Highway 18.

For the first nine miles, the drive traverses ancient basalts and mudstones formed about fifty million years ago. Some of them are visible in the banks of the Salmon River, which parallels the highway. H.B. Van Duzer Forest

State Park, with a hiker\biker camp, and fishing, signals the beginning of a magnificent nine-mile corridor of stately Douglas firs, Oregon oak, and alder. At the lumbering community of Grand Ronde, Highway 18 merges with Highway 22, which extends northwest to U.S. Highway 101.

At Willamina, a scenic side road loops north of town through the Coast Range foothills then rejoins the main highway near Sheridan. The loop takes you past Willamina Falls and a large rock known as an erratic, which was moved here by an ice age glacier. A nearby park and arboretum feature more than 120 trees and native and exotic wildlife.

Near Sheridan the merged highways split, and Highway 22 angles thirty miles southeast to Salem. Highway 18 leaves the forest and bisects low rolling hills of open farmland as it heads 9.5 miles east to Amnity and enters the northwestern corner of the Willamette Valley. The Yamhill River, weaving in and out of the roadside east to Dundee, is fished for trout, steelhead, salmon, bass, crappie, and blue gill.

The Willamette Valley's rich soil was the main attraction and prime motivation for the thousands of emigrants who endured the hardships of the Oregon Trail. From Amnity to Tigard, you'll cross valley farms and orchards that grow cherries, plums, wheat, nursery stock, grass seed and ninety per cent of the nation's filberts. Several communities along the highway reflect the pioneer heritage.

McMinnville, six miles east of Amnity, exhibits the traditional main street of small town America by preserving fifty-two commercial buildings spanning the 1880s to the 1930s. Taking Highway 99 from McMinnville, you'll pass Linfield College, a comprehensive liberal arts school established in 1849.

Lafayette, four miles east, straddles the highway with a few blocks of historic buildings and a large antique mall. At Yamhill Locks Park, you can picnic and fish on the Willamette River bank overlooking the crumbling cement walls of locks that aided navigation from 1900 to 1954.

The Dundee Wine Company's Elk Cove Tasting Room on Highway 99 is situated across the road from a filbert orchard and shares its parking lot with Argyle Vineyards. Both are open seven days a week from 11 a.m. to 5 p.m. Argyle's fifteen-minute tour takes you through the sparkling wine process from chilling and pressing grapes to bottling.

At Newberg, a mile east, you can take a self-guided walking tour of more than fifty homes and buildings built from 1880 to 1928. They include a variety of architectural styles and portions of two Donation Land Claims. Hoover-Minthorn Museum House, one block south of Highway 99 at 2nd and River streets, was the boyhood home of Herbert Hoover from 1885-1889. It exhibits many original furnishings, photographs, and souvenirs. Hoover Park, across the street, offers a pleasant picnic spot with a variety of trees, a rhododendron garden, and stone creek-bank retaining walls built during the 1930s by the Work Progress Administration.

On the concluding twenty miles to Tigard, Highway 99 cuts across the low hills of the westernmost edge of the Columbia Plateau basalt lava flows while passing clusters of businesses and open fields.

12 MOSIER, ROWENA DELL, MARYHILL LOOP

General description: A fifty-mile drive on the eastern portion of the Historic Columbia River Highway and into Washington State.

Special attractions: Columbia River Gorge National Scenic Area and Historic Highway, buildings and sites, Tom McCall Wildflower Preserve, The Dalles Dam, Horsethief Lake State Park, Maryhill Museum of Art, Stonehenge Replica, fishing, boating, sailboarding.

Location: Columbia River Gorge between Mosier and Biggs.

Drive route numbers: U.S. Highway 30, U.S. Highway 197, Washington Highway 14, U.S. Highway 97.

Travel season: All year. Some roads become extremely icy in winter.

Camping: In Washington, three U.S. Army Corps of Engineer sites offer primitive camping; two state parks, one with standard sites and one with hookups. In Oregon, there are no campgrounds on the loop but several with hookups are situated in the immediate area on Interstate 84.

Services: All services at The Dalles, Biggs. Limited Services at Mosier and Rowena.

Nearby attractions: Hood River Valley Scenic Drive, Mount Hood Loop, Columbia River Gorge Scenic Drive, Sherman County Loop Tour, Goldendale Observatory.

For more information: The Dalles Area Chamber of Commerce, 404 W. 2nd St., The Dalles, OR 97058. (541) 296-2231, (800) 255-3385 (USA).

The drive: When it was completed in 1922, the historic Columbia River Highway extended from The Dalles to the Pacific Ocean and was considered an engineering masterpiece. One newspaper said it "possesses the best of all the great highways in the world, glorified."

Starting at Mosier, the drive incorporates the first fourteen miles of the historic highway (U.S. Highway 30) as it travels east atop the ridges of the Columbia River Gorge National Scenic Area, affording magnificent views of the river and Washington countryside. Descending into The Dalles, it crosses the Columbia River, and follows Washington Highway 14 east to Maryhill and the Stonehenge replica while offering continuous views of Oregon's Columbia Gorge. The drive concludes by returning to Oregon at Biggs. Travelers can join the drive at Biggs, The Dalles, and several Interstate 84 exits west to Mosier. For the most direct access to Mosier take Exit 69 and travel 0.5 mile south into town. Traffic is usually light on the historic highway and moderate on Highway 14.

Temperatures from the mid-nineties to over 100 degrees are common during summer. Travelers will find spring and fall days between the upper forties and the low sixties. Winter days range from below freezing to the low

MOSIER, ROWENA DELL, MARYHILL LOOP

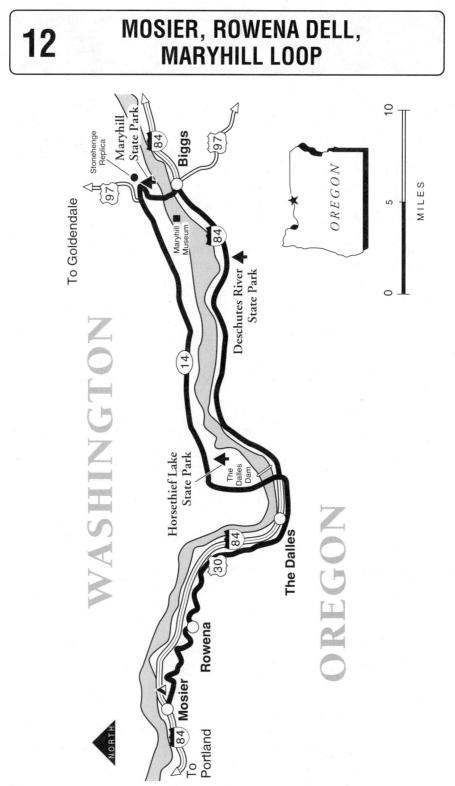

forties, and gorge winds often create extremely icy conditions between November and February.

The drive begins by crossing the picturesque Mosier Creek Bridge. At 120 feet long it is the second longest single arch on the highway. It was built in 1920 and was the first bridge designed by Conde B. McCullough. Later, he became world famous for his bridges on the Oregon Coast and Central America's Inter-American Highway.

After the bridge, the road climbs abruptly and curves around hills of scrub oak and pine, and by apple and cherry orchards protected by rows of Lombardy poplars. Looking north, you will see the Columbia River below and Washington across the water. Two miles east of Mosier, the road passes a large Georgian home with a two-story portico nestled on a north hillside. It was built in 1913 by wealthy Bostonian Mark Mayer, who donated the land for Mayer State Park.

Unmarked Memaloose Overlook, one mile east of the home, was established as a memorial to the Indian burial grounds on the Columbia's Memaloose Island, which is visible below. Memaloose State Park is near the island and accessible only to westbound travelers on Interstate 84; it contains forty-three full hookup and sixty-seven tent camping sites.

U.S. Highway 30 continues east for several miles along the flat-topped ridges and terraced lava outcroppings of Rowena Dell. With its sparse vegetation, the terrain is somewhat reminiscent of the southwestern United States and known locally as the "Grand Canyon" of the gorge. Formed about fifteen million years ago and refined by ice age glaciers and floods 12,000 years ago, the Dell is a protected nature preserve. From February through May, it presents Oregon's premier wildflower displays. One of the gorge's most picturesque bridges spans Dry Canyon Creek.

At Rowena Crest Viewpoint, the drive reaches its highest level, about 1,000 feet above the river. From the viewpoint, the Columbia River and its canyon seem to stretch east to infinity; and U.S. Highway 30 serpentines around bluffs below. On clear days, your 360-degree view encompasses 11,235-foot Mount Hood, plus Washington's 12,276-foot Mount Adams and the Klickitat River Canyon.

The Dell and Governor Tom McCall Preserve, across the highway, lie in a transition zone between the moist west side and the dry prairie east of the mountains. The 230-acre Nature Conservatory site supports 300 species of plants. Thompson's broadleaf lupine, waterleaf, Columbia desert parsley, and Hood River vetch, are unique to the gorge. Mule deer, golden eagles, osprey, Lewis woodpeckers, and numerous other birds inhabit the area. Watch for rattlesnakes, ticks, and poison oak if you decide to take the short walk through the meadows to the steep cliff edge.

The highway gradually descends from the steep viewpoint for several miles in a series of sweeping curves. Called the Rowena Loops, they were built to fulfill the stipulation of the highway's engineer, Samuel Lancaster that "the maximum grade of any ascent/descent should not exceed five percent." The decorative stonework along the loops were made by Italian stonemasons and extend several miles east to a turnoff to Mayer State Park.

The Columbia River Gorge Highway (U.S. 30) features classic bridges and decorative stonework.

The park, accessible from a one-mile side road over Interstate 84, is a favorite Columbia River picnicking, swimming, and boating site. From the shoreline, you have outstanding views of the gorge's steep cliffs and Washington's terraced hills. Pier fishing usually lands smallmouth bass, chub, and carp. In the main channel, you may be rewarded with catfish, salmon, sturgeon, and steelhead.

From the park, you can travel to The Dalles by Interstate 84 or return to the historic highway through the community of Rowena. Until 1845 when the Barlow Road provided an alternate route to Oregon City, the Rowena area was a staging point for Oregon Trail emigrants who made the final leg of their journey by floating down the Columbia.

As U.S. Highway 30 nears The Dalles, it traverses some of the area's best preserved scablands. The barren slopes were created 13,000 years ago when ice-age floods washed away topsoil and loose bedrock.

Entering The Dalles, the drive crosses Mill Creek Bridge, which was built in 1920 as part of the original highway. Williams House Bed and Breakfast is about 500 feet east of the bridge. The stately Queen Anne home, furnished with Georgian and Victorian antiques, is on the National Register as are many of the 19th century Italianate and Gothic homes in Trevitt Addition, one block east. One block north of U.S. Highway 30, which becomes Third Street in downtown, the original Wasco County Courthouse contains local artifacts and photos. In 1854, the small frame building became the seat of government for the largest county ever created in the United States. Wasco County covered 130,000 square miles and extended from the Cascades to the Rockies.

Old St. Peter's Church, on Third Street, was built in 1897. A six-foot-high rooster caps the spire of this beautiful red brick Gothic Revival structure.

About two miles east of town, you turn north on U.S. Highway 197, pass the entrance to The Dalles Dam and visitor center, and cross the Columbia River into Washington. At the visitor center, you can see Native American petroglyphs, history and environmental exhibits, and take a free train ride to the dam's fish ladder and powerhouse.

On the Washington side, roads lead from the main highway to the dam, Port of Klickatat Industrial Area, and two Corp of Engineer-operated parks near the shores of twenty-four-mile-long Lake Celilo Reservoir. High bluffs protect the lake from strong winds, making it an ideal spot for beginning and intermediate sailboarders and a popular spot for boating, waterskiing and fishing. The shoreline is a habitat for bald eagles, nesting Canada geese, and mule deer. Spearfish and Hess parks, as well as nearby Avery Boat Ramp offer primitive camping, beaches, and boat ramps.

Turning east on Washington Highway 14, you follow the lake's shore to Horsethief Lake State Park. Through the centuries Native Americans came from throughout the Northwest to Horsethief Lake and Celilo Falls to trade and catch annual supplies of salmon. Artifacts found here indicate that the trade network extended as far east as Michigan.

While most campsites have been covered by water, you can still see original petroglyphs on a five-minute walk from the parking lot. The many recreational opportunities range from fishing and sailboarding to hiking, rock climbing, and overnighting in twelve standard campsites.

From Horsethief Lake, the highway starts four miles of climbing and curving through dry grass hills. Several turnouts afford magnificent views of Oregon's Columbia Gorge and the river's traffic of boaters, waterskiers, sailboarders, large barges filled with lumber, gravel, grain, and other commodities. The highway peaks at a summit overlooking the site of Celilo Falls and the community of Wishram. Until they were inundated by dam backwaters in 1957, Celilo Falls was the major obstacle to water travel on the Columbia.

St. James Mission Church in Wishram retains reminders of the town's past as a major Burlington-Northern Railroad switching point by displaying relics from a mobile railroad chapel car. The mission's bell came from a train engine.

The drive exits the Columbia River Gorge National Scenic Area by descending through a winding canyon with rustic barns and homes made of black Columbia River basalt.

A few miles beyond, Maryhill Museum of Art sits on a flat plain, literally in the middle of nowhere. Built in 1907 as a mansion by businessman and world traveler Samuel Hill, it houses original bronzes, plasters, watercolors, and sketches by Auguste Rodin. Many include his fingerprints and signature. Maryhill's "The Thinker" is the only plaster cast of the reduced version in existence. Other exhibits include extensive collections of Native American artifacts, chess sets, 19th century American, Dutch, and French paintings, weaponry, and the Queen of Rumania's gold-leafed furniture.

A steam locomotive is a centerpiece at Maryhill State Park, three miles east near the junction of highways 14 and U.S. 97. It offers swimming, boating, picnicking, and a fifty-hookup trailer campground.

Stonehenge replica, a mile east of the junction, was also built by Samuel Hill. The full-sized reproduction of England's Stonehenge was started in 1918 and completed in 1929 as America's first World War I memorial. A diagram at the replica suggests how the original, built around 1350 BC, may have been used by ancient astronomers to measure time and mark seasons of the year through observing positions of the sun and moon.

The drive concludes by returning to U.S. Highway 97 and crossing the Bridge to Biggs, Oregon. From Biggs, your can return to The Dalles through the gorge on Interstate 84 or take the Oregon Trail route along the rim and through Fifteen-Mile Canyon.

13 COLUMBIA RIVER GORGE HISTORIC HIGHWAY

General description: A sixty-five-mile drive on paved roads through the most scenic section of the Columbia River Gorge from river level to 893 feet.
Special attractions: Spectacular gorge scenery, seven roadside waterfalls, Oregon Trail terminus and water route, Bonneville Dam, Hood River sailpark, sailboarding, hiking, west coast rain forest.
Location: Northern Oregon border between The Dalles and Troutdale.
Drive route numbers: Interstate 84 and U.S. Highway 30.
Travel season: All year.
Camping: Three state park campgrounds, two with full hookups, and one with electricity; four forest service campgrounds with picnic tables, fire rings, flush or vault toilets, drinking water.
Services: All services in The Dalles, Hood River, Cascade Locks, and Troutdale.
Nearby attractions: Mount Hood Scenic Loop, Hood River Valley Scenic Loop, Biggs-The Dalles-Oregon Trail Drive, Sherman County Loop, Washington State's Maryhill Museum and Stonehenge Replica, Fort Vancouver National Historic Site.
For more information: The Dalles Area Chamber of Commerce, 404 W. 2nd St., The Dalles, OR 97058, (541) 296-2231, (800) 255-3385 (USA). Hood River County Chamber of Commerce, Port Marina Park, Hood River, OR 97031, (541) 386-2000, (800) 366-3530 (USA). Columbia River Gorge National Scenic Area, Wacoma Center Suite 200, 902 Wasco Avenue, Hood River, OR 97031 (541) 386-2333.

The drive: The most scenic section of the Columbia River Gorge lies on the forty-three miles between The Dalles and Troutdale. From The Dalles to exit 35 and the Historic Columbia River Highway (U.S. Highway 30), it follows

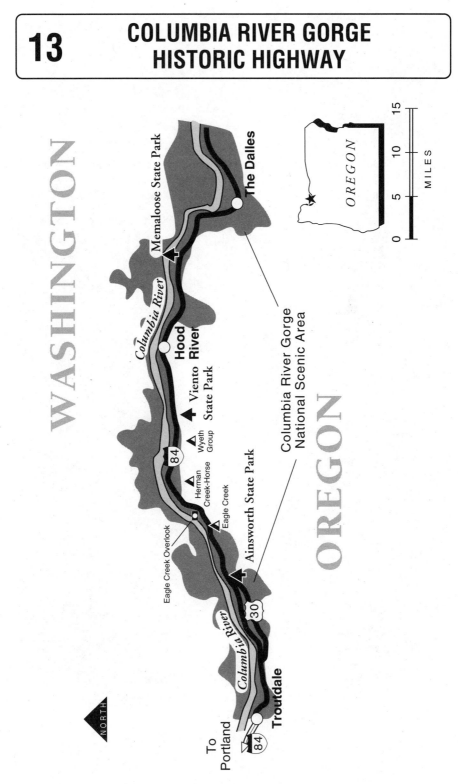

OREGON

MILES

15 10 5 0

WASHINGTON

OREGON

Memaloose State Park

The Dalles

Columbia River

Hood River

Viento State Park

Wyeth Group

84

Herman Creek-Horse

Eagle Creek

Eagle Creek Overlook

Ainsworth State Park

Columbia River Gorge National Scenic Area

30

Columbia River

To Portland

Troutdale

84

NORTH

Spectacular Multnomah Falls plunges 620 feet in two stages. A steep trail leads to the bridge and the top of the falls.

Interstate 84 on a water-level roadbed with the serene Columbia River ever present on the north, and towering cliffs on the south. The final twenty- two miles climb a southern ridge lined with seven major waterfalls and viewpoints overlooking the gorge, Columbia River, and Washington State. Mileposts begin with zero at Portland, and exit numbers on Interstate 84 roughly correspond to the number of miles from Portland.

When it reaches Oregon, the Columbia has flowed 1,000 miles through British Columbia and Washington. The gorge you travel through today is the aftermath of forty million years of ashfalls, mudslides, lava flows, and erosion. During the last ice age, about 13,000 years ago, the gorge was refined by a series of 600-1,000-foot deep floods that swept away hillsides, leaving streams to drop over cliffs as waterfalls and exposing tilted rocks and ancient lava flows. Evidence of virtually every type of geologic violence can be seen— including tablelands uplifted and tilted at forty-five-degree angles; giant slides of mud, rock and sand; outcroppings from lava flows; columnar basalt; and erosion caused by wind, water, and ice-age floods.

Summer travelers will find temperatures in the 90s and 100s in The Dalles and about five to ten degrees cooler from Hood River westward. Spring and fall days range from the upper forties to the low sixties. The gorge is usually colder in winter than surrounding areas as temperatures dip to the low thirties and forties. Icy roads are common and occasionally Interstate 84 may be closed briefly because of snow.

The Dalles has been a meeting place for Native Americans for more than 12,000 years, a Lewis and Clark campsite, and a Hudson's Bay Company post. Prior to the opening of the Barlow Road around Mount Hood in 1845, The Dalles marked the end of the overland portion of the Oregon Trail. From The Dalles and Rowena, travelers, with their wagons, livestock, and belongings, were rafted and portaged down the Columbia to the Willamette River and Oregon City.

A National Register Historic District exhibits Italianate, Gothic, Queen Anne and other 19th century homes. Other historic sites include the original 1854 courthouse and Fort Dalles Surgeon's Quarters, established in 1847. The Dalles Dam includes a Lewis and Clark exhibit, a petroglyph collection, and offers free train rides to viewpoints of the dam and spillway.

From The Dalles, the drive heads west with Interstate 84 sandwiched between high tiers of stone benches, table rocks, and columnar basalt that all compete for attention with the placid Columbia River and the moss-colored rolling hills of Washington. Rowena, at exit 76, and Mosier, at exit 69, are gateways to a nine-mile segment of the Historic Columbia River Highway (U.S. Highway 30) that can be driven as an alternative to Interstate 84 or incorporated as a loop. The U.S. Highway 30 segment features several points of interest: a picturesque bridge; Tom McCall Preserve, which contains diverse plants and animals; Rowena Dell, a protected botanical area known for its spring wildflowers; and Mayer State Park, which offers a sweeping vista of the eastern area.

Memaloose State Park Rest Area, a few miles west on Interstate 84, overlooks an Indian burial ground on a Columbia River island. The camp-

The view from Portland Woman's Forum State Park encompasses Crown Point, Vista House, the Columbia River, and Washington state.

ground includes forty-three full hookups and sixty-seven tent sites on the river's edge.

From Mosier past Hood River, Interstate 84 hugs the banks of the Columbia River. The gorge opens into a giant mountain-rimmed bowl covered with Christmas tree sized Douglas firs. Columbia River Sailpark, at exit 63, was built to accommodate thousands of sailboarders who have made Hood River world famous as a sailboarding hot spot. The facility incorporates the Port of Hood River, Hood River Convention and Visitor's Bureau, a boat basin, swimming and sailboard launching beaches, and a county museum. This exit is also the starting point for the Mount Hood Loop and Hood River Valley Loop drives on Highway 35. White Salmon Bridge, which spans the Columbia River, connects to Washington Highway 14 west to Vancouver and east to Maryhill Museum.

Hood River has been famous for apples and other fruit since at least 1900. The main business district retains several brick and stone buildings from the 1920s. Hood River Hotel, built in 1910 and renovated in the late 1980s, and the Hood River Railroad Depot are listed on the National Register of Historic Places. During spring and summer, Mount Hood Railroad operates scheduled sightseeing excursions through orchards and mountain foothills.

The Columbia Gorge Hotel, at exit 62, is situated on a section of the historic highway on a high bluff overlooking the river. At this Spanish mission-style hotel built in 1921, you can stay in rooms furnished with antiques and four poster and brass beds. Stone bridges and guard rails are indicative of the stonework on the historic highway, and overlook a 200-foot waterfall that plunges from the bluff to the river below.

West of Hood River, the gorge varies from the moss-colored hues of Douglas fir to the yellowish greens of cottonwoods and alders. Viento State Park, at exit 56, has fifty-eight electrical and seventeen tent sites. Wyeth Group Campground, at exit 51, and Herman Creek Horse Camp, at exit 47, are operated by the forest service and contain a total of twenty-five sites.

Exit 44 provides access to Cascade Locks, commercial RV parks, and Bridge of the Gods Historic Site. According to an Indian legend, this was the site of a natural stone arch that spanned the Columbia. When two "warrior god" volcanos—Oregon's Mount Hood and Washington's Mount Adams—fought over the "goddess" volcano, Mount St. Helens, the bridge collapsed, causing the Cascades of the Columbia.

The cascades, actually caused by rock slides, were considered the most treacherous part of the 2,000-mile Oregon Trail. After locks were built in 1896, river traffic was able to bypass the dangerous rapids. Rendered obsolete with the construction of Bonneville Dam, they are part of a park with two museums, one of which is the home of a former lock tender. Sternwheeler cruises through Columbia River Gorge also originate at the park. The steel-trussed Bridge of the Gods connects Oregon with Washington's Highway 14. Cascade Locks is also a trailhead for the Pacific Crest Trail, which extends from Canada to Mexico. West of Cascade Locks, two forest service campgrounds, Eagle Creek and Eagle Creek Overlook, provide a total of sixty sites.

Bonneville Dam, at exit 40, features a multi-leveled visitor center with fish ladders and an underwater viewing room. At a shaded pond area, you can see trout, salmon, sturgeon, and other local species.

Exit 35 is the eastern access to the Historic Columbia River Highway. Built between 1913 and 1920, it is still considered an engineering marvel. Samuel Lancaster, the Highway's chief engineer, saw the project as a unique opportunity to reconcile nature and civilization. His purpose, he said, was "to find the beauty spots, or those points where the most beautiful things along the line might be seen to the best advantage, and if possible, to locate the road in such a way as to reach them."

Lancaster's road incorporated the era's most up-to-date standards. Graceful bridges complement natural settings and blend with the environment. Stone guardrails, dry masonry, and rock walls, which appear intermittently throughout the drive, are characteristic of the stonemason's artistry and training in old world road building traditions. Virtually the entire route is shaded. Lancaster succeeded so well in attaining his objectives that the drive is sometimes referred to as a mystical experience.

The historic highway begins by winding through a typical Cascade rain forest of fir, maple, and alder, enhanced by moss and thick ground covers of fern and wildflowers. Ainsworth State Park, one mile west of exit 35, offers forty-five full hookup campsites in an idyllic setting along with a 1.25-mile hiking trail. Nearby Horsetail Falls drops in a rushing torrent. A 1.3-mile trail takes you to an upper cascade called Pony Tail Falls. Horsetail is one of seven major waterfalls along the highway. Each has space for parking.

Oneonta Gorge, two miles west, is a forest service botanical area with more than fifty species of wildflowers, flowering trees and shrubs. If you

The highlight for many gorge visitors is a stop at Multnomah Falls where facilities include a rustic lodge-styled restaurant, gift shop, and trails.

want to see the falls, wait until summer when the stream is low. Bring rubber boots; you'll need to hike up 900 feet of the creek bed.

The Gorge's centerpiece, Multnomah Falls, drops from a ledge, two miles west. At 620 feet, it is the fourth highest waterfall in the United States. You can take a trail to a bridge at the sixty-nine-foot lower falls, then zigzag your way to the top.

Multnomah Falls Lodge was built in 1925 as a traveler's way station. The stone Cascadian-styled structure includes a lounge, restaurant, patio dining, and coffee and gift shop.

Westward from Multnomah Falls, the highway climbs 600 feet in eight miles. In keeping with Lancaster's decree that the road would have a maximum grade of five percent and a curve radii of not less than 100 feet, much of the route is a series of figure eight curves. You'll see four waterfalls in this section: Wahkeena, mile 31; Bridal Veil, mile 29; Shepperd's Dell, mile 27; and Latourell, mile 26; plus several historic private residences, bridges, and barns.

Like virtually everything on the highway, Vista House at mile 24, was part of Lancaster's vision. Crown Point State Park, where it sits, was, according to Lancaster, the ideal site for "an observatory from which the view both up and down the Columbia could be viewed in silent communion with the infinite." He also envisioned it as a memorial to Oregon pioneers that could "serve as a comfort station for the tourist and the travellers of America's greatest highway." Although the igloo-shaped Vista House is only open in summer, the parking lot and circular lower promenade are accessible all year. The view from 733-foot Crown Point encompasses extinct volcanos in Washington, the Columbia River, Beacon Rock—a 800-foot-high volcanic plug—and the spectacular eastern rim of the gorge.

Portland Woman's Forum State Park, at mile 10, offers the magnificent view of the entire gorge amphitheater. This is the place to photograph Vista House perched on Crown Point, with the Columbia below and the gorge wall in the background, just as you've seen it in thousands of pictures.

The remaining ten miles to Troutdale pass through thick forest by Dabney and Lewis and Clark state parks and the Sandy River, which is known for its spring smelt runs. Both parks are day-use facilities.

From Troutdale, travelers have the option of continuing west to Portland via Interstate 84, or traveling three miles south to Highway 26 and taking the Mount Hood Loop drive.

14   MOUNT HOOD LOOP

General description: A ninety-mile paved signed loop around the southern slopes of Mount Hood and through the Hood River Valley to the Columbia River Gorge Scenic Area. When the Columbia River Gorge drive is added from Hood River to Troutdale, the total mileage is 130 miles.

Special attractions: Spectacular mountain scenery, six ski areas, rivers, Mount Hood National Forest, Oregon Trail historic sites, Hood River Valley.

Location: Southern slope of Mount Hood between Gresham and Hood River.

Drive route numbers: U.S. Highway 26, Oregon Highway 35.

Travel season: All year.

Camping: Thirteen forest service campgrounds with picnic tables, fire pits, flush or vault toilets. Some have drinking water. Two county parks, one with hookups and one with tent sites.

Services: All services at Gresham, Sandy, Government Camp, and Hood River. Limited services at Rhododendron, Zigzag.

Nearby attractions: Mount Hood Wilderness, Warm Springs Indian Reservation, Badger Creek Wilderness, Salmon-Huckleberry Wilderness, Fort Vancouver National Historic Site, Columbia River Gorge Scenic Drive, Mosier-Maryhill Scenic Drive, Sherman County Scenic Drive, Biggs-The Dalles Oregon Trail Route, Hood River Valley Scenic Drive.

For more information: Portland/Oregon Visitors Association, 26 S.W. Salmon, Portland, OR 97204 (503) 222-2223, (800) 962-3700. Gresham Area Chamber of Commerce/Visitor Information Center, 150 W. Powell, P.O. Box 1768, Gresham, OR 97030, (503) 665-1131. Sandy Area Chamber of Commerce, 39260 Pioneer Blvd, P.O. Box 536, Sandy, OR 97055, (503) 668-4006. Hood River County Chamber of Commerce, Port Marina Park, Hood River, OR 97031, (541) 386-2000, (800) 366-3530 (USA). Mount Hood National Forest, 2955 N.W. Division St., Gresham, OR 97030, (503) 666-0700. Hood River Ranger Station, 6780 Highway 35, Mount Hood-Parkdale, OR 97041, (541) 352-6002. Columbia River Gorge National Scenic Area, Wacoma Center, Suite 200, 902 Wasco Avenue, Hood River, OR 97301, (541) 386-2333.

The drive: Mount Hood dominates the Oregon skyline as a giant cylindrical white-topped cone. At 11,235 feet elevation, it is Oregon's tallest mountain and a recreational area for all seasons. It offers spring wildflower meadows, camping, hiking, and climbing during summer, fall foliage, and skiing year-round.

Native Americans called it Wy'East, and according to their legends, it was a great chief who had been turned into a mountain as punishment and retaliated by spouting fire and boulders. In 1792, it was renamed Hood to honor an English navy admiral.

The mountain was formed between one and ten million years ago in a series of eruptions that extended over thousands of years. Six minor

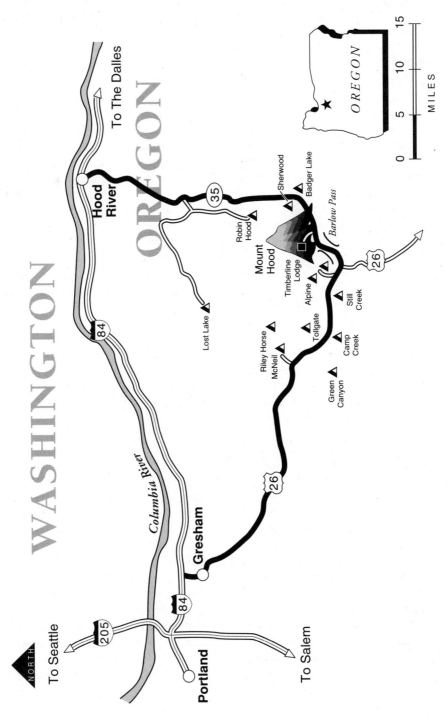

OREGON

MILES

0   5   10   15

To The Dalles

OREGON

WASHINGTON

Hood River

35

Sherwood

Badger Lake

Barlow Pass

Robin Hood

Mount Hood

Timberline Lodge

26

Alpine

Still Creek

84

Lost Lake

Riley Horse

Tollgate

Camp Creek

McNeil

Green Canyon

Columbia River

Gresham

26

205

To Seattle

84

NORTH

Portland

To Salem

eruptions occurred between 1804 and 1907.

U.S. Highway 26 follows the general route of the historic Barlow road, which was established in 1845 and offered Oregon Trail travelers an alternative to reaching western Oregon without fording the treacherous rapids of the Columbia River. The drive circles Mount Hood's southern slope and along ridges affording magnificent views of thick forest covering a sea of canyons, cliffs, hills, and mountains. After reaching a maximum elevation of 6,000 feet at Timberline Lodge, it concludes by taking Highway 35 through the picturesque orchards of the Hood River Valley. The Mount Hood Loop is often combined with the Columbia River Gorge Drive. For the best progression of scenery, begin in Gresham and end in Hood River or continue with the Columbia River Gorge Drive to Troutdale. Traffic is usually moderate during the week and heavy on week-ends.

Temperatures in the Hood River Valley average in the mid-sixties in summer. Winters range from thirty-three to forty- three degrees. Spring days are usually between forty-nine and fifty-six degrees. Autumn temperatures average in the high fifties. Temperatures at Mount Hood are unpredictable, but average five to ten degrees less than in the valley. Snow flurries can fall at Timberline Lodge in late spring and early summer.

If you are starting the drive from Portland, follow Interstate 84 east and take exits 13 to 16A 3.5 miles south to Gresham. Turning east on U.S. Highway 26, on the nine miles to Sandy, you'll pass open meadowlands and begin climbing into the Cascade foothills.

Five miles east of Sandy, the farmlands end abruptly. Dark green forest closes in and remains virtually unbroken until the Hood River Valley. The stately 150-foot evergreens are primarily Douglas fir, with a rich mixture of western red cedar and western hemlock. Oregon oak, cottonwoods, and alder add burnt yellow accents to the dark evergreens. Wild rhododendrons add splashes of red, white, and purple during springtime, and vivid reds and yellows of oaks and vine maples brighten autumn. On the eastern horizon, a mountain ridge forms an amphitheater for tree covered hills.

On the fifteen miles to Mount Hood Ranger Station at Brightwood, the drive parallels the Salmon River as it passes a candy factory and trout fishing farm. If you're planning to camp, cross country ski, or climb Mount Hood, you need to stop for maps and permits. Although there is no hiking trail to the summit, Mount Hood is the most frequently climbed glaciated peak in North America. Lists of minimum equipment necessary for a safe ascent are available at ranger stations, along with fact sheets on day hikes from forest service roads and trailheads along the highway.

Mount Hood RV Park, across the street, is a multi-purpose, full-service resort with space for 550 recreational vehicles, river frontage, indoor pool and sauna, and a 350-acre recreational park. Wildwood Recreation Area, east of the station, offers the first of several roadside hiking trails into the cool, inviting forest. The Resort At The Mountain, east of the recreation area in Welches, is a 212-room complex with golf, tennis courts, and a pool. Condominiums, a Swiss restaurant, and shops featuring hand-crafted gifts and antiques are nearby.

Snow capped Mount Hood dominates the northern Oregon skyline and is a major ski area and favorite of mountain climbers.—Oregon Department of Transportation photo

Zig Zag Ranger Station, a mile east of Welches, has been an administrative office since 1907. The eighteen buildings were constructed by the Civilian Conservation Corps between 1933 and 1942. Wy'East Rhododendron Gardens, which surround the offices, contain more than fifty varieties of rhododendrons that bloom during May and June.

From Zigzag, a road leads north to McNeil Campground with thirty-four sites and Riley Horse Camp with fourteen sites. Green Canyon Campground, a couple miles south of Zigzag has fifteen sites.

East of the station, the highway enters the 1,059,240-acre Mount Hood National Forest, which extends east past Hood River. On the twelve miles to Government Camp, it is easy to envision the hardships pioneers faced in crossing the mountains as the road climbs dramatically and serpentines along the ridge of a valley filled with trees from roadside to horizon. As it clings to the mountainside, virtually every inch is a viewpoint.

Tollgate Campground, with fifteen campsites, features a replica of the Barlow Road's western toll gate. Nearby Camp Creek Campground has eighteen sites. Several forest service roads start at the highway and lead to scenic viewpoints or trailheads. This is a winter recreation area, and signs warn of the need for carrying traction tires or chains. From November through April, permits are required to use sno-parks.

Laurel Hill, at milepost 46, was the most difficult section of the Barlow

U.S. Highway 26 crosses Laurel Hill, which proved to be a stiff challenge for Oregon Trail wagons moving west on the Barlow Road.

Road. Wagons were lowered down the steep slopes by makeshift winches made with ropes lashed to trees. The hill provides eastbound travelers with the first view of Mount Hood's snow-capped peak.

Government Camp, a few miles further east, was named for an Army detachment that camped here in 1849. Today, the resort community is a winter sports center serving six ski areas that stretch east for about twenty miles. Numerous cross-country ski trails also start from Government Camp. Alpine Campground, north of town, has sixteen sites, and Still Creek, near the highway, contains twenty-seven sites.

Mount Hood Ski Bowl, across the highway from Government Camp, is America's largest night skiing area. Its facilities include a lodge, four double chairlifts, and five surface tows. In summer, you can enjoy the mountain scenery from an alpine slide, ride in go carts, or rent horses to explore the backcountry.

Summit Ski Area, two miles east, rents tubes and discs for non-skiers. The three miles of trails are excellent for beginners.

Two miles east, a steep, six-mile side road leads to Timberline, at the 6,600-foot level, passing seasonal waterfalls and vistas of seemingly endless forests, peaks, and valleys. While most come to enjoy year-round day and night skiing, Timberline is also a major stop for sightseers. Timberline Lodge, constructed during the 1930s as a Works Progress Administration project, is a National Historic Landmark and an impressive monument to the skill of its builders. It contains seventy-one rooms, a lounge, and outdoor pool.

Easy access to Trillium Lake, two miles south of U.S. Highway 26, has made it a favorite rest and picturesque picnicking spot. Some of the thirty-nine campsites can accommodate oversized trailers. Nearby Still Creek Campground has twenty-seven sites.

Snowbunny is three miles east of Timberline's road and is a snowplay area with a sliding hill and snack bar. The area was the site of a Barlow Road toll house and pioneer campground. A small cemetery near Snowbunny contains graves of several children and adults who perished on the Barlow Trail.

A few miles further, the drive turns onto Oregon Highway 35 and U.S. Highway 26 continues southeast to Vale. A gravesite near the junction marks the final resting place of a pioneer woman. Shortly after the junction, U.S. Highway 35 crosses the Pacific Crest Trail, at 4,157-foot-high Barlow Pass.

The loop road reaches its highest point at 4,647-foot Bennett Pass. Mount Hood Meadows, near the summit, encompasses the mountain's largest ski area. It covers 2,000 acres, sixty slopes and trails, and can move 12,000 skiers per hour on nine chairlifts. From the lounge with its 120-foot glass wall, you have a magnificent close-up view of the mountain's white-capped peak.

The nine miles to Cooper Spur Ski Area feature some of the best highway scenery as the road winds through canyons, by cliffs, and along the white-capped Hood River. En route it passes several campgrounds, hiking trails, and forest service roads. Sherwood, Badger Lake, and Robin Hood campgrounds feature a total of fifty-three sites.

The Cooper Spur access road is a historic district. Cloud Cap Inn, built in 1889, was the first structure constructed on Mount Hood. It offers a superb view of the snow-capped peak. Other sites include an 1889 wagon road, a 1900s log clubhouse, cookstoves constructed of native rock, and a public shelter built in 1939 by the Civilian Conservation Corps. Tilly Jane Campground, built in 1926, and Cloud Cap Saddle contain a total of eighteen sites that are open only during summer. The panoramic view of Washington's Mount Adams, Mount Rainier, and Mount St. Helens from Inspiration Point has graced numerous post cards and calendars. Cooper Spur Ski Area caters to families and includes a restaurant, a rope tow, warming hut, and T-bar lift.

As Highway 35 leaves the Mount Hood National Forest, it passes through stands of alder and cottonwoods brilliant green in spring and bright yellow in autumn. Routson Park, near the boundary, offers river fishing for trout and steelhead. Because of the steep climb, the twenty campsites are not recommended for trailers.

Fruit orchards have been the center of the Hood River Valley economy since 1900 and come into view near the ranger station by the community of Mount Hood. Toll Bridge Park, at Mount Hood, features twenty full-service and twenty-five tent sites.

The remaining fifteen miles overlap the most scenic portion of the Hood River Valley circle tour as it continues north through the fragrant orchards and vistas of the valley's fields and forests. Panorama Point, three miles east of the highway near Hood River, offers a sweeping view of the valley capped by Mount Hood in the background. The drive concludes by entering the Columbia River Gorge National Scenic Area and Hood River, where Highway 35 crosses Interstate 84.

General description: A forty-seven-mile loop tour on paved roads from the Columbia River Gorge through the Hood River Valley's fruit orchards, business and residential areas.

Special attractions: Hood River Valley, Columbia River Gorge National Scenic Area, hotel and sailpark; fruit orchards, outstanding views of Mount Hood, sailboarding, sailing, camping. Laurence Lake Reservoir and Lost Lake (optional).

Location: Hood River Valley in the Columbia River Gorge on northern Oregon border.

Drive route names and numbers: Oregon Highway 35, Parkdale Road, Baseline Drive, Lost Lake Road, Green Road, Oregon Highway 281, U.S. Highway 30.

Travel season: All year. The best time to drive the route is between mid-April and early May when the fruit trees are blossoming. An annual blossom festival is usually held the third weekend in April and features arts and crafts displays, bake goods, a flea market, wine and distillery open houses, and other events along the route. If Easter falls on the third weekend, the festival is held a week earlier. The road to Lost Lake is usually open from mid-May until it is closed by snow in late October.

Camping: Two county campgrounds, one with tent sites and one with hookups are on the route. Three forest service campgrounds with picnic tables, fire pits, drinking water, and flush or vault toilets are situated within ten to twenty miles of the route. Two county campgrounds, one with tent and the other with primitive sites are near the route. Viento State Park, eight miles west on U.S. Highway 30, has fifty-eight electrical and seventeen tent sites.

Services: All services at Hood River. Limited services at Mount Hood and Parkdale.

Nearby attractions: Columbia River Gorge Scenic drive, The Dalles, Mount Hood Loop and National Forest.

For more information: Hood River County Chamber of Commerce, Port Marina Park, Hood River, OR 97031; (541) 386-2000, (800) 366-3530 (USA). Hood River Ranger Station, 6780 Highway 35, Mount Hood-Parkdale, OR 97041, (541) 352-6002. Columbia River Gorge National Scenic Area, Wacoma Center, Suite 200, 902 Wasco Avenue, Hood River, OR 97301, (541) 386-2333.

The drive: The Hood River Valley lies between the Columbia River and the ever-looming presence of Mount Hood on the southwestern horizon. Shellrock Mountain, twelve miles west, is one of two ridges between Portland and The Dalles that were formed about ten million years ago when an igneous rock called diorite pushed its way through the Columbia Gorge basalt. A large fault east of Hood River has raised the valley about 1,000 feet over several million years. The protected valley's climate and annual thirty inches of rain are ideal for growing fruit and have made the county famous for its apples, pears,

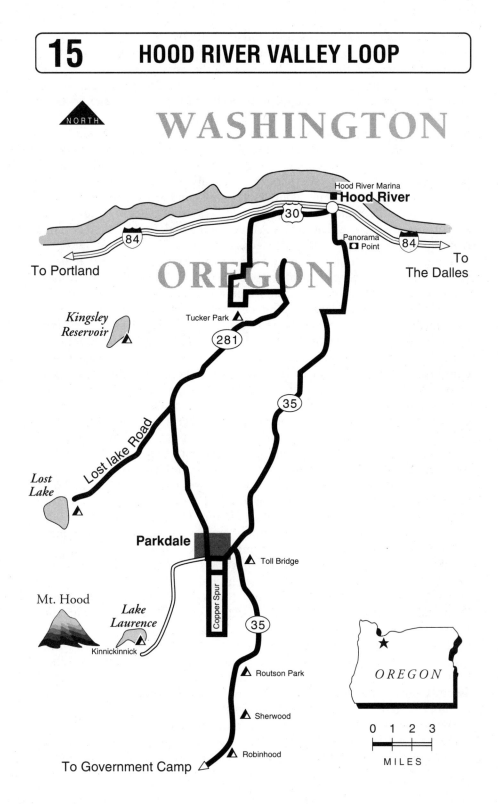

85

cherries, peaches, and grapes since the early 1900s.

The drive begins at the Columbia River Sailpark and proceeds south on Oregon Highway 35 through orchards along the eastern edge of the valley. At the community of Mount Hood, it turns west for a few miles, affording outstanding views of Mount Hood and the Hood River. Returning north, the view extends to the state of Washington's rolling hills as the drive continues through orchards and a wooded canyon on the western side of the valley. The sailpark is situated at exit 63 on Interstate 84, and the tour can be taken in reverse by starting at exit 62. Since the tour stays on main roads and takes you through the heart of the valley, traffic is usually moderate to heavy.

Summer temperatures in the mid-sixties are common and make pleasant travel weather. Travelers will find spring days usually between forty-nine and fifty-six degrees, and autumns average in the high fifties. Winters range from thirty-three to forty-three degrees.

Winds in the Columbia River Gorge average sixteen miles per hour all year. When combined with the river's downstream current, they create ideal conditions for sailboarding. The combination has made Hood River America's sailboarding capital, and the Columbia River Sailpark was built to accommodate the thousands who congregate to participate in world-class competitions and recreational water sports. It also contains the Port of Hood River, and includes jogging trails, swimming and sailboarding launching beaches, and equipment rental shops for sailboarders and fishermen. Ducks and geese waddle across lawns with picnic tables overlooking the boat basin.

Before departing on the drive, you may want to stop at the Hood River County Visitor's Center in the sailpark for the drive's brochure. Next door a museum traces area history from the first inhabitants to the development of the fruit industry. Hotels, a small mall of specialty shops, and several fast food restaurants are situated across the highway in Hood River Village.

From the sailpark, the drive heads south, crosses Interstate 84, and follows Oregon Highway 35 past the junction to U.S. Highway 30. In the first mile, the route climbs through the northeast edge of Hood River and enters the scenic corridor. A four-mile side road to Panorama Point loops off the main highway and through forest and farmland. From the point, you have a sweeping view of a patchwork of meadows, mills, fruit orchards, the Columbia River, Mount Hood, and the city below.

Apple and pear orchards surround the highway south of the point. Diamond Fruit Packers, on the loop, conducts tours of its packing and cold storage plants.

Rejoining Highway 35 four miles south of Hood River, you pass Hanel Lumber Company, which also offers tours of its mills and production processes. During the next few miles the route leaves valley farmlands and ascends a tree-lined ridge. Turnouts provide ample opportunities to photograph the pastoral farms and orchards in the valley below.

At the community of Mount Hood, fifteen miles south of the sailpark, the drive turns west to Parkdale. Hood River Ranger Station, a mile south of the turn-off, issues camping, hiking, and snow park permits. Cherry and peach orchards bordering the ranger station parking lot provide colorful fore-

Hood River Sailpark is a mecca for sailboarders and includes a marina, visitor center, museum, and picnic area.

grounds for frame-filling photos of Mount Hood, which appears to be only a few miles behind them.

Four campgrounds are located along Highway 35 between one and twelve miles south of the Ranger Station. Toll Bridge with forty-four sites and Routson Park with twenty, are operated by Hood River County Parks. Routson's steep grade limits its availability to large trailers and motorhomes. Sherwood, with fourteen sites and Robinhood with twenty-four, are forest service campgrounds. All offer fishing access to the Hood River's trout, fall salmon, and steelhead.

Mount Hood fills the horizon in front of you, and Douglas fir and alders line the highway as you drive west on Parkdale Road. The east fork of the Hood River crosses under the road as a series of white water riffles.

Turning north onto Baseline Drive and continuing through Parkdale, the roadside fills with berry fields and apple orchards. Kinnickinnick Campground, ten miles south of Parkdale, is situated on the shores of Laurence Lake Reservoir. It has eight no-fee campsites. Boating on the lake is limited to craft with electric motors.

After a few miles, the Hood River reappears along the roadside as the drive dips in and out of a wooded ravine. As it traverses hilltops, you can see the rolling, grass-covered hills of the Columbia River Gorge's Washington shoreline. Small valleys and hills to the west, covered with Douglas fir, provide vistas of dark greens and varying shades of blues and purples.

At Dee Junction, travelers have a choice of continuing north on Highway 242 or turning southwest and taking Forest Service Road 13 up Mount Hood's eastern slope to Lost Lake. The lake is about twenty miles from the junction.

The Columbia Gorge Hotel, built in the 1920s, features decorative stonework, a waterfall that drops 200 feet, and rooms furnished with antiques.

Lost Lake, at 3,200 feet, is one of Oregon's scenic icons, and has graced countless calendars, post cards, book and magazine covers. It is anything but lost, and during the season, you can expect heavy traffic on roads and services straining to meet the needs of campers, fishermen, and sightseers.

The rewards are the magnificent scenery of a tranquil lake and forest of Douglas fir, mountain hemlock, cedar and white pine with snow-capped Mount Hood ever present in the background. Otter and beaver inhabit the shore, and deer, black bear, and bobcats roam the hills. Motorboats are not allowed on the lake, which draws fishermen for its brook, rainbow, brown trout and kokanee. A forest service concessionaire campground with ninety-one tent and trailer sites and seven cabins are usually booked months in advance.

Kingsley Reservoir and Wahtum Lake, a few miles west of Dee are also popular water recreation spots with small campgrounds.

At O'Dell Crossroads, the loop leaves the main highway and climbs to 863 feet on Summit Road, then follows Lynne and Wy'east roads through more orchards. Returning to Highway 282, it winds by roadside stores and stands that sell seasonal fresh fruit.

At Oak Grove store, the drive turns north on Country Club Road. You may see pheasants flying in open fields that share the countryside with a fruit packing plant and a residential area mixed with older two-story homes and modern ramblers. Tucker Park, on the banks of the Hood River, has twenty campsites with hook-ups, and offers a relaxing, shaded spot for a picnic. This section has some curves, signs warn that it is slippery when icy and frequent patching has left a rough roadbed.

Turning west and then north, you pass Hood River Golf and Country Club, which is one of the region's oldest courses. With nine holes and double tees, the public course is compact but very scenic as its fairways are framed by Mount Hood, the western slopes of the Cascades, and the valley's orchards.

Continuing north on Country Club Road, you wind through a wooded area, pass Three Rivers Winery, which offers tours and tastings, and reach a junction with U.S. Highway 30 and Interstate 84 at exit 62 to the Columbia River Gorge Hotel.

The hotel was built in 1921 by lumber baron Simon Benson and is a National Historic Landmark. Some rooms include antiques, fourposters, and brass beds. A seven-course farm breakfast is included with room rentals or can be purchased separately. The grounds offer a fine view of the river and gorge, along with Wah-Gwin-Gwin Falls, which plummets 200 feet into the Columbia River Gorge below. There is also a formal garden, and elaborate stone walkways, retaining walls, and bridges.

From the hotel, travelers can return to Hood River by Interstate 84, or a three-mile segment of the historic Columbia River Highway (U.S. Highway 30).

16 BIGGS, THE DALLES, OREGON TRAIL ROUTE

General description: A twenty-two-mile drive through the Columbia River Gorge National Scenic Recreation Area on a segment of the Oregon Trail.
Special attractions: Original Oregon Trail route and ruts, Deschutes State Park and River, Columbia River Gorge scenic views, The Dalles.
Location: Columbia River Gorge between Biggs and The Dalles.
Drive route names: Old Frontage Road, Old Moody Road, 15 Mile Canyon Road.
Travel season: All year.
Camping: One Oregon state park with primitive sites.
Services: All services at Biggs and The Dalles.
Nearby attractions: Columbia River Gorge Historic Highway, Tom McCall Preserve, Horsethief Lake State Park, Maryhill Museum of Art, Stonehenge Replica, Goldendale Observatory, Sherman County Loop, Hood River Valley, Mount Hood Loop and National Forest.
For more information: The Dalles Area Chamber ofCommerce, 404 W. 2nd St., The Dalles, OR 97058. (541) 296-2231, (800) 255-3385 (USA). Columbia River Gorge National Scenic Area, Wacoma Center, Suite 200, 902 Wasco Ave., Hood River, OR 97031. (541) 386-2333.

The drive: For travelers on the Oregon Trail, this twenty-two-mile segment was a welcome site, for it meant the end of the overland journey was near.

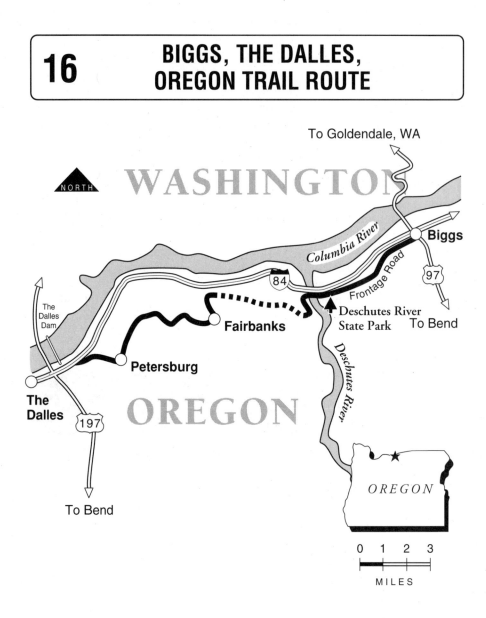

16 BIGGS, THE DALLES, OREGON TRAIL ROUTE

To Goldendale, WA

NORTH

WASHINGTON

Columbia River

Biggs

84

Frontage Road

97

Deschutes River State Park

To Bend

Fairbanks

Deschutes River

Petersburg

The Dalles Dam

The Dalles

197

OREGON

To Bend

OREGON

0 1 2 3

MILES

Today, it offers travelers an opportunity to see the same landscape the pioneers crossed and to escape Interstate 84's fast lane for the quiet backroads and rural countryside.

Starting at Biggs, the drive proceeds west through Deschutes River State Park and then follows a gravel road over the rim of the Columbia River Gorge. Some of the land is private property, so you will want to confine your photo stops and roadside hikes to areas near pullouts. At Fairbanks, it returns to pavement and travels north through the hay fields and farms of scenic 15 Mile Canyon. Climbing a ridge, the drive enters The Dalles by The Dalles Dam, and concludes downtown. The tour can be joined at Biggs or The

Dalles. While traffic is usually light, narrow roads, a few sharp curves, and occasional slow-moving farm machinery necessitate a leisurely pace.

During summer, temperatures range from the 90s to over 100 degrees. Winter days fall between the low thirties and forties with occasional dips into the twenties and teens. Spring and fall days range from the upper forties to the low sixties.

To begin at Biggs, take exit 104 off Interstate 84 and then turn west at the Deschutes State Park sign and onto Old Frontage Road. The road is situated between the Columbia River and the original route of the Oregon Trail.

Biggs' restaurants, motels, and service stations straddle Old Frontage Road and serve primarily Interstate 84 and U.S. Highway 97 travelers. About one mile west of the service area, you'll see a historical marker and viewpoint. It was from this point that most Oregon Trail travelers who came west between 1843 and 1863 had their first look at the Columbia River. Because of the Columbia Plateau's difficult terrain, most wagon trains came across the plains from Pendleton to Biggs and stayed south of the river until this point.

Along with river traffic and the backwaters of The Dalles Dam, you'll see Maryhill Museum of Art standing in glorious isolation on the Washington side. Mount Hood's 11,235-foot snow-capped peak is directly in front of you.

One mile ahead, look for a dark wooden post on the road's south side. By taking the short path up to the bench, you will be able to see original Oregon Trail ruts.

Descending these slopes, the immigrants crossed the river at Deschutes River State Park, three miles west. For thousands of years prior to the arrival of the pioneers, the park grounds had been a trading center for Native Americans from various tribes who came to fish the Columbia. In exchange for trade goods, they often assisted the pioneers by taking women and children across the river in canoes. The Deschutes was forded by floating the wagons and swimming the livestock. When the stream was high and the ford dangerous, the island at the river's mouth was often used as a bridge and temporary stop to rest horses and cattle.

When Oregon Trail travelers arrived at the site of Deschutes River State Park, they camped in sagebrush that still covers roadside hills. Today's visitors can overnight in thirty-four primitive sites and enjoy the shade of planted locus, willow, and poplar groves. Situated at the confluence of the Deschutes and Columbia, the park is a staging area for boating on both rivers, plus hikes and mountain bike ventures into the surrounding hills.

The Deschutes is one of nineteen rivers managed as a Oregon Scenic Waterway. It has a reputation as an exciting whitewater rafting stream and as a superb steelhead and trout fishery. This section is limited to fly fishing, and you'll need a pass if you want to boat on the lower 100 miles, which includes the segment by the state park. Passes can be purchased at sporting goods stores and regional park offices.

The mouth of the Deschutes is a favorite spot for fishing the Columbia. Fish taken here often average fifteen to thirty pounds, and occasionally up to fifty pounds. In addition to trout, steelhead, and salmon, you may catch bass, walleye, and sturgeon.

The Oregon Trail route from Biggs to The Dalles offers sweeping views of the Columbia River from atop the gorge's rim.

The 253,500-acre Columbia River Gorge National Scenic Area starts at the Deschutes and extends west eighty-five miles to the Sandy River near Troutdale.

After crossing the river, wagon trains climbed the hills and continued to The Dalles along roughly the same route that you will travel. On the west bank, the drive follows Old Moody Road, which bisects Heritage Landing's boat ramp and parking lot. At the end of the landing, it starts seven miles of gravel, passes under an old railroad bridge, and climbs a short but steep ridge to the top of the gorge rim.

The road is well maintained, but narrow, and not recommended for long trailers. Atop the rim, you'll start by traveling through sagebrush and dry grass broken by scattered poplars and lava outcroppings.

The rim rocks have provided geologists with important information on lava flows and the distances that molten rock can move as a continuous river from its source. Rocks in this area erupted as lava from the Grand Ronde volcano in northeastern Oregon, and flowed as far west as The Dalles. Thousands of years later, at the end of the last ice age, they were refined and sculpted by the world's largest floods. When ice-age glaciers melted, they formed a large lake that extended east to Missoula, Montana. Eventually the rim of ice that dammed the water broke and the whole lake rushed through eastern Washington and down the Columbia River. The cycle was repeated at least thirty-five times as the ice dam reformed and broke apart. The largest floods released walls of water 2,000 feet high, eroding some areas and depositing gravel and sediment in others.

As the road cuts across private land, you'll see rustic farms with aging barns, corrals, and windmills sitting in the middle of wheat fields and meadows of grazing cattle. Distant horizons are filled by the Columbia River

An abandoned school is a prominent local landmark at Petersburg.

east and west, cliffs and tablelands to the south, and the rolling buckskin-colored hills of Washington on the north. On some sections the road hugs the cliff's edge, and you can see the river, bridges, and boat traffic below.

The gravel ends at 15 Mile Road in the farming area of Fairbanks. A large tree, on the right side of the junction, shelters another Oregon Trail marker. This was an important Oregon Trail junction, for from here the trail paralleled 15 Mile Creek north to the Columbia River. The creek and canyon were named by pioneers because a road crossed the stream about fifteen miles from The Dalles.

You'll have a definite feeling of driving through a canyon as you continue north on 15 Mile Road, surrounded by hills of lava outcroppings, and wide bottomlands filled with sagebrush, wheat fields, and farms.

The original one-room school house at Petersburg, about midway, is a regional landmark. Dating back to the turn of the century, it sits vacant north of the highway on the community's western edge and near the route of the Oregon Trail.

Leaving Petersburg, the drive moves through pear and cherry orchards, and begins a leisurely climb to a ridge where you have a sweeping view of The 1.5-mile-long Dalles Dam, its visitor center, and the Columbia River.

Until 1845, the Oregon Trail terminated at The Dalles. After arriving near the present-day dam's visitor center site, early travelers followed the shoreline to Chenowith Creek or Rowena—nine miles west—and began the hazardous trip down the Columbia. Others veered inland along present-day 10th, Lewis, and Fourth streets.

With the completion of the Barlow Road in the 1840s, they had the option of going by river or through the thick forest, sheer cliffs, and steep grade of Mount Hood's south slope.

The Dalles Mission, established in 1838, provided a temporary respite for weary travelers. In 1847, when hostilities between settlers and Cayuse Indians increased, The Dalles became a base for military operations. With the construction of Fort Dalles in 1850, the military's presence was extended westward from Fort Laramie in the Wyoming Territory.

Several sites have survived The Dalles pioneer era. They include Fort Rock, where Lewis and Clark camped. The Fort Dalles Museum is housed in the original surgeon's quarters and displays horse-drawn vehicles, pioneer and Indian artifacts. Frontier missionaries preached at Pulpit Rock, which is still used for Easter sunrise services. The city park contains a marker that was placed there in 1906 by Oregon Trail pioneer Ezra Meeker to commemorate the 50th anniversary of the historic route.

17 FRENCH PRAIRIE LOOP
99 East

General description: A sixty-mile drive through northwestern Oregon's Willamette Valley and French Prairie's agricultural lands and historic areas.
Special attractions: Oregon Trail terminus, Willamette Falls, Aurora Historic District, French Prairie historic churches, Champoeg State Park, Willamette River, camping, wildlife observation, museums.
Location: Northwestern Oregon between Oregon City and Newberg.
Drive route names and numbers: Oregon Highway 99 East, Oregon Highway 219, Champoeg Park Road.
Travel season: All year.
Camping: One state park campground with forty-eight electrical and six tent sites.
Services: All services in Oregon City, Canby, Woodburn, Newberg. Limited Services in Aurora, St. Paul.
Nearby attractions: Portland, Columbia River Gorge, Multnomah Falls, Salem, Silver Falls Loop, Mount Hood Loop, 99 West Scenic Drive, Washington County Loop.
For more information: Oregon City Chamber of Commerce, 1795 Washington St., Oregon City, OR 97045, (503) 656-1619, (800) 424-3002. Portland/ Oregon Visitor's Association, 26 S.W. Salmon, Portland, OR 97204, (503) 222-2223, (800) 962-3700. Canby Area Chamber of Commerce, 266 N.W. 1st, #C, P.O. Box 35, Canby, OR 97013, (503) 266-4600. Woodburn Area Chamber of Commerce, 2233 Country Club Rd., P.O. Box 194, Woodburn, OR 97071, (503) 982-8221. Newberg Area Chamber of Commerce, 115 N. Washington, Newberg, OR 97132, (503) 538-2014. Champoeg State Park, 7679 Champoeg Road NE, St. Paul, OR 97137, (503) 633-8170.

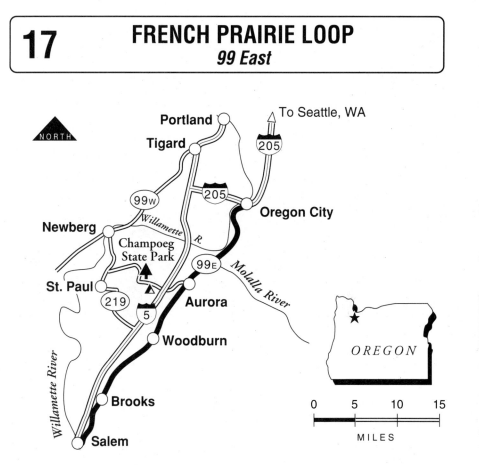

17 FRENCH PRAIRIE LOOP
99 East

The drive: Several versions of this drive exist, including separate itineraries for the Highway 99 East and French Prairie segments. This drive, which combines the two, can be taken from Portland by traveling thirteen miles southeast to Oregon City. It can also be joined from Interstate 5 at exit 263 at Brooks, exit 271 at Woodburn, or exit 278 at Aurora/Donald.

History and architecture take precedence over natural scenery that includes the Willamette River, hop and berry fields, and open farmland. It was this rich soil and abundant wildlife along the Willamette that attracted the first fur trappers and later Oregon Trail emigrants to the area.

From Oregon City, the drive moves south along the banks of the Willamette River to the Aurora Historic District then passes through hop yards and berry fields en route to Brooks. After retracing about five miles, it turns northwest, passing several small crossroads communities that are distinguished by their unique churches. The drive concludes along the banks of the Willamette River at Champoeg State Park. Traffic is usually moderate to heavy on Oregon Highway 99 East, and light on the backroads in the French Prairie section.

McLoughlin House, built in 1846 by Dr. John McLoughlin of the Hudson's Bay Company, is one of the most visited sites in Oregon City's historic area.

In the Willamette Valley, generally mild temperatures prevail all year. Winters average in the low fifties and drop into the forties at night. Summers range in the seventies and eighties. Spring days usually fall in the sixties, and in the low seventies in fall. Winter and early spring mornings may bring heavy fog, which lifts before noon or can last for days.

Oregon City was the western terminus of the Oregon Trail. It dates to 1829 when Dr. John McLoughlin, chief factor and superintendent of the Hudson's Bay Company at Fort Vancouver, claimed the land. Oregon's first provincial legislature met here in 1843, and it was the territorial capital from 1845 to 1852.

The city is divided with the business section situated at river level and residential areas sprawling along a cliff overlooking the waterfront. The areas are connected by streets and a 130-foot-high municipal passenger elevator, which is within walking distance of both city center and the historic sites on the upper levels.

McLoughlin House, a National Historic Site, stands two blocks east of the elevator on Center Street. It was built by Dr. John McLouglhin in 1846 and contains his gaming table, china, bed, and other possessions. The McLoughlin Historic District, surrounding the home, is part of his original plat and includes several blocks of picturesque dwellings and churches reflecting architectural styles from the 1840s to the 1930s.

The End of The Trail Interpretive Center, approximately five blocks east of the elevator, highlights travel on the trail with exhibits of covered wagons, river rafts, firearms and other relics. Some artifacts were brought west over the Oregon Trail.

By walking south about four blocks from the elevator you have a magnificent overview of Willamette Falls, which spills about forty feet over a rocky basalt horseshoe. You can also take an exhilarating cruise through the rock-walled waterway. A second scenic viewpoint, situated on the highway 0.6 mile south of city center, offers a closer, water-level view of the falls.

South of the falls, the drive follows the wide Willamette River as it weaves through mixed stands of oak and cottonwoods. The river begins more than 100 miles south in the Cascade foothills near Eugene and is one of the few that flows north. Turning onto NE Territorial Road at Canby, you follow the directional signs west and north to Molalla River State Park. The Canby Ferry, near the park, transports cars and passengers across the Willamette River to a west side connecting road.

The day-use park, near the mouth of the Molalla River, is known for its large rookery of great blue herons. A 1.5-mile trail will take you through a lush undergrowth along the Willamette's shoreline to a boat ramp.

Canby is a service center for the flower, berry, and dairy farms along the highway south of town. The Depot Museum on Highway 99 interprets its history.

Turning east on Barlow Road, the drive cuts through a landscape reminiscent of the European countryside on the 4.4-mile side trip to St. Josef's Wine Cellars. A rustic German tasting room and picnic grounds are open all year.

The Aurora National Historic District, two miles south on 99 East, was started as a commune in 1856 by William Keil, a Prussian tailor, self-proclaimed physician, and fundamentalist preacher. At its peak, the colony numbered 600 people and covered 15,000 acres.

Although the commune was disbanded after Keil's death in 1877, the town has retained several blocks of historic buildings and is also known for its many antique and collectible shops. Most buildings are large, reflecting the communal ownership and German architectural influence. The Old Aurora Colony Museum complex includes an ox barn, two homes, a communal wash house, and a farm machinery building. On a short walking tour, you can see thirty-three buildings from the 1865-1933 period, twenty of which are on the National Register of Historic Places.

Near Aurora, The Willamette River veers west. Highway 99 East cuts through Christmas tree farms, hop yards, and berry fields en route to Woodburn and Brooks.

At Brooks, you turn west onto Brookdale Road and cross Interstate 5 to the Antique Powerland and Truck Museum. It exhibits huge antique steam tractors, thrashing machines, and railroad cars. Trucks include a 1917 Packard, a 1923 Mack logging rig, and a 1917 Maxwell.

After returning to 99 East and traveling north a couple of miles, the drive turns west at Gervais and enters the southern edge of French Prairie. The community has a unique square steepled church, and a historic cemetery that contains a section for Old Russian Believers.

From Gervais to the conclusion of the drive, you'll be passing through the heart of the Willamette Valley's French Prairie farmlands. Cattle and sheep farms mingle with a patchwork of fruit orchards and field crops. Among them are sugar beets, grass for grass seed, corn, hops, apples, peaches, cherries, berries, vegetables, and poultry. The valley was formed about thirty-five million years ago when a section of the Pacific shoreline was uplifted and also created the Coast Range mountains. Floods following the last ice age deposited the rich silt that forms the basis of the productive croplands.

Four miles west at St. Louis, a picturesque white country church, built in 1889, sits at the intersection of Highway 219. Turning north on Highway 219, which is also signed as French Prairie Road, you cut through the center of the prairie, passing oak and cottonwood thickets, pasturelands, and picturesque farm houses and barns.

After seven miles, you turn onto Blanchet Road and, on the mile west to St. Paul, travel by hopyard trellises and farmlands, and a stately colonial home built in 1882. Look north as you approach town and you'll see a beautiful French cross towering above large, elaborate headstones in St. Paul Cemetery. Many of the graves date to the 1800s.

Today, the town is better known for its annual rodeo, which attracts national performers, than for its history. St. Paul was the core of French Prairie and second only to Astoria in the order of white settlement in Oregon. French Canadians began settling here as early as 1828, attracted by the water transportation and the location on the brigade trail that connected the area to Fort Vancouver.

A brick in the chimney of an old cabin west of town is dated 1832, and ten other sites and buildings are linked to the French Canadian era. They range from churches, missions, and cemeteries to boarding houses. The Catholic church, which dominates the skyline, was built in 1846 as a cathedral for the archdiocese.

Continuing north on Highway 219, you travel through seven miles of grasslands and nursery stock gardens to the Willamette River and Champoeg Road. A marker 0.25 mile north of the intersection remembers the site of the Willamette Valley's first trading post. It was established in 1811 by the Astor Company and subsequently was operated for ten years by the Northwest Company. The post was instrumental in bringing the first trappers, adventurers, and settlers to the French Prairie region.

Turning east on Champoeg Road, you travel 2.5 miles through a wooded corridor to the Robert Newell House, a reconstruction of an 1850s pioneer home. It contains governor's wives' inaugural gowns, antique guns, Native American artifacts, and basketry. A one-room school house, with 1850s furnishings, and an original wooden jail are also on the grounds.

A quarter mile east, Champoeg State Park's visitor center sits on a ridge overlooking lawns and forests on the riverbank below. Displays interpret the natural setting, fur trade, French Canadian settlers, and the struggle for the Oregon Country.

Champoeg was an early hub for river travel and contained a settlement of thirty buildings and 200 people. Until the 1840s, the Oregon country was shared by the United States and Great Britain under a "joint occupancy agreement." On May 2, 1843, settlers met at Champoeg and voted to establish

Highway 99 East offers the closest view of horseshoe-shaped Willamette Falls thundering over a basalt ledge at Oregon City.

a provisional government. It was the first organized American government in the Pacific Northwest.

Group picnic areas, forty-eight electrical and six tent sites, and hiker/biker camps are tucked away in a forest of black cottonwoods, Douglas fir, western red cedar, Oregon white oak, and big leaf maple. Deer, coyotes, beaver, and mink are sometimes seen along hiking trails, and sheep graze in adjacent fields. A boat ramp provides access to Willamette river salmon and steelhead fishing.

Although floods destroyed the town, several historic sites are marked, including a pioneer grave and cemetery. A pioneer mother's cabin museum overlooks the Willamette River. Its antiquities include a mastodon tooth found in the park and relics brought over the Oregon Trail.

From Champoeg, you can conclude by traveling thirteen miles east to Aurora and Interstate 5 or west five miles to Newberg.

18

EUGENE TO TIGARD DRIVE
99 West

General description: A 122-mile signed scenic drive through Willamette Valley cities, farms, vineyards, and historic areas.

Special attractions: Historic sites, wildlife refuges, wineries, McDonald Experimental Forest, Peavy Arboretum, valley scenery, Willamette River.

Location: Western Willamette Valley between Eugene to Tigard.

Drive route names and numbers: Oregon Highway 99, Oregon Highway 99 West.

Travel season: All year.

Camping: No campgrounds on the route. Champoeg State Park Campground with forty-eight electrical and six tent sites, is situated about eight miles south of Newberg. A Bureau of Land Management campground at Alsea Falls has sixteen tent sites and is located approximately fourteen miles west of the route.

Services: All services in Eugene, Junction City, Corvallis, Monmouth, McMinnville, Newberg, and Tigard.

Nearby attractions: Albany Historic Districts, Dorena Lake, covered bridges, Salem, Alsea River Back Country Byway, Columbia River Gorge, Silver Falls Loop, 99 East—French Prairie Loop Scenic Drive, Eugene-Willamette Pass Scenic Drive, Washington County Loop.

For more information: Eugene Convention and Visitor Association of Lane County Oregon, 115 W. 8th, Suite 190, P.O. Box 10286, Eugene, OR 97440, (541) 484-5307, (800) 547-5445. Junction City-Harrisburg Area Chamber of Commerce, 565 Greenwood St., P.O. Box 401, Junction City, OR 97448, (541) 998-6154. Corvallis Convention and Visitors Bureau, 420 N.W. 2nd., Corvallis, Oregon 97330, (541) 757-1544, (800) 334-8118 (USA). Monmouth-Independence Area Chamber of Commerce, 148 Monmouth St., Independence OR 97351, (503) 838-4268, (800) 772-2806. McMinnville Chamber of Commerce, 417 N. Adams, McMinnville, OR 97128, (503) 472-6196. Newberg Area Chamber of Commerce, 115 N. Washington, Newberg, OR 97132, (503) 538-2014. Tigard Chamber of Commerce, 12420 S.W. Main St., Tigard, OR 97223, (503) 639-1656. Willamette Valley Visitors Association, 300 S.W. 2nd Ave., P.O. Box 965, Albany, OR 97321, (541) 928-0911 (800) 526-2256 (USA). Champoeg State Park, 7679 Champoeg Road NE, St. Paul, OR 97137, (503) 633-8170.

The drive: Oregon Highway 99 was the main north-south avenue through the fertile Willamette Valley for over thirty years. Today, it offers travelers an opportunity to bypass the hustle and bustle of Interstate 5, a few miles east, and take a leisurely trip through the valley's rich farmlands, small historic communities, and quiet college towns. Along the way, visitors travel through a variety of croplands producing Christmas trees, grass for grass seed, wheat, nursery stock, cherries, prunes, grapes, and nuts. Numerous wineries along the route offer tours and tastings.

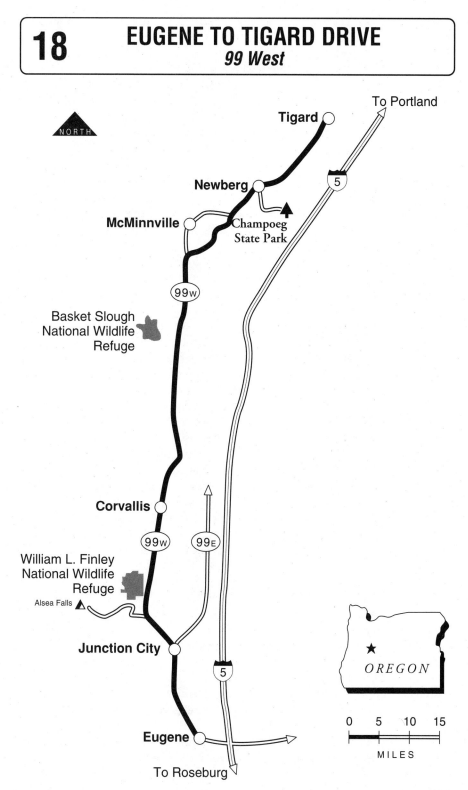

18 EUGENE TO TIGARD DRIVE
99 West

NORTH

To Portland

Tigard

Newberg

McMinnville

Champoeg
State Park

5

99w

Basket Slough
National Wildlife
Refuge

Corvallis

99w   99E

William L. Finley
National Wildlife
Refuge

Alsea Falls

Junction City

5

OREGON

0   5   10   15

MILES

Eugene

To Roseburg

The valley is a series of basalt ridges and basins filled with rich silt and gravel transported to western Oregon from as far away as Montana. They were deposited some 12,000 years ago by huge floods following the last ice age. The valley was raised above sea level about 35,000 years ago at the same time the Coast Range mountains were lifted by shifting of tectonic plates. Gradually, through faulting and shifting, the valley was lowered and widened.

The loop begins on 99 West in downtown Eugene and continues in a straight line, north through Corvallis to McMinnville. Turning east, it passes through several historic communities before concluding at Tigard. Most of the route is flat farmland, broken by thickets of Oregon oak, ash, and maple. On clear days you can see the lofty peaks of the Cascades to the east and the forested slopes of the Coast Range to the west. From Interstate 5, the drive can be joined at connecting highways at exit 249 in Salem, exit 233 in Albany, and exit 194 in Eugene.

Usually travelers will find winter temperatures ranging from the low thirties to forties. Summer highs are usually in the low eighties. Spring and autumn days average in the low seventies.

Eugene, Oregon's second largest city, is the home of the University of Oregon and a major cultural and wood products center. National entertainers appear at Hult Center for the Performing Arts, which is recognized for its architectural design and acoustics. Hendricks Park Rhododendron Garden displays over 6,000 rhododendrons. The Willamette and McKenzie rivers, are productive trout fisheries and offer the serenity of tranquil streams, and lush forest along a network of parks, bike paths, trails, and picnic areas.

From Eugene, Highway 99 extends seventeen miles north to Junction City, where it divides into two roads. Ninety-nine East continues to Harrisburg and Albany, while 99 West leads north to Monroe and on to Corvallis and Tigard.

Blue Star Wayside, midway between Eugene and Junction City, is a popular stocked trout fishing hole about three car lengths from the road. At Washburn Wayside, between Junction City and Monroe, you can picnic in the shade of an oak grove and take a short trail through the woods and meadows. Broadley Vineyards Winery and Cafe, housed in an old brick building on the banks of the Long Tom River in Monroe, offers tastings of its pinot noirs.

About twelve miles north, a short well maintained gravel road leads through William L. Finley Wildlife Refuge. At the 5,325 acres of marshland and forest, you may see Canada geese, deer, a resident herd of elk, and five species of woodpeckers.

The Fiechter House, adjacent to the park headquarters, was built in the 1850s and is a prime example of Classical Revival architecture.

A few miles north of the refuge, Tyee Wine Cellars, on Greenberry Road, produces Pinots, Chardonnays, and Gerwurztraminers. It opens for tastings, vineyard hikes, and picnicking on weekend afternoons from May through October.

Willamette Park, at Corvallis's southern city limits, provides a pleasant spot to relax while enjoying the lazy river and its passing parade of water

A short side trip off 99 West will take you east to the turn-of-the-century buildings of Independence's main street.

skiers, boaters, and barges. The boat launch's unique concrete plank floats on the water. North of the park, Highway 99 crosses U.S. Highway 20, which extends eleven miles east to Albany and west to Newport. Albany's collection of more than 150 homes and buildings represent several 19th Century architectural styles, and are preserved in three historic districts.

In Latin, Corvallis means "Heart of the Valley." The name is appropriate, for Corvallis is the county seat, a major commercial and industrial center, and the home of Oregon State University. The Victorian Italianate-styled Benton County Courthouse, is the oldest in Oregon still used for its original purpose. With a Visitor's Bureau walking brochure, you can see twenty-five buildings dating from the 1850s to the 1920s.

At Peavy Arboretum, 5.5 miles north on Highway 99, more than 160 trees and shrubs are maintained by Oregon State University's College of Forestry. You can feed ducks, hike two trails, and take several treks, horseback rides, and drives into adjacent McDonald Experimental Forest. The 7,000 acres of old- and new-growth timber surround two lakes. A short scenic drive on Barry Creek and Tampico Roads passes eleven historic sites.

Adair Village is a few miles north and today is a small community of about 500 people; the town is bordered by forest and low rolling hills. During World War II, it was the second largest city in Oregon; more than 100,000 men from all forty-eight states were trained here for overseas combat. A sign north of the Village commemorates the divisions that trained here.

During the next ten miles, the highway bisects flat meadows and rolling hills. Helmick State Park's grove of trees serve as a day-use area for picnickers.

At Monmouth, a side trip of a few blocks takes you west to the beautiful campus of Western Oregon State College. The college's Paul Jensen Arctic

Rodgers Boat Landing at Newberg provides a pleasant riverbank for picnicking and watching the variety of boats and crafts that ply the Willamette.

Museum contains a unique collection of more than 3,000 artifacts from the far north.

Independence, two miles east of Monmouth on Highway 51, offers a quick step into the past. The city park, on the banks of the Willamette River, displays a railroad car, covered wagon and a 100-year-old carriage. Look across the street, and you'll see a business district with charming early 1900s buildings. Several buildings house antiques and collectibles shops. The nearby Heritage Museum is filled with Native American artifacts, an 1888 covered wagon, and recreations of a schoolroom and parlor.

At the junction of U.S. Highway 99 and Oregon Highway 22, a turn west will lead five miles to Dallas. Basket Slough National Wildlife Refuge, north of Dallas on Highway 22, was established to protect Canada Geese, but about 200 other species of wildlife also use it. You can see them from several viewpoints and roads that meander through the habitats.

Dallas City Park covers thirty-five acres with a small arboretum of Oregon plants, a Japanese garden, creek, and tennis courts. Next door at Muir and McDonald Co., you can watch as cow hides are turned into leather using a vegetable tanning process that has remained unchanged since the company was founded in 1863.

Rejoining Highway 99 West, five wineries in the nine miles to Amity signal the first of seventeen vineyards in Yamhill County. Most offer public tastings of Pinot noir and Chardonnay, plus specialties such as Chenin blanc, Riesling, vintage brut, and cabernet sauvignon. The area is also a breeding ground for thoroughbred horses, and you're likely to see fields with grazing Morgans, Tennessee Walkers, Arabians, and Clydesdales.

The area between Amity and Tigard also grows ninety per cent of the nation's filberts.

The historic Amity Church of Christ, on Highway 99 West, was founded in 1846. It is the oldest Christian church west of the Rockies.

By taking an eight-mile side trip northeast on Highway 223, you can see an original 1856 blockhouse from Fort Yamhill in Dayton's city park. A picturesque brick Baptist church across the street was built in 1886.

Highway 99 continues north to McMinnville, which preserves fifty-two commercial buildings spanning the 1880s to the 1930s. Linfield College, on Highway 99, was established in 1849 and is a comprehensive liberal arts school.

Lafayette is a few miles west and contains an interesting museum with twenty showcases of pioneer memorabilia housed in an 1892 church. Yamhill Locks Park, filled with tall shade trees, offers a refreshing picnic spot and fishing on the Willamette River bank. It overlooks the broken cement walls of locks that served navigation from 1900 to 1954.

En route to Dundee, you'll pass several orchards and wineries. Argyle Vineyards shares a parking lot with Dundee Wine Company's Elk Cove tasting room on Highway 99 in Dundee. A fifteen-minute tour takes you through the sparkling wine process from chilling and pressing grapes to aging wine. A filbert orchard is across the street.

Newberg is the home of George Fox College, started by Quakers in 1885 and named after the founder of the Friends Church. The college's most famous alumnus, Herbert Hoover, is memorialized in the Hoover Academic Building, which contains a variety of his memorabilia. From 1885 to 1889, he lived at the Hoover-Minthorn Museum House, one block south of Highway 99 at 2nd and River streets. It exhibits many original furnishings and souvenirs of his boyhood.

Rodgers Boat Landing, 1.7 miles south of the home, provides access to the Willamette River. From the landing you may see a variety of Willamette River traffic including jet boaters, fishermen, and large commercial barges.

The Highway 99 West drive concludes by passing clusters of businesses, stands of trees, and open fields on the twenty miles east at Tigard.

19 BENTON COUNTY LOOP

General description: A 109-mile signed scenic loop through Willamette Valley farms, vineyards, and foothills of the Coast Range mountains.
Special attractions: Waterfalls, South Fork of the Alsea River, Willamette River, William L. Finley National Wildlife Refuge, McDonald Experimental Forest, Peavy Arboretum, mountain and valley scenery historic sites, wineries.
Location: Western Willamette Valley between Corvallis and Alpine.
Drive route names and numbers: Alpine Road, County Road C-03-45120,

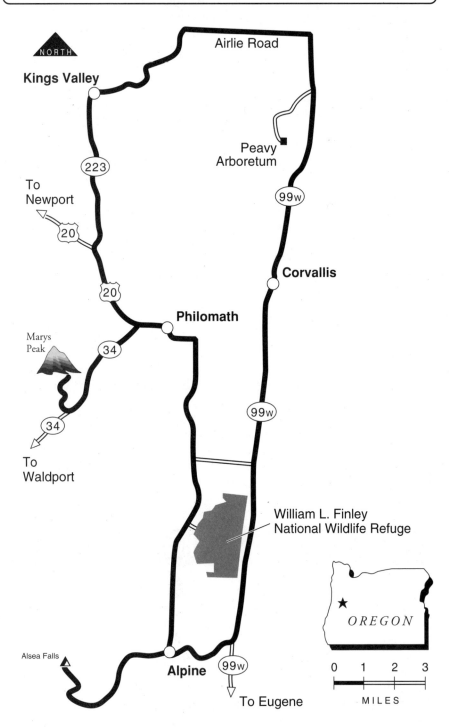

NORTH

Kings Valley

Airlie Road

Peavy Arboretum

223

99w

To Newport

20

20

Corvallis

Philomath

Marys Peak

34

34

99w

To Waldport

William L. Finley National Wildlife Refuge

Alsea Falls

Alpine

99w

To Eugene

OREGON

0   1   2   3

MILES

Bellfountain Road, U.S. Highway 20, Oregon Highway 223, Airlie Road, Oregon Highway 99 West.

Travel season: All year, although Road C-03-45120 to Alsea Falls and the access road to Marys Peak may close temporarily due to snow.

Camping: One Bureau of Land Management campground with picnic tables, fire rings, vault toilets and drinking water.

Services: All services in Corvallis. Limited services in Philomath and Alpine.

Nearby attractions: Albany historic districts, Linn County Covered Bridges Scenic Drive, 99 West—Eugene—Tigard Scenic Drive.

For more information: Corvallis Convention and Visitors Bureau, 420 NW 2nd., Corvallis, Oregon 97330, (541) 757-1544, (800) 334-8118 (USA). Philomath Area Chamber of Commerce, 2395 Main St., P.O. Box 606, Philomath, OR 97370, (541) 929-2454. Willamette Valley Visitors Association, 300 S.W. 2nd Ave., P.O. Box 965, Albany, OR 97321, (541) 928-0911, (800) 526-2256(USA).

The drive: In the past, there have been several versions of this drive. While some routings start at different points, all follow essentially the same quiet backroads through forest, farmland, and several small communities that are little more than a crossroads with a store or a church. The current version begins at the southern end of Benton County and travels west through the heavy forests of the Coast Range. From Alpine, it heads north through forest, Christmas tree farms, and wineries to Philomath. Returning to forests it makes a brief swing west on U.S. Highway 20 before continuing north through woodlands and wineries. It concludes by taking Oregon Highway 99 south to Corvallis. Traffic is usually light on the backroads, and moderate to heavy on 99 West. Most of the route traverses pillow basalts that formed underwater and were part of the Pacific Ocean floor about fifty-sixty million years ago. The area was raised above sea level about thirty-five million years ago.

Usually, travelers will find winter temperatures ranging from the low thirties to forties. Summer highs are generally in the low eighties. Spring and fall days average about seventy degrees. Most of the forty inches of rain per year falls in winter.

The drive begins fourteen miles south of Corvallis at the junction of 99 West and Alpine Road. Taking Alpine Road west, you travel along a ridge covered with oak trees that overlooks rolling hills and meadows. The road ends 3.5 miles west at Alpine where a general store and a few homes are clustered around an intersection.

From Alpine, you can take a scenic side trip to Alpine Vineyards and Alsea Falls by traveling west on Foster Road and turning south on County Road C-03-45120. The winery and picnic area overlook the scenic foothills of the Coast Range and the twenty-six-acre vineyard. While enjoying the scenery, you can sample Chardonnay, Pinot noir, Riesling, Gerwurztraminer, Cabernet Sauvignon, and White Cabernet.

After a short stretch of pastoral valley farms, the paved county road climbs into the Coast Range foothills and becomes a Bureau of Land Management National Back Country Byway. The rewards for negotiating hair pin turns and frequent log trucks are lush Douglas fir forests, an abundance of columbines, foxgloves, and other wildflowers, and flaming vine maples in autumn. From pullouts you'll see an endless dark green forest filling hills, valleys, peaks, and ravines.

Deer and elk are prevalent, and the scenic Alsea River's South Fork, which parallels much of the route, is a good stream to try your luck at catching coho and chinook salmon, steelhead, and trout. Alsea Falls is a rushing white water cascade just a short walk from the roadside parking lot or a one-mile riverside hike from the sixteen-unit BLM campground.

The 10.6 miles from Alpine to the falls is generally usable all year without special equipment. From the falls, the pavement continues west, then turns to gravel east of Alsea where it joins Oregon Highway 34.

Returning to Alpine, the drive traverses two miles of oak-covered hills as it takes Bellfountain Road north. Look east at Bellfountain and Dawson roads, and you'll see Bellfountain Community Church, an excellent example of 19th century Queen Anne church style architecture. By turning west at Dawson Road, you can picnic in the shade of huge Douglas firs at Bellfountain Park. Established in 1851, it is the county's oldest park and contains the longest picnic table in the United States cut from a single piece of wood. Hull-Oakes Lumber Company, west of the park, operates one of the nation's last steam-driven sawmills. You can tour it by calling in advance.

Two miles north of the intersection a well maintained gravel road meanders through the 5,325 acres of William L. Finley Wildlife Refuge to an eastern entrance on U.S. Highway 99 West. Its marshes, creeks, and meadows attract virtually every species of birds found in the Willamette Valley. While it was established to protect Canada geese, you may see wood ducks and hooded mergansers nesting in summer. Ruffed grouse, ring-necked pheasants and mourning doves are also seen along with deer and a resident herd of elk. The Woodpecker Loop Trail meanders through a mixed forest of Douglas fir, maple, Oregon ash, and oak that is a habitat for five species of woodpeckers. Several historic buildings near the headquarters include a barn and an 1850s Classic Revival-styled home.

Two miles north, Bellfountain and Tyee Wine cellars offer tastings, vineyard hikes, and picnicking. Both bottle Pinots, Chardonnays, and Gerwurztraminers.

Bellfountain Road cuts across rolling hills dappled with Christmas tree farms, hay fields, and dairy farms as it continues five miles north to Philomath.

Philomath is a combination of Greek words meaning "lover of learning," and was named after a local college which closed in 1929. The imposing college building houses the Benton County Historical Museum, which contains Calipooia Indian artifacts, Camp Adair photographs, logging equipment, and other collections. A second-floor gallery features changing exhibits of local arts, crafts and photography.

Oregon Highway 34 starts at Philomath and ends at Newport on the Oregon Coast. This highway provides an opportunity for a scenic side trip. About ten miles south of Philomath, a side road spirals off of Highway 34 to

Alsea Falls, situated 10.4 miles southwest of Alpine, climaxes a scenic trip into the Coast Range mountains.

the summit of Mary's Peak where sweeping views of mountain and valley forests, streams, and meadows stretch to the far horizons. At 4,097 feet elevation, it is the highest peak in the Coast Range and often has snow during winter.

A few miles south, you can visit Alsea River Trout Hatchery, which raises cutthroat trout and steelhead. At the community of Alsea, your options include taking the graveled and paved county road to Alsea Falls and Alpine, or continuing on Highway 34 to Waldport. West of Alsea, the highway passes by several county parks with boat launches. Hayden Covered Bridge (World Guide Number 37-02-05) 1.5 miles west of Alsea, was built in 1918 and is still in use.

From Philomath, the drive follows U.S. Highway 20 west for five miles through a forested corridor. At Wren, it passes Harris Covered Bridge (World Guide Number 37-02-04) and turns north onto Highway 223. The bridge was built in 1936 and is still used. Motor-home crossings are not recommended due to limited clearance.

Deer are so plentiful along the nine miles to Kings Valley, that signs ask you to watch for them. You'll also see sheep farms, magnificently dilapidated barns, thickets of Douglas fir forest, and the last Christmas tree farms.

Kings Valley Community Chapel, at the junction of Maxwell Creek Road and Highway 223, is an excellent example of the Gothic Church style that was prevalent here during the 19th century. Paul M. Dunn Forest, nearby, is an Oregon State Research Project where you can study and photograph plants.

Turning east onto Maxwell Creek and Airlie Roads, you'll pass low rolling hills covered with Serendipity and Airlie vineyards. Serendipity Wine Cellars makes Muller Thurgau, Chenin blanc, Chardonnay, Cabernet Sauvignon, Zinfandel and Marechal Foch. Airlie Winery specializes in Pinot noir, Chardonnay, Marechal Foch, Müller-Thurgau, Riesling, and Gewürztraminer.

After three miles, turn south onto Oregon Highway 99 West, and you will pass through Adair Village. During World War II, the army training center covered 50,000 acres. The area east of the highway was a base camp, and hills to the west were used for maneuvers. To simulate actual conditions, full-scale models of European towns were built. Few of the buildings remain.

Tall Fir trees line the highway as it continues south to Corvallis. Peavy Arboretum, two miles south of Adair Village is maintained by OSU's college of forestry, and exhibits more than 160 trees and shrubs from the United States and several nations. In the adjacent McDonald Experimental Forest, you can hike through 7,000 acres of new and old growth timber, by lakes, and historic sites.

The drive concludes 5.5 miles south in Corvallis, The towns attractions include twenty-five historic buildings displaying a variety of architectural styles from the 1850s to the 1920s, Oregon State University, and Avery Park's rose garden, picnic areas, and playgrounds. Benton County Courthouse, is the oldest in Oregon still used for its original purpose. It is a prime example of Victorian Italianate architecture and contains local history displays.

20 LINN COUNTY COVERED BRIDGES LOOP

General description: A fifty-one-mile drive on paved two lane county roads through farmlands and crossroads communities to five covered bridges.
Special attractions: Five covered bridges, fish hatchery, historic church, Santiam River.
Location: Eastern Willamette Valley between Albany and Lyons.
Drive route names and numbers: U.S. Highway 20, Oregon Highway 226, Gilkey Bridge Road, Shamanek Bridge Drive, Richardson Gap Road, Fish Hatchery Road.
Travel season: All year.
Camping: There are no campgrounds along the route.
Services: All services in Albany. Limited services in Crabtree and Scio.
Nearby attractions: Albany historic districts, North Santiam Canyon Scenic Drive, Santiam Scenic Loop Drive, Silver Falls Scenic Loop Drive.
For more information: Albany Visitors Association, 300 Second Ave., S.W., P.O. Box 965, Albany, OR 97321, (541) 928-0911, (800) 526-2256 (USA). Willamette Valley Visitors Association, 300 S.W. 2nd Ave., P.O. Box 965, Albany, OR 97321, (541) 928-0911, (800) 526-2256 (USA).

The drive: Five of Oregon's fifty-three covered bridges are included on the

Larwood Covered Bridge sits at the confluence of the Roaring River and Crabtree Creek. Nearby, a small park provides a relaxing picnic spot and good angle for photographing the bridge.

drive, which forms a rectangle as it extends through a small valley framed by the Cascade foothills and western ridges. The route can be driven from Interstate 5 by traveling east from exit 238 on Jefferson/Scio Road, then turning south on Robinson Road and starting at Gilkey Bridge, or by taking exit 233 at Albany to U.S. Highway 20. Highway 22 travelers can join by exiting at Lyons and following Highway 226 southwest eight miles to Hannah Bridge. While traffic is usually light, allow time for leisurely driving, as posted speeds sometimes drop to fifteen and twenty miles per hour.

All of the bridges are identified by name and cataloged in the World Guide Number System, which is a national indexing system used to identify covered bridges. The six-digit number identifies the state, county, and bridge location. Since Oregon is number thirty-seven when states are listed alphabetically, the first number for each Oregon Bridge is thirty-seven.

While they are wistful reminders of a horse and buggy past, covered bridges served a multitude of purposes beyond providing access across streams. During prohibition, illegal liquor was often stored in them, and outlaws used them for cover while awaiting their victims. Political rallies, dances, and church meetings were sometimes held in them.

Because timber was abundant, they were economical to build. By covering them, they were protected from Oregon's rainy weather, and their life span was doubled.

Travelers will find moderate temperatures in the Willamette Valley. Summer highs rarely rise above the mid-eighties. Spring and fall days average

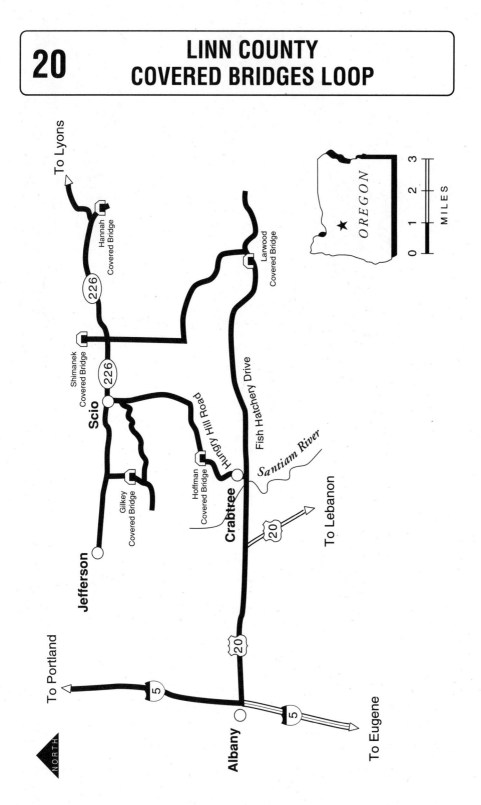

To Lyons

Hannah Covered Bridge

Larwood Covered Bridge

OREGON

0 1 2 3

MILES

226

Shimanek Covered Bridge

226

Scio

Hungry Hill Road

Fish Hatchery Drive

Hoffman Covered Bridge

Santiam River

Crabtree

Gilkey Covered Bridge

20

To Lebanon

Jefferson

To Portland

5

20

5

Albany

To Eugene

NORTH

in the low seventies. Winter days hover between the low thirties and low forties. Temperatures in the middle to high sixties are common in spring and fall. Mornings can bring heavy fog that obliterates surrounding countrysides.

From Albany, you begin by traveling nine miles east through open farmland on U.S. Highway 20. Turning onto Oregon Highway 226, which is signed as Crabtree Road, you cross the Santiam River, lined with flat fields and clumps of oak trees. A turn north onto Cold Springs Road takes you 0.25 mile into Crabtree where you join Hungry Hill Road one block east of the first cross street.

During the 1.5 miles to Hoffman Bridge, there is a wistfulness of times gone by as you pass classic weather beaten barns with diamond-shaped windows, austere two-story houses, and grazing cattle. A bed of Volcanic ash, deposited thirty to thirty-five million years ago, when this section had a subtropical climate, provides the fertile base for the dairy farms and fields of hay, wheat, and vegetables, which you'll pass along the route.

Hoffman Bridge (World Guide Number 37-22-08) was built in 1936 and is surrounded by woods and rests on original hand-hewn timbers, which were cut at Hungry Hill and hauled down by teams of horses. Instead of the exposed trusses common to most covered bridges, it displays unique gothic style windows. Crabtree Creek meanders out of the hills, under the bridge, and into an open field.

Old barns and modern ranches with brick homes and white board fences stand on rolling hillsides and grasslands as Hungry Hill Road and Highway 226 stretch north toward Scio. One mile south of Scio, the drive turns west at Gilkey Road and follows it four miles to Goar Road and Gilkey Bridge (World Guide Number 37-22-04). The one-lane bridge, built in 1939, spans Thomas Creek and once stood next to a covered railroad bridge. At 120 feet, it is the area's longest existing covered bridge.

From Gilkey Bridge, you can travel east to Scio on either the Jefferson-Scio Road or by backtracking on Gilkey Road. Scio Depot Museum contains an interesting collection of Willamette Valley artifacts. You can enjoy a picnic lunch on a shaded creek bank next to the 100-year-old railroad station.

Highway 226 cuts through potato and hay fields on the seven miles to Camp Morrison Road. Hannah Bridge (World Guide Number 37-22-02) crosses Thomas Creek about 100 feet south of the intersection. It has been there since 1936 and is among the most picturesque. It is situated at the mouth of a forested canyon and was designed with rounded portals and exposed trusses.

After backtracking through two miles of wooded countryside and postoral farmlands, you turn west onto Shimanek Bridge Drive. It ends at Shimanek Bridge (World Guide Number 37-22-03), situated at the intersection of Richardson Gap Road.

Since 1861, five bridges have occupied this site. The present structure was built in 1966 and is the county's newest. Its louvered windows, red paint, and old style portal design with squared rather than rounded corners are unique.

After following Richardson Gap Road 4.5 miles south through flat hayfields and rolling oak and alder covered hills, you turn east on Fish

Gilkey Bridge is one of fifty-three covered bridges in Oregon and is situated between Jefferson and Scio.

Hatchery Road, and travel 3.6 miles to Larwood Bridge (World Guide Number 37-22-06).

The bridge dates to 1939 and is near the confluence of the Roaring River and Crabtree Creek. A small creek-bank park next to the bridge is a delightful picnic and swimming spot and provides a good angle for photographing the bridge. A restored waterwheel across the stream adds a bit of nostalgia.

Roaring River Park and Fish Hatchery are about one mile east of the bridge. At the park, you can fish the Roaring River, enjoy a large day use area with picnic shelters and playground equipment, walk a plant identification trail, and take short hikes from the parking lot through the dense forest to the river's edge.

The Oregon State Department of Fish and Wildlife operates Roaring River Fish Hatchery. It produces about one million rainbow trout per year, along with some 225,000 winter and summer steelhead. Each pond holds about 20,000 fish. You'll also see the settling basins and a display pond with sturgeon, albino cutthroat, brook and brown trout.

After returning to Richardson Gap Road, the drive concludes one mile south at Providence Pioneer Church. The picturesque church was founded in 1853 by Oregon's first circuit rider and is still in use. From its hilltop, you have a commanding view of the valley below.

To rejoin U.S. Highway 20, take Fish Hatchery Road west. By turning south to Sweet Home, you can see three more covered bridges on the Santiam Loop Scenic Drive to Brownsville.

21 EUGENE, WILLAMETTE PASS, U.S. 97 JUNCTION

General description: A ninety-one-mile drive from the Willamette Valley through the Central Oregon Cascades and over Willamette Pass.

Special attractions: Outstanding mountain scenery, Willamette Valley, mountain and reservoir lakes, waterfalls, covered bridges, Willamette and Deschutes national forests, camping, hiking, waterskiing, canoeing, boating, snowmobiling, cross-country and downhill skiing.

Location: West central Oregon between Eugene and Willamette Pass.

Drive route number: Oregon Highway 58.

Travel season: All year.

Camping: Two Corps of Engineer campgrounds; twenty-three forest service campgrounds with tables, fire pits, flush or vault toilets. Some have water.

Services: All services at Eugene and Oakridge. Limited services at Westfir.

Nearby attractions: Lane County covered bridges, Dorena Lake, Diamond Peak Wilderness, Newberry Crater National Monument, Cascade Lakes Highway, Waldo Lake Wilderness, Crater Lake National Park, Robert Aufderheide Scenic Byway.

For more information: Eugene Convention and Visitor Association of Lane County Oregon, 115 W. 8th, Suite 190, P.O. Box 10286, Eugene, OR 97440, (541) 484-5307, (800) 547-5445 (USA). Oakridge-Westfir Chamber of Commerce, P.O. Box 217, Oakridge, OR 97463, (541) 782-4146.

The drive: This busy corridor connects Eugene, the state's second largest city, with central Oregon. It is also one of Oregon's most magnificent drives, affording the eastbound traveler roadside views of the Willamette River, the valley floor, and Lookout Point Reservoir, framed by a continuous panorama of thick forested mountain slopes and peaks. The westbound traveler begin on the Cascade's eastern slopes, surrounded by steep cinder cones and several glacier-carved lakes which are accessible from short side roads. Crossing Willamette Pass at 5,128 feet, the road descends amidst towering fir-covered mountains. The final forty-four miles west of Oakridge offer roadside views of the reservoir and river. In addition to a diversity of man-made and natural scenery, the route includes fascinating geology, and virtually unlimited opportunities for outdoor recreation.

Traffic is usually fairly heavy. You will want to stay within the fifty-five-mile-per-hour speed limit and use the frequent turnouts to let semis and logging trucks pass before descending the six-percent downgrades with runaway truck ramps. The route is heavily patrolled by the state police.

During the summer, you can expect temperatures in the high seventies and low eighties. Winters average in the high forties and low fifties. Spring days are usually in the mid-sixties, while autumn temperatures range from the mid-sixties to mid-seventies.

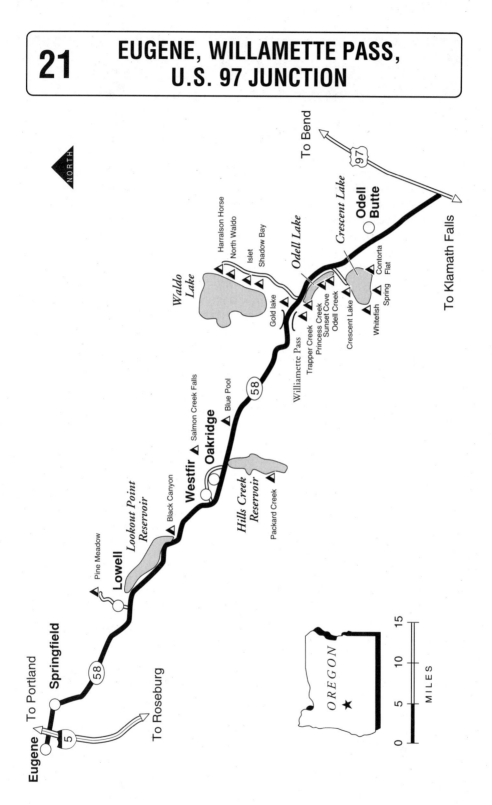

NORTH

To Bend

97

Odell Butte

Crescent Lake

Odell Lake

To Klamath Falls

Harralson Horse
North Waldo
Islet
Shadow Bay

Waldo Lake

Contorta Flat
Spring

Gold lake

Whitefish

Trapper Creek
Princess Creek
Sunset Cove
Odell Creek
Crescent Lake

Williamette Pass

58

Salmon Creek Falls
Blue Pool

Westfir
Oakridge

Black Canyon

Lookout Point Reservoir

Hills Creek Reservoir

Packard Creek

Pine Meadow

Lowell

To Portland

Springfield

58

To Roseburg

5

Eugene

OREGON

0   5   10   15
M I L E S

In the Eugene-Springfield area, the drive starts at Interstate 5 exit 188. Howard Buford Recreation Area, two miles east of the exit, is situated on the banks of the Coast Fork of the Willamette River. It includes Mount Pisgah Arboretum, where you can walk five miles of trails by wildflower and rhododendron species gardens and through groves of incense cedar, redwoods, Douglas fir, and Oregon white oak. At the visitor center, you can participate in a "touch me" nature exhibit.

After passing five miles of picturesque barns and farmland, you'll enter the community of Pleasant Hill and cross a side road leading three miles north to Jasper. Within seven miles of Jasper, you can see five of Lane County's covered bridges as you follow the north bank of the Willamette to rejoin Highway 58 at Lowell.

At Pleasant Hill, Highway 58 starts the gradual climb which continues through Willamette Pass. This section was formed between fifteen and thirty million years ago during a period of intense volcanic activity. The dark roadside rocks are basalts mixed with lighter colored andesites.

Elijah Bristow State Park, 3.7 miles east, offers sixteen miles of hiking, biking, and equestrian trails, and the opportunity to fish the Willamette for trout, salmon, steelhead, walleye, small and large mouth bass. Dexter Park, 2.5 miles east, provides a large picnic area, boat launch, and a sweeping water level view of Dexter Lake and Dam. Dexter and Lookout Point Reservoir, a few miles east, are Corps of Engineer earth-and-gravel-fill dams and operate as a single unit to provide flood control, irrigation, improved navigation and power generation. At both, you can fish all year and enjoy seasonal waterskiing, sailing, swimming, picnicking, and hunting.

Lowell Covered Bridge, built in 1945, (World Guide Number 37-20-18), stands near an intersection, 2.3 miles east. The side road connects to the north shore's Wimberly County Park, Lowell Ranger Station, a marina, and a viewpoint of 14,360-acre Lookout Point Reservoir stretching through a narrow fir-forested canyon. A paved side road near the Corps of Engineer's ninety-two-site Pine Meadow Campground angles northeast along twenty-two miles of Fall Creek Reservoir. Three forest service campgrounds, with a total of twenty-nine sites, are situated along the timbered shoreline of the 1,852-acre reservoir. The nearby Fall Creek Trail has been designated a National Recreation Trail.

Two miles east, the route passes Lookout Point Dam. Across the highway you'll see a granite cliff. It is a magma plug, about one mile in diameter and was formed from molten lava that pushed into solid rock and cooled slowly without reaching the surface.

After following the reservoir for several miles, the highway enters the 1.6-million-acre Willamette National Forest, which encompasses eight wilderness areas, seven major Cascade mountain peaks, and 1,400 miles of trails. Cutting through a Douglas fir and oak corridor, you pass public boat ramps, small county park camping areas, private RV parks, and the forest service's seventy-two site Black Canyon Campground.

Seventeen miles east, the route reaches Westfir Junction. By traveling two miles north, you can see Office Covered Bridge (world guide number 37-20-

39) in the community of Westfir. The 180-feet-long bridge is the town's dominant landmark. The junction is also the southern access to the Robert Aufderheide National Forest Service Scenic Byway, which extends fifty-five miles north along the Wild and Scenic North Fork of the Middle Fork of the Willamette River and the South Fork of the McKenzie River.

The Middle Fork of the Willamette River runs through Oakridge, a mile east of the junction. At Green Waters Park, on the river bank, you can swim, fish, and walk a nature trail. Salmon Creek Falls' fourteen-unit campground offers an overnight on a mountain slope north of town.

Hills Creek Lake, three miles southeast of Oakridge, fills 2,735 acres of a narrow, forested canyon, surrounded by rugged mountains. You may see waterfowl, black tailed deer, wintering elk, bald eagles, and osprey along the forty-four miles of shoreline. The lake is a popular waterskiing and sailboarding spot, and fishermen are rewarded with catches of kokanee, rainbow trout, crappie, large mouth bass, and catfish. Larison Cove on the northwest end, is reserved for canoes and non-motorized boats. It offers a beautiful forested shoreline, tranquility, and picnic sites which are accessible only by trail or canoe. The forty-four sites at Packard Creek and Sand Prairie campgrounds on the western shore overlook the scenic lake. Sacandaga Campground, several miles south on the Willamette River banks, has seventeen sites.

East of Oakridge the highway enters the high Cascades by passing McCredie Springs and Blue Pool Campground's twenty-four sites. Ahead of you waves of trees fill mountainsides as the road disappears into a canopy of mixed Douglas fir, maple, oaks, poplars, western red cedars, and hemlocks. Many are so tall you won't be able to see their tops from inside your vehicle. Soon you begin a five-mile, six-percent climb, pass through a tunnel, dip into a ravine, and start another six-percent climb. Many of the deep ravines crevasses and basins that became mountain lakes were gouged out by glaciers during the last ice age.

At the top of the second climb, Salt Creek Falls, Oregon's second highest waterfall, drops 286 feet over a basalt ledge. Looking west from the viewpoint Salt Creek weaves a thin line through a narrow forested ravine. By following a 2.5-mile trail along the canyon rim you'll see several more cascades en route to Diamond Creek Falls.

Two miles east, a side road leads northeast along thirteen miles of Waldo Lake. Carved out of the Cascades at an elevation of 5,414 feet, it is Oregon's second largest natural lake. The water is so clear that on calm days you can see to a depth of 100 feet. A twenty-one-mile loop trail around the lake will take you by isolated beaches, coves, and meadows and into the adjacent Waldo Lake Wilderness. It is used by hikers, horses, and mountain bikers. The lake is also a popular spot for sailboarding and canoeing. Five forest service campgrounds along the access road provide a total of 232 sites.

After passing two viewpoints overlooking the 35,400-acre Diamond Peak Wilderness, the highway reaches Willamette Pass summit. Also, watch for a side road that leads north to tiny Gold Lake, which is open to fly fishing. The pass is a favorite ski area and capable of moving 8,400 skiers per hour on four triple and one double chair. Its total skiable terrain covers 1,100 acres with five beginner, eleven intermediate and thirteen advanced/expert runs. Facilities include a lodge, day-care and children's learning center, and Oregon's only snow-making system.

East of the pass the trees are smaller and the undergrowth thins because the mountains, acting as a shield, cut off rain and snow. Much of the soil is covered with yellow pumice that erupted from Mount Mazama about 7,000 years ago.

About four miles east of the summit, the Willamette National Forest ends, and the 1,600,616-acre Deschutes National Forest begins. The highway crosses the Pacific Crest Trail that winds south by Odell Lake, through the Diamond Peaks Wilderness, and on to California. Through the trees on the south side of the highway you can see beautiful Odell lake ringed by a thick forest of dark blue-green trees and framed by the Diamond Peaks. Short side roads lead to its tranquil shore and boat ramps that are usually busy as fishermen launch in search of trout. Its easy access makes it one of Oregon's busiest lakes and supports a year-round resort at the east end, a trailer park on the west end, and four forest service campgrounds, nestled in the trees around its shoreline. They contain a total of 126 sites.

Two miles east, a short side road leads south to its sister, Crescent Lake. A small service community with a mini-mart, marina, motel, and gas station, surrounds the lake. Like Odell, it is a year-round favorite of trout fishermen and cross-country skiers. The four forest service campgrounds ringing the lake offer 144 sites.

East of Crescent Lake, the highway passes a side road leading four miles north to Davis Lake and five forest service campgrounds with seventy sites. Continuing east, you'll see the tall, perfectly cylindrical cone of 7,037-foot Odell Butte punctuating the horizon. Crescent Creek Campground, north of the butte, has ten sites. A few miles further, the highway enters an area of dead trees killed by pine beetles, crosses the Little Deschutes River, and ends at a junction with U.S. Highway 97. From the junction, you can travel north twenty-four miles to LaPine or south eight miles to Chemult.

22 EUGENE, FLORENCE, JUNCTION CITY

General description: A 139-mile drive along two-lane paved highways through Willamette Valley farmlands and Coast Range mountains.
Special attractions: Beautiful forests, low mountains, reservoir park, river valley, scenic lake, covered bridges, sand dunes, ocean beach scenic drive.
Location: West-central Oregon between Eugene and Florence.
Drive route numbers: Oregon highways 126 and 36.
Travel season: All year.
Camping: Three Bureau of Land Management and four forest service campgrounds with tables, fire pit, flush or vault toilet. One state park campground with full hookups, electrical and tent sites. One Lane County

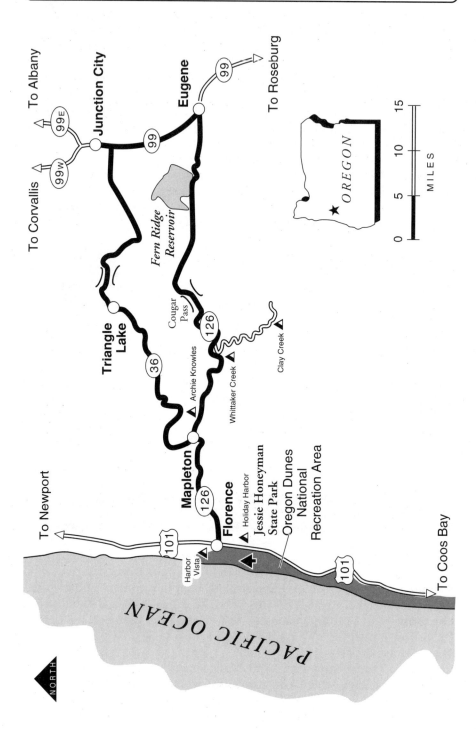

Park campground with electricity, and one Siuslaw Port Commission RV park with hookups.

Services: All services at Eugene and Florence. Limited services at Noti.

Nearby attractions: McKenzie River, 99 West Scenic Drive, Highway 58-Eugene-Willamette Pass Scenic Drive, William L. Finley National Wildlife Refuge, Lane County covered bridges, Dorena Lake.

For more information: Convention and Visitor Association of Lane County Oregon, 115 W. 8th, Suite 190, P.O. Box 10286, Eugene, OR 97440, (541) 484-5307, (800) 547-5445 (USA). Siuslaw National Forest, 4077 Research Way, P.O. Box 1148, Corvallis, Oregon 97339, (541) 750-7000. Florence Area Chamber of Commerce, 270 Hwy. 101, P.O. Box 26000, Florence, OR 97439, (541) 997-3128.

The drive: From Eugene, Highway 126 takes travelers through the western Willamette Valley and over the crumpled ridges of the Coast Range to Mapleton, then follows the Siuslaw river into Florence. En route, it passes 100-year-old farms, covered bridges, small roadside communities, tiny ponds, creeks and rivers. The return on Highway 36 stays in the rugged Siuslaw River Canyon, offering a roadside of rocky cliffs, narrow ravines, and a river that changes from slow and meandering to rushing cascades as the road climbs a basalt ridge to serene Triangle Lake. It concludes with the Willamette Valley farmlands. During the week, traffic is usually light to moderate on both highways and moderate to heavy on weekends. The rural countryside, a narrow road, and some sharp turns dictate a slow pace.

Summer travelers can expect temperatures in the high seventies and low eighties. Winters average in the high forties and low fifties. Spring days are usually in the mid-sixties, while autumn temperatures range from the mid-sixties to mid-seventies. Rainfall averages ninety inches per year on the coast and 120 inches in the mountains.

Oregon Highway 126 starts as a business loop in downtown Eugene and winds its way west on Garfield and 11th streets. Shedding the city's congestion, it cuts through grasslands and oak-covered ridges. After about seven miles, it passes Fern Ridge Reservoir, which extends north 4.5 miles as it fills a shallow lowland. Although you're likely to have only moderate success at catching crappies, bass, cutthroat, and stocked rainbow trout, you'll find it an excellent lake for sailboarding, power boating and waterskiing.

Six parks on the graceful curve of the western shore overlook the reservoir and draw heavy use from picnickers, swimmers, and wildlife watchers. The marshlands are nesting and stopover habitats for gulls, ducks, geese, herons, egrets, and raptors. You may see nesting osprey in the large oaks, willows, pines, and apple trees in Perkins Peninsula Park along Highway 126. A pullout, 0.6 mile west, overlooks a breeding ground for yellow-headed blackbirds and purple martins. Bird checklists and viewing area guides are available at Fern Ridge's headquarters. In fall, the surrounding lands are open to shotgun and archery hunting for waterfowl and deer. A private concession near the park operates thirty-seven tent/trailer campsites.

West of Fern Ridge, the highway continues for a few miles through the

After meandering through a scenic wooded canyon, Highway 36 reaches picturesque Triangle Lake where fishermen can cast for stocked rainbow trout, wild cutthroat, and bass.

valley's flat grasslands and low, oak-covered hills, as it passes several farms that have been here more than 100 years. A mile west at Venita you can purchase gas, groceries and liquor at roadside stores. A few miles beyond, you'll cross the Long Tom River and pass three vineyards, which offer tastings of Chardonnay, Pinot noir, and Rieslings.

After the highway passes several ponds frequented by ducks and geese, the ascent into the Coast Range starts in stands of alders. Two miles west, you're into a continuous forest of Douglas fir, western hemlock, and western red cedar. Except for small valley meadows, squeezed in the flatlands of wooded hills and mountains, the forest will be your constant companion during the thirty-two miles to Mapleton. When the highway dips down into Noti, you'll see log decks and lumber yards extending from one end of the community to the other.

Passing clearcuts, Christmas tree farms, and roadside meadows with a few head of grazing cattle and horses, the quintessential Oregon forest begins with gorgeous, huge Douglas firs enclosing the highway. A series of curves and patched highway signals the ascent to the 769-foot summit of Cougar Pass. A few miles east of Walton, which has a gas station and store, Wildcat Creek starts meandering along the roadside. A couple miles west, Walton Wildcat Covered Bridge (World guide number 37-20-04) straddles Turner Creek. The bridge was built in 1925 and is located at Austa Wayside boat ramp. By turning south on County Road 4390 at the bridge, you can use Whittacker Creek Campground as your base for salmon and steelhead fishing in an arm of the Siuslaw River. The Bureau of Land Management campground has thirty-one tent and trailer sites, a boat ramp, playground, and swimming areas. Kentucky Falls Recreation Trail, about twelve miles south of the campground, is a four-mile round trip hike to eighty-ninety-foot twin waterfalls. BLM's Clay Creek Campground, nearby, offers twenty-two sites, a group picnic shelter, and softball field surrounded by rugged mountains and evergreens.

The descent from the mountains is exceptionally scenic. Stands of alders and moss-draped trees create a natural tunnel, and sandstone and igneous rock outcroppings frame a small canyon. The mountains were created about thirty-five million years ago, when they were uplifted from the ocean floor. Prior to the lifting, volcanism covered existing sandstone with molten lava. The rocks you see on the along the highway are actually part of the ancient sea floor, which has been exposed layer by layer as streams eroded down through the rock.

Turner Creek is a good trout stream and meanders alongside Highway 126 for about four miles. A small BLM campground with seven sites is situated south of the highway near the west end of the creek. The forest service's Archie Knowles Campground, three miles east of Mapleton, provides a relaxing environment for enjoying the scenery, fishing, and short hikes. It has three sites.

At Mapleton, Highway 126 meets Oregon Highway 36, then follows the Siuslaw River westward. If you're planning to hike or camp in the Oregon Dunes Recreation Area, or other parts of the forest, the Siuslaw National Forest's Mapleton office, on Highway 126 can assist you with trail maps, camping permits, hiking, hunting, and fishing information.

Between Mapleton and Florence, the river spreads into two channels separated by small islands and mudflats and is lined with lumber yards, boat basins, and a golf course. The Siuslaw Port Commission's Holiday Harbor Campground, on the river's shore in Florence next to a marina, includes seventy tent and trailer sites with electricity.

Highway 126 ends at a junction with U.S. Highway 101. By continuing straight ahead, you can take the 2.4-mile Siuslaw Estuary Scenic Drive, which cuts through stands of dwarfed lodgepole pines and ends at the Pacific Ocean on a sandy beach and grass jetty. At the jetty, you can cast a line in the surf for salmon, perch, and ling cod, dig crabs, fly kites, and comb the beach for shells, driftwood, and other treasures washed ashore by the tides.

A viewpoint at Harbor Vista Park offers a sweeping vista of white-capped waves, sandy beaches and the shoreline forest. The park, at the end of the estuary drive, has twenty-seven campsites. Most have electricity and water.

By turning south at the end of the access road, you'll follow the picturesque shoreline to Florence's waterfront district. The district is a combination of specialty shops, restaurants, theaters, a boat basin, converted warehouses and picturesque commercial buildings. A Fly Fishing Museum at 280 Nopal Street, displays work of the best west coast fly tiers.

Several attractions along U.S. Highway 101 are within a few miles of Florence. Heceta Lighthouse, Sea Lion Caves, Darlingtonia Botanical Gardens, and the Sutton Recreation Area, are five to twelve miles north of town. Sutton Creek and Lake campgrounds, situated in a sand dune area, feature a total of nine tent and sixty-three tent trailer sites.

The Oregon Dunes Recreation Area begins south of Florence and stretches for forty-seven miles along the coast. Jesse M. Honeyman State Park, two miles south of town, contains magnificent 500 foot-high sand dunes, three fresh water lakes, and sixty-six full hookups, seventy-five electrical, and 240 tent sites.

North Fork Siuslaw Road, one mile east on Highway 126, leads seventeen miles to North Fork Campground where you'll find five group-sized sites and a boat launch. You can use the campground as a base for salmon, steelhead, and cutthroat trout fishing, as well as hikes to an old homestead on a river bank, and along a 4,000-foot nature trail.

As the Coast Range mountains fill the horizon and picturesque homes and boat basins frame the highway, the return to Mapleton seems more scenic than it did on arrival.

From Mapleton, Highway 36 stays in the narrow Siuslaw river canyon. En route to Deadwood you can photograph the slow-moving stream against a background of mountains filled with magnificent trees from several viewpoints and waysides offering boat ramps, swimming, and access to fishing holes. Around Swisshome the highway stretches along a ridge, with white water cascading below then cuts through dairy farms as it passes Deadwood Covered Bridge (World guide number 37-20-06). The bridge was built in 1928 and stands about 100 feet south of the highway; it also is known as Lost Creek and Nelson Creek Bridge.

The river scenery is most spectacular at Lake Creek Wayside, where it boils and churns in series of whitewater cascades that twist, turn, and rush over basalt slabs and boulders.

About one mile east, the drive reaches its highest point as it climbs out of the canyon at Triangle Lake. The lake is at 1,000 feet elevation and is stocked with rainbow trout. Wild cutthroat, kokanee, catfish, blue gill, and bass make it a fisherman's dream come true. It also sees heavy use by water skiers, boaters and swimmers. A quaint church, at the southern end, was built in the 1950s but looks as if its been here for centuries.

After Triangle Lake, the highway leaves the lush-green mountains and descends into the wide-open meadows of the Willamette Valley. On the remaining twenty miles it passes aged barns—including one that is round—isolated stores, and Christmas tree farms, and the Long Tom River. Reaching U.S. Highway 99 West, you can conclude the drive by either traveling north two miles to Junction City, or south fifteen miles to Eugene.

General description: A ninety-mile drive on paved roads starting near sea level in Salem and rising to 4,500 feet at Hoodoo Ski Bowl.

Special attractions: Detroit Lake, Willamette National Forest, fishing, hiking, hot springs, alpine, and cross-country skiing.

Location: West-central Oregon between Salem and the Cascade Mountains.

Drive route numbers: Oregon Highway 22, Oregon Highway 126/U.S. Highway 20.

Travel season: All year.

Camping: Eleven forest service and two Bureau of Land Management campgrounds with tables, fire pits, vault or flush toilets, some with drinking water. One state park campground with full hookups, electrical and tent sites.

Services: All services in Salem. Limited services at Stayton, Lyons, Mill City, and Detroit.

Nearby attractions: McKenzie-Santiam Pass Scenic Byway, Silver Falls Loop Drive, Covered Bridges Drive, Mount Jefferson and Middle Santiam wildernesses, headwaters of the Metolious River.

For more information: Salem Convention and Visitors Association, 1313 Mill St., S.E., Salem, OR 97301, (503) 581-4325, (800) 874-7012. Stayton/Sublimity Chamber of Commerce, 1203 N. 1st., P.O. Box 121, Stayton, OR 97383, (541) 769-3464. North Santiam Chamber of Commerce/Visitors Information Center, P.O. Box 222, Mill City, OR 97360, (503) 897-2865. Willamette National Forest, Supervisor's Office, 211 E. 7th Ave., Eugene, OR 97401, (541) 465-6521. Detroit Ranger Station, HC73 Box 320, Mill City, OR 97360, (503) 854-3366.

The drive: Starting at exit 253 off Interstate 5 in southeast Salem, the drive climbs gradually from an elevation of 154 feet to 4,500 feet at Hoodoo Ski Bowl. The first fifteen miles are straight and flat as the route crosses eastern Willamette Valley farmlands and clumps of trees underlaid by basalts. On the section to Detroit Lake State Park, tree-lined corridors alternate with canyon bluffs, the riffling North Santiam River, Big Chief and Detroit Lake reservoirs. The remaining forty miles are virtually a continuous corridor of Douglas fir, with occasional views of surrounding snow-capped peaks. Week-day traffic is usually moderate, but includes large trucks. Since ninety percent of the recreational users come from the surrounding area, traffic is heavy on weekends and holidays.

Weather is conducive to recreation all year. An average rainfall of thirty-nine inches supports a luxuriant mixed forest of Douglas fir, maple, oak, and alder, together with wild rhododendron and scotch broom displays in the spring. Summer temperatures are usually in the low eighties. Five to twenty mile per hour breezes help cool evenings. Winters range from daytime highs in the low fifties to below freezing in the mountains. Spring days are usually

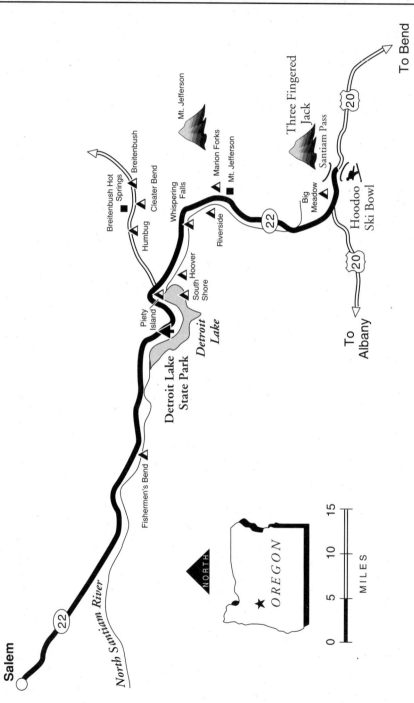

Salem

22

North Santiam River

Fishermen's Bend

Detroit Lake State Park

Detroit Lake

Piety Island

South Shore

Hoover

Humbug

Breitenbush Hot Springs

Breitenbush

Cleater Bend

Whispering Falls

Riverside

Marion Forks

Mt. Jefferson

Mt. Jefferson

22

Big Meadow

Santiam Pass

Three Fingered Jack

Hoodoo Ski Bowl

20

20

To Bend

To Albany

NORTH

OREGON

MILES

0   5   10   15

in the mid-sixties, while autumn temperatures range from the mid-sixties to mid-seventies.

From exit 253 at Interstate 5, the North Santiam Highway (Oregon Highway 22), starts as four lanes and stretches east through dairy farms, grasslands, and field crops, punctuated by isolated stands of willows, alders, and oaks. The Cascade foothills are a constant hazy blue on the horizon ahead. During the first five miles, the road passes the Oregon State Reformatory and the exit to Highway 214, which is the southern access to the Silver Falls Scenic Loop Drive.

At mile 11.5, Sublimity and Stayton lie about a mile north and south of the highway respectively. Both are small service communities. You'll find two city parks in Sublimity and two streams running through Stayton which is situated on the banks of the Santiam River. It is also the home of a historic woolen mill and four city parks. Jordan Bridge (World guide number 37-24-02) was built in 1937 and moved to Stayton from Linn County in 1988.

East of Stayton, the highway narrows to two lanes and remains so to the end of the drive. The farmlands and flood plain are replaced by the western Cascade foothills. They were formed through repeated volcanic eruptions, and as the road continues to climb, the rocks become younger, for flows from each succeeding volcano covered older rock.

As the road parallels the Santiam River, it appears to divide the foliage. Alders and oak line the river bank, south of the highway while Douglas fir and pine cover northside hills and ridges. You can expect to see fishermen angling off banks and boats, for the Santiam is renowned as a prime steelhead, rainbow trout, and salmon stream. The forests also support deer and elk, which are often seen along the road and in a narrow canyon en route to Mehama.

Highway 22 and Oregon Highway 226 meet at Mehama. Highway 226 continues one mile south to Lyons, and then angles southwest to Scio. The northern segment of the Linn County Covered Bridges Loop starts seven miles east of Scio on Highway 226.

Old Mehama Road loops northeast on ten miles of pavement and about eight miles of gravel to the Elkhorn region and the Little Santiam Recreation Area before rejoining Highway 22 at Gates. The Elkhorn region balances summer homes and a golf course with ranching, logging, copper, lead, and zinc mining.

At the Recreation Area, you can picnic in a thick forest, take extended wilderness hikes, and swim in natural pools along the pristine Little Santiam River. The Bureau of Land Management provides twenty-three tent sites in its Elkhorn Valley Campground.

Between Lyons and Mill City, seven miles east, you can camp along the roadside on the banks of the North Fork of the Santiam River at the BLM's Fishermen's Bend Campground. It has thirty-eight sites. Nearby North Santiam State Park provides a good view of the riffling river that is partially hidden by trees along the roadside. The park offers a shaded picnic area, fishing, and short trails for walks along the river bank.

In keeping with its name, lumber mills line the highway through Mill City, at mile 28. A travel information center has brochures and fact sheets on local recreation. At Gates, three miles east, you'll find a live bird exhibit, motel, RV park, and restaurants.

East of Gates the highway enters a canyon, which is particularly striking in autumn when maples turn to russets and yellows and are highlighted by evergreens and columnar basalt cliffs. Roadside stops include: Maples Rest Area; Paddlesaddle Park, with a boat ramp, trails, picnic tables, and fire pits; and Niagara County Park, where you can walk a trail down to the river.

Big Cliff Dam, at mile 38.5, is a Corps of Engineers project and part of the Detroit Lake system. As a reregulating dam and small reservoir, it smooths power generation water release from Detroit Dam and controls the downstream river level fluctuation. Reregulations at Big Cliff may cause the lake level to fluctuate as much as twenty-four feet daily. The dam offers good views of the Santiam River and classic cement highway barriers.

Three miles east, the road enters the Willamette National Forest and Detroit Lake Recreation Area. At 1.6 million acres, the national forest is approximately the size of New Jersey. It ranks first among 156 national forests in producing lumber, and is used by campers, boaters, swimmers, hikers, fishermen, skiers, and snowmobilers.

Rocks surrounding the dam have been bleached greenish gray by hot water and steam. Some absorbed water while they were underground molten lava and cooled to become granite.

Detroit Dam rises 463 feet from its foundation in the narrow, steep, rocky slopes of North Santiam Canyon to create a lake with thirty-two miles of shoreline. The concrete gravity structure has public restrooms and barriers that protect fishermen and sightseers from traffic. It can be toured by prior arrangement. From May to September, the lake is kept at the highest possible levels for the enjoyment of water skiers, swimmers, and other visitors who fill shoreline day use areas, trailer campgrounds, and boat launches.

At Marigold Day Use Area, four miles east of the dam, you can camp in a fragrant Douglas fir and Engelmann spruce forest at Piety Island's twelve sites. It was named for a former highway construction camp (covered by the lake) and serves water recreation needs with a swimming area, bath house, a wide, paved boat launch, and a separate launching area for water skiers.

Two miles east, Detroit Lake State Park and the Detroit Ranger Station straddle the highway. At the ranger station, you can get trail maps, campground information, and secure sno-park permits.

The state park offers a magnificent roadside viewpoint with snow-capped Mount Jefferson on the southern horizon and Detroit Lake in the foreground. On the lake's north shore, the campground contains eight loops with 134 tents, seventy electrical, and 107 full-hook-up sites scattered through a Douglas fir forest. Conveniences range from hot showers, boat ramps and docks to evening amphitheater programs.

Detroit, a few miles east, is a roadside community with seasonal accommodations, RV parks, two boat docks, and boat rentals. Check your fuel gauge before continuing east, for Detroit has the last gas station for fifty-five miles. Nearby, Hoover South Shore Campground includes twenty-nine

Fishermen are among the many users who find recreational opportunities at the lake created by the backwaters of Detroit Dam.

single and eight double sites, plus a group camp capable of accommodating up to seventy people. A short distance west, South Shore Campground's thirty-two sites overlook the lake.

Although Breitenbush Hot Springs, ten miles north of Detroit, is a retreat and conference center, it is usually open to the public on weekends. Set in forests and meadows, the artesian hot springs carry thirty minerals; some believe the springs contain curative agents. Swim suits are required in hot tubs and sauna, while nude bathing is acceptable in meadow pools overlooking the river and mountains. Several trails start at the center and meander through an ancient forest. The Breitenbush Gorge Trail has been designated a National Recreation Trail. Four forest service campgrounds with a total of sixty-five sites are located on or near the road between Detroit and Breitenbush.

After Detroit, the highway enters a forested corridor which continues virtually unbroken for the twenty-seven miles to the junction with U.S. Highway 20. The beauty is in the trees, which cluster tightly together and display a smattering of oaks and light green vine maples among the thick Douglas and white fir. Wild rhododendrons add splashes of reds and pinks in late May and early June. At periodic turnouts, you have ample opportunities to photograph the Santiam's riffles, Mount Jefferson, and occasional roadside cascades.

Every few miles a campground lies tucked away in the woods and close to the river. They start with Whispering Falls' sixteen sites, at elevation 2,000 feet. Then comes Riverside with thirty- seven sites, Marion Forks with eight fee and seven free sites, and Big Meadows with nine camp spots, plus corrals, loading ramp, and troughs for horses.

Marion Forks Restaurant at milepost 68, is open seven days a week and has the only food along this stretch. Migrating salmon and steelhead intercepted at Minto Station egg collection facility, four miles west of Big Cliff Dam, are fertilized and transported to nearby Marion Forks Salmon Hatchery. When they reach fingerling size, they are released to continue their normal migratory cycle.

At elevation 3,000 feet, you enter a snow zone and winter recreation area. In winter, traction tires and devices are mandatory. You need a permit, available at forest service ranger stations, to park at Big Springs Sno-Park. The park is a staging area for cross-country skiing and snowmobile runs.

Highway 22 meets U.S. Highway 20 at mile 83, and the route overlaps the McKenzie—Santiam Pass Scenic Byway on the remaining eight miles to Hoodoo Ski Bowl. As you spiral east up the steep grade, Three Fingered Jack is a continuous presence on the northeastern horizon.

Hoodoo Ski Bowl, west of Santiam Pass Summit, is a family-oriented ski area with a triple chair, two double chairs and a rope tow. The top elevation is 5,703 feet, with thirty percent of the terrain geared to beginners, forty percent to intermediate, and thirty percent for advanced skiers. Big Lake Campground, nearby, offers twenty-one sites on a scenic lake surrounded by thick forest and towering mountain peaks.

From Hoodoo, you have the option of continuing east over 4,617-foot Santiam Pass Summit and driving about seventeen miles to Sisters or following U.S. Highway 20 fifty-five miles west to Albany.

24 SANTIAM LOOP

General description: A sixty-seven-mile arc on two lane paved highways through open farmland, thick forests, and historic communities.

Special attractions: Willamette National Forest, Foster and Green Peter lakes, covered bridges, fish hatchery, museums, Menagerie Wilderness, historic districts, Santiam Canyon, fishing, hiking, recreational gold panning, rock hounding.

Location: Western Central Oregon between Albany and Brownsville.

Drive route numbers: U.S. Highway 20, Oregon Highway 228.

Travel season: All year.

Camping: Four forest service and one Bureau of Land Management campgrounds with tables, fire pits, vault or flush toilets, some with drinking water. One state park campground with primitive sites. Several commercial RV parks are also situated on the route.

Services: All services in Albany, Lebanon, and Sweet Home. Limited services at Brownsville.

Nearby attractions: Salem, Eugene, McKenzie-Santiam Pass Scenic Byway, North Santiam Canyon Scenic Drive, Linn County Covered Bridges Scenic Drive.

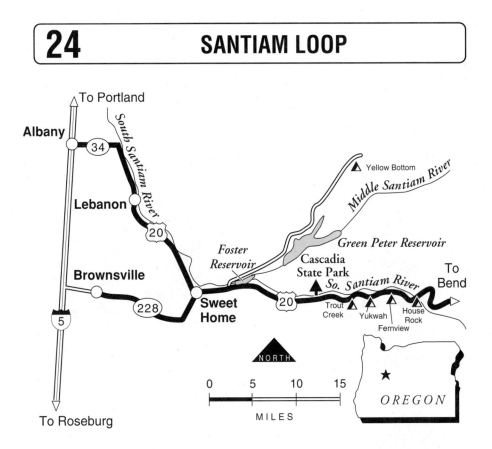

For more information: Albany Visitors Association, 300 Second Ave. S.W., P.O. Box 965, Albany, OR 97321, (541) 928-0911, (800)-526-2256 (USA). Lebanon Chamber of Commerce, 1040 Park St., Lebanon, OR 97355, (541) 258-7164. Sweet Home Chamber of Commerce, 1575 Main St., Sweet Home, OR 97386, (541) 367-6186. Willamette National Forest, Supervisor's Office, 211 E. 7th Ave., Eugene, OR 97401, (541) 465-6521. Sweet Home Ranger District, 3225 Highway 20, Sweet Home, OR 97386, (541) 367-5168.

The drive: From Albany, the drive extends southeast through the farmlands of the Willamette Valley to Sweet Home. Foster Lake, the Santiam River, and the dense Willamette National Forest offer striking scenery as the route heads east into the Cascade foothills. Returning to Sweet Home, it concludes by traveling west to the Brownsville Historic District. Traffic is usually moderate to heavy. The tour can be joined at Interstate 5 by driving east from Exit 216 to Brownsville, or by taking Exit 233 at Albany onto U.S. Highway 20.

Travelers will find summer temperatures in the low eighties. Winters range from daytime highs in the low forties to the low fifties and below freezing on the slopes of the mountains. Spring days in the mid-sixties are

Brownsville's historic district contains some of Oregon's finest examples of Victorian, Greek Revival, and Italianate architecture.

common. Autumn temperatures range from the mid-sixties to mid-seventies.

At Albany, self driving tour maps are available for three historic districts of 350 homes that include every major architectural style popular in the United States since 1850. Visitors can see the insides during an annual Historic Interiors Tour on the last Saturday in July or a Christmas Home Tour on the third Sunday in December.

The Albany Timber Carnival brings national attention every 4th of July weekend. Competitors come from as far as Australia, Spain, Canada, and the Eastern Seaboard to show their skill in log cutting, tree climbing, and other events.

Monteith Riverpark, on the banks of the Willamette, is a pleasant spot to picnic and jog. It also hosts outdoor concerts and is a departure point for river rafting and fishing. The Willamette River runs through the western edge, and the Calapooia River also crosses near town.

From Albany, the drive begins by traveling nine miles east through sheep and dairy lands to Crabtree Road where it swings south. Crabtree Road (Oregon Highway 226) is the access point for the fifty-mile-long Linn County Covered Bridges Drive . If you decide to include it, it will add about two-and-one-half hours to your driving time.

Lebanon, eight miles south of the junction, is a major producer of strawberries. Each year, during an annual festival, 17,000 pieces of shortcake are given away. Ponderosa Vineyards opens its tasting room on Sunday afternoons from June through September. It is the county's only winery, and bottles sauvignon blanc, chardonnay, vin rose, and pinot noir. Gill's Landing at the Santiam River, has a boat ramp, swimming, playgrounds, and overnight camping. At Ralston Square, you can picnic by a canal.

South from Lebanon, trees intermingle with grass lands. East of the highway, Waterloo County Park, on the banks of the South Fork of the Santiam River, offers a boat ramp and covered picnicking along with short hiking and nature trails. At McDowell Creek Falls a few miles further, you can walk a short path to a small waterfall.

Scenic tree-covered hills signal the approach to Sweet Home, thirteen miles south of Lebanon. U.S. Highway 20 meets Oregon Highway 228 at the western end of town. At the junction, a lawn full of wagon beds, tractors, and farm equipment are part of the East Linn Museum. Inside you'll see firearms, china, Native American relics, and a large polished rock collection.

Sweet Home sits on the site of a prehistoric forest and has become a rockhounder's hot spot. Surrounding hills, streams, and lowlands have yielded everything from seventy different kinds of petrified wood, to arrowheads, crystal-lined geodes, and fish-eye agates. You can obtain lists of local minerals and their locations at the museum and Chamber of Commerce. Although fossil leaves can be taken from a public dig, many sites are on private land, and you'll need the owners permission before you dig.

Weddle Bridge (World guide number 37-22-05), downtown in Sankey Park, has been reconstructed as part of an exhibition of Northwest forest resources. When it was built in 1937, it straddled Thomas Creek near Scio. The park makes an ideal outing for small children who can romp on playground equipment and fish for steelhead in Ames Creek, which flows under the bridge.

Within a couple of miles of the intersection as you continue east on U.S. Highway 20, you'll pass the Chamber of Commerce, and Willamette National Forest's Sweet Home Ranger Station. If you're planning on backcountry hiking, stop at the station for maps and recreation information.

About one mile east, signboards at Foster Lake Viewpoint provide basic information on services, parks and recreational opportunities along Foster and Green Peter lakes. Both are Corps of Engineer projects. Foster Lake, which spreads along 3.5 miles of U.S. Highway 20, is a highly scenic reservoir encircled by a huge Douglas fir forest that starts at the water's edge. The scenery and languid waters have made it a favorite of boaters, photographers, and fishermen who take stocked rainbow trout and blue gills. It's also used for jetboat races and waterskiing.

Crossing Foster Lake Dam, the scenic North River Road takes you to a fish hatchery and three parks along the Santiam River, which is known for its salmon and steelhead. At the hatchery, you can feed fish and see winter steelhead and summer salmon brood stock.

To see Green Peter Lake, turn north on Quartzville Road at the east end of Foster Lake. This magnificent drive on a two-lane paved road begins in a thick evergreen forest, and follows the north shoreline of the ten-mile-long lake as it crosses several creeks en route to the Quartzville area at elevation 4,418 feet.

Quartzville was platted in 1865, and following the discovery of gold, lead and silver, it grew to 1,000 people. By 1871, it was a ghost town. While nothing remains of the town, you can still try your luck at recreational gold panning in the region's creeks.

Commercial campgrounds along the twenty-seven-mile route are Sunnyside with a three-lane boat ramp, fifty-two tent and RV hook-ups with cable TV; Whitcomb Creek features a boat launch and thirty-four tent and RV hookups. The Bureau of Land Management's Yellow Bottom Campground, near the summit, has twenty-two sites. Green Peter Lake is considered a good chinook salmon and bass fishery.

East of Foster Lake, the Willamette National Forest becomes so thick and dark it virtually envelopes U.S. Highway 20, and at times it almost seems like you are driving through a tunnel. Cascadia State Park, twelve miles east of Sweet Home, is nestled in huge Douglas fir trees at the base of the mountains. In the secluded park, with twenty-six primitive campsites, you can pump mineral water from natural springs, walk through a mixed forest of fir, maple, oak, and alder down to the scenic river canyon, or take a two-mile hike to a waterfall. Short Covered Bridge (World guide number 37-22-09), near the park, has been reconstructed several times since the original was built in 1845.

Trout Creek Campground, the first of several Willamette National Forest camping areas along the highway, is about eight miles east of the park. In addition to fishing and enjoying the fragrant pine scented forest from twenty-four tent sites, you can hike to an adjacent elk refuge and into the Menagerie

Top: A brilliant winter sunset silhouettes Twin Rocks, near Rockaway on the northern Oregon coast.

Bottom: Low tide attracts beachcombers and seagulls to the tidepools around Haystack Rock at Cannon Beach on the northern Oregon coast.

Colorful kites of all sizes and shapes take flight at Lincoln City on Oregon's central coast.

Boardman State Park on Oregon's southern coast offers magnificent views of rugged headlands and offshore rocks.

Top: Early morning light on yellow lupine and purple foxglove with Humbug Mountain and Three Sisters Rocks on the southern Oregon coast.

Bottom: Built in 1931, the historic St. John's Bridge spans the Willamette River in Portland, Oregon.

Top: Oregon's tallest peak, Mount Hood, 11,235 feet, rises behind Lost Lake in the Mt. Hood National Forest.

Bottom: Sunset at Crown Point commands a view of the Vista House and the Columbia River Gorge.

Below:
The Wild Cat
Covered Bridge
spans the Suislaw
River in Oregon's
Lane County, home
to more covered
bridges than any
county west of the
Mississippi.

Oregon's Opal Creek cascades through
the North Santiam Canyon, where
there are stands of old-growth forest.

Spring blooms at Iverson's Tulip Farm in Oregon's Willamette Valley.

Beautiful clouds are reflected in central Oregon's Todd Lake as they float by 9,060 foot Mount Bachelor.

Top: Hart Mountain, 7,710 feet, in the high desert region of southeast Oregon, is a natural wildlife refuge for antelope, bighorn sheep, migrating birds, and twelve species of sagebrush.

Bottom: Beautiful clouds and Wizard Island reflect into Oregon's Crater Lake National Park.

Sweet Home's Sankey Park includes restored Weddle Covered Bridge and Ames Creek, an ideal fishing spot for young people.

Wilderness area. Yukwah Campground, 0.25 mile east of Trout Creek, also has nature trails, fishing, and twenty-one sites suitable for RVs. Fernview, three miles east of Yukwah, contains eleven sites and a two-mile trail to Rooster Rock viewpoint.

House Rock, twenty-six miles east of Sweet Home, features thirteen tents and four tent/trailer sites. A 0.8-mile trail leads to forty-foot House Rock Falls through primeval forest and along the Santiam Wagon Road where original ruts are still visible. It ends at House Rock, an overhanging boulder that once sheltered travelers from winter storms.

After returning to Sweet Home, as you travel west on Highway 228, you'll pass Crawfordsville Covered Bridge (World guide number 37-22-15). It was built in 1932 but bypassed by a newer road. McKircher Park, one mile south of the bridge, offers an idyllic picnic spot overlooking a rushing cascade.

Some of the headstones in Crawfordsville's cemetery, also along the highway, are more than 100 years old. As you continue west, roadside stands invite stopping to purchase fresh tomatoes onions, squash, berries and filberts.

Brownsville, seven miles west of Crawfordsville, is the third oldest continuing settlement in Oregon. It began in 1846 and was named after one of its founders.

You'll see the aftermath of an 1880s building boom in a collection of buildings that represent styles from the 1850s through the 1920s. Greek Revival "box" construction, Queen Anne Victorian, Italianate—you'll find them all and more on a self-guiding walking tour of thirty sites.

The Moyer House is Brownsville's pride and joy. The 1881 Victorian Mansion was inspired by contemporary Italianate Villa architecture. Interiors feature hand-painted landscapes, floral stenciling, and turn-of-the-century styled furnishings. The Moyer House and many other buildings are listed on the National Register of Historic Places.

The Railroad's heritage is represented in the Linn County Historical Museum that is housed in a depot and several boxcars. Inside are artifacts brought over the Oregon Trail, Native American relics, and natural history exhibits. Replicas of a general store, bank, barber shop, and other buildings of the period are also displayed.

Other museums, within walking distance of each other, include the Pioneer Picture Gallery, which features large collections of historic photos, and the American Military Museum. Its exhibits are chronological and trace the evolution of uniforms, awards, and insignias. Displays cover early pioneer militia, the Civil War, Indian campaigns, Spanish American War, and World War I.

Upon concluding your sightseeing, you can reach Interstate 5 by traveling four miles west on Highway 228.

25 WOODBURN, SILVER FALLS, SALEM LOOP

General description: A signed thirty-five-mile drive on paved two-lane roads through the eastern Willamette Valley's agricultural lands and forest to the Cascade Mountains foothills, and Oregon's largest state park.

Special attractions: Mount Angel Abbey, Silver Falls State Park with ten waterfalls, Christmas tree farms, covered bridge, historic sites, horseback riding, hiking, camping.

Location: Eastern Willamette Valley between Silverton and Salem.

Drive route numbers: Oregon Highway 214, Oregon Highway 22.

Travel season: All year.

Camping: One state park campground with electrical hookups.

Services: All services in Woodburn and Salem. Limited services in Mount Angel and Silverton.

Nearby attractions: Oregon City historic attractions, 99 East-French Prairie Loop Drive, Albany Historic Districts, Linn County Covered Bridges Drive, North Santiam Canyon Scenic Drive. Table Rock Wilderness.

For more information: Salem Convention and Visitors Association, 1313 Mill Street SE, Salem, OR 97301, (503)-581-4325, (800) 874-7012. Silver Falls State Park, 20024 Silver Falls Highway SE, Sublimity, OR 97385, (503) 873-8681. Silverton Area Chamber of Commerce, 421 S. Water, P.O. Box 257, Silverton, OR 97381. (503) 873-5615. Stayton/Sublimity Chamber of Commerce, 1203 N. 1st, P.O. Box 121, Stayton, OR 97383, (541) 769-3464.

To Portland

NORTH

99E

Woodburn

Mount Angel

Silverton

5

214

Salem

22

99E

214

5

22

Silver Falls
State Park

To Eugene   To Bend

OREGON

★

0   5   10   15

MILES

Woodburn Area Chamber of Commerce, 2233 Country Club Rd., P.O. Box 194, Woodburn, OR 97071, (503) 982-8221.

The drive: This signed scenic route begins in Woodburn at the junction of Oregon Highway 214 and 99 East and travels southeast through hop yards and berry fields to Mount Angel's Benedictine Abbey. It continues southeast through the quiet rural community of Silverton, climbs a ridge of foothills, and enters the dark forest of Silver Falls State Park. From the park, it concludes through rolling hills to downtown Salem. The route can be joined from Interstate 5 by taking exit 271 east to Woodburn, or by driving the itinerary in reverse from exit 253 at Salem. Traffic is usually moderate.

Summer temperatures are usually in the low eighties. Winters range from daytime highs in the low forties to the low fifties and near freezing on the slopes of the mountains. Days in the mid-sixties are common during spring, and autumn temperatures range from the mid-sixties to mid-seventies.

From the busy intersection of Oregon highways 99 East and 214, the scenic drive quickly exits the congestion. After two blocks, you've left the business and fruit processing plants and are traveling through hop yards. The yards are intriguing even in winter when the strings are bare and the eighteen-foot-high poles stand in stark relief. As the season unfolds, they will be bustling with activity as mazes of strings are reconstructed and vines are hand wrapped around them. In the warmth of springtime, the vines grow up to eight inches per day, and by late summer they form a lush golden green canopy over the yard. Hops are natural preservatives which enhance the foam and quality of beer, and after the September harvest, they will be sold to brewers.

During the six miles to Mount Angel, hop yards vie for attention with rustic barns and farmhouses, dairy herds, berry fields, and an occasional corridor of trees.

At Mount Angel, a Benedictine Monastery crowns a hill, 1.5 miles east of the route. Along the entrance road, you'll see a grotto and stations of the cross nestled in a quiet forest. A tiny cemetery chapel, near the entrance, was built in the 1880s and is the oldest building.

About 100 monks, who are members of Mount Angel Abbey, maintain the impeccable courtyard and elegant multi-storied brick buildings. A self-guiding walking brochure details the history and functions of the buildings and will take you along paths to viewpoints which encompass the Willamette Valley below, Mount Hood, fifty miles north, and Washington's famed Mounts Rainier and St. Helens.

You may also wish to stop at the library. It is an architectural masterpiece designed by famed architect, Alvar Aalto. A rare book room exhibits ancient hand-written volumes which predate the printing press. The small museum displays Native American relics (not religious artifacts), miniature books, Civil War memorabilia, military medals, and a fine collection of the region's stuffed birds and animals.

Coming and going from the abbey on Church Street, you'll pass the cathedral-like St. Mary's Church. The Neo-Gothic brick building is a National Historic Site. It was built in 1910 in the form of a Latin cross, and its twenty-two stained glass windows, paintings, and statues were designed as a religious picture story. Inside, you'll find a brochure explaining the art.

Silverton, 2.5 miles south, is an agricultural center where commercial crops range from strawberries and produce to flowers and Christmas trees. With many older homes perched on hillsides, you'll find Silverton quaint, charming, quiet, and beautiful. Silver Creek flows gently through town, and at Silverton Reservoir, along the highway, you can fish for trout, salmon, and steelhead, enjoy an afternoon of boating, and relax with a picnic lunch on the peaceful shoreline.

Cooley's Gardens, two miles west of town, operates the world's largest iris nursery. While the display gardens are open all year, they are at their colorful best from mid-May to early-June when they become a riot of color. Three million plants, covering 200 acres, turn fields bright yellow, deep purple, pink, orange and blue.

Gallon House Bridge (World guide number 37-24-01) 1.5 miles northeast of Silverton, via either Downs or Hobart Road, spans Abiqua Creek near its confluence with the Pudding River. Built in 1917, the National Historic Site received its name during Prohibition when whiskey sold for ten cents a gallon, and it became a gathering place for illegal liquor sales.

On the fourteen miles south to Silver Falls State Park, the highway winds and climbs into the Cascade foothills. The hills are underlaid with basalt which flowed down the Columbia River from eastern Oregon about twenty million years ago and are covered with 10.8-million-year-old volcanic ash.

As the road clings to a cliff and becomes rough with patches, posted mileages drop to twenty-five and thirty miles per hour. You can also expect to meet farmers on tractors and heavy equipment as it enters a belt of Christmas tree farms where hillsides are covered with Nobel and Douglas fir seedlings. At the southern end, an excellent all weather road cuts into stately groves of Douglas fir, which form a virtual canopy over the highway as it approaches Silver Falls State Park.

Silver Falls, Oregon's largest state park, fills 8,700 acres of meadows and a ravine cut by Silver Creek and covered with second-growth Douglas fir, western hemlock and a thick undergrowth of giant ferns, salmon berry, salal, and the state's flower, Oregon grape. The quiet, cathedral-like forest is laced with a network of paths that include three miles of jogging, four miles of biking, and fourteen miles of horse trails.

The "Trail of Ten Falls" is the most popular and takes you through Silver Creek's canyons to ten waterfalls. You can walk behind three of them, and you'll see others ranging from a 178- foot drop to twenty-seven-foot cascades. Some, like Winter Falls, are accessible by short walks from roadside turnouts. As you walk this seven-mile National Recreation Trail, watch for the state animal, the beaver, along with deer, rabbits, squirrels, and chipmunks. If you have a license, you can also fish Silver Creek.

In addition to fifty-three electrical and fifty-one tent sites, accommodations include youth, group, and horse camps, plus a conference center with four lodges, meeting rooms, and dining hall. There are also two ranches with dormitory accommodations, outdoor swimming pool, activity fields, and picnic areas. The lodge-like visitor center's snack bar operates seven days a week in summer and on winter weekends.

Because of its thick vegetation and its location in the Cascade foothills, Silver Falls is usually cool, even in the heat of summer. Prepare for your visit by bringing at least a light jacket.

West of the park, the highway winds through farmlands and rolling hillsides planted in commercial grass seed and Christmas trees ranging from seedlings to full sized. Silver Falls Winery, in the community of Sublimity, offers pinot noir tasting and tours daily from June through September.

Twelve miles east of Salem, you turn onto Oregon Highway 22 and follow it west to downtown where it becomes Mission Street. Along Mission Street you'll find Bush Barn Art Center, with two exhibition galleries and Northwest arts and crafts for sale. Bush House, on the grounds, was built in 1877-78. The Victorian mansion houses original furnishings, gaslights and ten marble fireplaces. Deepwood Estate, nearby, displays an elegant Queen Anne home built in 1894. It is surrounded by six acres with a nature trail,

At Silver Falls State Park, visitors can hike to ten waterfalls, and enjoy camping, horseback riding, and picnicking.

original carriage house, English tea house and a garden with a wrought iron gazebo.

A gilt-covered twenty-three-foot statue of a pioneer crowns Oregon's State Capitol, approximately eight blocks north of Mission Street. The Vermont marble building contains an exhibit area with extensive murals and a gift shop.

26 ROBERT AUFDERHEIDE MEMORIAL DRIVE

General description: A fifty-seven-mile National Forest Service Byway on a paved highway through a typical Cascade Mountain forest and along a Wild and Scenic River.

Special attractions: Old growth forest, Cougar Reservoir, Wild and Scenic North Fork of the Middle Fork of the Willamette River, Waldo Lake, French Pete and Three Sisters wilderness areas, colorful wildflowers and autumn foliage, camping, horse and mountain hiking.

Location: West-central Oregon in the Willamette National Forest, between Blue River and Westfir, about forty-one miles east of Eugene.

Drive route number: Forest Service Road 19.

Travel season: The byway opens and closes depending on snow, with the season usually starting in early June and closing at the end of October.

Camping: Nine national forest campgrounds with toilets, drinking water, picnic tables and fire grates, plus numerous undeveloped sites.

Services: No services on the byway. All services in nearby Oakridge, Blue River, and McKenzie Bridge.

Nearby attractions: McKenzie Pass-Santiam Pass Loop, Cascade Lakes Highway Loop, and North Santiam Canyon.

For more information: Willamette National Forest, 211 E. Seventh Ave., Eugene, OR 97401, (541) 465-6521. District Rangers: Oakridge Ranger District, 46375 Highway 58, Westfir, OR 97492, (541) 782-2291. McKenzie Ranger District, 57600 McKenzie Hwy., McKenzie Bridge, OR 97413, (541) 822-3381.

The drive: Robert Aufderheide was the Willamette National Forest supervisor from 1954 to 1959. The Memorial Drive starts midway between Blue River and McKenzie Bridge and extends north-south to Westfir along the South Fork of the McKenzie River and North Fork of the Middle Fork of the Willamette River. It is a popular bicycling route with elevations ranging from 1,052 to 3,728 feet. Since most of the drive is through a forested corridor that blocks views of rivers, cliffs, and hills, you will see some of the best scenery along the numerous hiking trails that start at the roadside. Mile-by-mile directional audio tapes of the drive are available free of charge at McKenzie

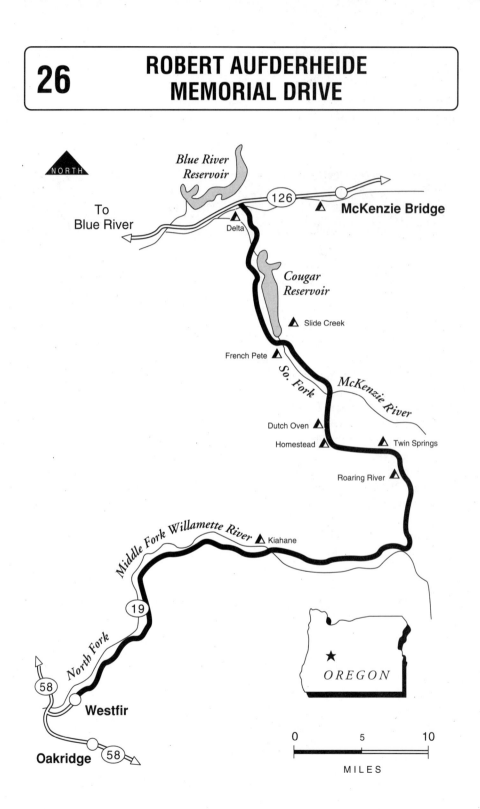

NORTH

Blue River Reservoir

To Blue River

126 ▲ **McKenzie Bridge**

Delta ▲

Cougar Reservoir

▲ Slide Creek

French Pete ▲

So. Fork *McKenzie River*

Dutch Oven ▲
Homestead ▲   ▲ Twin Springs

Roaring River ▲

Middle Fork Willamette River ▲ Kiahane

19

North Fork

58

Westfir

58 ▲

Oakridge

★

OREGON

0   5   10

M I L E S

Cougar Reservoir fills a six-mile-long forested canyon on the western slopes of the Cascade Mountains.

Bridge and Westfir ranger stations.

Temperatures average thirty degrees in winter and ninety degrees in summer. Spring and fall temperatures peak at about sixty degrees. The area receives seventy-one inches of rain per year, with most of it falling between November and May, and intermittently throughout the travel season.

The Blue River region was settled in the 1860s. By 1892, it was a successful mining community with a general store, livery stable, mill, and hotel.

Delta Campground Nature Trail, at the Blue River entrance, provides a good introduction to the byway's plants and trees. The half-mile trail offers a refreshing walk through an old-growth forest of 200-500-year-old trees that tower over thirty-nine campsites.

At Cougar Reservoir powerhouse, one mile south of the campground, you may see beaver and other wildlife on a half-mile trail along a side channel which feeds three small riparian ponds. The reservoir covers the site of a Molalla Indian summer camp and was named for cougars which are seldom seen but still inhabit the area. The 452-foot dam is Oregon's tallest rock-filled structure, and when full, its backwaters create a lake six miles long. During summer months, the Corps of Engineers keep it at a high level for scenic and recreational enjoyment, and in fall the surplus water is released for power generation. You'll find it an excellent lake for stocked rainbow trout fishing, water skiing, and boating. Several boat launches and three U.S. Forest Service campgrounds with sixteen sites are situated on or near the shore.

Because of pedestrians, bicyclists, and sharp curves, speeds vary from twenty-five to thirty miles per hour along west rim cliffs and shoreline. Rocks

The McKenzie River flows through a forested corridor at the northern end of the Robert Aufderheide Memorial Drive.

from the basalt cliffs were used to fill the dam structures and were sheared off in tiers to prevent rock from falling into the valley below. As you continue along the western rim, watch for osprey nests in tree snags. Northern bald eagles and western red tailed hawks often soar across the lake.

From a viewpoint at milepost 5, you have a magnificent panorama of the lake, small islands, and the French Pete addition to the Three Sisters Wilderness, which begins on the eastern shore. You can enter the wilderness by hiking or horseback from several trailheads along the South Fork of the McKenzie River.

The only roadside waterfall plunges into a creek near milepost 7 where a pullout with parking provides a good view of the lake and a 0.3-mile-long trail up a steep embankment to Terwilliger Hot Springs. Six pools at the springs attract nudists and other bathers.

After passing two miles of day-use area, you cross the South Fork of the McKenzie River and wind through its canyon lined with cottonwoods and willows. The McKenzie is free flowing from its headwaters to the reservoir, and because of its outstanding scenery, fishing, wildlife, and hiking opportunities, it has been studied for wild and scenic river status.

During the next twelve miles, the river appears intermittently as a series of whitewater riffles surrounded by cliffs and forest. Occasionally, you'll see seasonal cascades rushing through the lush growth on the east side of the highway. Groves of old growth Douglas fir, hemlock, and moss-draped maples along with lush undergrowth of wild flowers, ferns, and late summer huckleberries add to the visual delights and create habitats for wildlife. You'll also pass trees sporting antique telephone insulators that provided communications with the fire guard station. There is also an old maple that was saved by building the highway in a curve around it as well as timber standing at seemingly impossible angles on sloping ground.

This section is laced with campgrounds and hiking trails. Slide Creek Campground features sixteen sites and a boat ramp. French Pete Campground at milepost 11 includes sixteen tent sites and a trail leading to the French Pete Wilderness. Rebel trailhead at milepost 13 was named for a Civil War sheepherder. The steep and strenuous twelve-mile-loop trail rewards you with lush meadows and mountainsides filled with wildflowers. Homestead and Twin Springs campgrounds near McKenzie Bridge offer overnights in a stately Douglas fir forest with a ground cover of ferns, alders, oak, and maples.

At Frissel Crossing and Olallie campgrounds, you'll find a total of twenty-nine sites, horse camps, and trails to the Three Sisters Wilderness. Roaring River Campground is unique in that it is reserved for up to fifty people.

At Roaring River, the highway begins climbing to Box Canyon. The river is the major source of water for the South Fork of the McKenzie and is named for the sound it makes as it rushes over rocks and down the canyon in a series of whitewater cascades. Its constant temperature of thirty-seven degrees makes it an excellent stream for fish reproduction. At a turnout, you are within yards of the river and on the edge of its brush-filled canyon. Wild rhododendrons brighten the dark forest in May and June, and you may see deer and elk. They are attracted to the area by the lichens that hang like hair from trees.

The road reaches its highest point at Box Canyon where elk sometimes graze in meadows beside a replica of the first fireguard station. An information station, built in 1933 by the Civilian Conservation Corps and used by the forest service as a fire station, is open during summer. The complex also contains a horse camp with corrals and information signs on the spotted owl and Robert Aufderheide. Several trails meander into The Three Sisters Wilderness and the Chucksney Mountain Roadless Area. The beautiful high vistas of the Roadless Area are habitats for bear, grouse, deer, elk, and bobcat.

Nearby, the arduous Shale River Trail offers the road's most spectacular hike as it takes you along the river that drops 2,400 feet in three miles and plunges over thirty-four separate waterfalls. As you hike through stands of Pacific yew and western hemlock, you'll pass the source of the McKenzie's north fork and the forest's largest-in-diameter western red cedar.

Two miles south, fish creek empties into the river. Fish Creek Trail is over six miles long and starts at the highway and crosses the smaller stream twice as it wanders through the Waldo Wilderness, then switchbacks up steep ridges to scenic Winchester Lake.

The highway continues through a blowdown area, known for its spring and fall displays of dogwoods and rhododendrons. At milepost 38, you cross the North Fork of the Middle Fork of the Willamette River, which parallels the highway to Westfir. It has been designated a wild and scenic river because of its water quality, geology, scenery, hiking, kayaking, and other recreational opportunities.

Roadside maples form a natural tunnel over the highway en route to Kehanie Campground, one mile south of the crossing. It offers twenty-one tent and trailer sites in a beautiful setting adjacent to a three-mile-long, deep canyon. The canyon has protected 400- to 500-year-old Douglas firs, allowing them to reach heights of 270 feet.

During the next six miles, several forest service roads branch off the main highway. They include Road 1934 to Blair Lake, ten miles east, and Road 1928, which loops back sixteen miles to Oak Ridge. It was built in the 1940s for a logging camp at milepost 45. While nothing remains of the camps, you'll see scars left by logging from the 1920s to the 1960s south to Westfir.

The drive concludes by following the Willamette River as it twists and turns through a deep canyon with 1,000-foot-high walls. Rocks in the gorge were covered with lava 300 million years ago and are some of the oldest in the area. In spring, this section is a favorite of river rafters and kayakers, fishermen, and wildlife observers. It is restricted to fly fishing for chinook salmon and wild trout. The lush stands of alders and tall trees attract osprey and beavers.

Westfir, at milepost 57, is the drive's southern terminus. Office Covered Bridge (World guide number 37-20-39) stretches for 180 feet beside the highway and is Oregon's longest covered bridge. The town was founded in 1923 as a result of a timber sale that stipulated a stable community be established to encourage family life. Remains of the mill that operated into the 1980s and homes owned by the lumber company still stand. A forest service office and nursery are also located in Westfir. Several trailer parks are situated near the community.

From Westfir, you can take Highway 58 west to Eugene, or east over Santiam Pass to U.S. Highway 97.

27 MCKENZIE, SANTIAM PASS

General description: A 130-mile signed scenic loop through high mountain lava fields, past lakes and waterfalls. The loop portion from Sisters is a National Forest Service Scenic Byway.

Special attractions: Outstanding views of ten spectacular mountain peaks, McKenzie Lava Beds and Dee Wright Observatory, two national forests, headwaters of the Metolius River, llama, elk, and reindeer farms, several waterfalls, Pacific Crest National Scenic Trail.

Location: West-central Oregon between Redmond and the western Cascade Mountains.

Drive route numbers: Oregon highways 126, 242, 126, U.S. Highway 20, U.S. highways 20/126.

Travel season: All highways except 242 are open all year. Highway 242 closes from November to late June or early July, depending on snow fall and melting.

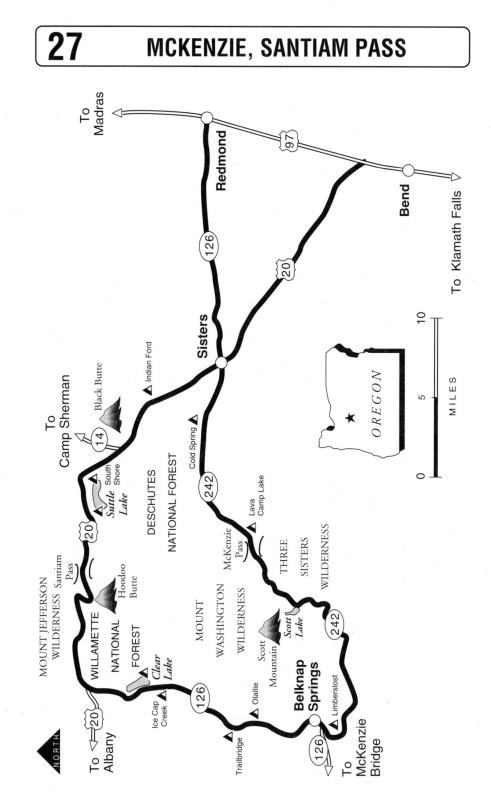

To Madras

Redmond

97

Bend

To Klamath Falls

126

20

Sisters

Indian Ford ▲

To Camp Sherman

Black Butte ▲

14

OREGON

★

MILES

0   5   10

Cold Spring ▲

DESCHUTES NATIONAL FOREST

Suttle Lake ▲ South Shore

242

20

Lava Camp Lake ▲

McKenzie Pass

THREE SISTERS WILDERNESS

MOUNT JEFFERSON WILDERNESS   Santiam Pass

Hoodoo Butte ▲

WILLAMETTE NATIONAL FOREST

MOUNT WASHINGTON WILDERNESS

Scott Mountain ▲   Scott Lake

242

Clear Lake ▲

Ice Cap Creek ▲

Belknap Springs ▲ Limberslost

20

126

To Albany

Olallie ▲

Trailbridge ▲

126

To McKenzie Bridge

NORTH

Camping: Seventeen forest service campgrounds with tables, fire rings, and toilets. Some have drinking water.

Services: All services in Redmond and Sisters. Limited services at McKenzie Bridge and Camp Sherman.

Nearby attractions: Three Sisters Wilderness, Cove Palisades State Park, Robert Aufderheide Memorial Drive, Smith Rocks State Park, Crooked River National Grasslands.

For more information: Central Oregon Visitors Association, 63085 N. Hwy. 97, No.104, Bend, OR 97701, (541) 328-8334, (800) 800-8334. Eugene Convention and Visitor Association of Lane County Oregon, 115 W. 8th, Suite 190, P.O. Box 10286, Eugene, OR 97440, (541) 484-5307, (800) 547-5445 (USA). Metolius Recreation Association, P.O. Box 64, Camp Sherman, OR 97730, (541) 595-6117. Redmond Chamber of Commerce, 446 S.W 7th, Redmond, OR 97756, (541) 548-5191, (800) 574-1325. Deschutes National Forest, 1645 Highway 20 E, Bend, OR 97701, (541) 388-2715. Sisters Ranger District, Hwy. 20 and Pine St., Sisters, OR 97759, (541) 549-2111. Sisters Area Visitor Information Center, 231 E. Hurd St., Suite D, P.O. Box 430, Sisters, OR 97759, (541) 549-0251. Willamette National Forest, 211 E. 7th Ave., Eugene, OR 97440, (541) 465-6521.

The drive: Several communities and organizations incorporate the McKenzie-Santiam Loop in their local drives. From Eugene, it can be joined by taking Highway 126 east fifty-five miles along the scenic McKenzie River to Highway 242. It is also often included as extensions of the Highway 22 North Santiam Canyon Scenic Drive. From Bend, you can join by taking U.S. Highway 20 west to Sisters. The most direct access is Highway 126 west from Redmond.

The central loop takes you to some spectacular high country and a variety of scenery, from magnificent snow-capped peaks, to lava beds and graceful waterfalls. Since Highway 242 is sixteen feet wide, steep and winding, it is not recommended for trailers, and vehicles over fifty feet long are prohibited.

Elevations range from about 2,300 to 5,325 feet. Summer temperatures average between seventy and ninety at Redmond and sixty-five to eighty in the mountains. Winter days are usually in the thirties and forties with nights falling to the low twenties in the mountains. Spring and fall range from the thirties to the fifties.

In Redmond, the Fantastic Museum features Hitler's stamp collection, antique arcade machines, and automobiles. Petersen's Rock Garden, south of town, displays an intricate network of miniature bridges, towers, and castles built of various rocks.

The Three Sisters provide a magnificent backdrop as you travel west on Highway 126. During the nineteen miles to Sisters, you pass a reindeer ranch and may see llamas grazing near the roadside. Cline Falls State Park, on the Deschutes River bank, offers a picnic area shaded by juniper and willow trees. As you approach Sisters, your panoramic view encompasses nine major mountain peaks.

Sisters entices travelers to linger in its western false-front buildings and

Dee Wright Observatory, constructed of lava blocks, sits atop 5,325-foot McKenzie Pass. Observatory windows provide viewing of Mount Hood, Mount Jefferson, Three Fingered Jack, and several other Cascade peaks.

homey restaurants. The Deschutes Ranger Station, at the junction of highways 126, 242 and U.S. Highway 20, is a must stop for trail maps, and backcountry, snow park, and wilderness permits.

In the first five miles, Highway 242 passes an elk breeding ranch, enters the Deschutes National Forest, climbs through ponderosa pine, and reaches the drive's high of 5,325 feet at McKenzie Pass summit. En route, you'll pass Cold Springs Campground with twenty-three sites, and the 7.6-mile Black Crater summit trail. Portions of the roadway follow an 1860s wagon route, and the next seventeen miles have been designated a historic highway.

At McKenzie Pass, you enter the edge of a sixty-five square mile lava flow. Dee Wright Observatory, on the summit, is built of lava. Its viewpoints isolate Mount Hood, Mount Jefferson, Three Fingered Jack, Mount Washington, North Sister, and Middle Sister.

The lava flows originated about 2,600 years ago and are some of the nation's most recent and impressive examples of volcanic activity. Since it is extremely dangerous to walk on the piles of sharp, chunky rock, take the signed 0.5-mile Lava River Trail Loop through lava gutters, pressure ridges, levies and crevasses.

After crossing the Pacific Crest Trail, a mile west of the Observatory, you wind through a mixed forest of Douglas, white, and sub-alpine fir, scrub pine, and spruce. The descent starts with views of Belknap Crater, North and Middle Sister, Craig Lake, and several large roadside ponds. At Scott Lake, accessible from a north-side road, you can see the Three Sisters reflected in the mirror-smooth waters. Obsidian trailhead, nearby, is one of the most popular routes into the 283,402-acre Three Sisters Wilderness. You can explore it on 433 miles of trail that lead across its many peaks and cones.

At Deadhorse Grade, about nine miles west of the summit, the road drops from 4,749 to 3,566 feet in 0.2 mile. The grade received its name when a horse died of exhaustion trying to climb it.

Alder Springs Campground is near the base of the grade and is a Willamette National Forest Service site with seven tent spots. Nearby, a trail leads to Linton Lake. Proxy Falls, a mile west and poorly marked, is accessible by a half-mile trail. It takes you from the parking lot across several lava flows to a waterfall that drops in two stages of 200 feet each.

The next eight miles are a mixture of peaceful setting and sharp curves. A forested bowl frames the roadway as it meanders through a quiet glade of thick ferns and towering trees that shroud everything in perpetual shade.

Crossing White Branch Creek, fed by Oregon's Largest glacier, you pass Limberlost Campground, with four tent and ten tent/trailer sites. Two miles west, Highway 242 reaches its junction with Highway 126. Gas, food, and groceries are available at McKenzie Bridge, six miles west on Highway 126.

About two miles north on Highway 126, side roads lead to Lost Creek and Belknap Hot Springs Resort. Crossing the McKenzie River, you continue north through a fir and alder corridor with a mountain of Douglas fir in front of you. At Olallie Campground two miles north of the hot springs, you can camp at seventeen sites on two levels by the banks of the river and Olallie Creek. A reservoir, a few miles north, offers boating and fishing from a jetty, trails around the small lake, and a connection to the McKenzie River National Recreation Trail, which follows the river upstream.

Five miles north, Ice Creek Campground shares an access road with Koosah Falls, which is linked to Sahalie Falls by a 0.3-mile riverside hiking trail. The campground has eight tent/trailer and two tent sites. Rocks at the precipice separate Koosah Falls into several graceful curtains. Sahalie, with a separate access, parking lot, and restrooms, thunders over a lava cliff. You can overnight in the quiet forest one mile north in thirty-five tent/trailer sites at Cold Water Cove Campground.

Clear Lake, east of the highway, is known for the exceptional clarity of its water. Fed by numerous springs, the lake is the headwaters of the McKenzie River and was created about 3,000 years ago when the stream was dammed by a lava flow. You can see a submerged forest at the bottom of the 195-foot-deep lake, which produces fair to good catches of brook trout, cutthroat, and stocked rainbows. A shoreline resort operates a store, restaurant, campground, and cabins.

Two miles north, another McKenzie River National Recreation trailhead leads to superlative mountain and river scenery and the last vestiges of the 1860s Santiam Wagon Road. Fish Lake, accessible by a dirt road near the trailhead, usually dries up by mid-summer. A campground with eight tent/trailer sites is situated near the basin.

Two miles north, Highway 126 joins U.S. Highway 20, and they continue east as a joint highway to Sisters. Three Fingered Jack, 7,841 feet, fills the

Sahalie Falls thunders over a cliff less than 0.4 mile off U.S. 126 and is connected by a short trail to Koosah Falls.

horizon in front of you as the road climbs toward Santiam Pass. At Sawyers Ice Cave, a mile east of the junction, a short trail from the parking lot offers a refreshing walk into a series of caves which usually retain ice until late summer. East of the cave, Highway 22—the North Santiam Scenic Drive— intersects your route as you enter the fifteen-mile-long Metolius River Recreation Area near Hoodoo Ski Bowl.

Hoodoo's 1,035-foot vertical rise is served by three lifts. Facilities include two lodges, rental, and repair shops. A campground with hookups can be reserved by the season that usually runs from November through March.

Several side roads lead to snow play and cross-country ski areas. Big Lake, three miles south on Hoodoo's access road, is shallow but yields good fishing for brook and cutthroat trout in spring and fall. In summer, boaters, waterskiers, and sailboarders hold sway, and in winter the road becomes a cross-country ski and snowmobile trail. You can camp on the lake side in the shadow of tall mountain peaks in two forest service campgrounds with thirty-five tent/trailer sites.

Shortly after Hoodoo, you cross the Pacific Crest Trail and Santiam Pass Summit at 4,817 feet. A pullout offers a superb view of 7,794-foot Mount Washington, and its 52,516-acre wilderness.

Suttle Lake Resort and Marina, three miles east, operates as a spring-through-autumn bed and breakfast with gas and a store. Deer, black bear, bald eagles, not to mention boaters, waterskiers, sailboarders, and fishermen are attracted to its glacier-carved bowl and large German brown, rainbow trout, kokanee, and whitefish.

At Blue Lake, two miles north, you'll also find several forest service campgrounds, each with a few sites. Blue Lake offers a full-service resort with horse stables and pack service, horse and hiking trails, a restaurant and store, twelve cabins, and forty campsites. Eleven feature water, electricity, sewer, and television sets. In winter, the trails become cross-country and snowmobile routes, and the lake turns into an ice skating rink.

The picture postcard lake sits in a small volcanic crater surrounded by a mixed forest of pines and firs. Hungry eastern brook and German brown trout, kokanee, whitefish, and monthly stockings of rainbow trout keep fishermen returning. Because of its popularity, reservations are recommended, and there is a service fee for day-use areas.

One mile east, a trail leaves the main highway for the 111,177-acre Mount Jefferson Wilderness. A worthwhile side trip begins near the trailhead and includes the Camp Sherman Resort area, numerous forest service campgrounds, and a state fish hatchery with viewing ponds. The ten-mile round trip will also take you to the headwaters of the Metolius River where it emerges in full stream from underground springs at the base of Black Butte. An exceptionally scenic viewpoint overlooks the headwaters, lush meadows, and 10,497-foot Mount Jefferson. For the first nine miles, the Metolius is a fly fishing only, catch- and-release stream for native rainbow, Dolly Varden, brown, and brook trout. It is heavily fished in summer with only fair results.

With 6,436-foot Black Butte looming beside you, the main highway passes Indian Ford Campground, which has twenty-five tent/trailer sites. The remaining ten miles to Sisters are on a gentle downgrade through a ponderosa pine forest with a bitterbrush undergrowth. From Sisters, you conclude the drive by retracing Highway 126 back to Redmond.

28 CASCADE LAKES HIGHWAY

General description: An eighty-seven-mile signed highway through the Central Cascade Mountains, skirting nine alpine lakes.
Special attractions: Mount Bachelor Ski Area, nine alpine lakes, two reservoirs, resorts, Three Sisters Wilderness, Deschutes River, camping, hiking, fishing, boating.
Location: Central Oregon between Bend and LaPine.
Drive route numbers: Oregon highways 46 and 42.
Travel season: Open all year from Bend to Mount Bachelor. The remaining section closes because of snow, but usually opens in early June and closes in November.
Camping: Twenty-five forest service campgrounds with tables, fire rings, and toilets. Some have drinking water. Additional forest service and private campgrounds are situated near the route.
Services: All services in Bend, Sun River and LaPine. Limited services along the route.

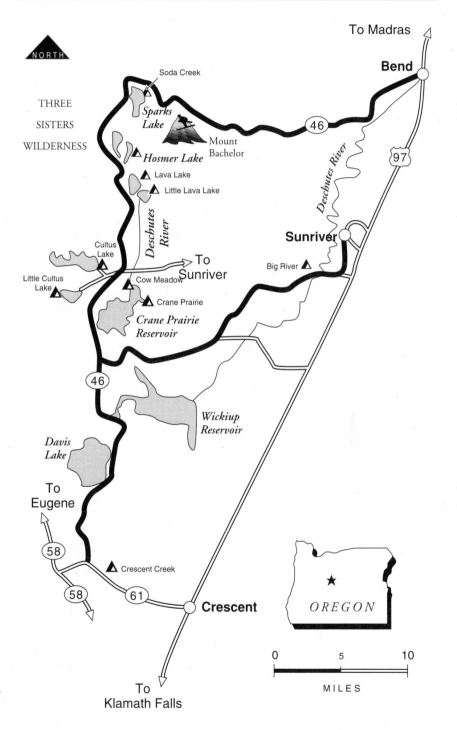

NORTH

To Madras

Bend

THREE
SISTERS
WILDERNESS

Soda Creek

Sparks Lake

Mount Bachelor

46

Deschutes River

97

Hosmer Lake

Lava Lake

Little Lava Lake

Deschutes River

Sunriver

Cultus Lake

To Sunriver

Big River

Little Cultus Lake

Cow Meadow

Crane Prairie

Crane Prairie Reservoir

46

Wickiup Reservoir

Davis Lake

To Eugene

58

Crescent Creek

58

61

Crescent

OREGON

0   5   10

MILES

To Klamath Falls

Nearby attractions: Crooked River Gorge, Smith Rocks State Park, High Desert Museum, Newberry Crater National Monument, Three Sisters Wilderness, Cove Palisades State Park.

For more information: Bend Chamber of Commerce/Convention and Visitors Bureau, 63085 N. Hwy. 97, Bend, OR 97701, (541) 382-3221. Central Oregon Visitors Association, 63085 N. Hwy. 97, No. 104, Bend, OR 97701, (541) 328-8334, (800) 800-8334. Deschutes National Forest, 1645 Highway 20 E, Bend, OR 97701, (541) 388-2715. LaPine Chamber of Commerce, P.O. Box 616, LaPine, OR 97739, (541) 536-9771. Sunriver Area Chamber of Commerce, Sunriver Village, Bldg. 15, P.O. Box 3246, Sunriver, OR 97707, (503) 593-8149.

The drive: From central Oregon's high desert, the drive climbs to about 6,000 feet at Mount Bachelor. As it moves south and east, the drive follows portions of Indian trails and wagon roads, and crosses forested slopes explored by Nathaniel Wyeth, John C. Fremont, and Kit Carson. Although the route extends through a corridor of trees, lakes are easily accessible and usually within a mile of the main road. They are stocked frequently with rainbow trout, and contain other species. Most of the route is straight and with gradual slopes, and traffic is light to moderate during the week. From U.S. Highway 97, the drive can be joined either in Bend, Sunriver, or LaPine.

While improvements have shortened the route, some signs and brochures still call it the Century Drive, in reference to its original 100 mile length. It is also called The Cascade Lakes Tour. Portions have been designated a National Forest Service Scenic Byway.

Summer temperatures average sixty to eighty degrees, and winter days generally fall between twenty and forty degrees, with cold nights. Significant snowfall occurs in higher elevations. Spring days range from about fifty-seven degrees to the high sixties, while fall temperatures are usually in the high seventies.

In Bend, the drive begins at U.S. Highway 97 and Franklin Ave. Drake Park, on the route, stretches along the Deschutes River's eastern bank, offering in-town fishing for crappie and bass, and eleven acres of lawns shaded by junipers and oaks.

As you drive west, you'll see the Cascade peaks on the horizon. After about ten miles, the scatterings of bitterbrush, sage, and ponderosa pine thickens as you enter the National Forest Service Scenic Byway. During the next few miles, the road climbs to 5,600 feet and passes the Deschutes River Recreation Area, several snow parks, and the Swampy Lakes region. Several hiking, bicycle, and snowmobile trails, two to ten miles long, branch from the highway and into the mountains.

Mount Bachelor fills the horizon as it rises out of a valley covered with jack and sugar pine, ponderosa, Douglas fir, western and Engelmann spruce. The mountain is a geologic infant and probably formed about 14,000 years ago when the earth's crust cracked and cooling lava created its symmetrical cone. Mount Bachelor's ski season generally begins around Thanksgiving and ends by July 4th. A network of nine lifts serve ten alpine runs, and there are also sixty kilometers of groomed cross-country tracks. At the resort, you can relax in six day lodges and rent mountain bikes. Summer services include a Deschutes National Forest Ranger Station with seven interpretive guides.

For the best overview of the Cascades, take the chairlift to the 7,000-foot timberline, or the 9,065-foot summit. The view from the top encompasses three states, and The Three Sisters Wilderness, alpine lakes, cinder cones, volcanic domes, lava and pumice fields, chasms and calderas. Tumalo Mountain Trail, which begins near the ski area, extends around the peak's rim.

In the next three miles, the highway enters Dutchman Flat, a pumice field of sparse vegetation with an outstanding view of Broken Top Mountain, and passes Todd and Sparks lakes. Brook and stocked rainbow trout thrive in Todd Lake which has a walk-in campground. A 0.4-mile walk from the parking area puts you on a trail encircling the beautiful lake, framed by a thick fir and spruce forest and Broken Top's summit. Tiny wildflowers decorating the landscape include a proliferation of alpine stars, columbine, elephanthead, and poison larkspur.

Sparks Lake has a ten-mile-per-hour speed limit and fly fishing limited to stocked rainbow trout. It covers about 250 acres with a maximum depth of eight feet. With no surface outlets, it is gradually turning into a marsh as it fills with sediment. Three trails of two to four miles each invite hiking through the pleasant forest and chunky lava to Moser Lake at the south end. You can also explore the terrain on mountain bikes and horse trails.

Green Lakes trailhead, near Sparks Lake Road, offers one of several entries into the 200,000-acre Three Sisters Wilderness. Numerous trails wind through the wilderness to 111 lakes, volcanic peaks, and Oregon's largest glacier.

Several springs surface at Devil's Hill and Garden, west of the trailhead, and feed a small meadow of thick marsh grass, lupines, and Indian paintbrush. Astronauts trained on the 2,000-year-old lava, and a rock from Devil's Hill was deposited on the moon. Archaeological finds indicate that Indians inhabited this region some 8,000 years ago, and several rocks still retain their pictographs.

As the route turns south, roadside evergreens shrink to the size of potted plants. Devil's Lake, crystal clear and emerald green, offers canoeing, fishing, horse and hiking trails, and camping in six sites at an elevation of 5,446 feet.

Elk Lake Recreation Area stretches for four miles along the roadway. The 390-acre lake is a scenic highlight, framed by Mount Bachelor and South Sister and ringed by lodgepole pine, fir, and hemlock. A resort with gas, dining room, and boat dock operates all year serving sailboarders, sailboaters, and skiers who follow cross-country trails to its shores in winter. Brook, brown and rainbow trout make it attractive to fishermen. You have a choice of staying in the resort's twelve cabins, or 100 sites in several shoreline campgrounds. The recreation area features horse camps and hiking trails.

Horner Lake, a mile south, is one of the few western lakes stocked with Atlantic salmon. Reserved for sports fishermen, it is limited to ten-mile-an-

Broken Top Mountain is one of several prominent Cascade peaks that are seen along the Cascade Lakes Highway.

hour speeds and fly fishing only with barbless hooks on a catch-and-release basis. In addition to campgrounds and hiking trails, a picnic area with six tables and fire grills has one of the route's few sandy beaches. While eating lunch, you have a superb view of Mount Bachelor and a forest which turns to varying shades of blue and green as it stretches from the water's edge to the distant mountains. An easy 3.5-mile Elk Lake Trail touches the shoreline of both lakes.

As the highway descends, trees gradually increase in height from eight to forty and fifty feet. Lava Lake and its resort are surrounded by lodgepole and Douglas Fir. In addition to brook and rainbow trout fishing, you can rent boats, and stay in 243 full-hookup campsites. Food, gas, and showers are available. Little Lava Lake, nearby, is the headwaters of the Deschutes River, which you will see briefly on the highway's east side as it flows south through lush meadows. Two campgrounds near Little Lava Lake have a total of eighteen sites.

During the next eleven miles, as you travel through an avenue of ponderosa pine, Douglas fir, white fir, white pine, lodgepole spruce, and mountain hemlock—watch for deer, elk, martens, marmots, porcupines, and ground squirrels. This section offers access to several trails and campgrounds, Cultus Corral Horse camp, and the Cow Meadow area with fishing and tent camping.

Cultus Lake Resort is two miles west of the highway and offers food, lodging, gas, and two area campgrounds with sixty-nine sites. Cultus Mountain separates it from remote Little Cultus Lake, which has a ten-site

Sparkling alpine lakes, Mount Bachelor, and thick fir forests provide a magnificent setting for the Cascade Lakes Highway.

campground.

Osprey Point, on the west bank of 3,850-acre Crane Prairie Reservoir, is the drive's prime spot for wildlife viewing. A 440-yard trail takes you along a ponderosa covered shoreline to a viewing area where migratory ospreys and Canada geese nest in tree snags and on artificial nesting poles. Over half of Oregon's ospreys nest here and can usually be seen between April and October.

Watching ospreys catch their dinner is a highlight. They soar into the sky, pause in mid air, then power dive into the water, catch their prey, and glide to a tree limb. Eagles sometimes steal their catches in mid-air. These magnificent birds share the habitat with great blue herons, deer, otters, and sandhill cranes. By taking the trail 170 yards north, you'll pass a historic tree and grave and end at the Quinn River's headwaters that gush from a giant spring and over moss-covered rocks. Three western shore campgrounds provide ninety-three sites.

From the reservoir, the Forest Service Scenic Byway continues south on Highway 46 for twenty-one miles to a junction with Highway 58. En route, it passes Davis Lake, an old lava flow, three campgrounds with over sixty sites and skirts the eastern foothills of 7,037-foot Odell Butte.

The Cascade Lakes Tour turns east onto Highway 42. About four miles east of the junction, a short side road leads to Crane Prairie Resort on the reservoir's east bank. The resort area is an excellent place to see eagles, osprey, deer, elk, geese, and a variety of ducks. Crane Prairie Campground has 147 sites, and the resort offers a full hookup RV park, marina, store, and restaurant.

A mile east on Highway 42, a side road takes you south to Twin Lakes and Wickiup Reservoir. Twin Lakes Resort opens with fishing season and closes in October. It services lakes and reservoir users with a store, restaurant, and twenty-two full-hookup campsites containing water, sewer, electricity, and picnic tables. Four forest service campgrounds within a mile provide an additional 400 sites. The lakes are stocked several times a year with rainbow trout. Although power boats are not allowed, you can swim, paddleboat, and kayak at Twin Lakes.

At Wickiup, you can powerboat and waterski, enjoy great fishing for heavily populated kokanee, and brook and brown trout.

A few miles east, Highway 42 meets Highway 43, which leads thirteen miles south to LaPine. If you begin or end the drive at LaPine, on Highway 43, you'll pass Pringle Falls about four miles southeast of the junction. You can camp on both sides of the river and use it as a base for good fishing, canoeing, drifting, watching osprey and deer, and exploring Pringle Falls Experimental Forest.

Northwest of LaPine, Highway 43 begins and ends by crossing the Little Deschutes River. It meanders 120 miles north to empty into the main Deschutes near Sunriver. The Little Deschutes is a popular innertubing and drifting stream.

Highway 42 continues northeast through seven miles of ponderosa pine corridor to the Deschutes National Forest Guard Station. Fall River's headwaters emerge from springs behind the station. The four miles of the river between the station and Fall River Fish Hatchery is stocked at least every other week during summer with rainbow trout. This is also a scenic hiking and camping area with opportunities to see osprey, eagles and, other wildlife.

Fall River Hatchery, near the Deschutes National Forest boundary, offers a refreshing respite in a setting of ponderosa pines, and beautiful lawns on the banks of the rippling stream. The hatchery releases 170,000 rainbow and 400,000 brook trout annually. In addition to feeding fish, you can picnic and fly fish the river from the hatchery grounds. Cross-country skiers use the area for staging winter trips.

From the hatchery, the road drops through waves of lodgepole pines. Big River Campground, also set in a forest overlooking the river, is a favorite departure point for rafting parties.

The drive concludes with farms, open fields, and a crossing of the Little Deschutes River. As you near Sunriver, Mount Bachelor and other peaks are a continuous presence on the western horizon. Sunriver Nature Center offers a last bit of sightseeing with hands-on activities for young children, a botanical garden, observatory, and a 0.4-mile nature trail through various habitats.

From Sunriver, your options for other scenic drives include The Bend-Newberry Crater itinerary and the Lake-Klamath County Loop Drive.

General description: A 110-mile loop through rolling hills of the Oregon wheat country, the Deschutes River Canyon, and into Washington state. Add about twenty miles for the Maupin Loop.

Special attractions: Oregon Trail routes, waterfalls, Wild and Scenic Deschutes River, museums, Columbia River Gorge, Stonehenge, Maryhill Museum of Art, fishing.

Location: North-central Oregon between The Dalles, Maupin and Biggs.

Drive route numbers: U.S. Highway 197, Oregon Highway 216, U.S. Highway 97.

Travel season: All year.

Camping: Two city park campgrounds, One state park campground with table, fire ring, toilets, and boat ramp. One state park campground with primitive sites, about four miles off the loop; Two Bureau of Land Management campgrounds with tables, fire rings, and toilets about five and ten miles off the loop.

Services: All services at The Dalles, Biggs. Limited services at Dufur, Maupin, Grass Valley, and Moro.

Nearby attractions: Columbia River Gorge Historic Highway, Mount Hood, Warm Springs Indian Reservation, Hood River Sailpark, Goldendale Observatory.

For more information: The Dalles Area Chamber of Commerce, 404 W. 2nd St., The Dalles, OR 97058. (541) 296-2231, (800) 255-3385 (USA). Central Oregon Visitors Association, 63085 N. Hwy. 97, No.104, Bend, OR 97701, (541) 328-8334, (800) 800-8334. Greater Maupin Area Chamber of Commerce, P.O. Box 220, Maupin, OR 97037, (541) 395-2599.

The drive: The Oregon Trail crosses the drive at several points as it begins in the Columbia River Gorge National Scenic Area at 175 feet elevation and climbs to about 3,000 feet. Distant Cascade peaks and forested foothills provide a magnificent contrast with the roadside scenery that is a succession of grasslands, wheat, and barley fields. Depending on crop rotation and season, they form a colorful patchwork of bright greens, yellows, magentas, and sandy to chocolate browns. At Tygh Valley, travelers have an option of taking a short route on Highway 216 or adding twenty miles by motoring south to Maupin and returning by the Deschutes River Canyon.

Summer in the Columbia River Gorge usually brings highs averaging in the mid-eighties while the southern portion reaches into the nineties. Winter days average twenty-two degrees in the southern section and have dropped to record lows of minus thirty-nine degrees. In the gorge, winter days in the thirties and forties are common. Spring days range from fifty-seven to sixty-five degrees, and fall brings temperatures between sixty-three and seventy-four degrees.

The drive starts at U.S. Highway 197 near The Dalles Dam and climbs a dry grass hill overlooking a ravine of oak and popular trees. At mile marker 2, it passes Bonneville Dam's Celilo Converter Station, which can be toured with a self-guiding brochure available at the administration building. The station exhibits working examples of all stages of direct current technology.

Leaving the Columbia River Gorge National Scenic Area, you climb through rolling hills of wheat and grass, alternating with freshly plowed and unplowed ground. The land is mostly loess—wind-blown glacier silt that mixed with residual soil from underlying basalt and small layers of volcanic ash. It receives less than twelve inches of rain per year. To maximize production, crops are rotated and fields are planted every other year. In the off years, they lie fallow. Sherman County, which you will see later, uses this method to produce 304,138 acres of wheat and barley, leaving 200,000 acres for beef pasture.

As the road tops hills and dips into ravines, Mount Hood stands in bold relief on the western horizon. The landscape and vegetation changes to vibrant greens, golden wheat fields, and varying shades of earth. Except for poplars planted as windbreaks, trees are virtually nonexistent. Dufur, thirteen miles south, was settled in 1893. A log cabin museum, built as a family home in 1900 and used into the 1970s, retains its original floor plan and logs. It contains collections of war memorabilia, padlocks, early 1900s clothing, and household furnishings. The Balch Hotel, next door, dates to the early 1900s, has been renovated as a bed and breakfast and is furnished with period reproductions.

Dufur City Park has eight tent/trailer sites with showers, a picnic area and swimming. A commercial RV park offers seventeen spaces with full hookups and a laundry.

If you are planning to fish the area's streams and camp, you'll want to stop at the Barlow Ranger Station of the Mount Hood National Forest. Some streams are protected to increase steelhead runs.

Eight miles south of Dufur, the route reaches its high point of 2,665 feet elevation at Tygh Ridge then twists down through a rugged canyon. Unlike today's relaxing scenic drive, the rock walls and waves of ridges that converge ahead of you posed severe challenges for early wagon and automobile roads.

About eight miles south of the summit, Highway 197 crosses a junction, seemingly in the middle of nowhere. The crossing is near the point where Oregon Trail wagons began the rugged ascent of Mount Hood's eastern slopes over the Barlow Road. The road opened in 1845-46 and was the first route over the Cascades slopes and later became the final segment of the Oregon Trail.

Oregon Highway 48 heads west through the settlement of Tygh Valley, known for its annual Native American rodeo, and parallels the Barlow Trail for about fourteen miles to Forest Creek Campground. The pavement ends at the campground, which offers eight tent/trailer sites. The remaining portions of the trail are on the National Register of Historic Places. It is a narrow, rough dirt road, and some parts are impassable. If you intend to explore it, check with the Barlow Ranger Station for road conditions and a

160

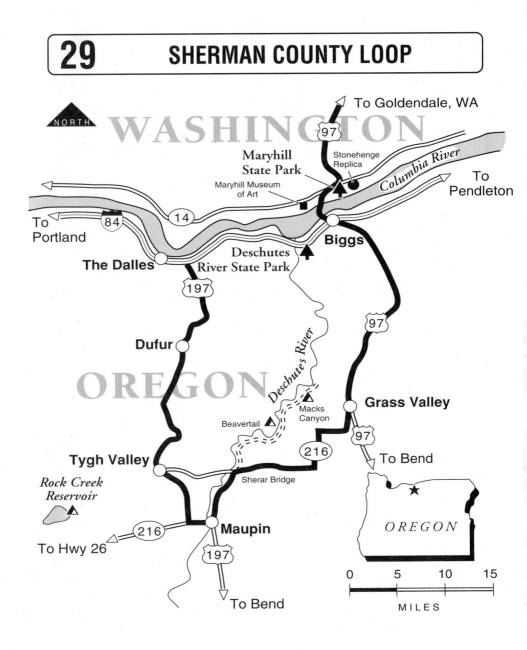

29 SHERMAN COUNTY LOOP

To Goldendale, WA

97

WASHINGTON

NORTH

Maryhill
State Park

Stonehenge
Replica

Maryhill Museum
of Art

Columbia River

To
Pendleton

To
Portland

84

14

Biggs

The Dalles

Deschutes
River State Park

197

Dufur

OREGON

Deschutes River

Grass Valley

Macks
Canyon

97

Beavertail

97

Tygh Valley

216

To Bend

Sherar Bridge

Rock Creek
Reservoir

Maupin

216

197

To Hwy 26

To Bend

OREGON

0   5   10   15

MILES

self-guiding brochure. You'll also need a vehicle suited to rugged conditions.

From the junction, you can either continue south on U.S. Highway 197 to
Maupin, or take Oregon Highway 216 east. Maupin has a hotel which dates
to the early 1900s and is a center for white water rafting, kayaking, and other
outdoor recreation. A handicapped-accessible fishing ramp is situated near
the Deschutes River Road, which you will follow north to Highway 216
near Sherar Bridge. This portion of the Lower Deschutes is a National

Mount Hood, Oregon's tallest peak, frames the western horizon behind the roadside community of Dufur on U.S. Highway 197.

Wild and Scenic River and an Oregon State Scenic Waterway. En route, you may see deer, bald eagles, Canada geese, antelope, wild turkey, and pheasants.

If you elect to take the shorter route and travel east on Oregon Highway 216, after about five miles you'll come to Tygh Valley State Park. Often called White River State Park, it offers a refreshing spot to enjoy river and canyon scenery from a picnic ground shaded by poplars and oaks. From the overlook, you have a close-up view of White River Falls that drops in two stages and several curtains of water. To the east, deep in the red rocks of the canyon, an abandoned power station sits on a seemingly impenetrable ledge. You can also fish the White River for trout and steelhead.

Two miles east, the road descends into the lava outcroppings, benches, and ridges of the Deschutes River Canyon. The river rushes and boils through Sherar Bridge. This section has been a traditional Native American fishery and was a campground for Oregon Trail wagon trains. They followed roughly the same route as the highway from Grass Valley, winding down steep basalt ridges and traveling west over the Barlow Road. A narrow wooden bridge that spanned the Deschutes became the gateway to central Oregon, despite the heavy tolls charged by its owner, Joseph Sherar.

Today, Native Americans still stand on wooden platforms and dip salmon while others cast for trout and steelhead from the rocky shore. Pictographs, drawn centuries ago, are still visible on the west bank. Two Bureau of Land Management campgrounds, about five and ten miles northeast, offer thirty-eight sites in the rugged canyon.

Tygh Valley State Park is a scenic wayside offering a close-up view of White River Falls, access to river fishing, and a view of an abandoned power station perched on a canyon ledge.

The highway continues through several miles of rugged cliffs, then climbs the plateau to merge twenty-two miles east with U.S. Highway 97 at Grass Valley.

Grass Valley sits at altitude of 2,350 feet. The 150 residents, grain elevators, gas station, motel, restaurant and RV park with full hookups are surrounded by wheat and barley fields and cattle ranches that stretch north to the Columbia River. According to legend, when the first settlers arrived they found native grasses taller than a man's head even when he was sitting atop a horse. Situated in Sherman County, Grass Valley became a division point on the pioneer stage line between The Dalles and Canyon City.

Moro, nine miles north, also has an economy tied to agriculture. With 310 people, it may be among America's smallest county seats. The picturesque pioneer courthouse is a regional landmark. An agricultural experiment station has stood at the eastern edge of town on an original homestead since 1909, developing grains and testing them for diseases, winter hardiness, and yield. The Sherman County Museum, established in 1893, contains period rooms and a large collection of local cattle brands.

Three miles north on U.S. Highway 97, De Moss Memorial Park sits in the shadow of a dilapidated grain elevator. The park was once a well known local health resort, with streets named for musicians and avenues honoring poets. It was founded by a family of itinerant musicians who traveled from town to town entertaining cowboys and settlers. By 1893, they were famous and became the official songwriters for the Chicago World's Fair. The park has a few picnic tables and offers informal camping.

Ten miles north of Moro, side roads branch from U.S. Highway 97 east to Wasco and northwest to rugged Fulton Canyon. Nearby, an Oregon Trail spur crossed a pioneer road linking the Columbia to the interior.

Mount Hood, in Oregon, and Mount Adams, across the Columbia in Washington state, stand as two snowcapped cones as you enter another canyon five miles south of Biggs. Oregon Trail wagons descended to this point from the inland portion of the Columbia Plateau, and headed north to the river. Small farms with aging barns and quaint windmills lie protected by the slopes of converging ridges. After a few miles, the Columbia Gorge opens in front, and you can see Maryhill Museum across the river in Washington.

Crossing the bridge at Biggs and entering Washington, you pass Maryhill State Park. It displays a steam locomotive and offers swimming, boating, picnicking, and fifty hookup sites. Stonehenge replica, a mile east of the park, is a full-sized reproduction of England's Stonehenge and was America's first World War I memorial.

Maryhill Museum of Art, about three miles west on Washington Highway 14, sits isolated on a flat plain, literally in the middle of nowhere. Nothing can prepare you for the imposing structure, and you are likely to come away somewhat overwhelmed by this curiosity and its fine art. It houses original bronzes, plasters, watercolors, and sketches by Auguste Rodin and extensive collections of chess sets as well as 19th Century American, Dutch, and French paintings.

You can conclude by returning to Oregon on U.S. Highway 97 to Biggs or by following Highway 14 west and crossing the bridge to The Dalles. From Biggs, your options are to return to The Dalles through the gorge on Interstate 84 or take the Oregon Trail route along the rim and through 15 Mile Canyon. Deschutes River State Park, four miles west of Biggs, has thirty-four primitive sites.

30 COVE PALISADES LOOP

General description: A thirty-one-mile scenic drive through an agricultural plain to spectacular high desert canyons surrounding an artificial lake fed by three rivers.

Special attractions: Round Butte Observatory, Lake Billy Chinook, Cove Palisades State Park, views of ten Cascade mountain peaks, fishing, camping, water recreation.

Location: Central Oregon west of Culver and Madras.

Drive route names: Belmont Lane, Mountain View Drive, Frazier Drive,

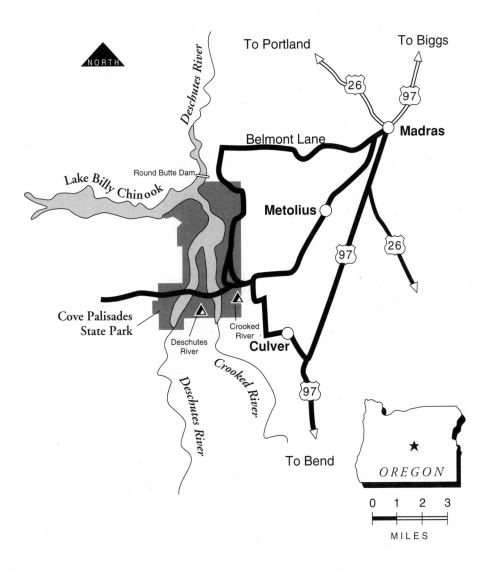

Fisch Lane, Feather Drive, Huber Lane.

Travel season: All year. Park campgrounds and facilities close during winter.

Camping: One state park campground with two sections featuring full hookups and electricity.

Services: All services at Madras. Limited services at Lake Billy Chinook and Culver.

Nearby attractions: Ogden Scenic Wayside, Smith Rock State Park, Crooked River National Grasslands, Crooked River Gorge, Headwaters of the Metolius River, Pelton Dam and park, Warm Springs Indian Reservation, Kah-Nee-Ta Resort.

For more information: Central Oregon Visitors Association, 63085 N. Hwy. 97, No.104, Bend, OR 97701, (541) 328-8334, (800) 800-8334. Culver Visitor Information Center, 411 1st St., P.O. Box 86, Culver, OR 97734, (541) 546-6032. Greater Maupin Area Chamber of Commerce, P.O. Box 220, Maupin, OR 97037, (541) 395-2599. Madras-Jefferson County Chamber of Commerce, 197 S.E. 5th St., P.O. Box 770, Madras, OR 97741, (541) 475-2350 (800) 967-3564.

The drive: Several Cascade Peaks dominate the horizon as the drive extends west through flat farmland. Lake Billy Chinook and its canyons are hidden until you reach the gorge edge, where the route follows the eastern rim to spectacular viewpoints and into the park and canyons. The drive concludes by traveling southwest though commercial field crops.

Summers in central Oregon average highs of sixty-two to eighty-two degrees, with occasional jumps into the nineties but rarely over 100. Winter highs generally fall between thirty-five and forty-one degrees but seldom drop below zero, even though this is high desert country and the area does receive snow. Visitors can expect balmy spring days in the high fifties to mid-sixties and autumns around seventy degrees.

Madras, with a population of 3,570, and an elevation of 2,245 feet, was founded in 1911. According to legend, it was named after a bolt of cloth.

Surrounding areas are frequented by rockhounds who gather here every July 4th for an annual convention and to mine landscapes for fossils, agates, and petrified wood. Several ranches offer digs for jasper, thundereggs, moss and rainbow agates.

Exiting Madras, you travel west through grasslands, farms, and low hills covered with sagebrush and isolated junipers. On clear days, you may be able to see more than 100 miles of the Cascade Range and its most prominent peaks.

After 7.5 miles, the drive turns south on Mountain View Road. Junipers have thickened into a forest and provide a cool corridor on the 1.7 miles to Round Butte Observatory.

The observation building, operated by Portland General Electric Company, overlooks Round Butte Dam, 400 feet below, and hints at the spectacular scenery to come as the vista encompasses Lake Billy Chinook, the Deschutes River, and sheer canyon walls. The rock-filled dam is one of the nation's largest earthen dams and holds back the Deschutes, Metolius, and Crooked rivers.

Information boards explain the geology, local history, Round Butte and Pelton Dam projects, and identify local fish and birds. The site has restrooms and drinking water. A three-acre picnic area is a pleasant spot to savor the scenery.

You'll also find information on facilities at Pelton Dam and Park. Situated seven miles north of the observatory and also operated by the power

Swimmers, boaters, sunbathers, and fishermen find plenty of space to enjoy their recreational activities on the shorelines and waters of Lake Billy Chinook.

company, Pelton Park features eighty campsites and a store with food, fishing supplies, boat rentals, and moorage space.

During the next five miles, four roadside pullouts on the rim of the gorge offer a variety of striking views. At the first viewpoint, you can see the Deschutes River curve around the tall island butte, merge with the Crooked River, and continue as one stream north into a narrow canyon. A second viewpoint is directly across from the tip of the island, with Lake Billy Chinook below and the gorge walls seeming to converge to the north.

The third viewpoint is a prime spot for seeing the lake and canyon walls and ten of the Cascade's most prominent peaks. They include Mount Adams in Washington State, and Oregon's Mount Hood, Mount Jefferson, Three Fingered Jack, Mount Washington, Black Butte, The Three Sisters, Broken Top, and Mount Bachelor. From the last viewpoint, you look out at Mount Jefferson, the island between the rivers, and see boaters and picnickers below.

Less than a mile south, the road enters Cove Palisades State Park and takes you down to Lake Billy Chinook's shoreline. Crooked River Campground, by the entrance, overlooks the lake several hundred feet below. It has ninety-one sites with hookups for trailers and tents.

The near vertical canyon walls were formed over millions of years. Between ten and twelve million years ago, the Deschutes and other rivers were rerouted by lava flows that formed the Cascade Mountains' base. As the foundation raised, land around Cove Palisades sank. Ancient rivers carried sediment from the mountains into the basin. Over an eight million year period, sediment, volcanic ash, cinders, and lava created a 1,000 foot thick layer.

Later, lava flows capped the rimrock palisades and virtually filled the

Four viewpoints on the eastern rim of Lake Billy Chinook offer sweeping panoramas of the lake, ten mountain peaks, and the shorelines below.

canyon, and rivers cut through the flow to their original depths.

Cove Palisades has a been a favored fishing and recreation area since the late 1800s. Until the early 1960s when Round Butte Dam was constructed, the state park was situated on the Crooked River's banks 900 feet below the canyon rim and 200 feet below the lake's present-day water level. In 1963, it was relocated to the peninsula that separates the river arms. It remains one of Oregon's most visited recreation areas.

Lake Billy Chinook, with three arms and seventy-two miles of shoreline, was named for a local Native American who helped guide Captain John C. Fremont through the region in 1843. In addition to waterskiing and other water sports, you have a good chance at landing a variety of fish from kokanee, chinook salmon, Dolly Varden, and smallmouth bass to rainbow and German brown trout. Several years ago the lake produced record twenty- and twenty-three-pound bull trout.

About ten miles of paved road meander through the canyon and park. On the east rim, the road ends at Cove Marina, three miles north of the Park entrance. At the marina you can rent boats, motors, waterskiing equipment, and moorage space. The store carries groceries, ice, and fishing permits, and the restaurant opens at 6 a.m. for fishermen and early risers.

Crooked River Day Use Area, 0.5 mile south of the marina, is a large lakeside picnic grounds and a launching site for boaters and waterskiers. Russian olives, black locus, European beech, poplars, and other non-native trees have been planted to shade day use areas along the shorelines.

The road clings to a thirty- to fifty-foot ridge as it continues south two miles, crosses a bridge, and makes a moderately steep climb to the shallow gap that connects the peninsula to the mainland. On the west side, the land opens into a flat plain.

At Deschutes River Camp, on the Peninsula, you can sleep at the base of towering rock walls in ninety-four tent sites and eighty-seven spots with hookups for water, sewer, and electricity. Facilities include central restrooms, hot showers, and a fish cleaning station. A nearby group camp has three areas capable of accommodating twenty-five people in each.

The Crooked River Petroglyph, a basalt boulder that was moved here, is situated between the two camps at the base of the often photographed "Ship" formation. It is covered with symbols carved by prehistoric Indians.

Lower Deschutes Day-Use Area sits at the base of The Island, and Upper Deschutes Day-Use Area is on the southwestern shore near the end of the pavement. Area hikes are rewarding but watch for rattlesnakes. In addition to rugged scenery, you may see mule deer, otters, ground squirrels, and raccoons. Bird life ranges from geese to magpies, red-tailed hawks, and meadowlarks.

A dirt forest service road connects to Camp Sherman and the headwaters of the Metolius, about twenty miles southwest.

Forest Service Road 1139, also unpaved, heads inland along the western rim to the forest service-operated Perry South Campground on the Metolius River.

Irrigation has turned the high desert south of the rim into a productive agricultural area. Leaving the park, the Three Sisters provide a scenic backdrop on the five miles to Culver as you travel by fields planted for grass and carrot seed, potatoes, alfalfa, garlic, and a variety of grains. The area is particularly aromatic in late summer during the peppermint harvest.

If you are interested in country crafts, a stop at Culver's Old Court House Mall can be rewarding. From Culver, your options for additional sightseeing include the Prineville Loop Tour, the McKenzie Santiam Loop, and the Cascade Lakes Highway.

31 MADRAS-PRINEVILLE LOOP

General description: A seventy-mile loop through rolling grass, sagebrush- and juniper-covered hills, and the Crooked River Gorge.
Special attractions: Crooked River National Grasslands, Crooked River Gorge, Smith Rock State Park, Ogden Scenic Wayside, three reservoir lakes, rock climbing, rock hounding, fishing.
Location: Central Oregon between Madras and Prineville.
Drive route names and numbers: U.S. Highway 26, U.S. Highway 126, Oregon Highway 27, O'Neil Road, U.S. Highway 97.
Travel season: All year.
Camping: Three state park campgrounds, one with full hookups, one with primitive sites, and one with an informal walk-in bivouac area; One forest service campground and one Bureau of Land Management campground with

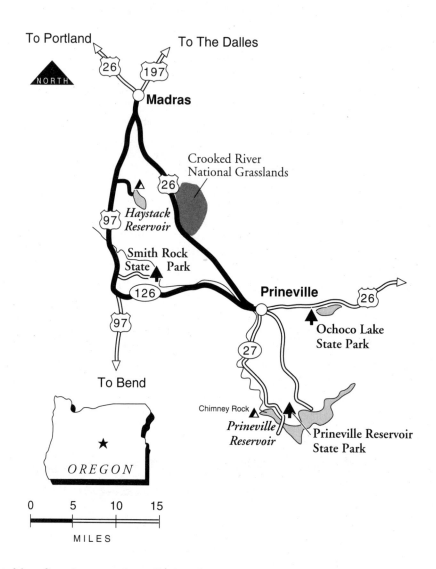

tables, fire rings, vault or flush toilets, and drinking water.

Services: All services at Madras and Prineville.

Nearby attractions: Cascades Lakes Highway, Three Sisters Wilderness, Pine Mountain Observatory, High Desert Museum, Lava Butte, Lava Cast Forest, Benham Falls, Sunriver Nature Center, Cove Palisades State Park, Lake Billy Chinook. McKenzie Pass-Santiam Loop, headwaters of the Metolius River, Pelton Dam, Warm Springs Indian Reservation, Kah-Nee-Ta Resort.

For more information: Central Oregon Visitors Association, 63085 N. Hwy. 97, No.104, Bend, OR 97701, (541) 328-8334, (800) 800-8334. Madras-

Jefferson County Chamber of Commerce, 197 S.E. 5th St., P.O. Box 770, Madras, OR 97741, (541) 475-2350. Prineville-Crook County Chamber of Commerce, 390 N. Fairview, Prineville, OR 97754, (541) 447-6304.

The drive: From Madras, the route proceeds southeast across sagebrush and rolling hills through the Crooked River Grasslands to Prineville and the rugged Crooked River Canyon. Turning west it extends through the sheer basalt cliffs of the rugged Crooked River Gorge to Terrebonne. As the route returns north on U.S. Highway 97, it is framed by the snow-capped peaks of the Cascades to the west and the high desert's low hills and prairie near the roadside. Traffic is usually moderate on U.S. Highway 26 and Oregon 126, light on Oregon 27 and O'Neil Road, and moderate to heavy on U.S. Highway 97.

Between fifteen and twenty million years ago, most of the area was covered by basalt lava to a depth of several hundred feet. Over time the Crooked River cut through the rock, creating the sheer-walled deep canyons, which you travel through on the southern section of the drive.

Summers in central Oregon register from the 60s to the 80s and 90s, but rarely over 100 degrees. While the area does receive snow, temperatures seldom drop below zero and usually stay between thirty-five and forty-one degrees. Spring days are usually in the high fifties to mid-sixties, with autumn temperatures hovering around seventy degrees.

Madras, the Jefferson County seat, is the center of an agricultural area with cattle ranches and commercial crops of vegetable seeds, garlic, grain, potatoes, alfalfa, clover, and mint.

The drive begins in south Madras where the route leaves U.S. Highway 97 and heads southeast on U.S. Highway 26. It starts by cutting through fields of hay, juniper, and sagebrush, framed by a low eastern ridge. After about three miles, a wooden-framed structure, east of the highway, marks the site of one of central Oregon's many commercial cinnabar mines.

During the next fifteen miles you travel through the rolling rangeland of the 105,000-acre Crooked River National Grasslands, which spread into deep canyons and across scattered volcanic buttes. The grasslands are managed by the Ochoco National Forest to provide a habitat for antelope, wild horses, elk, and upland game. At Rimrock Springs viewpoint five miles further south, you can walk a nature trail to a grassy ridge with an observation platform overlooking a small reservoir. As you walk the 1.5-mile trail, watch for bald eagles, ducks, quail, chukars, and mule deer.

Leaving the grasslands, the highway tops Grizzly Pass. Hay fields and cattle ranches fill the valley between the summit and the ten miles to Prineville. You'll enter town by traveling under the Railway Express overpass. The railroad is one of the few in the United States that is owned by a municipality.

Prineville is the only incorporated city in Crook County. When it was settled in 1868, it became central Oregon's first town. Native American artifacts, antiques, guns, and other regional relics are preserved in the

Bowman Museum, which is housed in a 1910 stone bank building.

The surrounding hills, cliffs, and lowlands contain an abundance of thunder eggs, agates, fossils, petrified wood, and jaspers. Prineville is a focal point for rockhounds, who gather for annual conventions and digs. You can obtain lists and maps of digging sites from the Chamber of Commerce. While you can dig on public lands free, some sites are on private land and fees are charged.

Local reservoirs have long been known for outstanding fishing. Scenic Barnes Butte Lake, three miles north of town on Barnes Butte Road, has been featured on nationally-syndicated television fishing shows for its world class bluegill and largemouth bass. It is limited to single barbless hooks and catch-and-release trout fishing.

Six miles east of town alongside U.S. Highway 26, Ochoco Reservoir fills a wooded ravine between wooded hills. Situated on the centennial bike route and impounded by 125-foot Ochoco Dam, it is a favorite recreation area with year-round rainbow trout fishing, boating, and waterskiing. You can enjoy its peaceful setting from twenty-two primitive and hiker/biker campsites at nearby Ochoco Lake State Park.

The area's best scenery lies south of Prineville on Highway 27. During the first few miles, you'll travel through the center of beautiful farms with impeccable buildings and white board fences, bordered by high ridges and lava outcroppings. After about seven miles, the Crooked River starts meandering along the roadside. It begins in the Ochoco Mountains and flows west 107 miles to empty into the Deschutes near Madras.

About mile marker 12, the route enters the steep reddish brown basalt palisades of the Lower Crooked River canyon and becomes a Bureau of Land Management National Scenic Byway. This section is also a national Wild and Scenic River and a popular canoe route. Riverside rattlesnakes temper local fishermen's enthusiasm somewhat for runs of hungry brown and rainbow trout. Other wildlife to watch for are coyotes, deer, and raptors. You can enjoy a picnic lunch at several BLM picnic areas and overnight in sixteen campsites at Chimney Rock Recreation Area.

At mile marker 20, rolled-earth and rock-filled Arthur R. Bowman Dam rises 245 feet from a 1,100-foot-wide base. It creates twelve-mile-long Prineville Reservoir. Built for irrigation and flood control, it a favorite of waterskiers and boaters during summer weekends. Scrappy largemouth and smallmouth bass, catfish, native and stocked rainbow trout make it a year-round fishery.

The pavement ends at a boat launch on the western shoreline. If you elect to return to Prineville, you'll have a completely different view of the palisades. As you drive north, the cliffs tower above you as a giant natural amphitheater. The BLM byway continues south for twenty-two miles as a narrow washboardy, all-weather gravel road with sharp turns through high desert sagebrush.

Prineville Reservoir State Park, on the eastern shore, offers twenty-two full hookups, forty-eight tent sites, a boat ramp, and a dock. It attracts boaters, waterskiers, and swimmers; rock collectors come to hunt a variety

Smith Rocks natural amphitheater attracts rock climbers from around the world.

of agates and petrified wood. Evening slide programs are presented in the campground's outdoor theater. The park is not accessible from Highway 27, but can be reached on a separate side road that leads seventeen miles south from Prineville.

Returning to Prineville, the loop drive continues by crossing the Crooked River on Highway 126, makes a sharp turn north at the top of the first hill and enters Ochoco Wayside. From the small park, the sweeping view encompasses the valley, gorge, and surrounding area. Afterward, you continue west on O'Neil Road along the scenic Crooked River rim. A house across the valley at mile marker 11 became famous in a book titled "House Under the Rimrock," and was the home of former Governor Tom McCall. O'Neil Road ends at a junction with U.S. Highway 97 near Terrebonne.

Smith Rocks State Park, four miles east of Terrebonne, is one of Oregon's scenic icons, and the drive's highlight. Juniper, ponderosa pine, and sagebrush stud its canyon floor. The Crooked River is a winding blue ribbon separating sheer talus rocks on the north and the rimrock plateau to the south.

A climber's favorite since the 1940s, Smith Rocks has acquired an international reputation as one of the nation's best rock climbing areas. Three of its more than 600 routes have received the highest difficulty rating of 5.14. But the park offers excellent climbing for beginners and intermediates as well as experts. If you're not a climber, you can explore the 623 acres of scenic wonders on seven miles of hiking trails. You can also fish the river, picnic at a panoramic overlook, and camp beside the beauty in a walk-in bivouac or tent camping area that is open year-round.

As U.S. Highway 97 continues north, on clear days, you'll see Mount Jefferson and several lesser peaks on the western horizon.

Ogden Scenic Wayside, three miles north of Terrebonne, offers a delightful rest stop and a closeup view of the Crooked River Gorge. The walls of the gorge expose basalt flows that buried five- to ten-million-year-old blankets of volcanic ash and dust. The wayside honors Peter Skene Ogden who led a Hudson's Bay Company trapping party on the first recorded journey into central Oregon in 1825. As he roamed the West, Ogden became an important figure in the early fur trade.

The route continues north through the grasslands and isolated junipers of the high desert, passing shallow ridges and swales. Six miles north, you pass a side road to Culver and the southern entrance to the Cove Palisades Scenic Drive. Round Butte Dam and Cove Palisades Recreation area, about ten miles west, offer boating, tent camping, fishing, and visitor information. The exit is in the middle of farmland and sagebrush/juniper grasslands with a good view of snow-capped mountains to the northwest.

A mile further, Jericho Lane heads five miles east over juniper-covered hills to Haystack Reservoir. In early spring and late fall, it yields good catches of crappie, bass, catfish, kokanee, bullhead, and stocked rainbow. Speedboats and waterskiers take over during summer. A forest service campground provides twenty-four sites, a boat ramp, and swimming area, and a KOA campground with full hookups is situated on the access road, 0.5 mile east of U.S. Highway 97.

The drive concludes seven miles north at the junction of U.S. Highway 97 and U.S. Highway 26. Access to the Cove Palisades Loop is 1.5 miles north off U.S. Highway 97 in Madras.

 BEND-NEWBERRY CRATER

General description: A 42.3-mile drive through pine forests and lava beds to the summit of Newberry Crater National Volcanic Monument.

Special attractions: High Desert Museum, Lava Butte, Lava Cast Forest, Benham Falls, Sunriver Nature Center, Lava River Cave, LaPine Recreation Area, Deschutes National Forest, Newberry Crater National Volcanic Monument.

Location: Central Oregon between Bend and LaPine.

Drive route numbers: U.S. Highway 97, Forest Service Road 21.

Travel season: All year. Newberry Crater receives significant snow and is a center for cross-country skiing and winter recreation. East Lake Resort closes from mid-October to mid-May, and Lava River Cave closes in mid-September.

Camping: Eight forest service campgrounds with tables, fire rings, vault or flush toilet, drinking water. One Oregon State Park campground with full hookups. East Lake Resort campground with full hookups.

Services: All services in Bend and Sunriver. Limited services at Newberry Crater National Monument.

Nearby attractions: Cascade Lakes Highway, Smith Rocks State Park, Crater Lake National Park, Three Sisters Wilderness, Pine Mountain Observatory, Fort Rock State Park, Hole-In-The- Ground.

For more information: Central Oregon Visitors Association, 63085 N. Hwy. 97, No.104, Bend, OR 97701, (541) 328-8334, (800) 800-8334. Bend Chamber of Commerce/Convention and Visitors Burau, 63085 N. Hwy. 97, Bend, OR 97701, (541) 382-3221. Deschutes National Forest, 1645 Highway 20 E. Bend, OR 97701, (541) 388-2715. LaPine Chamber of Commerce, P.O. Box 616, LaPine, OR 97739, (541) 536-9771. Sunriver Area Chamber of Commerce, Sunriver Village, Bldg. 15, P.O. Box 3246, Sunriver, OR 97707, (541) 593-8149.

The drive: Starting in Bend, the drive follows U.S. Highway 97 south, then turns east and climbs to over 6,000 feet elevation to the National Monument. The first twenty-five miles are a flat, tree-lined corridor and the last eighteen miles are a steep, mostly straight climb with views of forested mountains and valleys. As Central Oregon's main north-south corridor, U.S. Highway 97 is generally busy with traffic particularly heavy during the 8-9 a.m. and 5-6 p.m. rush hours. Highway 21 to Newberry Crater is a signed Corridor 97 Association tour, which usually has light traffic during the week and heavy on weekends.

Volcanism forged the landscape between Bend and Newberry Crater. The last volcanic activity occurred only 1,300 years ago. Newberry Crater National Volcanic Monument gained its monument status in 1990 and preserves 56,000 acres of lakes, lava flows, and other geological formations. Over ninety-five percent of the world's geologic features are visible here, including ash flows, cinder cones, pumice rings, and rhyolitic domes.

Summer temperatures average seventy-three to eighty-two degrees, while winter days generally fall between twenty and forty degrees with cold nights. Although the area receives only about twelve inches of precipitation per year, significant snowfall occurs at Newberry Crater. Spring days average about sixty degrees, while fall days are slightly warmer at about sixty-seven degrees.

Before leaving Bend, at 3,628 feet elevation, you may wish to visit the Deschutes Historical Center. It exhibits artifacts from Lava Island Rock Shelter and other areas you will see on the drive.

From Bend, U.S. Highway 97 heads south in a straight line through a ponderosa pine forest. After about seven miles, you arrive at the High Desert Museum. The 150-acre complex is virtually a must for anyone interested in the high desert's history and wildlife. Many displays are interactive. You can trace the area's history from prehistoric to present times and step into a settler's cabin, a sheepherder's wagon, and the forestry learning center. A nature exhibit features burrowing owls, kangaroo rats, lizards, bats, rattlesnakes, and other desert animals that are seldom seen.

During the next three miles, the route enters the Deschutes National

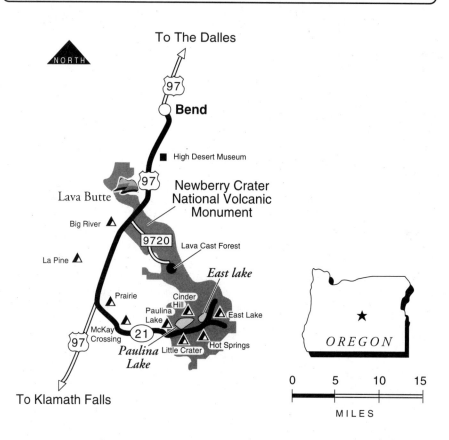

Forest and crosses the northwestern tip of panhandle-shaped Newberry Crater National Volcanic Monument. The panhandle section includes Lava River Cave, Lava Cast Forest, and Lava Butte, which can be seen west of the highway as you continue south 0.7 mile to Lava Lands Visitor Center.

Shuttles operate from the center to Lava Butte's summit, 500 feet above the plain. At the summit, you'll look down into a 150-foot crater. The outstanding view from a short paved rim trail encompasses Newberry Crater, The Three Sisters, Mount Bachelor, the high desert, Smith Rocks, and a 6,100-acre lava field. Visitor center videos and displays interpret the area's geology and archaeology. You can also walk a short trail from the center across lava flows to the butte's base.

At Benham Falls, four miles west of the visitor center, lava filled the channel of the Deschutes River for several miles to a depth of fifty feet and forced the stream over an ancient lava dome. A 0.5-mile trail through a stand of old growth ponderosa connects the idyllic river bank picnic area with the falls that are really rapids. If they look familiar, it may be because you've seen

At Newberry Crater, a developed trail leads through a jumbled landscape of obsidian to a view of Lost Lake.

them in "Rooster Cogburn and the Lady," "The Indian Fighter" and other films.

Back on U.S. Highway 97, the drive continues south one mile to Lava River Cave, set in a ponderosa pine forest with a ground cover of bitterbrush, manzanita, and snow brush. It is Oregon's longest known uncollapsed lava tube and has a main tunnel 5,200 feet long. You can rent lanterns and take a self-guided tour of its lava and ice stalactites and stalagmites, echo hall, and sand gardens. The 2.4-mile trail, including the walk to and from the parking lot, is relatively easy despite stairs and an uneven surface. Bring a jacket; the cave temperature is a constant forty degrees.

Continuing south, you temporarily leave the national forest and monument. Sunriver Nature Center, 2.5 miles south of the cave, and 3.4 miles west of U.S. Highway 97 is located on sediments deposited by ancient lake beds that were created when lava flows dammed the Deschutes River. Many of the center's activities are geared to children, and there are also natural history displays and exhibits of local ancient stone artifacts.

From Sunriver, a bumpy, dirt forest service road (9720) heads east nine miles to the Lava Cast Forest. Tree molds in this five square mile area were created about 6,000 years ago when a Newberry Crater eruption spilled into the ponderosa, lodgepole, and white fir forest. As the lava cooled, the intense heat burned the wood and left the molds. You can see them on a one-mile trail through lava logs, lava lakes, and a lava sea surrounding a forested island. The area is at its best in early summer when purple penstemon and Indian paintbrush add a bit of color to the landscape.

U.S. Highway 97 exits the national monument and forest, passes the entrance to the Fall River/Cascade Lakes Highway, and continues south 7.5

miles to the LaPine State Recreation Area. At the park's entrance four miles west of the highway, a sign directs you to Oregon's largest ponderosa pine. It has a circumference of 326 inches and is 191 feet tall. From a lookout, you have a commanding view of the Deschutes River and the devastation caused by the mountain pine beetle. It has infested many lodgepole pines and deprived them of nutrients. As they die, the branches turn red.

A day-use area on the winding Deschutes River provides picnic tables, fireplaces, and drinking water. Although the river has a slight current, a bathhouse and swimming beach offer a welcome break from the summer heat. The campground, one mile west, provides fifty sites with electricity, tables and water, and ninety-five sites with full hookups for water, sewer, and electricity.

About one mile south, the route leaves U.S. Highway 97 and turns east on Forest Service Road 21 to climb the western slopes of Newberry Volcano. From the beginning at roughly 4,000 feet, the road rises dramatically during the eighteen miles to 6,371 feet at East Lake. Prairie Campground with sixteen sites and McKay Crossing with ten, are situated near the base in jackpine scrub forest on sandy soil. A group camp is also nearby.

As the road climbs through a lodgepole and ponderosa forest, several pullouts invite photographs of the forested slopes, cones, lava flows, the valley, and Cascade Mountains to the west. After passing an area of dead timber devastated by beetles at mile marker 12, you reenter the national monument.

The crater you see today is the end result of millions of years of volcanism. Numerous ash and pumice avalanches swept down its sides spreading a base twenty-five miles wide and covering 500-square miles. Named after J.S. Newberry, a scientist attached to an 1853 railroad surveying party, it is one of the United State's largest volcanos. During a series of major eruptions, the top collapsed into empty lava chambers leaving a caldera of seventeen-square miles, five miles across. It is so vast that the rim appears to be a separate mountain range.

The crater holds two scenic lakes, which were once a single body of water but were separated by lava and mud flows. East Lake is about 170 feet deep and covers 1,000 acres. Paulina Lake spans 1,500 acres and is about 248 feet deep. In the monument, you can hike, horseback, snowmobile, or cross country ski more than 100 miles of trails. Some are short, easy lakeside jaunts; others will take you on a twenty-five-mile crater rim loop or along the 8.5-mile Peter Skene Ogden National Recreation Trail that passes twenty waterfalls on Paulina Creek.

Most of the facilities and sites are situated near the monument entrance. A dirt side road to 7,984-foot Paulina Peak, the highest point on the volcano, is easily accessible by car and offers a view of the two lakes, the Cascade Mountains, central Oregon, Washington, and California. You can reach Paulina Creek Falls picnic area and the 100-foot falls on a short walk from the parking lot. At Newberry Crater Wildlife Refuge, also near the entrance, you may see bear, eagles, ducks, geese, badger, bobcats and occasionally, elk.

Paulina Lake, behind the falls, is known for trophy-sized brown, rainbow, and brook trout as well as kokanee salmon. You'll find it a pleasant and scenic setting for canoeing, boating, sailing, and waterskiing. A year-round resort on the lakeshore, housed in a 1929 log cabin, operates a restaurant, rents ten cabins and boats, and sells groceries, tackle, and gas. Four forest service campgrounds on or near the lake provide 132 sites, a group camp, and stables for twelve horses.

From the entrance, the road continues north to the obsidian flow. It occurred about 1,300 years ago and is the last known volcanic event at Newberry. When it reached the surface, the lava cooled quickly creating a spectacular hill of black glass and volcanic foam. A 0.4-mile hike on an improved trail is moderately strenuous as it climbs to the top of the flow and overlooks tiny Lost Lake.

After passing three forest service campgrounds with 191 sites, the pavement ends at East Lake Resort. A dirt road, not recommended for passenger cars, continues around the mountain and back to Bend.

At East Lake, you have an opportunity to sailboard in a volcano. Your efforts at still fishing, trolling, and fly-fishing are likely to be rewarded, thanks to planted Atlantic salmon, annual plantings of 225,000 ravenous rainbow trout, plus native eastern brook and German brown trout. East Lake Resort rents boats, eleven cabins and has an RV park with full hookups. It operates a store, cafe, and boat house. From the resort, you have the best view of the pretty lake and the caldera, which are obscured by trees along the roadside.

On the return to the monument boundary, you have a much better view of Paulina Peak that looms above the roadside and a second opportunity to see interesting outcroppings and gravel slides you may have missed on the initial trip.

From Newberry Crater, you can return to Sunriver or Bend and take the Cascade Lakes Highway, or travel south and drive the Lake County-Klamath County Scenic Loop.

33 BLUE MOUNTAIN SCENIC BYWAY

General description: A 130-mile paved route from the Columbia River grasslands into the forested Blue Mountains.

Special attractions: Oregon Trail site, lakes and reservoir, elk herds, forest views, Wild and Scenic North Fork John Day River, bird watching, hunting, hiking.

Location: Northeastern Oregon, starting at Exit 147 west of Boardman, and ending in the Blue Mountains, northwest of Sumpter.

Drive route numbers: Oregon Highway 74 and 207/74, U.S. Forest Service roads 52, 51, and 73.

Travel season: Oregon Highway 74 to Heppner is open all year. Forest service roads are not plowed in winter, but are used by snowmobilers and

This stately courthouse in Heppner was built in 1903 and is on the National Register of Historic Places.

cross-country skiers. They are usually open from June 15 to October 15.

Camping: One county park campground with full hookups. One state park Campground with primitive sites. Four forest service campgrounds with picnic tables, vault toilets, and fire rings.

Services: All services in Heppner and Ukiah. Limited services in Ione, Lexington, and Granite.

Nearby attractions: Columbia River Gorge, Elkhorn Scenic Byway, John Day Fossil Beds National Monument, Battle Mountain State Park, Strawberry Mountain Wilderness, Interstate 84 Oregon Trail Route, Lehman and Ritter Hot Springs.

For more information: North Central Oregon Promotion Committe, 404 W. 2nd St., P.O. Box 1053, The Dallas, OR 97058, (541) 296-2231, (800) 255-3385. Umatilla National Forest, 2517 SW Hailey Ave., Pendleton, OR 97801, (541) 278-3716. District Rangers: Heppner Ranger District, 117 S. Main St., Heppner, OR 97836. (541) 676-9187. North Fork John Day Ranger District, P.O. Box 158, Ukiah, OR 97880. (541) 427-3231. Heppner Chamber of Commerce, West May St., P.O. Box 1232, Heppner, OR 97836, (541) 676-5536.

The drive: For the first sixty miles, you're likely to wonder why this route has been designated a Forest Service Scenic Byway. The only trees are stands of poplars planted as windbreaks, oaks by creek banks, and a few isolated junipers on distant hillsides. Meanwhile, you'll travel through wheat fields, grasslands, sagebrush, lava outcroppings, small cattle and sheep farms, and scattered settlements of a few hundred people. This segment is relatively flat

33   BLUE MOUNTAIN SCENIC BYWAY

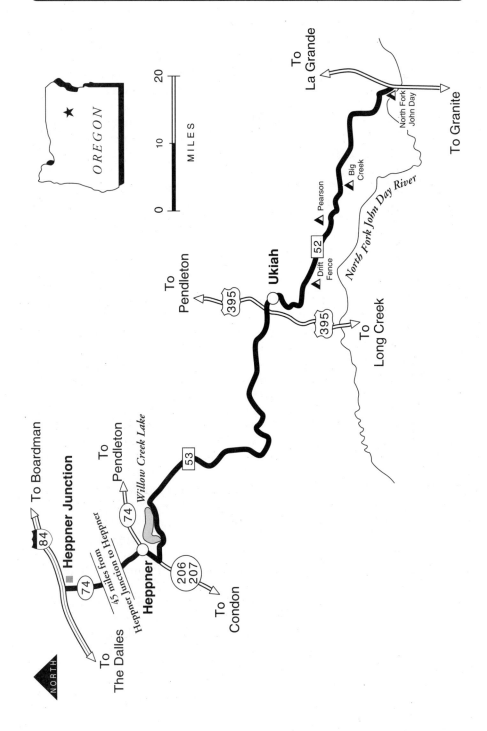

OREGON

MILES

0   10   20

NORTH

To La Grande

To Granite

North Fork John Day

North Fork John Day River

Pearson

Big Creek

52

Drift Fence

To Long Creek

395

Ukiah

395

To Pendleton

53

Willow Creek Lake

To Pendleton

74

Heppner

206 207

To Condon

74

45 miles from Heppner Junction to Heppner

Heppner Junction

84

To Boardman

74

To The Dalles

and winding. A creek and railroad tracks meander a few feet from the road, which stays in a valley between rolling hills and distant mountains.

After Heppner, the route starts climbing, eventually reaching an elevation of about 6,000 feet. Once it enters the Umatilla National Forest, it follows a ridge top to Ukiah then dips into a valley and climbs back into the mountains. Small meadows and firewood cutting areas break into the tree lined corridor.

Traffic is usually moderate between Interstate 84 and Heppner. Forest service roads are less heavily traveled except during hunting season when 20,000 hunters invade the area. As you travel the byway, keep your binoculars handy. The Umatilla National Forest supports 324 species of wildlife, and grasslands provide feed for deer and a variety of birds.

In the lowlands, travelers can expect summer temperatures of ninety and sometimes 100 degrees. Winters plummet to the twenties, thirties, and, at times, to near zero. Spring averages about sixty-five degrees, while autumn days fall between sixty-four and seventy-seven degrees.

A few homes stretch around a curve at the base of a ridge in Cecil, fourteen miles south of exit 147. From 1849 to 1853, the Oregon Trail passed nearby. By traveling fourteen miles east from the Oregon Trail sign on Highway 74, you can see the actual trail ruts at Wells Spring along with an information center and kiosk.

At Morgan, six miles further, a green valley and buckskin brown hills surround three water towers. Continuing south, you'll see a couple of grain elevators standing in the middle of nowhere, and possibly cattle and sheep on the hillsides. At Ione, population 275, look for the picturesque country church and some turn-of-the-century two-story buildings. A restaurant, lounge, several grain elevators, and another Oregon Trail sign line the highway. Eight miles southeast is Lexington with 280 people. It sits in the middle of a large agricultural area.

Heppner, the area's largest town, fills a small valley with 1,415 people and a few blocks of brick buildings. A museum on the highway displays photo collections, local relics, and period rooms depicting a school and post office. The stately courthouse, built in 1903, is on the National Register of Historic Places.

Willow Creek Dam, at the southern end of town, became the world's first roller-compacted concrete dam when it was built in 1961 by the Corps of Engineers. From downtown, you can take a short, easy walk to the twelve-acre reservoir at the bottom of a wide expanse of hills with long gradual slopes that extend to the horizon. A day-use area, boat launch, and docking facilities are scattered around the rim where people gather year-round to fish for bass and trout and enjoy summer boating and waterskiing.

For an interesting side trip, take Oregon Highway 206/207 twenty miles south to Hardman. During the late 1800s, this semi-ghost town was a stopover for freight wagons and stagecoaches. Several buildings still stand. The dance hall has been renovated to offer travelers some of the flavor of the lively past.

From Heppner, the route follows Willow Creek Road and Forest Service Road 53 as it climbs a ridge overlooking the reservoir. About midway, you'll

Heppner's museum displays period rooms depicting a post office and school, and the grounds offer a shaded lawn with picnic tables.

find a beautiful roadside picnic area facing the lake and mountains across a valley dotted with small farms and grasslands.

As it winds through hills and canyons, trees replace meadows, the road narrows, and long curves become hairpin turns. After about seventeen miles, you enter the Umatilla National Forest, and for the rest of the drive you'll be traveling through a corridor of mixed lodgepole pine, Douglas fir, western larch, ponderosa pine, and white fir. At higher elevations, you'll also see sub-alpine fir.

The 1,399,342-acre national forest serves many purposes. As you continue east, watch for some of the 10,000 cattle and 8,000 sheep that graze on these lands. You can also expect to see wood cutters and pickup trucks stacked with firewood. Hikers, horseback riders, and mountain and dirt bikers depart from the highway to some of the 700 miles of trails.

Cutsforth Forest Park, near the entrance, offers a pleasant break and the opportunity to overnight in the thick forest in a campground featuring twenty-four hookups and fifteen tent sites with electricity, sewer, and water. Children can romp on playground equipment, explore a nature trail, and fish a creek or a handicapped accessible pond that are stocked twice yearly with rainbow trout.

Penland Lake, eight miles east and five miles south on a side road, offers swimming, trout fishing, and boating with electric motors. While most of the seventy-acre lake's shoreline is privately owned, a day-use area and five-site Penland Lake Campground provides public access.

On the seven miles between Penland Lake and Potamus Point access roads, lines of spindly lodgepole pine, and room-sized Christmas trees are broken by small meadows, firewood cutting areas, and snags of dead trees. Each year about 15,000 cords of firewood are cut throughout the forest, and more than 2,000 personal-use Christmas tree permits are issued.

From Potamus Point, eight miles south of the main highway, your view overlooks several mountain lakes, rocky crags and outcroppings, and the Wild and Scenic North Fork John Day River drainage. In late fall and early spring, you may also glimpse herds of elk in distant meadows.

After several miles of traveling through sub-alpine fir, lodgepole and ponderosa pine, the forest disappears a few miles west of Ukiah, and you descend into a lake basin that was permanently emptied by an ancient earthquake. The area is particularly pretty in spring when bright blue camas covers meadowlands.

Ukiah, with about 250 people, has a restaurant, store, and gas. Check with the John Day Ranger Station if you need trail maps, wilderness permits, or are exploring the back country. At Ukiah-Dale Forest State Park, three miles southwest of town on U.S. Highway 395, you can camp in twenty-five primitive sites on the North Fork John Day River banks.

Crossing Camus and Pine Creeks, the route quickly climbs back into mountains and forest. Bridge Creek Wildlife Area, about four miles east of Ukiah, was developed in the 1860s by miners who built pole bridges over area streams. Today, it is a wintering habitat for one of the nation's largest herds of Rocky Mountain elk. In addition to approximately 16,500 elk, the forest is home for mule and whitetail deer, big horn sheep, black bear, and mountain lions. During your drive, you are likely to see bald eagles, peregrine falcons, barred, flammulated and great gray owls, and pileated, black-backed, and three-toed woodpeckers.

The North Fork John Day Overlook, about nine miles east, is a convenient pullout with an excellent view of the John Day Wilderness to the north, and the Strawberry Mountains on the south. Bridge Creek elk herds can sometimes be seen from the viewpoint along with logging operations on distant mountainsides.

Several trails begin near the highway between Bridge Creek and North Fork John Day Campground, twenty-five miles east of the overlook. They range from easy to difficult and from short hikes to extended treks through forested valleys, up mountain slopes, and into the John Day Wilderness. A sparse undergrowth invites short roadside explorations into the ponderosa pine forest. A dirt road leads north to 6,790-foot Tower Mountain where the view includes the Elkhorn Range to the east, Malheur National Forest on the South, Washington State to the north, and the Cascades to the west. Big Creek and Drift Fence campgrounds are situated near the highway and offer a total of five tent sites.

The Blue Mountain Byway ends at North Fork John Day Campground where U.S. Forest Service roads 52 and 51 meet. Seven tent/trailer sites are frequented by hunters, hikers and horseback riders. Fishermen find the North Fork John Day River a rewarding stream for Chinook salmon, steelhead, Dolly Varden, and rainbow trout.

Taking Forest Service roads 51 and 73 south from the junction, the Blue

Mountain and Elkhorn Scenic Byways overlap on the ten miles south to Granite.

A few miles south of the junction, the route passes Chinese Walls that were built by oriental miners more than 100 years ago. Gold was discovered at Granite on July 4, 1862. Several decades of varied mining activity produced more than $9 million in gold and a town with two hotels, three stores, five saloons, and many homes. Today, only a few buildings and residents remain.

A nearby dirt road will take you eight miles west to the remains of the Fremont Powerhouse. It was constructed in 1908, used until 1967, and is listed on the National Register of Historic Places. Parts of the pipeline that provided water from Olive Lake are still visible along the road from the power plant to the lake.

From Granite, you can conclude your sightseeing either by traveling north twenty-seven miles to Anthony Lakes and on to Haines or continue southeast to Sumpter and Baker City.

34 ELKHORN SCENIC BYWAY

General description: A 106-mile paved loop through the desert valleys of the Baker and Powder rivers, agricultural lands, and into the Blue Mountains and Elkhorn Range.

Special attractions: Oregon Trail Route and Interpretive Center, lakes and reservoirs, historic gold mining area, ski resort, mountain lakes, forest views, Wild and Scenic North Fork John Day River, wildlife watching, recreational gold panning, hiking.

Location: Northeastern Oregon west of Baker and Haines.

Drive route numbers: Oregon Highways 7 and 410, Forest Road 73, Baker County Road 1146, U.S. Highway 30.

Travel season: From Baker, roads to Granite, and from Haines to Anthony Lakes are open all year. Between Granite and Anthony Lakes, routes are not plowed in winter and usually open around July 4th.

Camping: Eight national forest campgrounds with picnic tables, fire grates, flush or vault toilets. One has hookups.

Services: All services in Baker. Limited services in Sumpter, Granite, Haines.

Nearby attractions: Interstate 84 Oregon Trail route, Blue Mountain Scenic Byway, John Day Fossil Beds National Monument, Strawberry Mountain Wilderness, Battle Mountain State Park, Lehman Hot Springs, La Grande-Ukiah-Weston Scenic Drive, Farewell Bend State Park.

For more information: Baker County Visitor and Convention Bureau, 490 Campbell St., Baker, OR 97814, (541) 523-3356, (800) 523-1235 (USA). Wallowa-Whitman National Forest, 1550 Dewey Ave., P.O. Box 907, Baker, OR 97814, (541) 523-6391. Umatilla National Forest, 2517 SW Hailey Ave., Pendleton, OR 97801, (541) 278-3716.

ELKHORN SCENIC BYWAY

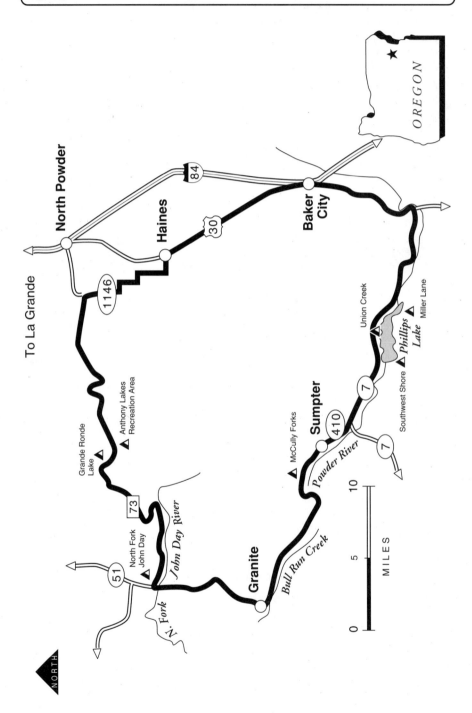

OREGON

North Powder

To La Grande

Haines

84

30

1146

Baker City

Union Creek

Miller Lane

Phillips Lake

Southwest Shore

7

Anthony Lakes Recreation Area

Sumpter

McCully Forks

410

7

Grande Ronde Lake

Powder River

73

John Day River

North Fork John Day

51

N. Fork

Granite

Bull Run Creek

10

5

MILES

0

NORTH

The drive: From Baker City, the drive follows the Powder River west to Sumpter where it climbs into the Blue Mountains. Passing the semi-ghost town of Granite, it continues through magnificent mountain scenery to Elkhorn Pass and the Anthony Lakes Recreation Area. The descent is through a steep canyon back to the Baker Valley, then briefly crosses the original route of the Oregon Trail on the return to Baker City. Although the drive can be joined at Haines, Sumpter, or from the Blue Mountain Scenic Byway at North Fork John Day Campground, forest service route brochures start in Baker City.

Summer travelers can expect hot days with temperatures ranging from the 80s to over 100 degrees in the Baker Valley, and 10 to 15 degrees cooler in the mountains. Winters are cold and snowy with temperatures dipping to below zero, the teens, twenties, and low thirties. Spring days are usually in the mid-sixties, while fall ranges from sixty-four to seventy-seven degrees.

In Baker City a walking/driving tour includes more than 100 elegant stone buildings and Victorian homes. At the National Historic Oregon Trail Interpretive Center, three miles east of town, paths lead from the center atop Flagstaff Hill to the original wagon ruts. The outstanding view encompasses the Blue Mountains and Baker Valley.

Leaving Baker City, on Highway 7, the drive begins in dry grasslands, enters a canyon with rugged lava outcroppings, scattered juniper-covered hills and creek bottom willows, then crosses the Powder River. The Powder River meanders for several miles along the roadside. After about thirteen miles, the route makes the first of several entrances into Wallowa-Whitman National Forest. As you travel through Sumpter to Elkhorn Summit, lodge-pole pine is the forest's dominant species and is mixed with western larch, Douglas fir, and ponderosa pine. Douglas fir dominates east of Elkhorn summit.

Near the forest boundary, you'll see Mason Dam and Phillips Lake south of the highway. The 167-foot-high dam holds back a reservoir covering five miles and a surface area of 2,450 acres. Powder River and Phillips Lake are fished for rainbow trout, coho salmon, and bass.

Union Creek Recreation Area offers camping in shady ponderosas beside the serene lake, and is a launching pad for boating, waterskiing, and swimming. The campground's fifty-eight sites feature twenty-four with sewer, water, and electrical hookups.

Several habitats intermingle at nearby Mowach Loop Picnic Area and attract waterfowl, eagles, raptors, mule and white tail deer, elk, coyotes, and weasels. Osprey nest on artificial snags. Southwest Shore Campground includes twenty tent/trailer sites on the lake. Deer Creek Campground has only six sites but offers the allure of recreational gold panning. Any gold you find is yours. Area campgrounds fill early during deer and elk season and are also staging areas for cross-country skiing.

A short side road leads south to the Sumpter Valley Railroad Park, where you'll find a brightly painted depot, water tower, rolling stock, and short nature trails where you may see deer, cranes, and ducks. The restored train operates on summer weekends and includes the original 1915 gear and steam-driven, wood-burning Heisler locomotive.

Highway 7 turns south near the railroad access. You leave the national forest and continue west on Highway 410 past fields of dredge tailings on the three miles into Sumpter.

With about 150 people, Sumpter is barely a shadow of its glory days when it had 3,000 people, eighty-one businesses and produced more than $10 million in gold ore. Today, a gas station, general store, restaurant, and a few residences straddle the highway. At the southern end of town, you can see the gold dredge sitting idle in its pond.

Leaving Sumpter, the highway enters a thick forest, which will fill the roadside for most of the sixteen miles to Granite. A side road heads north to Bourne, a picture-perfect ghost town with another abandoned dredge you can see by hiking 0.5 mile up Cracker Creek. The town was at the center of hard-rock mining, and a few privately owned claims are still producing. About three miles west, you reenter the national forest at McCully Fork Campground, where you can try your luck in the designated gold panning area and camp in a pine forest with six tent sites.

Near the campground, the road starts a dramatic climb, winding around ridges with distant forests and towering mountain peaks providing some of the drive's most striking scenery. The formations represent three distinct types of rocks from three time periods. Initially, ancient sea sediments hardened into sandstone. Later, molten rock solidified into granite and was covered by more recent volcanic basalt flows. Glaciers, wind, and water have refined the mountains and valleys into the craggy peaks and steep slopes you see today.

Blue Springs Summit, at 5,864 feet, is a popular snowmobile area and signals the beginning of several miles of live, dead, downed, and logged trees that were victims of a mid-1970s Pine Mountain beetle infestation. Boundary Guard Station, north of the summit, was built during the Depression by the Civilian Conservation Corps and is worth a stop to see its many unique details.

Granite, a few miles further north, is also nearly a ghost town with a booming past tied to gold. A store, a few residences, and abandoned buildings stand isolated among the evergreens.

For a venture into the deep woods, take Forest Road 10 five miles south to Fremont Powerhouse. Built in 1908 and used until 1967, it still contains massive turbines and some other equipment. You'll see portions of the wood and steel pipeline that supplied water from Olive Lake along Road 10.

Granite represents the last services for fifty-seven miles. Forest Service Road 73, which you take north and east twenty-six miles to Anthony Lakes, starts with eight miles of patchy, rough road through the Crane Creek area. Deer and elk are often seen along here in early mornings and evenings. The road also passes the Chinese Walls—large boulders and rock embankments that were worked by Oriental miners more than 100 years ago.

The Elkhorn and Blue Mountain scenic byways meet at North Fork John Day Campground. With seven tent/trailer sites, the campground is a jumping-off point to the John Day Wilderness, plus area hiking and horseback

Scenic Anthony Lake is surrounded by mountains, forest, a ski resort, and several smaller lakes.

trails. The river supports one of the largest spawning populations of wild spring chinook and summer steelhead. About fifty-four miles are set aside as a National Wild and Scenic River.

The Elkhorn loop continues east, passing alpine meadows and clear cuts with majestic peaks forming a huge amphitheater for smaller mountains and valleys.

After about sixteen miles, Highway 73 crosses Elkhorn Mountain Summit. At 7,392 feet elevation, it is the highest point on the drive. A summit pullout overlooks the headwaters of the Grande Ronde River. Grande Ronde Lake sits nestled in a thick Douglas fir forest and is another prime spot for watching deer. Known for German brown trout fishing, it is also popular with cross-country skiers. A lakeside campground has eight sites but is not suitable for large trailers or motorhomes.

Anthony Lakes, a mile east of Grande Ronde Lake, has been a family ski area since 1933 and is famous for its powder snow. It has a base elevation of 7,100 feet, sixteen downhill runs, and serves as the hub for more than 400 miles of cross-country skiing and snowmobile trails. The season generally starts around Thanksgiving and lasts through mid-April. Facilities include a day lodge with food service, deli bar, and lounge.

A national forest recreation area surrounding the ski complex, provides hiking and biking trails and camping and fishing at mountain lakes. Mud Lake Campground has seven tent sites. Anthony Lakes Campground offers twenty-one tent and sixteen tent-trailer sites in one of eastern Oregon's most picturesque settings. The lake, a fifty-yard stroll from the ski lodge, is ringed by thick Douglas fir, tamarack, lodgepole, and white fir with a towering mountain behind it. Eleven to fourteen-inch brook trout are common catches, along with German brown and rainbow trout. From campsite, fishing area, or boat, you may see elk, deer, and other wildlife.

The 22.5-mile Elkhorn Crest National Recreation Trail begins near the ski area. It links with several shorter trails, takes you through valleys, by remote lakes and spectacular peaks, and into the North Fork John Day Wilderness.

From Anthony Lakes, the drive descends eight miles of steep grade through a narrow, brushy canyon. A midway viewpoint overlooks the pastoral Baker Valley and the distant Wallowa Mountains near the Idaho border. Dutch Creek Flat Trail, three miles east, offers a final trek into the high country with a eleven mile walk through beautiful meadows by secluded Dutch Flat Lake and then joins the Elkhorn Crest Trail.

As the road straightens and enters the flat, open fields of the Baker Valley, you'll pass an entrance to Pilcher Creek Reservoir, where you can fish for rainbow trout. The valley is a major livestock, hay, and grain producer, and you can expect to see modern farms, meadows, and aging barns. South to Haines and Baker, your drive concludes with roadside pastures framed by the majestic peaks of the Blue Mountains, which rise abruptly from the plain and are often tinged with a purple haze.

Haines, with about 370 people, has a quaint country church and general store that looks like a survivor from the 1800s. Eastern Oregon Museum preserves some of the region's rowdy past with brewery wagons, bootlegger's stills, a saloon bar, steam powered threshing machines, and arrowheads.

At Haines, the route joins U.S. Highway 30, which briefly parallels the Oregon Trail. You may wish to make a final stop at Wallowa-Whitman National Forest Ranger Station on U.S. Highway 30 in Baker for information on Hells Canyon and other recreational opportunities in this vast forest. The station also issues backcountry permits, trail maps, and campground information.

35 LA GRANDE, UKIAH, WESTON LOOP

General description: A 170-mile paved loop drive along the Grande Ronde River, through a wildlife test area, wheat and farmlands, and into the Blue Mountains.

Special attractions: Oregon Trail and Walla Walla Historic Trail routes, state parks and waysides, two national forests, elk habitat test area, Lehman Hot Springs, mountain and valley scenery, Umatilla Indian Reservation, Spout Springs Ski Area.

Location: Northeastern Oregon between La Grande, Ukiah, Pendleton, and Weston.

Drive route numbers: Interstate 84, Oregon Highway 244, U.S. Highway 395, Oregon Highway 11, Oregon Highway 204, Summerville Road.

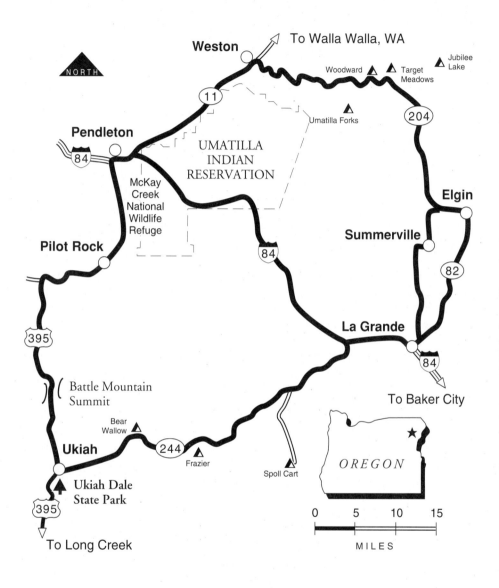

35 LA GRANDE, UKIAH, WESTON LOOP

Weston

To Walla Walla, WA

NORTH

Woodward
Target Meadows
Jubilee Lake

11

Umatilla Forks

204

Pendleton

84

UMATILLA
INDIAN
RESERVATION

Elgin

McKay
Creek
National
Wildlife
Refuge

Summerville

Pilot Rock

84

82

395

La Grande

84

Battle Mountain
Summit

To Baker City

Bear
Wallow

244

Ukiah

Frazier

Spoll Cart

OREGON

Ukiah Dale
State Park

395

0   5   10   15

MILES

To Long Creek

Travel season: All year. Snow and ice can create extremely dangerous driving conditions on U.S. Highway 395 at Battle Mountain State Park and on Oregon Highway 204.

Camping: Six forest service campgrounds with picnic tables, vault toilets and fire rings; some with water. Two state park campgrounds with primitive sites.

Services: All services in La Grande and Pendleton. Limited services in Ukiah, Pilot Rock, Weston, Tollgate.

Nearby attractions: Oregon Trail route, Oregon Trail Interpretive Center, Blue Mountain Scenic Byway, Elkhorn Scenic Byway, Whitman Mission National Historic Site, Farewell Bend State Park.

For more information: La Grande-Union County Chamber of Commerce, 1912 4th St., No. 200, La Grande, OR 97850, (541) 963-8588, (800) 848 9969. Pendleton Chamber of Commerce/Visitor and Convention Bureau, 25 S.E. Dorion, Pendleton, OR 97801, (503) 276-7411, (800) 547-8911 (USA). Wallowa-Whitman National Forest-La Grande Ranger District, 3502 Highway 30, Highway 30, La Grande, OR 97850, (541) 963-7186. Umatilla National Forest, 2517 SW Hailey Ave., Pendleton, OR 97801, (541) 278-3716. North Fork John Day Ranger District, P.O. Box 158, Ukiah, OR 97880, (541) 427-3231.

The drive: From La Grande at 2,788 feet elevation, the drive crosses a variety of terrain and vegetation as it heads southwest through the Grande Ronde River bottomlands and plateaus to Ukiah. Turning north, it crosses Battle Mountain and descends to flat rolling wheat fields and agricultural lands near Pendleton where it parallels the historic Walla Walla Trail and the Umatilla Indian Reservation northeast to Weston. Taking Highway 204 southeast, the drive climbs through the Umatilla National Forest, to over 5,000 feet near Spout Springs, then returns through a steep canyon and farmlands.

At lower elevations summer travelers can expect temperatures in the high 80s, low 90s, and over 100 degrees. While winter days sometimes drop to near zero, the teens, and twenties, temperatures usually average between thirty-nine and forty-nine degrees. Pendleton usually has a little milder weather. Spring days usually average about sixty-five degrees. Autumn temperatures range from sixty-four to seventy-seven degrees.

La Grande was named for its beautiful setting. As you travel north on Interstate 84, drive about one mile and take exit 252 southwest on Highway 244, you are treated to an awesome landscape of steep mountains, isolated monoliths, deep valleys, and ravines.

Hilgard Junction State Park, at the junction of the two highways, sits on the north bank of the Grande Ronde River. From campground and picnic areas, you can look across the river and see the sheer bluffs where Oregon Trail wagons and livestock were lowered by ropes to the river bank. The park is a departure point for river rafters, trout, salmon, and steelhead fishermen. You can camp in the shadows of the high bluffs and on the river bank in eighteen primitive campsites. At Red Bridge State Park, four miles west, the shallow river invites wading and fishing, and paths meander under tall oaks and ponderosa along the north bank.

During the next ten miles, the road leaves the forested corridor of the canyon and cuts across flat hills. The river deepens, widens, and shares the landscape with lava outcroppings, isolated stands of pine, meadows laced with ravines, and occasional farms and corrals.

Near Forest Service Road 51, which provides access to the Blue Mountain and Elkhorn Scenic Byways, the Grande Ronde River bends south through meadows to its headwaters in the Blue Mountains. You leave the hills, as Highway 244 enters 2,383,159-acre Wallowa Whitman National Forest.

The thin ribbon of national forest which you cross contains the Starkey Elk Habitat and Wilderness Area. This one-of-a-kind test area encompasses 25,000 acres of forest and range where the effects of cattle, deer, and elk on managed forests are studied on a long-term basis. If you decide to stop and take a self-guided wildlife tour, you'll become part of the data for counters and cameras record vehicle traffic.

About five miles west, the road leaves Wallowa-Whitman and enters 1,399,342-acre Umatilla National Forest. Near the boundary, short roads lead south to Frazier Campground and Lehman Hot Springs. With five tent and twenty-seven tent/trailer sites, Frazier serves as a base for trail bikers, hunters and fishermen.

You'll find one of the area's largest hot spring pools at Lehman Hot Springs, where Nez Perce Indians once picked huckleberries. Berry picking is still a popular activity, along with cross-country skiing, snowmobiling, hunting, hiking, swimming, and gathering mushrooms.

On the sixteen miles to Ukiah, Camas Creek weaves in and away from the highway. It commands attention along a roadside of scrub brush, clearcuts with graying stumps, and low, rolling dry grass hills. Two Umatilla National Forest campgrounds sit in a stand of Ponderosa about six miles west of the hot springs. An interpretive trail at Bear Wallow Creek, which has five tent/trailer sites, explains the life cycle of salmon and their habitat requirements. Adjacent Lane Creek Campground offers four tent/trailer sites.

Ukiah draws autumn deer and elk hunters, and local rivers are known for their exceptional early spring steelhead fishing. Highway 244 meets U.S. Highway 395 west of town. Ukiah-Dale Campground, three miles south of the junction, is an Oregon State Park with twenty-five primitive sites on the North Fork John Day River.

North of Ukiah, U.S. Highway 395 splits the Camas Prairie flatlands, which are particularly scenic in spring when camas lily sunflowers and Indian paintbrush mix with sagebrush, grass, and juniper trees. After about thirteen miles, you begin weaving through yellow and white pine, tamarack and western larch on the climb to Battle Mountain's 4,270-foot summit. A general store with gas, groceries, and a few residences are scattered among the trees on the south slopes.

Battle Mountain State Park, about 0.4 mile north of the summit, offers a refreshing break with picnic tables and lawns on a ridge shaded by Douglas fir, ponderosa, and planted spruce. The park commemorates the decisive

Battle Mountain State Park, overlooking ravines and rangeland, commemorates an 1878 battle between the U.S. Army and Native Americans.

engagement of the Bannock War, which was fought in the Battle Mountain foothills on July 8, 1878. It marked the last major Indian uprising in the Pacific Northwest.

Leaving the forest as you continue north, the undulating line of the horizon is virtually unbroken, save for a lone grain elevator and a few horse corrals. Depending on the season and crop rotation, the fields are a blanket of fresh greens, golden wheat, dark and light browns, mixed with silver-blue sage, and dark green bitterbrush.

About twelve miles north of Battle Mountain, U.S. Highway 395 intersects Highway 74 to Heppner and the Blue Mountain Scenic Byway and heads east through a ravine where ice and water have created a series of dark lava benches. Watch the marshland and fields, south of the road, and you may see deer grazing, or hawks swooping from rock to meadows. Two miles east, at Pilot Rock, U.S. Highway 395 separates grain elevators, log decks, gas stations, and a motel.

McKay Creek National Wildlife Refuge, eight miles south of Pendleton, surrounds a reservoir that serves boaters and waterskiers. Warm-water game fish are plentiful, and the variety of crappie, smallmouth and largemouth bass, perch, catfish, and trout make it a fishing hot spot. You may also see bald and golden eagles, wintering Canada geese, and more than 33,000 ducks.

At Interstate 84, you turn east, and after a couple of miles, take exit 213 onto Highway 11. Traveling northeast through Pendleton, the highway follows the historic Walla Walla Trail, which was an Oregon Trail departure point for Washington bound wagons that followed the spur to Whitman Mission.

Woolen mills and rodeos have brought Pendleton enduring fame. The

The Grande Ronde River parallels Oregon Highway 244 as it flows east to La Grande.

lively history is interpreted at the Pendleton Round-Up Hall of Fame, in brochures for walking/driving tours of Victorian homes, and guided underground tours into tunnels constructed during the late 1800s by Chinese laborers. Pendleton Woolen Mills offers tours and a sales room.

In north Pendleton, you cross the Umatilla River, which extends about twenty-five miles northeast through the Umatilla Indian Reservation. Four miles north, you pass a side road leading east to a mission on the Umatilla Reservation. Although a Jesuit mission, established in 1888, burned decades ago, you can see a cemetery containing several graves of people who were born in the 1700s and tour a long house.

Twelve miles north, between Mission and Athena, the landscape becomes an geometric hodge-podge of squares, boxes, rectangles, and diamond-shaped green, brown, and yellow fields.

At Weston, with a store and a few residences, you turn southeast on Highway 204, which starts with a gradual six-mile climb up Weston Hill. At the top, the commanding view includes the Blue Mountains, Walla River, rugged Storm Canyon, Table Mountain, and a sea of wheat.

As you continue climbing, the roadside is sprinkled with meadows, stands of ponderosa pine, scattered homes, picturesque barns, and Christmas tree farms. Weston Lake is at mile marker 10 and sits near a cluster of homes and cabins; it attracts local trout fishermen. Clover, lupine, and other wildflowers add colorful touches and a fragrant aroma to springtime travel.

Reentering the Umatilla National Forest, the highway passes a winter recreation area. Several trails invite short hikes through a sparse ground cover and into a mixed forest of white fir, blue spruce, tamarack, ponderosa, and white pine.

North Fork Umatilla Trail begins near a roadside viewpoint and provides the nearest access to North Fork Umatilla Wilderness, a few miles west of the highway. The wilderness, which you'll see from the overlook, is nestled in the North Fork Umatilla River's narrow valley. Despite some steep, timbered cliffs, it is popular with day hikers and horseback riders.

Nearby, the tiny community of Tollgate spreads along the highway and around small, private Langdon Lake. Woodward Campground's eighteen tent/trailer sites serves as a base for trail bikers and provides public access to Langdon Lake for stocked rainbow trout fishing. Target Meadows Campground, two miles east of the highway, offers sixteen tent/trailer and four tent sites.

Jubilee Lake, twelve miles east of Tollgate via Forest Road 6413, is a favorite of boaters, waterskiers, swimmers and trout fishermen. At Jubilee Campground, you can overnight camp on one of the forty-seven tent/trailer or the four tent sites at 4,800 feet. The campground is surrounded by magnificent forests and mountain peaks.

The four miles between Tollgate and Spout Springs Ski area is a popular snowmobile route lined with blown down trees, which were leveled by a rare windstorm several years ago. Most of Spout Springs eleven ski runs serve beginning and intermediate skiers. There are also eleven miles of cross-country trails, which become hiking and mountain biking routes in summer. A chalet-styled lodge with a cafe operates year around.

A mile east of Spout Springs the drive crosses the Blue Mountains summit at 5,158 feet. You can spend the night near the summit in seven tent sites at Woodland campground. From the summit, you wind down the mountain on a steep grade through a deep, thickly forested canyon.

After about twelve miles, you exit the Umatilla National Forest and turn west on Summerville Road. Summerville, four miles south, was an Indian and Oregon Trail campsite. Established in 1865, it enjoyed a rowdy history with numerous saloons, twenty-four-hour poker games, and stagecoach holdups.

On the remaining thirteen miles to La Grande, field crops and low hills fill the eastern horizon. The forested slopes of the Blue Mountains rise from the valley floor to the west.

36 OREGON TRAIL ROUTE
Interstate 84

General description: A 190-mile drive on paved roads through desert, grasslands, and over the Blue Mountains while following the route of the Oregon Trail.

Special attractions: Oregon Trail ruts, campsites and Interpretive Center, State Parks, Blue Mountains, wildlife observation, historic sites, camping, boating.

Location: Northeastern Oregon between Ontario and Echo.

Drive route names and numbers: Interstate 84, U.S. Highway 30, Oregon Highway 86, Echo Road.

Travel season: All year. Deadman's Pass can become extremely hazardous in winter due to snow, ice, and steep grade.

Camping: Three state park campgrounds, one with full hookups, one with electricity, and one with primitive sites. One Bureau of Land Management campground with tables, fire rings, vault or flush toilets, and drinking water.

Services: All services in Ontario, Baker City, La Grande, and Pendleton. Limited services at Farewell Bend, Huntington, North Powder, and Echo.

Nearby attractions: Lake Owyhee Scenic Drive, Eagle Cap Wilderness, Wallowa Hells Canyon Loop Drive, La Grande-Ukiah-Weston Scenic Loop, Elkhorn Scenic Byway.

For more information: La Grande-Union County Chamber of Commerce, 1912 4th St., No.200, La Grande, OR 97850, (541) 963-8588, (800) 848-9969. Baker County Visitors and Convention Bureau, 490 Campbell St., Baker, OR 97814, (541) 523-3356, (800) 523-1235 (USA). Wallowa-Whitman National Forest, 1550 Dewey Ave., P.O. Box 907, Baker City, OR 97814, (541) 523-6391.

The drive: From 1841 through 1884, the Oregon Trail was the major east-west route from the Idaho border to Portland. Interstate 84 parallels and overlaps portions of the trail between Farewell Bend State Park and Pendleton.

The original trail followed centuries-old Indian paths that had been used by early explorers and fur traders, and wove over mountain passes, through valleys, and across rivers formed by more than 200 million years of geologic activity. The shape of the land has dictated routes of travel from the dawn of man to today.

From Ontario to Ladd Canyon, south of La Grande, the highway crosses flat desert, wide valleys, rolling sand, gray and brown hills and mountains. It is a land of little water, covered with sparse pale grass sprinkled with juniper trees. Between La Grande and Pendleton, the route climbs high into the Blue Mountains then abruptly descends to flat fields.

In summer, temperatures jump to the high 80s, 90s and over 100 degrees. Winter days drop to zero, but usually average between thirty-nine and forty-nine degrees. Spring days usually average around sixty-five degrees, and autumn about seventy degrees.

OREGON TRAIL ROUTE
Interstate 84

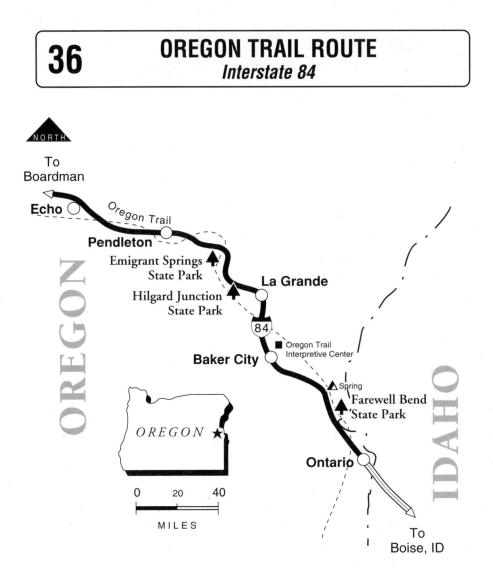

To Boardman

Echo ○

Oregon Trail

Pendleton ○

Emigrant Springs State Park ▲

Hilgard Junction State Park ▲

La Grande ○

84

■ Oregon Trail Interpretive Center

Baker City ○

▲ Spring

Farewell Bend State Park ▲

Ontario ○

OREGON ★

0   20   40

MILES

To Boise, ID

OREGON

IDAHO

The Oregon Trail entered the state about nine miles south of Ontario near Nyssa, meandered west, and extended north over rolling hills. About twenty-three miles north of Ontario, it entered Farewell Bend. Information boards at Ontario State Park, Exit 374, highlight the history of migration and life on the trail. The park is on the banks of the Malheur River and offers a pleasant, shaded spot for a picnic.

Seventeen miles north of Ontario, Interstate 84 passes tilted and faulted formations of fifteen-million-year-old rocks. Climbing a long hill, the Snake River spreads in a gently curving bay to the east.

At Farewell Bend, Exit 353, wagon trains saw the last of the Snake River, which they had followed for 320 miles. Here they rested and grazed livestock before attempting the mountainous terrain ahead.

The large, lake-like river, shaded picnic grounds and ninety-four-site campground with fifty-three electrical hookups, remains a popular site for catfish and bass fishing, waterskiers, jetboaters, and swimmers. Hotels, restaurants, and gas stations are situated along the one-mile entrance road.

From Farewell Bend, the Oregon Trail headed northeast over a low divide and into the Burnt River drainage to Huntington, then meandered along eastern ridges forty miles north to Flagstaff Hill. Huntington, a former frontier and cattle-shipping town, offers food, gas, and a BLM campground with fourteen sites and drinking water.

North of Farewell Bend, Interstate 84 enters the Pacific Mountain time zone and cuts through the almost 200-million-year-old sedimentary rocks of the Lower Burnt River Canyon. The rocks provided raw materials and jobs for 145 people at Lime's cement plant. About five miles north, on the highway's west side, you'll see the gray, terraced hillsides and buildings left abandoned when the plant closed in 1980.

Interstate 84 emerges from the Burnt River Canyon about four miles north. The canyon was a major obstacle for wagon trains, and it took them five to six days to cross the fifteen miles, which you will travel in a few minutes from Farewell Bend. The rigors of traveling this section are detailed at the Weatherby Rest Area at exit 335. Hills, rocks, and flatlands of the Conner Creek Fault, near the exit, are fragments of 170- to 280-million year-old-ocean floors and islands that were broken, fused together, and moved here when tectonic plates shifted.

The sandstone is processed into cement at Durkee's Ash Grove plant. Between Durkee, exit 330, and Pleasant Valley, exit 315, the Oregon Trail and Interstate 84 merge for about fifteen miles. The banks of the Burnt River near Durkee often yield colorful fire opals. Pleasant Valley was settled by Oregon Trail farmers.

The highway weaves between Iron Mountain, an ancient volcanic neck, and Elkhorn Ridge, a fragment of a 200-million-year-old ocean floor. As you continue to Baker City and La Grande, several western peaks dominate the horizon. From south to north they are: Elkhorn, 8,922 feet; Rock Creek Butte, 9,097 feet; Hunt Mountain, 8,232 feet; Red Mountain, 8,920 feet; and Twin Mountains, 8,920 feet.

North of Pleasant Valley you top a 3,998-foot summit and continue on to Baker City, while the Oregon Trail skirts mountain slopes and heads north to Flagstaff Hill.

By taking exit 302 at Baker City, seven miles east on Highway 86, you can see original Oregon Trail ruts at the base of 3,800 foot Flagstaff Hill. The Oregon Trail Interpretive Center, at the summit, features a gallery with life-sized figures in scenes depicting trail life. Six major trail themes are interpreted through diary excerpts, photographs and audio visual displays. From the observation platform, you have a magnificent view of the valley, mountains, and Baker City.

Interstate 84 heads north from Baker City, flanked on the east by sagebrush flatlands and the distant, white peaks of the Wallowa Mountains.

By contrast, the glacier carved Elkhorns rise behind green pasturelands to the west. The highway crosses The Oregon Trail at a rest area fourteen miles north of Baker and stays on or near the route through Pendleton.

Near the rest area, immigrants bartered with itinerant traders and found food and water for livestock. A few miles north, when you cross the 45th parallel, you are half way between the Equator and North Pole. At North Powder, the trail passes through town along E. Street. Three miles northeast on Highway 237 a monument commemorates the first recorded birth on December 3, 1811, of a white child born west of the Rockies. From the North Powder exit, you can travel west to the Anthony Lakes Ski Area and U.S. Highway 30, which overlaps portions of the trail near Haines.

The red and yellow steaks that you'll see in Interstate 84's embankments are layers of individual Columbia River basalt lava flows. Numerous eruptions between six and seventeen million years ago covered approximately 45,000-square miles of Oregon, Washington, and Idaho.

The hills open into Ladd Canyon, which gave up its lush green grass to wagon train live stock. Between 1843 and 1859, more than 350,000 settlers entered the Grande Ronde Valley near the Charles H. Reynolds Rest Area, at the canyon's southern edge.

By taking exit 268 to Foothill Road and traveling east two miles you can visit Hot Lake, another refreshment point on the trail. In the 1920s, Hot Lake was a famous resort. Although it no longer operates, and the eight acre lake is covered with lily pads, the main brick building still stands and is listed on the National Register of Historic Places.

You can follow the general route of the Oregon Trail west on Foothill Road, through Ladd Management Wildlife Area, where you may see deer and migrating waterfowl to a trail campsite at Bernie Park in southwest La Grande. From the park, the trail continued west on Avenue C to Fourth Street, then headed over forested hills to the south Bank of the Grande Ronde River.

Leaving La Grande on Interstate 84, you travel northwest about two miles through the rugged canyon of the Grande Ronde River to exit 252 and Hilgard Junction State Park where Oregon Trail travelers took advantage of the abundant water supply, before climbing the Blue Mountain slopes. Looking across the picnic area, campground, and Grande Ronde River, you can see cliffs where wagons, cattle and horses were lowered by ropes to the meadows below. Information boards highlight the route of the Oregon Trail from Hilgard Junction to the summit of the Blue Mountains, about fifteen miles northwest and 1,200 feet higher. The park contains eighteen primitive campsites and is a popular rafting and trout fishing spot.

Continuing northwest you'll follow essentially the same route as the wagon trains by traveling on forested ridges overlooking the narrow, twisting river canyon. After two miles, the highway crosses a small segment of 1.38-million-acre Wallowa-Whitman National Forest. During the next ten miles as the elevation increases, trees become shorter and the trunks smaller. Alpine meadows break the forest's continuity.

Reaching the Blue Mountains' summit, at 4,193 feet, the route passes

Dioramas, diary excerpts, and other exhibits interpret six major themes of pioneer life at the Oregon Trail Interpretive Center near Baker City.

Meacham where several immigrant graves are situated and you can see the deep ruts along short walking trails near the summit. At Emigrant Springs, exit 234, forest, springs, and meadows provided ready supplies of firewood, water, wild game, and grass for livestock. An Oregon Trail exhibit covers disasters and hazards, death and disease, and the importance of horses and oxen to pioneer travel. The state park includes a stone Oregon Trail monument dedicated by Warren G. Harding in 1923, a group picnic area, and meeting hall. Although the springs were destroyed by highway and pipeline construction, the park still offers camping at eighteen full hookup and thirty-three tent sites in a thick ponderosa, western larch, and Douglas fir Forest. From Squaw Creek Lookout north of the campground, you have a good view of Squaw Creek Canyon.

About four miles west, you enter the southern section of the Umatilla Indian Reservation, which was established in 1856. Deadman's Pass Rest Area, at exit 228, straddles the highway in two sections. At the southern segment, accessible by a tunnel under Interstate 84, you can see original Oregon Trail ruts by going through a gate and up a short trail. Information boards explain the trails numerous side routes. The pass was named after four freighters who were killed near here by Indians in 1878.

At Deadman's Pass, the highway starts six miles of six percent downgrade. Slower speeds are recommended even in the best of weather; winter weather can make this stretch extremely dangerous. The winding road has a brake-check area and two- runaway truck ramps. From a viewpoint, about 1.5 miles below the summit, your panoramic view includes the Cascade and Blue mountains, rumpled hills covered with forest and hazy grasslands, and a checkerboard of green, yellow and brown fields. At the mountain's base, the route leaves the Umatilla Indian Reservation and passes the turnoff to the Walla Walla Trail, which leads north to Whitman Mission in Washington state.

Rodeos and woolen mills have made Pendleton famous. The rodeo's memorable moments are preserved at the Pendleton Round-Up Hall of Fame, and you can also tour the woolen mills and shop for bargains in their sales room.

West of Pendleton, the trail veers southwest across twenty miles of wheat and farmland to Echo where tours of the ruts and an archaeological dig at the site of Fort Henrietta can be arranged through City Hall. The Fort was established as a Umatilla Indian Agency, destroyed during the Indian Wars of 1855 and rebuilt as a military stockade. You can reach Echo either by exit 193 to Echo Road or by continuing about twelve miles west of Pendleton on Interstate 84 and turning south at the Stanfield Rest Area.

37 IMNAHA RIVER-HAT POINT OVERLOOK

General description: A fifty-eight-mile drive on paved and dirt roads through scenic canyons and into the mountains of the Hells Canyon National Recreation Area.

Special attractions: Joseph, Wallowa Lake State Park, Wallowa-Whitman National Forest, Wild and Scenic Imnaha River, Hells Canyon National Recreation Area, Hat Point Overlook, North America's deepest gorge, Snake River.

Location: Northeastern Oregon between Enterprise and Hat Point.

Drive route names and numbers: Oregon Highway 82, Imnaha Road, forest service Road 4240.

Travel season: Forest Road 4240 to Hat Point is usually open from July through October. Oregon Highway 82 and Imnaha Road remain open all year.

Camping: One state park campground with full hookups, four U.S. Forest Service campgrounds with tables, fire rings, and pit or vault toilets.

Services: All services in Enterprise and Joseph. Limited services in Imnaha.

Nearby attractions: Hells Canyon Wilderness, Eagle Cap Wilderness, La Grande-Wallowa-Hells Canyon-Baker Scenic Loop Drive.

For more information: Wallowa County Chamber of Commerce, 107 S.W. 1st, P.O. Box 427, Enterprise, OR 97828, (541) 426-4622, (800) 585-4121. Wallowa-Whitman National Forest, 1550 Dewey Ave., P.O. Box 907, Baker City, OR 97814, (541) 523-6391. Eagle Cap Ranger District, 88401 Hwy. 82, Enterprise, OR 97828, (541) 426-4978. Hells Canyon National Recreation Area, 88401 Hwy. 82, Enterprise, OR 97828, (541) 426-4978.

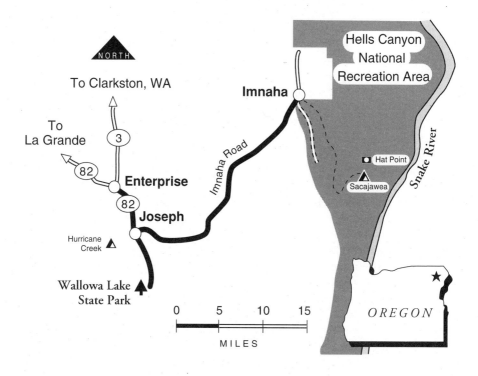

The drive: Beginning in Enterprise at 3,757 feet elevation, the drive travels the first fourteen miles through level farm country framed by the magnificent Wallowa Mountains. After descending into a rugged canyon for twenty-one miles, the pavement ends at the tiny community of Imnaha. The final twenty-four miles to Hat Point climbs to 6,982 feet on a narrow, rough, and rocky dirt road. The scenery is spectacular as the road clings to cliffs, weaves through forest, and winds by deep gorges, sheer cliffs, hills, and mountains. For many this final segment has an irresistible, almost mystical allure. Be forewarned, however. The forest service recommends 2.5 hours travel time one way, and that doesn't include sightseeing stops. If you value your vehicle's undercarriage, do not attempt this with a sports car or other low-clearance vehicles. Also, sharp turns and the one-lane road bed make it unsuitable for trailers and motorhomes. Leave your boat trailer at home or in Imnaha, for there is no place to launch it along the way.

Summer temperatures reach the high eighties in lower elevations and will be somewhat cooler at Hat Point. Winters bring significant amounts of snow as temperatures range from the mid-twenties to the low forties. Spring days average between sixty-one and seventy-one degrees, and autumn temperatures range from sixty-four to seventy-seven degrees.

Before leaving Enterprise, you may wish to stop at the Wallowa-Whitman National Forest Visitor Center one mile west of town on Highway 82. It offers displays on Hells Canyon Recreation Area and the Wallowa Mountains, plus maps and camping information. If you plan to drive the Hat Point segment, check on road conditions.

Joseph, four miles east, is a gateway to Hells Canyon and the Wallowa Mountains. During the 1980s the town of 1,135 became a mecca for artists. Many of the turn-of-the Century buildings have been converted into shops, boutiques, and studios for sculptors, potters, painters, and photographers. Valley Bronze of Oregon has acquired a national reputation for its bronzes, silver, sterling, and stainless steel sculptures. Foundry tours show you the production process from artists' clay models to the finished castings. They range from figurine size to several stories high installations for public buildings and parks.

If you are camping, you can choose between ten tent sites at the forest service's Hurricane Creek Campground, four miles southwest of Joseph on Forest Road 8205 or 121 full hookups and eighty-nine tent sites at Wallowa Lake State Park, six miles south of town on Highway 82.

The lake, framed by the towering glacial peaks of the Wallowa Mountains and a mixed forest of white pine, ponderosa, and spruce, offers one of Oregon's most exquisite scenes. Easily accessible from Highway 82, which hugs the northern and eastern shoreline, it is the hub for recreation that includes the state park, a resort, a mountain tramway and hikes into the 200,416- acre Eagle Cap Wilderness. Anglers pull trophy-sized rainbow trout, large catfish, kokanee, and mackinaws out of the water in summer and through winter ice. You can also waterski, boat, swim, and enjoy the magnificent surroundings from rented rowboats, canoes, and paddle bikes.

The region around the lake is often called the Little Switzerland of America. The Wallowa Lake Tramway has the steepest vertical lift for a four-passenger gondola in North America, and from lake level at 4,400 feet it takes you on a spectacular fifteen minute ride to the 8,200-foot summit of Mount Howard. At the top, the spectacular view encompasses the lake, snow-capped mountains of the Eagle Cap Wilderness, forested foothills, and pastoral farmlands.

Taking Imnaha Road east from Joseph, you travel through lush pastures of grazing cattle, white board fences, and distant farm buildings situated at the base of the Wallowa Mountains that rise majestically in steep steps from the valley floor. Ferguson Ridge Ski Area, four miles south of the highway, offers winter access to the mountains with a network of cross-country trails.

After ten miles, you weave down into a deep canyon with forested hills, past a few abandoned sheds, and along the side of the first of several creeks. Gradually, the forest disappears, and the gorge narrows to steep basalt walls. Watch for cattle, sheep, and horses grazing on the greenery near the creek, for much of the wayside is not fenced.

Most of the twisted, massive rock walls you pass through came from volcanos that erupted on Pacific Ocean islands more than 300 million years

The banks of the Wild and Scenic Imnaha River was once the home of Chief Joseph and the Nez Perce Indians.

ago. When the eruptions stopped, the region lowered into the ocean and sediment was deposited on the submerged platforms. Later geologic activity created basins that filled with sediments from surrounding streams and volcanic explosions of molten rock which crystallized into granite. During and after these geologic processes, the rocks folded, faulted, and tilted. Wind, rain, and ice continue to deepen ravines that start on hillsides and converge by roadside creeks. With every twist and turn of the road, a new vista unfolds, and there are ample wide spots and turns to stop and photograph the surroundings. Due to rugged cliff and steep embankments, opportunities for hiking and roadside treks are limited.

About five miles east of the canyon's entrance, the route begins riding the crest of low dry grassland hills and weaves by more converging mountain ridges and through stands of ponderosa pine. In late spring, the grass has an unusual moss brown and green velvet sheen. Near Imnaha you enter Wallowa-Whitman National Forest and the Hells Canyon National Recreation Area. At 2.38 million acres, Wallowa-Whitman is Oregon's largest national forest and stretches east into Idaho. The national recreation area includes the Hells Canyon Wilderness and the Rapid and Snake River segments of the National Wild and Scenic River System.

At Imnaha, thirty miles west of Joseph, the dirt road to Hat Point begins where the pavement ends at the community's sole restaurant-store. Look across the road, and you can see the nationally designated Wild and Scenic Imnaha River flowing out of the wilderness. It was from along the Imnaha's banks that Chief Joseph gathered the Nez Perce tribe in May of 1877 and began their famous fighting retreat to Canada, which ended in his defeat at Bear Paw Battlefield in Montana.

In the first five miles from Imnaha, you'll climb 2,655 feet. At Five Mile Viewpoint, you have the first of many views of the Imnaha Canyon, Wallowa Mountains, and Sheep Creek Divide—a razor sharp ridge that extends for miles.

Afterward, the road levels out and into ponderosa, lodgepole, and white pine. Watch the small meadows for Indian paintbrush, lupine, and several species of butterflies. You may hear the hoot of a horned owl and see mountain grouse and valley quail flutter from trees to rocks. Bobcat, cougar, and black bear also inhabit these woodlands but are rarely sighted.

At 9.7 miles, you'll see several small rock cairns at Monument Ridge, which are thought to be boundary markers. Historians are still debating whether they were built by Indians or sheepherders. About one mile further, the road crosses a narrow ridge overlooking the walls of Imnaha and Horse Creek canyons. At 17.1 miles, a short loop leads 0.8 mile to Granny Viewpoint where you can see the Imnaha River winding as a thin blue ribbon through pale yellow ridges 6,345 feet below. Saddle Creek Viewpoint and campground at mile 18.8 overlooks Hells Canyon, which is only accessible by foot, pack string, or boat.

Several marked trails begin near Hat Point's summit. Most are two to three miles long and lead down off the ridge into the gorge. Hat Point and Sacajawea campgrounds, 0.5 mile north of Hat Point, offer a total of ten tent sites. You'll need to bring all food and beverages as there are no services or running water beyond Imnaha. Short side roads near the point lead to spectacular overlooks of deep valleys, natural amphitheaters, caves, and endless vistas of ridges, hills, and ravines.

From Hat Point, you have the thrill of looking into North America's deepest gorge and seeing the Snake River more than one mile (6,982 feet) below you. Looking across the canyon into Idaho, you can see the craggy peaks of the Seven Devils Mountains. As you scan this land of serrated ridges, deep gorges, sweeping natural saddles, and plateaus, watch for elk in the valleys. Make sure to bring binoculars, for mountain goats may be seen on distant peaks and big-horned sheep on the high slopes.

For an even more encompassing view, you can climb a 100-foot-high forest service lookout tower that is manned during summer. A trail begins in the picnic area, meanders through wildflower meadows, and winds down the cliff to the canyon below.

On the return, you have a second opportunity to view the spectacular scenery. Because of the rumpled topography and twisting road, much of it will look very different from when you saw it driving to Hat Point.

38 WALLOWAS, HELLS CANYON LOOP

General description: A 270-mile scenic loop on paved roads through arid desert, lush farmlands, rugged canyons and forested mountains.

Special attractions: Historic sites, Joseph, Wallowa Lake State Park, Wallowa-Whitman National Forest, Wild and Scenic Rivers, Hells Canyon National Recreation Area, Oxbow Dam, Oregon Trail Interpretive Center, Eagle Cap Wilderness, wildlife observation, camping, fishing, hiking.

Location: Northeastern Oregon between La Grande, Enterprise, Copperfield, and Baker City.

Drive route names and numbers: Oregon Highway 82, Imnaha Road, U.S. Forest Service Road 39, Oregon Highway 86, Interstate 84, Oregon Highway 203.

Travel season: With the exception of U.S. Forest Service Road 39, all routes are open all year. Forest Service Road 39 usually opens about mid-June and closes because of snow in late October or early November.

Camping: Three state park campgrounds, two with primitive sites, and one with full hookups. Ten forest service campgrounds with tables, fire rings, vault or flush toilets. Some with drinking water.

Services: All services in La Grande, Enterprise, Joseph, Richland, and Baker City. Limited services in Elgin, Wallowa, Halfway, Copperfield.

Nearby attractions: Hells Canyon Wilderness, Hat Point, La Grande-Ukiah-Weston Scenic Loop, Elkhorn Scenic Byway, Farewell Bend State Park.

For more information: La Grande-Union County Chamber of Commerce, 1912 4th St., No. 200, La Grande, OR 97850, (541) 963-8588, (800) 848-9969. Baker County Visitors and Convention Bureau, 490 Campbell St., Baker, OR 97814, (541) 523-3356, (800) 523-1235 (USA). Wallowa County Chamber of Commerce, 107 S.W. 1st, P.O. Box 427, Enterprise, OR 97828, (541) 426-4622. Wallowa-Whitman National Forest, 1550 Dewey Ave., P.O. Box 907, Baker City, OR 97814, (541) 523-6391. Hells Canyon National Recreation Area and Eagle Cap Ranger District, 88401 Hwy. 82, Enterprise, OR 97828, (541) 426-4978.

The drive: From La Grande to Joseph, the route makes several crossings of the Wallowa and Grande Ronde rivers as it winds through commercial croplands, dairy farms, and a scenic canyon. Turning south on Forest Service Road 39, the drive extends through fifty-four miles of Wallowa-Whitman National Forest and the Hells Canyon National Recreation Area. With the road climbing mountains, dipping into canyons, and swirling around ridges, you'll see the forest from a variety of vantage points. Highway 86 also climbs mountains as it weaves west to Baker City through desert and arid grasslands along curves that are generally long, graceful, and open onto spacious vistas. The final portion on Highway 203 is divided between desert and forest. Because of the length, multiple attractions, and slow sections, plan a two-day trip with an overnight in either the Enterprise or Baker City areas. Traffic varies from light to heavy.

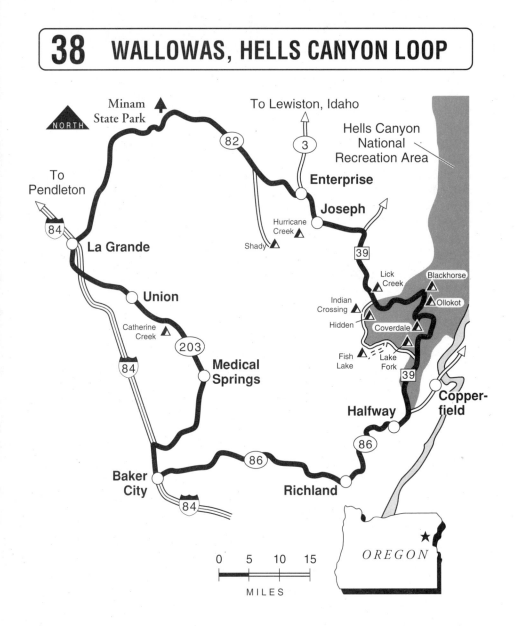

In the Oxbow, Baker City, and La Grande areas, summer temperatures rise into the 80s, 90s, and over 100 degrees. At Enterprise and in the Hells Canyon Recreation Area, it will usually be ten to fifteen degrees cooler. Winters are cold and snowy and temperatures may range from near zero to the mid-forties.

From La Grande, Highway 82 heads east through flat fields and small hamlets dominated by gray metal grain elevators. This area bills itself as the Grass Seed Capital of the World and also produces commercial crops of wheat and barley.

Elgin, about twenty miles east, was settled in 1882. The city hall and renovated opera house are listed on the National Register of Historic Places. Five miles east of town, look south from Highway 82, and you'll see an old log barn. It served as an 1878-settlers fort for anticipated attacks by Native Americans.

As the road climbs the 3,638-foot summit of Minam Hill, it affords continuing views of the valley sprinkled with farms, pastures, dry grass-lands, and the forested mountains of the Eagle Cap Wilderness to the south. Entering a canyon, steep walls rise in basalt benches, and a swatch of green oaks and willows, split by the Wild and Scenic Minam and Wallowa rivers, fills slopes of low hills and ridges covered with fir and ponderosa pine. You can enjoy trout fishing, rafting, and camping from twelve primitive sites at Minam State Park, two miles north of the highway. Wallowa Wayside offers a scenic roadside picnicking and fishing spot.

Exiting the canyon, the road winds through foothills then heads in a straight line across flatland dairy farms as it crosses the Wallowa and Lostine rivers. En route it splits the settlements of Wallowa and Lostine. Boundary Campground, nine miles south of Wallowa on Forest service Road 8250, offers eight tent sites and a trail into the Eagle Cap Wilderness. Four additional forest service Campgrounds, eleven to seventeen miles south of Lostine are accessible by Forest Road 8210. They have a total of thirty-six tent sites and are situated in the Eagle Cap Wilderness and near the Wild and Scenic Lostine River.

East of Lostine, farms set on vast meadows at the base of crumpled mountain slopes with silhouetted ridges of buff brown, mossy green, light and dark blue. The Wallowa-Whitman National Forest headquarters observation deck, one mile west of Enterprise, offers the best view of the farms and rugged peaks. Exhibits highlight the forest's geology, wildlife, and multiple uses.

At Joseph, four miles east, many early 1900s buildings have been converted into artists studios. At Valley Bronze of Oregon you can take a foundry tour through the production process from artists' clay models to finished castings.

Campers can choose between ten tent sites at the forest service's Hurri-cane Creek Campground, four miles southwest of Joseph on Forest Road 8205, or 121 full hookups and eighty-nine tent sites at Wallowa Lake State Park, six miles south on Highway 82.

The lake, at the base of the towering glacial peaks of the Wallowa Mountains, is one of Oregon's scenic jewels, and the centerpiece for the state park, a resort, and a mountain tramway to the 8,200-foot summit of Mount Howard. Recreation includes fishing, waterskiing, boating, and swimming.

Before leaving Joseph, make sure you have plenty of gas, for there are no services for the next sixty-nine miles. Ten miles east, you turn south off Imnaha Road and onto Forest Service Road 39. As you drive the fifty-four miles, weaving through the thick tree-lined corridor of tamarack, spruce, Douglas, white and red fir, watch for some of the 350 species of wildlife that inhabit the region. You may see deer, elk, several species of owls, hoary marmots, pileated woodpeckers, and golden eagles.

The drive starts with snow-capped peaks on the western horizon and quickly enters 2.38 million acre Wallowa Whitman National Forest. It stretches virtually unbroken as an ocean of tree-filled valleys, ridges, hills and mountains from here to the junction of Highway 86. At about fifteen miles, after passing Lick Creek Campground with twelve sites, you enter the Hells Canyon Recreation Area. Its 652,488 acres extend east across the Snake River into Idaho's Seven Devils Mountains.

Following a steep downgrade through eleven miles of canyon highlighted with brilliant red rock outcroppings, the highway reaches a junction with Forest Road 3955. It leads twenty-eight miles northeast along the rugged Imnaha River. This segment of the river, which flows alongside your route for several miles, has been designated a Wild and Scenic River.

Logs in Gumboat Creek, near the junction, were victims of the spruce bark beetle. They provide a habitat for fish and other aquatic wildlife and protect a riparian zone from grazing cattle. Blackhorse Campground, with seventeen tent-trailer sites and Ollokot, with twelve, serve rainbow trout and steelhead fishermen, whitewater rafters, and backpackers heading into the Eagle Cap Wilderness and Recreation Area. Four campgrounds, with a total of fifty sites, are also situated a few miles west on Forest Road 3960.

For the easiest access to the Hells Canyon's rim, take McGraw Lookout Road east about five miles. The gravel road, near Ollokot, leads to a viewpoint overlooking the deep gorge, the Snake River, and the mountains to the east.

Approximately fifteen miles south, Road 39 levels and straightens as it passes a rest area with information boards and area maps. A National Recreation Trail starts nearby and follows Steep Creek into the mountains. About five miles south, you exit the recreation area near Lake Fork Campground, which has ten units.

Reaching Highway 86, you can see more of Hells Canyon on a seven-mile side trip to Copperfield and Oxbow Dam. Watch for cattle running free on roadbeds and on the round, sandy foothills.

Oxbow Dam is one of three hydroelectric projects that have tamed the turbulent Snake River leaving tranquil lakes with a surface area of 19,000 acres for boating, fishing, and water sports. The others are Brownlee, twelve miles south, and Hells Canyon Dam, twenty-three miles north of Oxbow. At Oxbow, you'll find trailer and tent campgrounds with hookups and boat-launching facilities. Gas, groceries and lodging are available at Pine Creek, one mile west on Highway 86. By taking Snake River Road north from Oxbow, you can make a brief detour into Idaho while enjoying the rugged, steep walls and Snake River. The road ends at Hells Canyon Dam, where a park overlooks the Wild and Scenic portion of the Snake and is a departure point for jet boat and float excursions.

Returning west on Highway 86, you'll find gas, food, and lodging at the farming community of Halfway. Wildflowers are so abundant that a local business supplies wild floral displays to stores and boutiques nationwide. Pine Ranger Station, west of town, dispenses national forest maps and campground information.

Near Enterprise and Joseph, Oregon Highway 82 passes by pastoral farms, pastures filled with cattle, and the majestic Wallowa Mountains.

During the thirteen miles to Richland, Highway 86 climbs to 3,653 feet and overlooks vast expanses of flat fields, rolling hills, and distant rounded buff-colored mountain slopes dappled with sagebrush and junipers. Richland sits in flat, lush pastureland, surrounded by buckskin mountains. At Hewitt Park, south of town, you can camp beside a small lake and enjoy the shade of larch and poplars while fishing for bass, perch, catfish, and bluegill.

A few miles west, the Powder River meanders along the road, through a shallow canyon, and by a collapsed mountain slope that blocked the stream and highway several years ago. In late summer, the river is mirror smooth, but it can be a swift, rushing stream when full. About fourteen miles east of Interstate 84, the river bends north as the road tops a plateau and continues west through grazing land and hay fields.

The Oregon Trail Interpretive Center, at 3,800-foot Flagstaff Hill, marks the spot where pioneer wagon trains first saw the Baker Valley and Blue Mountains. A gallery, with life-sized figures, interprets life on the trail. From the observation platform, the view encompasses the valley, mountains, Baker City ten miles south, and paths leading to the original trail ruts.

Seven miles west, the route turns north onto Interstate 84 and travels six miles to exit 298 and Highway 203. After a few acres of grasslands, the road rides a series of ridges through a desert of sage and bitterbrush, crosses the Powder River, drops into an oasis-like valley of lush pasturelands, and arrives eighteen miles northeast at Medical Springs. An abandoned outdoor pool, log cabin, and a former forty-room hotel stand next to each other as a reminder of the days when this was a health resort.

Medical Springs marks a transition from desert to forest. With the magnificent Blue Mountains ahead and the Eagle Cap Wilderness to the east, you top a 4,178-foot summit four miles north and briefly reenter Wallowa-

Whitman National Forest.

A few miles further, Catherine Creek State Park lies in a gorge with steep lava walls, its picnic grounds and eighteen primitive campsites shaded by ponderosa pines and spruce. The shallow creek is a great spot to take children innertubing and picnicking.

About mid-way between the Park and Union, eight miles west, the forest ends at the edge of grassy farmlands. At Union on a short walk around town, you'll see a variety of Victorian architecture displayed in Gothic, Renaissance, Revival, Mansard, Queen Anne, Foursquare, and T-shaped buildings.

Hot Lake, a few miles northeast, was set aside by Indians as neutral ground and became known as The Valley of Peace. Later, its mineral waters rejuvenated Oregon Trail travelers and were the major attraction of a 1920s resort. You can see the eight-acre lake covered with lily pads and the main brick building that is listed on the National Register of Historic Places.

As you follow the route of the Oregon Trail north through Ladd Management Wildlife Area—watch for deer and a variety of migratory birds. The drive concludes twelve miles north in La Grande.

39 JOHN DAY FOSSIL BEDS LOOP

General description: A 119-mile loop through the colorful gorge of the Sheep Rock Unit of John Day Fossil Beds National Monument, and through northeastern Oregon orchards and mountains.

Special attractions: Sheep Rock Unit of John Day Fossil Beds National Monument, Picture Gorge, Kam Wah Chung Museum, Malheur National Forest, North, South and Main Forks of John Day River, colorful rock formations.

Location: Northeastern Oregon between John Day and Monument.

Drive route names and numbers: U.S. Highway 26, Oregon Highway 19, County Road 402, U.S. Highway 395.

Travel season: Routes are open all year. The national forest campground closes from October 15 through May 30.

Camping: One state park campground with electricity and hiker/biker sites; Two Bureau of Land Management campgrounds with primitive sites; One national forest service campground with tables, fire rings, vault or pit toilets. Several private RV parks.

Services: All services in John Day. Limited services in Mount Vernon, Dayville, Monument, and Long Creek.

Nearby attractions: Strawberry Mountain Wilderness, Black Canyon Wilderness, John Day Fossil Beds Painted Hills Unit, Wild and Scenic John Day River, Monument Rock Wilderness, Ritter Hot Springs.

For more information: Grant County Chamber of Commerce, 281 West Main St., John Day, OR 97845, (541) 575-0547, (800) 769-5664. John Day Fossil Beds National Monument, 420 West Main St., John Day, OR 97845,

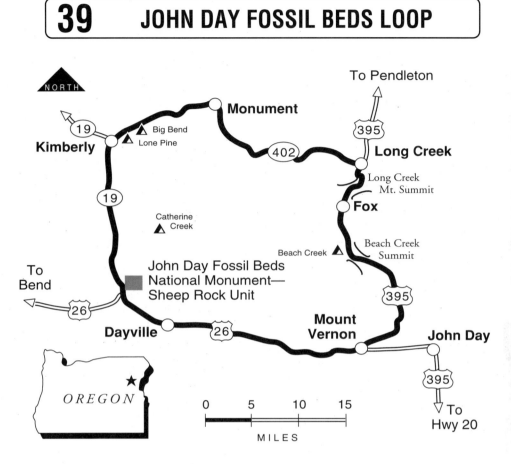

(541) 575-0721. Malheur National Forest, P.O. Box 909, John Day, OR 97845, (541) 575-1731.

The drive: Starting in the cattle country of John Day, the drive moves west, then switches to deep canyons of brilliant sandstone and lava as it heads north through the John Day Fossil Beds. Turning east at Kimberly, it follows a mountain ridge overlooking croplands and then returns south through the thick Malheur National Forest. The route crosses three branches of the John Day River several times, and the stream is a continuous presence during the first half of the drive. Although elevation ranges from 1,820 feet near Kimberly to 5,000 feet near Long Creek, grades are gradual with a minimum of curves. Traffic is usually moderate on U.S. Highway 26 and U.S. Highway 395 and light on Oregon Highway 19 and County Road 402.

The weather is characterized by cold winters and hot summers. Winter temperatures average twenty-five degrees to the low thirties and forties. Summer days are usually in the 90- to 100-degree range. Travelers can expect

Picture Gorge in the Sheep Rock Unit of John Day Fossil Beds National Monument exhibits colorful rock formations and contains a fossil record spanning sixty-five million years.

temperatures in the mid- sixties during spring and in the low seventies in fall.

John Day, Grant County's largest town, was named for a Virginia explorer and trapper who came west in 1811 with the William Price Hunt expedition. After becoming separated from the main party near the Snake River, he endured tremendous hardship while wandering across Oregon for nearly a year before reaching Astoria. Although Day's major achievement seems to have been simply surviving, his name has been given to two rivers, a national monument, a region, and a dam.

The Kam Wah Chung and Company Museum in the city park offers a fascinating glimpse into local 1880s Chinese culture. Listed on the National Register of Historic Places, the two story basalt building was constructed as a trading post in 1866-67. It contains thousands of original relics from its days as a combination Chinese fort, general store, pharmacy, doctor's office, temple, and home.

A stop at John Day Fossil Beds National Monument headquarters in town provides an excellent orientation to the drive and the monument, which comprises 14,000 acres in three separate units. Wall-sized information panels describe the geologic history and environmental changes that have taken place during the last sixty-five million years. "The Geologic History of The John Day Country," available for a nominal fee, is an excellent guide keyed to highway markers along the route.

The route follows U.S. Highway 26 west for thirty-eight miles as it parallels the John Day River through a countryside of meadows filled with huge herds of beef and dairy cattle, picturesque barns, and farm buildings.

Flat-topped, terraced and rolling hills with a sparse covering of scattered junipers, sagebrush, and bunchgrass frame the valley. The hills and rimrocks were created by numerous volcanic eruptions which deposited more than 100 feet of ash and lava on the John Day Valley during a 10,000-year period.

Clyde Holliday State Park, six miles west of John Day, offers a hiker/biker camp, thirty electrical hook-ups and fishing for trout and bass from a shaded riverside setting. The brick red basalts and sandstone terraces across the valley were uplifted approximately 1,000 feet forming a parallel step fault.

From nearby Mount Vernon, you can take a side trip southwest to Cedar Grove Botanical Area. It encloses a small grove of Alaska Cedars that are unique to the area and the last remnants of a prehistoric forest.

The main and south forks of the John Day River meet at Dayville. Six miles west of town, the route turns north onto Oregon Highway 19. It crosses Rattlesnake Creek, enters Picture Gorge, and the Sheep Rock Unit of John Day Fossil Beds National Monument.

Picture Gorge's colorful basalt and sandstone cliffs rise nearly 2,000 feet from the river base. Buried in the steep cliffs of the gorge and monument is one of the world's most complete fossil records. It spans the last sixty-five million years of geologic time and is a continuous record of the Age of Mammals—the time between the extinction of the dinosaurs and the beginning of the ice age.

The record indicates that 250 million years ago, this region was an ocean floor. After being covered with lava flows, it was submerged again about 180 million years ago. For the past sixty million years, volcanism, mountain building, and erosion have reshaped the land and changed the climate. Some fifty million years ago, this was a sub-tropical forest.

When the Cascade Mountains were born about thirty-five million years ago, eruptions showered the John Day country with ash. Fossils of more than 100 animals have been found in the beds and indicate that this was once home to saber-toothed cats, rhinoceroses, tapirs, dogs, horses, camels, sloths, peccaries, pronghorns, and ancestors of elephants. The fossil record is the only indication of the existence of extinct oreodonts, bear-dogs, and gomphotheres.

Sheep Rock Overlook, a mile north of the junction, affords an outstanding view of a graceful curve of the lazy John Day River, and the banded brown, yellow, and russet layers of the towering gorge walls. Information boards interpret the landscape twenty-five million years ago and the importance of fossils as indicators of past environments, climate, and plant and animal life. Collecting and removing artifacts is prohibited.

Sheep Rock's Cant Ranch House Visitor Center, nearby, was built in 1917 and is on the National Register of Historic Places. A museum displays fossils of a three-toed horse, rhinoceros bones, and the skull and teeth of a saber-toothed cat. Other rooms are furnished with antiques. In the laboratory, you can watch as fossils are cleaned and prepared for scientific study and future exhibits. Lawns, shaded by locust, willows, cottonwoods, apple and cherry trees, create a restful setting for picnicking and enjoying the scenic river and multi-colored cliffs.

North from the visitor center, the route continues through sheer cliffs banded with layers of mauve, pale greens, sulfur yellows, pinks, and reds. Goose Rock, named for Canada geese that nest at its base, is about 110 million years old. It is impregnated with leaf imprints and pollen grains deposited when it was an undersea channel.

At Blue Basin, a couple miles north, the easy, one-mile-long Island of Time Trail has interpretive plaques and fossil replicas and follows a creek into the blue-green canyons of the John Day Formation. For a longer, more strenuous hike, take the three-mile Overlook Trail. It gains 600 feet on the way to Blue Basin Rim where you have a spectacular view of the barren crumpled ridges of the valley badlands and an ancient 200 million year old landscape.

Cathedral Rock, a mile north, is a striking blend of greens, light and dark sand, and bright reds left by incandescent gas and volcanic debris. This giant bluff literally slid over a mile to its present position and forced the John Day River into a horseshoe bend at its base. A mile north, a hill topped with two prominent red and olive drab ash layers marks its original resting place.

The Foree area, nearby, offers a lovely picnic spot overlooking an eastern meadow, western limestone green fossil beds, and river banks lined with junipers and sagebrush. The 1.4-mile Flood of Fire Trail gently ascends a ridge to a view of the John Day River Valley and surrounding basalt cliffs. The Foree Loop Trail is an easy 0.4-mile hike skirting a basin of blue-green claystone that contain fossils of mammals who lived here twenty-five to thirty million years ago.

Although the Foree area marks the monument's northern boundary, brilliant reds, browns, and blue-green rocks frame the route as it weaves through nut orchards, dairy farms, silver sage-covered dry lands and tall terraced hills. Several volcanic dikes, formed when molten lava solidified in cracks, run through the cliffs as black, pink, and white bands.

From Kimberly's general store, the route follows the John Day River's North Fork fourteen miles northeast to Monument. This segment is at its most colorful and fragrant in spring. After passing a large orchard of cherry, apricot, peach and apple trees, the road opens into sweeping views of clover and mint fields; the river lined with cottonwoods and tall, stark hills sprinkled with boulders, sagebrush, and juniper. You can spend the night in the midst of the pastoral scenery at BLM's Lone Pine Park and Big Bend Park, one and three miles east of Kimberly. Each has four sites.

The north and middle forks of the John Day River meet near the small farming community of Monument. Usually this section has some of the best fishing in the river's system, and you stand a good chance of catching your limit on steelhead, rainbow trout, smallmouth bass, and catfish.

During the next eight miles, you'll gradually climb and wind along a ridge overlooking a valley of sage and junipers, rolling hills punctuated by red rocks, and distant mountains with landslide fans spreading at their base. The most impressive is Sunken Mountain, where a steep valley wall was undercut by stream erosion. A parking area near the jumbled rocks which slid down from near the summit offers a fine view of the area.

Long Creek Mountain, 4.5 miles east is an uplifted basalt block, 1,400 to

1,500 feet thick. You'll see the base of the basalt as you approach the mountain and on the descent into Long Creek.

At Long Creek, the route turns south on U.S. Highway 395, enters Malheur National Forest, and climbs to its highest point of 5,101 feet. From a rest area near the summit, you have a good view of eastern long, rolling, buckskin colored hills and narrow ravines.

The 1.46-million-acre forest features more than 200 miles of trails for hikers, horseback riders, cross-country skiers, and snowmobilers. It is a habitat for Rocky Mountain elk, mule deer, big horn sheep, black bear, bobcat, coyote, wintering bald eagles, and 235 species of birds. Forest streams contain northeast Oregon's largest wild runs of spring chinook salmon and summer steelhead.

After descending to Fox, a rustic mountain community where basalt flows converge from all sides to form a basin, the highway tops Beach Creek Summit at 4,708 feet. Nearby Beach Creek Campground is tucked into thick pine and firs with two tent and three tent/trailer sites.

Soon after, you leave the national forest. The drive continues through the tree-lined corridor for a few miles, descends into a canyon of converging hills, and concludes by coming full-circle at Mount Vernon.

40 ROSEBURG, LOWER UMPQUA RIVER, REEDSPORT

General description: A seventy-three-mile paved two-lane highway through farm and timber lands of the Umpqua River Valley to coastal rain forest and ocean.

Special attractions: Forest and river scenery, fishing, hiking, historic sites, elk observation, Oregon Dunes Recreation Area.

Location: Southwestern Oregon between Sutherlin and Reedsport.

Drive route numbers: Oregon Highway 138, Oregon Highway 38, U.S. Highway 101.

Travel season: The route is open all year. Winter brings icy mornings and evenings. Because many sections are shaded, ice and snow melt slower than in open areas.

Camping: Three Bureau of Land Management campgrounds with tables, fire rings, vault, or pit toilets.

Services: All services at Roseburg, Sutherlin and Reedsport. Limited services at Elkton.

Nearby attractions: Charleston-Seven Devils Loop scenic drive, Southern Oregon Coast, Umpqua Rogue Scenic Byway.

For more information: Roseburg Visitors and Convention Bureau, 410 S.E. Spruce, P.O. Box 1262, Roseburg, OR 97470, (541) 672-9731, (800) 444-9584 (USA). Sutherlin Visitors Center, 1470 W. Central, P.O. Box 327, Sutherlin, OR 97479, (541) 459-5829, (800) 371-5829. Lower Umpqua Chamber of

40 ROSEBURG, LOWER UMPQUA RIVER, REEDSPORT

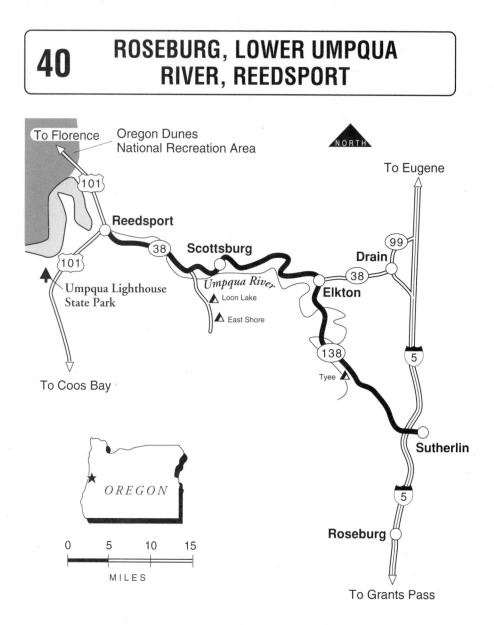

To Florence

Oregon Dunes National Recreation Area

NORTH

To Eugene

Reedsport

101

38 Scottsburg

Drain 99

Umpqua River

38

101

Umpqua Lighthouse State Park

Loon Lake

Elkton

East Shore

To Coos Bay

138

Tyee

5

Sutherlin

OREGON

5

0 5 10 15

Roseburg

MILES

To Grants Pass

Commerce, Hwy. 101 and Hwy. 38, P.O. Box 11, Reedsport, OR 97467, (541) 271-3495, (800) 247-2155.

The drive: Starting at exit 136 in Sutherlin, the drive follows Highway 138 northwest to Elkton, where it takes Highway 38 west to Reedsport. Since the route starts in the Umpqua River Valley and parallels the river to the coast the highway is situated in meadows, canyons, and rolling hills. The Coast Range mountains frame the horizon at the beginning and rise from the roadside as shear cliffs near the end.

The highways have a colorful history. Highway 138 was built after World

War II to meet needs of the local timber industry, which has placed Douglas County second among Oregon counties in producing wood and pulp products. An estimated three-fourths of the incense cedar for the world's lead pencils comes from this region.

Highway 38 began as a route for Hudson's Bay Company trappers and later became the main supply line for southern Oregon gold fields. Along with evidence of timber harvesting and historic sites, the area has lush and varied vegetation. Mileposts start at Elkton for Highway 138 and at Reedsport for Highway 38. Traffic is usually moderate on both highways.

Summer travelers can expect interior temperatures in the high eighties and low nineties, and in the sixty- to seventy-degree range on the coast. Winter temperatures on the coast range from averages of forty-seven to fifty-four degrees, and from forty-four to fifty-seven degrees near Sutherlin. Spring brings temperatures in the sixty-four- to seventy-two-degree range in the interior and in the high fifties on the coast. Autumn temperatures fall between sixty-nine and eighty-three degrees in the Umpqua River Valley and in the mid-sixties on the coast.

To start the drive from Roseburg, take Interstate 5 twelve miles north to exit 136 and turn west. The Sutherlin Visitor's Information Center at the exit has brochures on local tours such as side trips to several wineries. Rochester Covered Bridge (World Guide Number 37-10-04) is situated 0.4 mile east of Highway 138 at milepost 23. The eighty-foot-long bridge features a truss design with curved window tops. At Ford's Pond, south of the highway, you can fish a former log pond planted with blue gill and trout.

During the next nine miles, the highway crosses the Calapooia River, passes a varied landscape of pasturelands, thoroughbred horse farms, and the aftermath of logging activities that began in the 1850s and grew into a giant industry after World War II. Along with hills of old growth timber, you'll see second- and third-generation forests.

From here to the coast, many combinations of alder, black and white Oregon oak, madrone, big-leaf and vine maple mix with Douglas fir. Scotch broom, planted by pioneers to stabilize river banks, blooms bright yellow in spring. In autumn when oaks and maples change colors, the land is aflame with maroons, reds, and yellows.

At milepost 14, the highway bends in a horseshoe curve around the Umpqua River. The river varies from wide to narrow and meanders in and around the roadside for the duration of the drive. Large runs of shad, smallmouth bass, steelhead, coho, and chinook salmon have made this a favorite spot for fishermen, as well as great blue herons and ospreys. Their nests can be seen on snags across the river.

The world's largest black walnut tree stands at the northern end of the bridge, and bracken ferns proliferate on eastern hillsides. Three roads lead from the highway to separate boat ramps, and BLM's Tyee Campground, nearby, contains fifteen sites and a group picnic area on the river's bank.

Three miles north at milepost 11, you'll see sandstone outcroppings. They are ancient seabeds and were formed on the Pacific Ocean floor about fifty million years ago. After being submerged for about fifteen million years, they

The Umpqua River is a slow-moving stream as it flows near Oregon Highway 38 before emptying into the Pacific Ocean.

were raised above sea level when continental plates shifted, and the uplifting created the Coast Range.

At milepost 2, by leaving the main highway and traveling three miles east, you can tour the Oregon State Tree Nursery where several species of trees are produced in a controlled environment.

The junction of highways 138 and 38 in Elkton is near the site of the Hudson Bay Company's Fort Umpqua. From 1836 until its closure in the 1850s, the fort was the trade center for trappers. Its gardens and orchards supplied pioneers with fresh fruit, produce, and breeding stock.

At Elkton, you leave Highway 138 and travel west on Highway 38. It starts along a ridge and descends into the narrow Umpqua River Canyon. As it opens into sheep and horse ranches, sections of trees literally form a tunnel over the road.

Bunch Bar, at milepost 30, offers boat launching for fishermen and one of the best places for getting close to the river. At times, the Umpqua is so smooth that banks and trees are reflected with mirror-like clarity on the water's surface.

During the next several miles, sword and lady ferns dominate the abundant undergrowth, and clumps of Oregon myrtle and black cotton-woods, which are harvested for paper manufacturing, fill lowlands. In summer hills are covered with wild iris, flowering dogwoods, rhododen-drons, tiger lily, and foxglove. The lush vegetation supports a thriving population of black-tailed deer.

Agriculture came to the area as early as 1850. The farms and homes that you pass at mileposts 23 and 21 are both over 100 years old, and many of the roadside apple trees between Elkton and Scottsburg were planted by pioneers.

At Golden Creek by milepost 20, you can get closer to the river at a public boat landing that is a favorite spot for spring chinook and steelhead fishing. Scottsburg cemetery, across the road, contains many pioneer graves. Trailer and RV camps are available a mile west at Wells Creek.

Scottsburg, at milepost 17, was founded in 1850, when two surveying parties met here, joined forces, and platted the townsite. Because of its location at the head of the tidal zone of the Umpqua River, it soon became a major depot for supplies bound for southern Oregon and northern California goldfields. By 1855, it boasted a sheriff, doctor, two lawyers, a newspaper, eight stores, two hotels, and other businesses. The construction of an alternate route led to its decline, and after an 1861 flood swept away all but one of its thirty commercial buildings, it has endured as a small residential community, sandwiched between the river and grass and tree-covered bluffs. Haden store, on the highway, was built around 1851 and is the sole remaining structure from its glory days. A boat landing at Scottsburg Park is on the western fringe and empties into a section of the Umpqua known for its excellent striped bass and chinook salmon fishing.

West from Scottsburg, canopies of trees vie for attention with the river on the north and cliffs and mountains to the south of the road. The lower river valley's environment is similar to a rain forest, with moss-covered cliffs, ferns, big leaf maples, western red cedar, salmon, and thimble berries. About three miles west of Scottsburg, the highway crosses Elliott State Forest. In 1930, the 92,000-acre tract became Oregon's first state forest, and it is the only one that has never been privately owned. Although ninety percent of the timber was burned in an 1868 fire, the forest contains the oldest stands of state owned timber in Oregon. Most of it is second-growth Douglas fir mixed with red alder, western hemlock, cedar, and maple.

A short side road at milepost 13 winds into the Coast Range to Loon Lake Resort and magnificent Ash Valley. The lake is a mecca for waterskiers. You can trek through the rain forest to a lakeside waterfall and into the surrounding mountains. In addition to plenty of loons, you may see osprey, beaver, and otter along the shoreline. Two BLM campgrounds with a total of seventy-six sites are situated on the shore and represent the only developed recreation facilities in Elliott State Forest.

On the main highway, you can launch a boat and picnic at Umpqua Wayside State Park near milepost 10. The wayside overlooks Brandy Bar, where on August 6, 1850, the schooner *Samuel Roberts* ran aground during its maiden voyage to Scottsburg. While waiting for the tide to float the ship free, the crew consumed the brandy supply, giving the bar its name.

After the wayside, the highway cuts through the Umpqua River estuary. Because salt and fresh water meet and mix here, the area is a rich habitat for wildlife ranging from wood ducks, great blue herons, and red winged blackbirds to Roosevelt elk.

Elk are a continuing presence in roadside marshes. At milepost 7, Dean

Creek Elk Viewpoint's information boards cover virtually everything you will want to know about Oregon's largest land animal, including their speed, life span, seasonal activities, swimming and wading habits.

From the viewing area, Highway 38 cuts across marshes and lowlands and ends at a junction with U.S. Highway 101 in Reedsport. The headquarters of the Oregon Dunes National Recreation Area is situated at the intersection. It offers a twenty-minute film on the spectacular dunes, which stretch forty-seven miles along the coast from Florence to approximately North Bend. You'll also find information on varied recreational opportunities including dune buggy rides, tours, hikes, beach combing, camping, and fishing.

From Reedsport, you can take the Winchester Bay-Salmon Harbor-Umpqua Lighthouse Drive by continuing south four miles on U.S. Highway 101 and turning west on 8th Street.

Afterwards, your options for additional sightseeing include scenic Sunset Bay, Shore Acres and Cape Arago, twenty miles south near Coos Bay. At Gardiner, two miles north of Reedsport, virtually every home is eligible for the National Historic Register.

41 UMPQUA VALLEY WINE TOUR

General description: A thirty-five-mile loop through diverse agricultural lands, forests, canyons, historic roads and communities.

Special attractions: Wildlife Safari, eight wineries, historic buildings, North and South Umpqua rivers.

Location: Southern Oregon, west of Roseburg and Sutherlin.

Drive route names and numbers: Oregon Highway 42, County Highway 5C (Reston Road), Coos Bay Wagon Road, Melrose Road, Garden Valley Road, Oregon Highway 138.

Travel season: All year. Most wineries offer daily tastings between April or May and through September or October, and by appointment or on weekends the rest of the year.

Camping: No campgrounds on the route. Armacher County Park Campground at Winchester, midway between Roseburg and Sutherlin, has thirty tent/trailer sites, showers, toilets, and water.

Services: All services in Roseburg, Sutherlin, Winston. Limited services in Tenmile.

Nearby attractions: Roseburg-Lower Umpqua River-Reedsport Scenic Drive, Umpqua-Rogue Scenic Byway, Douglas County Museum, Oakland Historic District.

For more information: Roseburg Visitors and Convention Bureau, 410 S.E. Spruce, P.O. Box 1262, Roseburg, OR 97470, (541) 672-9731, (800) 444-9584 (USA). Sutherlin Visitors Center, 1470 W. Central, P.O. Box 327, Sutherlin, OR 97479, (541) 459-5829, (800) 371-5829.

The drive: Starting at Interstate 5, the loop travels through a variety of

41 UMPQUA VALLEY WINE TOUR

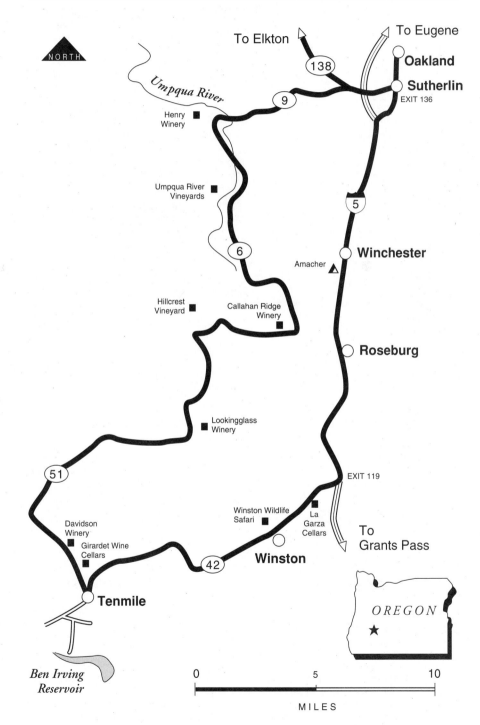

NORTH

To Elkton

To Eugene

138

Oakland

9

Sutherlin

EXIT 136

Umpqua River

Henry Winery

5

Umpqua River Vineyards

6

Winchester

Amacher

Hillcrest Vineyard

Callahan Ridge Winery

Roseburg

Lookingglass Winery

51

EXIT 119

Winston Wildlife Safari

La Garza Cellars

Davidson Winery

To Grants Pass

Girardet Wine Cellars

42

Winston

Tenmile

OREGON

★

Ben Irving Reservoir

0   5   10

MILES

The Umpqua Valley Wine Tour can be extended with an interesting sidetrip to the Oakland Historic District, off Interstate 5 at exit 138.

terrain ranging from shallow canyons to rolling hills and flat, open farmlands. The drive passes eight vineyards while offering a pleasant countryside of small crossroads communities, a historic wagon road, and the state's major wild animal park. It begins and ends at Interstate 5 and can be joined at either exits 119, 125, or 136. Traffic is usually moderate on highways 138 and 42, and light on county roads.

Protected by the Coast Range on the west and the Cascades to the east, the Umpqua River Valley's moderate climate sustains a variety of crops and animals. The area's clay soil, cool morning fogs, and gentle breezes make it ideal for growing wine grapes. Oregon's first vinifera vineyard was established here in 1961.

About fifty million years ago, the black basalt rocks in surrounding hillsides and canyons were part of the Pacific Ocean floor. Later they were covered with sediments that hardened into mud, sandstone, and topped with a rich loam.

Travelers can expect foggy and frosty mornings in fall and winter. The Roseburg/Sutherlin area receives an average rainfall of thirty-five inches. Summer temperatures average from lows of fifty-two to highs of eighty-four, and drop to between thirty-four and forty-eight degrees in winter. Spring temperatures range from sixty-four to seventy-two degrees, while autumns are usually between sixty-nine and eighty-three degrees.

If you are beginning at the north end, you can extend your sightseeing by taking exit 138 and traveling one mile east to the Oakland Historic District. Oregon's first organized historic district recognized by the National Register of Historic Places contains 136 properties and includes many 1890s brick buildings that are still in use.

To start the loop take exit 136 and follow Highway 138 west through Sutherlin. The Sutherlin visitor's information center, at Exit 136, has brochures on the wine tour and Roseburg historic districts.

After 0.5 mile, you turn onto Fort McKay Road and travel south. In the first ten miles, you'll pass picturesque vintage barns, grasslands, herds of dairy cattle and sheep, a small reservoir, and filbert orchards. The Coast Range rises in front of you as a natural shallow bowl filled with oak trees.

Approaching Henry Winery, the highway makes the first of the several crossings of the Umpqua River. A picnic area and a boat ramp, situated at the roadside, provide a pleasant spot to stop and enjoy the river that stretches from the Cascades to the Pacific Ocean and is famous for its native steelhead, spring chinook, and brown trout. During May and June, whitewater rapids challenge rafters and kayakers. Henry Winery, adjacent to the river, provides picnicking facilities and tastings of gewürztraminer, chardonnay, cabernet sauvignon, and pinot noir.

Backtracking to the Umpqua crossroads, the drive continues south on Garden Valley Road (County Road 6) through 8.5 miles of fruit orchards, sheep ranches, a short corridor of overhanging trees, and the small scenic canyon of the Umpqua River. A turn west on Hess Lane takes you to Umpqua River Vineyards. It features cabernet, sauvignon blanc, semillon, chenin blanc, and cabernet franc from grapes grown on the twenty-eight acre estate.

The North and South Umpqua rivers merge at River Forks Park, near Hess Lane and Garden Valley Road. The park has seventy-five picnic sites, and you can enjoy a beach area, playground, and pavilion or use the boat ramp to launch your river explorations. Singleton Park, a few miles south on Garden Valley Road, also offers a pleasant picnic ground and a pavilion.

At Melrose Road, the loop turns west, and a mile further, north onto Busenbark Lane and Callahan Ridge Winery. The winery is housed in an 1878 building with hand-hewn timbers and serves all the popular local varietal in a wheelchair-accessible tasting room and picnic area.

Continuing west on Melrose and then Doerner Road for about ten miles to the community of Melrose, you'll see more fields of vegetables and seed crops, horse ranches, and Christmas tree farms. About 3.5 miles west of Melrose, you can visit HillCrest Vineyard off Elgarose Loop Road. The thirty-five acres of Oregon's oldest vinifera vineyard yield grapes for riesling, cabernet sauvignon, and pinot noir.

The loop backtracks on Doerner Road to County Road 51 and then extends into the gently sloping hills and fields of the Lookingglass Valley on County Road 52. Lookingglass Winery, one mile east of Highway 52 on Lookingglass Road, offers samplings of pinot noir and cabernet sauvignon in a stone tasting room with blue-tiled roof and antique stained glass church windows.

Lookingglass Road continues east and joins Melrose Road, which connects

Douglas County Museum in Roseburg interprets local history with displays of steam-operated equipment, Native American artifacts, and natural history exhibits.

with Interstate Five at exit 124. Travelers who elect to join or terminate the loop by this route will travel through flat farmland, by exposed roadside rock walls, and top a hill with an outstanding view of the Lookingglass Valley and the Roseburg skyline.

At Lookingglass, one mile south of the winery, the general store is a gorgeous 1800s two-story false front. From the store, the loop heads west for two miles to the Coos Bay Wagon Road (County Road 5B). Built in 1867, it was the first road to link Roseburg and Coos Bay on the Oregon Coast. En route southwest to Reston Road, you'll pass several 1880s buildings and fragments of pioneer plum, apple, and pear orchards. The unique buildings include one of seven octagonal barns in Oregon and the Reston Stage Stop barn that still has the horse stalls in place.

Davidson Winery, near Reston Road Junction, was established in 1969 and is one of Oregon's first wineries. It specializes in pinot noir and chardonnay.

Speed limits slow to twenty-five miles per hour as the road becomes a bit windy and descends a ridge into a picturesque canyon lined with basalt bluffs, oak, and poplars. Acres of varietal and French cultivars spread over the hillsides around Girardet Wine Cellars. The vineyard produces blended wines in addition to riesling, chardonnay, pinot noir, and cabernet sauvignon.

Tenmile, a mile south of the winery, has a general store, gas, and several homes. An access road 0.3 mile west on Highway 42, leads to the 11,250-acre Ben Irving Reservoir, where you'll find twenty picnic sites, a large boat ramp, and small dock. The lake is a favorite of trout and bass fishermen and water skiers. From Tenmile, which is roughly ten miles west of Interstate 5,

Highway 42 cuts east through a pastoral countryside of horse and sheep farms.

At Winston, about eight miles east, you can see several buildings dating from 1887 to 1920 that exhibit bungalow, Queen Anne, and elements of Classical Revival architecture. The county-recognized historic district is situated south of the highway.

Winston Wildlife Safari, a mile east of town, is a prime example of the moderate climate's ability to sustain a variety of wildlife. More than 600 animals and birds, representing more than 1,000 species, roam free. The admission charge provides for two drives through the park. En route you'll see Roosevelt Elk and Damara zebra's grazing side by side with hippopotami, Bengal tigers, cheetahs, Asian deer and sheep, Canada geese, and North American timber wolves. At Safari Village, flamingos roam the grounds and children can pet Cameroon Pygmy goats, four horned sheep, and other exotic animals. You can also take an elephant ride, attend nature talks, browse in the gift shop, and dine in a restaurant overlooking the park.

The drive concludes by crossing the South Umpqua River and entering Interstate five at exit 119. If you're a fisherman, the South Umpqua is a stream to try, for it contains most of the area's fall chinook salmon along with wild and hatchery winter steelhead, coho salmon, cutthroat trout, and smallmouth bass.

La Garza Cellars, less than 0.5 miles west of the exit, produces cabernet sauvignon and is developing chardonnay and merlot.

You can add to your sightseeing at the south end by visiting Roseburg's Douglas County Museum and the Mill-Pine Neighborhood Historic District. Both can be reached by traveling four miles north on Interstate five and taking exit 123 east.

Outside, the Douglas County Museum displays a steam donkey, turbines from a dam, a railroad depot, farm equipment, and a carriage. Inside, you'll find four wings covering 8,000 years of Native American culture, natural history, and prehistoric animals. A spacious lot for parking RVs is adjacent to the museum.

The historic district was platted by the city's founder in 1887 and is on the National Register. This section is unique in that it is a neighborhood of lower middle class homes. Most of the 122 historic structures were built between 1887 and 1900.

42 REDWOOD HIGHWAY, OREGON CAVES

General description: A sixty-two-mile drive through southern Oregon's Rogue and Illinois river valleys and the Siskiyou National Forest to Oregon Caves National Monument.

Special attractions: Applegate, Illinois and Rogue rivers, wineries, Lake Selmac, Kalmiopsis Wilderness Area, Oregon Caves National Monument, Rough and Ready Botanical Wayside, Siskiyou National Forest, children's petting zoo, historical theme park, camping, fishing, hiking, water recreation.

Location: Southwestern Oregon between Grants Pass and the Oregon-California border.

Drive route names and numbers: U.S. Highway 199 (Redwood Highway), Oregon Highway 46.

Travel season: All year. Snow frequently accumulates between elevations of 2,000 and 3,000 feet. Chains and traction devices are necessary when driving to Oregon Caves in winter.

Camping: Two county campgrounds with hookups; six forest service campgrounds with tables, fire rings, flush or vault toilets, some with drinking water. Several commercial RV parks.

Services: All services at Grants Pass and Cave Junction. Limited services at settlements along the route.

Nearby attractions: Smith River National Forest Service Scenic Byway, Southern Oregon Coast, Redwoods National Park, Jedediah Smith Redwoods State Park, Six Rivers National Forest, Wild and Scenic Rogue River, Wolf Creek Tavern, Oregon Vortex, Grants Pass-Jacksonville Loop, Oregon Shakespearean Festival.

For more information: Grants Pass-Josephine County Chamber of Commerce, 1501 N.E. 6th St., P.O. Box 970, Grants Pass, OR 97526, (541) 476-7717, (800) 547-5927 (USA). Illinois Valley Chamber of Commerce, 201 Caves Highway, P.O. Box 312, Cave Junction, OR 97523, (541) 592-2631.

The drive: The route begins at 974 feet elevation in Grants Pass and peaks at Oregon Caves, elevation 3,970 feet in the Siskiyou mountains. From the beginning, distant forests and mountains provide a magnificent backdrop for farms, settlements, and a roadside of oaks, madrone, and Douglas fir.

The area is a geological mish-mash containing some of Oregon's older rocks. Two hundred million years ago this section was covered by an inland sea. Later there was violent uplifting, crushing and twisting, and the ocean floor was uplifted and rammed into an ancient mountain range. As a connecting link between the Coast Range and Cascades, the rocks, plants, and animals of both mingle along the way. Grants Pass sits on a platform of granitic rock called diorite. The area around Selma rests on a bed of 150-million-year-old slate. Oregon Caves dissolved out of 200-year-old limestone that has recrystallized into marble.

42 REDWOOD HIGHWAY, OREGON CAVES

U.S. Highway 199 was constructed in the early 1920s and follows the general route of an 1850s gold trail. Most settlements along the route date to the 1800s. Traffic is usually moderate.

Summertime temperatures average 79 to 90 degrees fahrenheit but can peak at over 100 degrees. Nights drop to fifty to sixty degrees. Winter days average forty-three to fifty degrees with nights falling between thirty-five and forty degrees. Travelers will find spring days in the mid-sixties and about seventy-six degrees the average in fall.

To drive the route from Interstate 5, leave the freeway at exits 55 or 58 at Grants Pass, and follow Sixth Street south through town. After approximately three miles, you'll cross Caveman Bridge and the Rogue River. Follow signs to U.S. Highway 199 and Crescent City.

Grants Pass began as a stopover on the California-Oregon stagecoach route and was named in 1865 in honor of General Grant's capture of Vicksburg. The Rogue River has long been a premier steelhead stream, and is also renowned for its coho salmon and trout fishing. Riverside Park, adjacent to Caveman Bridge, offers a shady picnic spot on the river's banks. The twenty-

Sailboats and sailboards share wind, water, and forest scenery at Lake Selmac.

five acres encompass playground equipment, a lighted softball diamond, an art center, bowling greens, and a gazebo.

Driving southwest from Grants Pass, the first nine miles of U.S. Highway 199 hint of the economy as you pass gladiolus fields, lumber mills, dairy farms, horse ranches, and vineyards. Rogue Community College, at mile marker 3, provides an opportunity for quiet walks past interesting sculpture, and modern architecture on a campus of rolling hills covered with scrub pine, oak, laurel, madrone, and Douglas fir. The college specializes in vocational/technical instruction and annually enrolls more than 10,000 people for full or part-time instruction.

Rogue River Vineyards, a mile west and 1.5 south of U.S. Highway 199, opens daily for tastings. Crossing Applegate Road, Riverbanks Road heads six miles north to Griffin Park where you can picnic, tent, and trailer camp in twenty sites and launch a boat into a long calm stretch of the Rogue.

The Applegate River, a tributary of the Rogue, is too shallow for boating but attracts rafters and swimmers and offers fair to good fishing for steelhead, cutthroat, and rainbow trout.

Entering a ravine cloaked with alder, cedar, Douglas fir, oak, and spruce, the highway bisects Wonder, where roadside businesses include an antique shop, second hand store, and a KOA campground. According to legend, the community received its name when a settler wondered how a local merchant hoped to earn a living in this once-isolated spot. Two miles south of Wonder, a partially paved and dirt road leads north over 4,438-foot Onion Mountain. Big Pine campground, with thirteen sites, and Sam Brown, with forty-three, are situated on the northern slopes and Spalding Pond with five sites is nestled on the western foothills.

A few miles west, you touch the edge of the 1.1-million-acre Siskiyou

230

Petrified Forest, made up of a collection of stalagmites, is one of numerous examples of underground beauty in Oregon Caves National Monument.—Oregon Department of Transportation photo

National Forest, climb 1,640-foot Hayes Hill, and enter the Illinois Valley. The national forest offers opportunities for hiking, bird and wildlife watching, and geologic and biological studies as it spreads over a mountainous terrain ranging from 100 to 7,055 feet.

Following an 1851 gold discovery on the Illinois River, the valley developed as a center for mining and timber. Together with tourism, they continue as the backbone of the economy.

Selma's restaurants, garages, and other businesses stretch for two miles along the highway. A road leads north from Selma five miles to thirty sites at Wild and Scenic Illinois River Campground. At the west end of town, a turn south on a paved road takes you two miles through the forest to the Lake Selmac Recreation Area.

The 160-acre man made lake is managed for trophy bass, and the limit is one bass per day, regardless of length. That shouldn't discourage you from fishing, for it also has plenty of hungry bluegill, catfish, crappie, and stocked rainbow trout. Although the ten-mile-per-hour speed limit eliminates water skiing, it makes the lake attractive to swimmers, board sailers, and sailboaters. A path circles the picturesque lake, and trails for horses, mountain bikes, and hikers wander into the mountains through mixed woodlands of Douglas fir, oak, madrone, cedar, cottonwoods, and yew.

Fishermen at Lake Selmac are rewarded with catches of bass, catfish, and stocked rainbow trout.

On the northern shore, the forest shades a campground with forty full hookups and sixty tent sites, plus picnic areas and a boat ramp. At Lake Selmac Resort, on the eastern shore, you can rent mountain bikes, canoes, rowboats, sailboats, and paddle boats. It also offers groceries, ice, a full-service RV camp, showers, bait, tackle, and a laundry.

Three miles west of the Lake Selmac turnoff, a road extends north from U.S. Highway 199 for seventeen miles to the 180,000-acre Kalmiopsis Wilderness Area. As the Siskiyou National Forest's largest wilderness area, it protects the very rare Kalmiopsis Leachiana, a miniature rhododendron-like plant that pre-dates the last ice age. The harsh and formidable landscape is a mass of rocky and brushy low-elevation canyons, lakes, and creeks. Recreation centers on hiking, wildflower displays, and wildlife observation. Babyfoot Lake and the Babyfoot Lake Botanical Area are scenic delights. If you want to see them, be prepared for a strenuous two-mile hike from the gateway at Onion Camp Campground. It has three primitive sites.

At Kirby, two miles west on Highway 199, local history is preserved at the excellent Josephine County Kirbyville Museum. In addition to a modern museum building, you'll step into a two-story 1871 home furnished with antiques, a one-room log cabin school that served seven children, and a barn-sized blacksmith shop. A small rock shop is illuminated with blacklights, and you'll see an assortment of vintage farm machinery displayed on the grounds.

Three miles west, U.S. Highway 199 and Highway 46 meet at Cave Junction. The latter winds southeast into the Siskiyou Mountains to Oregon Caves National Monument. By taking Holland Loop Road, approximately four miles east on Highway 46, you can tour the heart of the area's wine country. Bridgeview Vineyard, surrounded by seventy-four acres of vineyards grows grapes for pinot noir, chardonnay, riesling, gewürztraminer, Müller-thurgau, and pinot gris. Siskiyou Vineyards, a mile east, specializes in cabernet sauvignon, and features a picnic area and nature trail. Early muscat, and several experimental wines are produced at Foris Vineyards.

At Woodland Echos on Highway 64, you can walk through eight eras of history in a reconstructed Indian village, frontier town, and other depictions and overnight in a ten-acre campground or motel. Four miles east, Greyback Campground is situated on the edge of the Siskiyou National Forest at 1,800 feet. Stands of giant Douglas fir, ponderosa pine, yew, madrone, and live oak make this an inviting spot for swimming, fishing, hiking, or camping in thirty-seven tent and trailer sites along Sucker Creek. From the campground, the highway passes through dense timber as it weaves around sharp curves to Oregon Caves at 3,970 feet.

Poet Joaquin Miller called the cave the "Marble halls of Oregon." Its marble composition is unique among show caves for most are limestone. Let your imagination run wild on a guided tour, and you will find the River Styx, Passageway to the Whale, Ghost Room, George Washington's head, and Niagara Falls. Several steep steel and stone stairways have a total of 195 steps down and 345 up. Bring a jacket as temperatures average forty-one degrees.

From the cave entrance, you have a sweeping view of the forest and mountains which hold special pleasures for hikers. A 0.7-mile Cliff Nature Trail interprets the relationship of the cave to the surface and the plants of the forest. The 1.1-mile No Name Trail offers a quiet walk through a canyon and along a stream and waterfalls.

Facilities at Oregon Caves include a fifty-year-old chateau lodge with twenty-four rooms, plus several cabins. Cave Creek Campground, four miles from the cave, offers tent camping in eighteen sites at 1,900 feet.

A mile west of Cave Junction, Illinois River State Park provides a scenic setting for fishing and swimming. The park is situated at the confluence of the East and West forks of the Illinois Valley River, which provide good spring and summer fishing. While small trout are the main catch, you also have a chance at salmon and steelhead. You can explore the largely undeveloped 511-acre park on several hiking trails.

During the next few miles, the road passes two commercial RV campgrounds, a large lumber mill, and Noah's Ark Petting Zoo and Wildlife Park. The children's attraction features zebras, llamas, monkeys, and other exotic animals along with a restaurant and pony rides.

Depending on when you visit, Rough and Ready Wayside, may appear as a spring/early summer garden of wildflowers or little more than scrub brush and dying pine trees. Take a roadside trail into the preserve, and you'll see a variety of plants not found elsewhere, including Howell's mariposa lily, Piper's bluegrass, and Siskiyou butterwort.

After a final crossing of the West Fork of the Illinois River and Elk Creek, the highway reaches the Oregon-California border. A restaurant with motel and RV park on the Oregon side offer a pleasant break surrounded by the cool forest.

Highway 199 continues into California and runs into U.S. Highway 101 north of Crescent City. The California portion includes superlative scenery as the road twists around cliffs overlooking deep valleys and the steep canyon of the Smith River Scenic Byway.

43 GRANTS PASS, JACKSONVILLE LOOP

General description: A seventy-eight-mile loop drive through the Rogue River and Applegate valleys.

Special attractions: Riverside Park, Applegate River, Jacksonville National Historic Landmark, Table Rocks, Oregon Vortex, Rogue River, state parks.

Location: Southwestern Oregon between Grants Pass and Jacksonville.

Drive route names and numbers: Oregon Highway 238, Table Rock Road, Oregon Highway 234, Interstate 5.

Travel season: All year.

Camping: One state park campground with full hookups and electrical sites; one county park campground; eleven forest service campgrounds in vicinity of Applegate Lake, fifteen miles south of loop with tables, fire rings, flush and vault toilets. Some have water.

Services: All services at Grants Pass, Jacksonville, Central Point, and Rogue River. Limited services at Murphy, Applegate, and Gold Hill.

Nearby attractions: Crater Lake National Park, Oregon Caves National Monument, Oregon Shakespearean Festival, Kalmiopsis Wilderness, Redwood Highway-Oregon Caves Scenic Drive, Ashland-Howard Prairie-Hyatt Lake Loop, Wolf Creek Tavern.

For more information: Grants Pass-Josephine County Chamber of Commerce, 1501 N.E. 6th St., P.O. Box 970, Grants Pass, OR 97526, (541) 476-7717, (800) 547-5927 (USA). Jacksonville Chamber of Commerce, 185 N. Oregon St., P.O. Box 33, Jacksonville, OR 97530, (541) 899-8118. Rogue River Chamber of Commerce, 111 E. Main St., P.O. Box 457, Rogue River, OR 97537, (541) 582-0242. Southern Oregon Visitor's Association, P.O. Box 1645, Medford, OR 97501, (541) 779-4691, (800) 448-4856 (USA).

The drive: The loop begins at an elevation of 974 feet and remains relatively level as it heads southwest from Grants Pass to Murphy. Turning east, it moves through rolling hills and dips into small ravines as it passes through dairy farms and woodlands. From Jacksonville, the route heads northwest through orchards at the base of flat-topped mesas and returns to Grants Pass along the Rogue River. Distant forests, mesas and mountains command attention and provide a magnificent background for roadside farms, settlements, and tree-lined avenues.

The drive can be joined from Interstate 5 at exit 32 at Jacksonville and Central Point, exit 40 at Gold Hill, exit 43 at Valley of the Rogue State Park, exit 45 at Rogue River or exits 55 and 58 Grants Pass. Traffic is usually light

43 GRANTS PASS, JACKSONVILLE LOOP

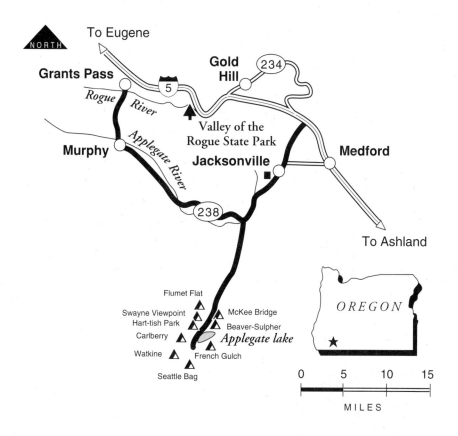

To Eugene

NORTH

Grants Pass

Gold Hill

234

5

Rogue River

Valley of the Rogue State Park

Murphy

Applegate River

Jacksonville

Medford

238

To Ashland

Flumet Flat

Swayne Viewpoint

McKee Bridge

Hart-tish Park

Beaver-Sulpher

Carlberry

Applegate lake

Watkine

French Gulch

Seattle Bag

OREGON

★

0   5   10   15

MILES

to moderate on the secondary roads and heavy on Interstate 5.

Summertime travelers will find temperatures in the 80s and 90s with highs over 100 degrees. Evenings level off into the sixties and seventies. Winters usually range from the mid-forties to the low fifties. Sunny days are common throughout the year as spring temperatures average in the mid-sixties and fall days are in the sixty-nine- to eighty-three-degree range.

To start in Grants Pass from Interstate Five, follow 6th Street south through town. After approximately three miles, you'll cross Caveman Bridge and the Rogue River. Continue straight ahead and follow signs to Highway 238 and Jacksonville.

Grants Pass is the gateway to Oregon Caves National Monument and Rogue River recreation areas. Before departing, you can tour twenty-three historic buildings on a self-guided walking tour.

The Rogue River, a relatively placid stream as it moves through Grants Pass, lives up to its name with turbulent rapids, rugged canyons, and swift riffles as it flows from the foothills of the Cascades near Crater Lake and meanders 215 miles to empty into the Pacific Ocean near Brookings. A thirty-two-mile segment west of Grants Pass was among the nation's first to be protected under the Wild and Scenic River Act and includes one of Oregon's most remote and rugged river courses. The Rogue has always been a premier steelhead stream and is also known for its excellent runs of coho salmon and trout.

Riverside Park, on the south bank of the Rogue and directly east of Caveman Bridge, offers shady picnic spots and departure points for boaters and jet boat excursions west through Hellgate Canyon.

From Grants Pass, Highway 238 extends west through residences and small farms, broken by clumps of scrub pine and mixed stands of oak, laurel, madrone, and Douglas fir. The Siskiyou Mountains frame the western and southern horizons as the drive passes Grants Pass Golf and Country Club and Fish Hatchery Park where you can picnic and fish from the banks of the Applegate River. Crossing the river and entering the lumbering community of Murphy, you'll see mills, a small marina, gas stations, and restaurants.

As the route turns southeast, the Applegate River, a tributary of the Rogue, parallels the highway for most of the way to Jacksonville. Too shallow for boating, it attracts river rafters and swimmers. Fishing for steelhead and trout is often sporadic in January and February but hot in March. The last Saturday in May signals the opening of generally good rainbow and cutthroat trout fishing that lasts through October.

During the next seven miles, you travel through shaded tree-lined avenues, by modern farm buildings, meadows with grazing horses and cattle, stately stands of oaks, dahlias and gladiolus nurseries, and a hereford ranch. East of Provost Store, laurel trees—dark brown with broken patches of bark—alternate with fields of lush grass, giving way to thicker forests and foothills that eventually rise to meet the distant mountains.

At mile marker 19, you cross the Applegate River and enter the town named in honor of pioneers Jessie and Lindsey Applegate. Through various endeavors, including blazing a trail into southern Oregon, they were instrumental in attracting the first settlers to the region. The town today is a few residences, stores, an RV park, and a cafe.

Cantrall-Buckley Park, approximately seven miles east and two miles south of the highway, provides camping, group reservation areas, interpretive displays, and fishing on the riverbank. Valley View Vineyard, a mile east of the park junction, offers daily wine tastings.

From Rush, a small roadside community at milepost 28, a paved road leads south fifteen miles to Applegate Lake. Perched on the Siskiyou's higher slopes, the lake is surrounded by some of Southern Oregon's most striking scenery. Ten- to fourteen-inch trout, large mouth bass, and landlocked steelhead have made it a local fishermen's favorite. Eleven forest service campgrounds with a total of seventy-nine sites are situated around the lake.

After Rush, the vegetation thins into dry grass. Cottonwoods, poplars, and other bottomland trees line the roadside as the route dips into a ravine and approaches Jacksonville.

The town of Jacksonville, with more than eighty buildings dating from the 1850s to the 1890s, is preserved as Jacksonville National Historic Landmark.

Jacksonville is a picture of times past when streets were lit with gas lamps, churches were small and white, and wall sized hand-painted tobacco signs adorned sides of buildings. More than eighty buildings in the community of approximately 1,950 people date from the 1850s to the 1890s. The whole town is preserved as a National Historic Landmark.

Jacksonville rose from an 1851 gold strike and ten years later numbered more than 5,000 people. The decline came when the railroad bypassed it in favor of Medford's flat lands, five miles east.

The former courthouse is one of the region's finest museums with collections of minerals, pioneer artifacts, Native American and Chinese exhibits. Next door, a children's museum offers hands-on exhibits. Stores throughout the town also display pioneer artifacts, mining equipment, and 1800s merchandise. The Peter Britt Music Festival is a summer-long affair devoted to dance, classical, bluegrass, and jazz.

From Jacksonville, the loop follows a former stagecoach route north to Central Point then turns west on Table Rock Road. The Table Rocks are two flat-topped mesas that dominate the horizon and stand in sharp contrast to the flat land orchards and rumpled mountain peaks.

They are remnants of ancient lava flows that covered the area 4.5 million years ago and have served as landmarks for pioneers, Indian battlegrounds, and treaty sites. Designated an area of environmental concern, they protect more than eighty rare and delicate plants. A species of dwarf meadow foam grows here and nowhere else. Brewer's rock cress, Henderson's fawn lily, and scarlet fritillaria mingle with common lupines, Indian paintbrush, honeysuckle, and three species of buttercup.

The rocks are accessible from trailheads off Highway 234 that you take

At Jacksonville, fading painted signs, brick buildings, and vintage farm equipment hint of times when life moved at a slower pace.

south to Gold Hill. The 1.5-mile hikes up the 800-foot rocks are moderately strenuous due to grades that sometimes exceed ten percent. In addition to sweeping views of cities, rivers, orchards and mountains, you'll see a patterned ground of grassy mounds, temporary pools surrounded by wildflowers, and possibly deer, bald eagles, and osprey. Watch for rattlesnakes in summer.

The Table Rock/Highway 234 segment is particularly outstanding during March and April when pear orchards bloom and add their special touches of pink and perfume. Table Rock Road also hosts Tou Velle State Park where you can fish the Rogue River, launch your boat, and picnic along the shoreline. About five miles north of Gold Hill, the Gold Nugget Recreation Area provides another opportunity to picnic beside the river in a laurel-and-oak-lined canyon.

By following Highway 234 west through Gold Hill and turning north on Sardine Creek Road, you can experience the unusual and seemingly improbable at the Oregon Vortex, which is also called The House of Mystery. The house is a former gold mining company assay office in a 165-foot spherical force field, half above and half below ground. Inside the circle, the majority of trees incline, toward magnetic north, people appear shorter when facing south than north, perspective is altered, and physical facts are reversed.

As you follow Interstate 5 from Gold Hill to Grants Pass, you'll overlook the Rogue River south of the highway and see steep forested hills and mountains on the north. The hills and rocks began as sea floor sediments and volcanics some 200 million years ago. Later they were compressed by the moving ocean floor, covered by other rocks, and intruded by lava flows. The heat baked and transformed them into crystalline granite.

Savage Rapids Park and Dam, at exit 45A, are popular spots for swimming and water skiing. Valley of the Rogue State Park and Rest Area, off exit 45B, provides camping in ninety-seven full hookup fifty-five electrical, and twenty-one tent sites in a shaded setting along with a boat ramp, riverside trails, and fishing. The City of Rogue River, accessible from exit 48, offers a local history display at the Woodville Museum, housed in a 1909 home. The annual Rogue River Rooster Crowing Contest has attracted national media attention and is held on the last Saturday in June.

As you return to Grants Pass, the highway climbs a ridge. Below, the city is nestled on the valley floor and surrounded by dark blue mountains.

44 ASHLAND, KLAMATH FALLS LOOP

General description: A 150-mile loop over the southern Oregon Cascade Mountains, along the western shore of Upper Klamath Lake and through the Rogue River and Bear Creek valleys.

Special attractions: Two national forests, Emigrant Lake, Upper Klamath Lake, Lake of the Woods, Fish Lake, Sky Lakes Wilderness, Mountain Lakes Wilderness, hiking, camping, mountain biking, cross-country skiing, wildlife, historic highway, and pioneer trails.

Location: Southern Oregon between Ashland, Klamath Falls, and Medford.

Drive route numbers: Oregon Highways 66, 140 and 62.

Travel season: All year, although portions of highways freeze and accumulate significant snow in winter, which, coupled with steep grades and sharp curves, create hazardous conditions.

Camping: Nine forest service and four Bureau of Land Management campgrounds with tables, fire rings, flush or vault toilets. Some have drinking water. In addition there are three county park campgrounds, two operated by Pacific Power and Light Company, and several commercial RV parks along the route.

Services: All services at Ashland, Medford, and Klamath Falls. Limited services at points along the route.

Nearby attractions: Oregon Vortex, Crater Lake National Park, Grants Pass-Jacksonville Loop, Redwood Highway-Oregon Caves Scenic Drive, Lake County Klamath County Loop, Mount Ashland Ski Area, Lava Beds National Monument.

For more information: Ashland Chamber of Commerce, 110 E. Main St., P.O. Box 1360, Ashland, OR 97520, (541) 482-3486. Greater Medford Visitors and Convention Bureau, 101 E. 8th, Medford, OR 97501, (541) 779-4847, (800) 469-6307. Klamath County Department of Tourism, 1451 Main St., P.O. Box 1867, Klamath Falls, OR 97601, (541) 884-0666, (800) 445-6728 (USA and Canada).

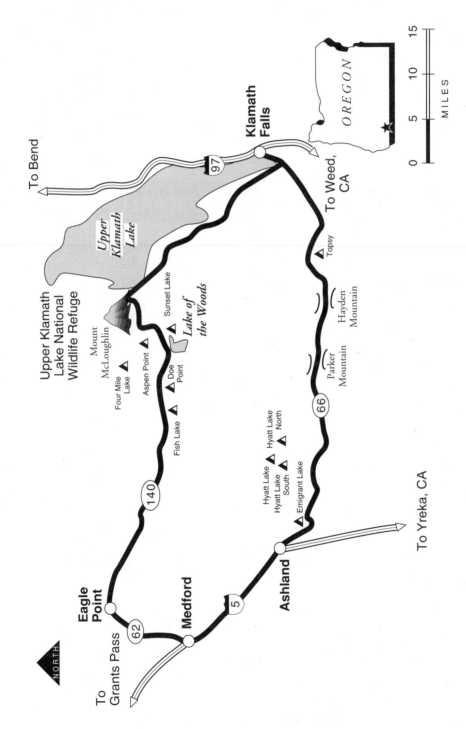

The drive: In the first seventeen miles, the drive climbs from about 1,900 feet elevation near Ashland to over 4,000 feet. Continuing east, Highway 66 remains on a plateau as it extends through a forested corridor of Douglas fir, enters a transition zone, and climbs through ponderosa pine to 4,696 feet, before descending through grasslands to Klamath Falls. Highway 140 follows the shoreline of Upper Klamath Lake north, travels west through dense forest, and peaks at 5,105 feet, before concluding in grass and farmlands. Both highways are essentially tree-lined corridors with the best scenery sometimes hidden by forest.

Stands of ponderosa pine with sparse undergrowth invites easy hikes from the roadside along Highway 66. On Highway 140, dense forest, lush undergrowth, and lava flows necessitate using forest service trails. Traffic is usually moderate to heavy on both highways. If you are driving the route in reverse, start at exit 30 at Medford.

In the Ashland/Medford and Klamath Falls areas, travelers can expect summer temperatures averaging from the low 80s to the high 90s with peaks near 100 degrees. Winter lows average thirty-two degrees and highs, fifty-two. In the mountains, snow accumulates above 3,000 feet with temperatures starting near zero and rising into the mid-thirties. Spring and fall are warm and sunny with temperatures in the high sixties and mid-seventies.

Ashland is the home of America's oldest Shakespearean festival. It began in 1935 and is recognized worldwide for its professional and innovative productions. Mount Ashland Ski Area, eighteen miles south of town, offers a magnificent view of the surrounding mountains and valleys. Skiing usually starts around Thanksgiving and continues into April.

From Ashland, take exit 14 and travel east on Oregon Highway 66. Three miles east of the exit, you enter the Emigrant Lake Recreation Area. The man-made lake holds bass, trout, and other sport fish and is also a favorite of board sailers, boaters, water and jet skiers. Scrub oak and madrone shelter a forty-one-site campground with water and restrooms, and a KOA campground is near the entrance.

The route follows the lake's shoreline for 5.5 miles. The next forty-one miles have been designated a state historic highway and was initially built between 1868 and 1873 as the Southern Oregon Wagon Road. It begins with an abrupt climb that takes you up more than 2,000 feet in eight miles. As the road swirls around ridges and hugs cliffs, take advantage of several strategically placed turnouts, for this section contains Highway 66's most spectacular roadside scenery. The view of the Bear Creek Valley below and deep canyons to the east become more awesome with each curve.

At Green Springs summit, the highway enters a thick Douglas fir forest that will be your companion for the next thirty miles. Two miles east, a paved side road leads north to Hyatt and Howard Prairie lakes. Both feature resort facilities, fishing, water recreation, and lodging. On winter weekends, the access road and lakes area are filled with cross-country skiers. Two campgrounds operated by the Medford Parks Department and three by the Bureau of Land Management overlook the lakes shores. A lodge-style restaurant is situated at the junction.

The Klamath River swells to a lake near Oregon Highway 66 as it feeds John Boyle Reservoir.

Tub Springs State Park, at mile marker 19, offers a water fountain and picnicking in the cool forest. In 1846, the spring was named by an exploration party led by Jessie Applegate. Between 1846 and 1860, the Applegate Trail, which the party blazed through the area, became an alternate to the Oregon Trail. It was used by immigrants traveling from Fort Hall in Idaho to the Rogue River and Willamette valleys. You can see remnants of the Applegate Trail and two wagon roads built in 1862 and 1873 near the park's north entrance.

The route roughly parallels the Applegate Trail to the Klamath River. Continuing east, you'll have a definite feeling of traveling on a high, broad plateau as the road stays flat before dipping into a shallow swale near mile marker 22 and the Pinehurst Inn. The Inn was a 1920s roadhouse, and has been restored as a bed and breakfast and dinner restaurant. Its six rooms, including two suites, feature antique furniture and clawfoot bathtubs. Green Springs Ranch, 0.5 mile east, offers the opportunity to vacation on a 1,000-acre working cattle ranch. With advance arrangements, you can tour the ranch and a small museum of Native American and pioneer artifacts.

The highway leaves a biological transition zone in which ponderosa, Douglas fir, and sugar pine mix and gradually climbs to Parker Mountain's 4,356-foot summit. Nine miles east you reach the road's highest point, 4,695-foot Hayden Mountain. After several curvy sections, a gentle downgrade takes you into open farmland and dry land grassy hills.

Six miles east of the summit, the route crosses the Klamath River, which widens into John Boyle Reservoir. The reservoir and river are favorites of water skiers and swimmers and offer good fishing for crappie, bass, and trout. You can camp near the reservoir in two Pacific Power and Light Company campgrounds or at BLM's Topsy Campground where you'll find twelve units, plus a hiking trail and boat launch. This section has been a crossing point since the days of the Applegate Trail.

During the remaining eighteen miles, you can experience fishing and picnicking on the Klamath River at Sportsman's Park. Panoramic views of the river are available on a ridge near the settlement of Keno. You'll also cross it one more time before entering the western city limits of Klamath Falls where highways 66 and 140 meet.

Klamath Falls was originally called Linksville. The name was changed to capitalize on a small falls, which has since been submerged by power dam backwaters.

Highway 140 begins by climbing rolling hills as it extends north through a few miles of thick ponderosa pines broken by cattle and horse ranches. A few miles further, it tops a ridge and descends to the western shoreline of Upper Klamath Lake's Howard Bay. Several pullouts and boat launches are situated along the shore.

Upper Klamath Lake, at 133 square miles and about 90,000 acres, is Oregon's largest body of fresh water. You're likely to see some of the 250 species of birds that are attracted to the lake and migrate along the Pacific Flyway.

After climbing a rim overlooking the scenic lake, the road reaches the summit of 4,766-foot Doak Mountain. About four miles north, you enter the 1.1 million-acre Winema National Forest. Odessa Creek and Malone Springs campgrounds, near the forest boundary, have a total of seven sites.

Highway 140 turns west in a few miles at a junction with West Side Road, which leads several miles north to small forest service campgrounds, several lakeside resorts, and the 14,000-acre Upper Klamath Wildlife Refuge. As you travel west through rows of quaking aspens and poplars, 9,495-foot Mount McLoughlin, southern Oregon's tallest mountain, stands behind an open meadow on the north. An endless forest fills the slopes of Brown Mountain south of the highway.

Mount McLoughlin is a relatively young volcano that began forming less than one million years ago. It is composed of alternating layers of cinders, scoria, volcanic ash, and basalt. After the last eruptions, about 12,000 years ago, ice age glaciers ground it down, removing massive amounts of earth and rock. Both Mount McLoughlin and Brown Mountain are thought to be active volcanoes. As you continue west to Fish Lake, watch for piles of rough blocks of lava along the roadside. Like Mount McLoughlin, they are products of recent eruptions.

Mount McLoughlin is part of the Sky Lakes Wilderness, which is accessible from Cold Springs trailhead, eleven miles north of the highway. Near the access road, you begin a long winding climb through a scenic pass where the highway meets Dead Indian Road. It skirts Lake of The Woods and heads forty miles southwest to Howard Prairie and Ashland.

Lake of the Woods, a few miles south, is a popular recreation area offering stocked rainbow trout fishing and boating, as well as cross-country skiing and other winter sports. An eight-unit resort rents boats and has meeting rooms, restaurant, and lounge, and RV facilities. At the Winema National Forest Visitor Center, you can obtain trail maps, permits, and tour a small museum. The NFS also operates Aspen Point and Sunset campgrounds, with a total of 122 tent/trailer and six tent sites. Trailheads for several hikes begin at the campgrounds and lead into the Mountain Lakes Wilderness where you'll find numerous small lakes inside a large crater-like basin surrounded by eight prominent mountain peaks.

Fourmile Lake Campground, situated six miles north of Highway 140 on Forest Service Road 3661, is also operated by the NFS. A difficult ten-mile round trip hike to Mount McLoughlin's summit begins near this road. The Pacific Crest Trail meanders between the lake and Mount McLoughlin before crossing Highway 140 a mile west of the visitor center. Fourmile Lake also enjoys heavy trout fishing and boating activity. In winter, access roads serve cross-country skiers and snowmobilers. A few miles west, Highway 140 reaches its high point of 5,105 feet. West of the summit, the forest thickens with Douglas fir, maples, and a dense ground cover. Lava, broken into large boulders and cracked by frost, provides a stark contrast to spring wild lilacs, lupine, trillium, and tiger lilies. As you enter the Rogue River National Forest, you'll see Fish Lake through the trees south of the road. At the lake, you can fish for rainbow and eastern brook trout in summer and try ice fishing in January and February. Several trailheads start near the shore and range from a 0.5 mile to across-the-Cascades treks of several days. Several routes serve mountain bikers, horseback riders, snowmobilers, and cross-country skiers. They include a twenty-seven mile groomed loop around Brown Mountain to Lake of the Woods.

Doe Point and Fish Lake campgrounds, operated by Rogue River National Forest, have forty-one tent/trailer sites. Fish Lake Resort offers rustic cottages, lakefront cabins, a cafe, store, and boat rentals.

Nearby, Forest Service Road 37 extends thirteen miles north to Willow Lake and Butte Falls. Three NFS campgrounds on this road contain twenty-nine tent and thirty-six tent/trailer sites. Willow Creek Campground also has facilities for horses.

As the highway continues west, it cuts across roadbeds of older volcanic and sedimentary rocks that were deposited on an ocean floor between fifty and seventy-five million years ago. The purple and greenish shades of some volcanic rocks were caused by steam and hot water.

You exit the national forest on a five-percent downgrade that stretches through seven miles of Little Butte Creek's north fork canyon then follows a high plateau of meadows and farmlands west to Eagle Point. At Jackson County Sports Park, near Eagle Point, you can watch drag and kart racing, shoot targets on four ranges, and fish for stocked trout in four ponds. The day-use area includes routes for all-terrain vehicles. Before turning south on Highway 62 at Eagle Point, you may wish to visit Butte Creek Mill. It is the West's last original water-powered gristmill.

Medford, ten miles south, marks the conclusion of the drive. With approximately 50,000 people, it is southern Oregon's largest city and the leading business, commercial, and professional center. Medford's economy is based in timber, agriculture, and tourism.

45 ASHLAND, HOWARD PRAIRIE, HYATT LAKE

General description: A 48.8-mile loop past three man-made lakes into the southern Oregon Cascade mountains and through the Bear Creek Valley.

Special attractions: Howard Prairie and Hyatt Lake resorts, Emigrant Lake, rugged mountain and valley scenery, fishing, camping, cross-country skiing, wildlife observation, historic highway.

Location: Southern Oregon east of Ashland.

Drive route names and numbers: Oregon Highway 66, Dead Indian Road, Howard Prairie-Hyatt Lake Road.

Travel season: Usually all year, although Bureau of Land Management portions of highways around Howard Prairie and Hyatt Lakes sometimes close because of heavy snow. Portions of highways freeze, and, coupled with steep grades and sharp curves, create hazardous conditions.

Camping: Three BLM campgrounds with tables, fire rings, flush or vault toilets, drinking water. Two Medford Park Department campgrounds with primitive sites. Several commercial campgrounds are also situated along the route.

Services: All services at Ashland. Limited services at points along the route.

Nearby attractions: Rogue River, Oregon Vortex, Crater Lake National Park, Mountain Lakes Wilderness, Lake of the Woods, Fish Lake, Grants Pass-Jacksonville Scenic Loop, Redwood Highway-Oregon Caves Scenic Drive, Ashland-Klamath Falls Scenic Loop, Applegate lake, Mount Ashland Ski Area.

For more information: Ashland Chamber of Commerce, 110 E. Main St., P.O. Box 1360, Ashland OR 97520, (541) 482-3486.

The drive: As the drive leaves the Bear Creek Valley at about 1,900 feet elevation, it climbs through forested ridges to over 5,000 feet in thirteen miles. Turning south, it continues through a forested highland prairie by two mountain lake resorts. The return is through a magnificent, but steep canyon, and along the shores of Emigrant Lake. Traffic is usually moderate on Oregon Highway 66 and light on Dead Indian and Howard Prairie-Hyatt Lake Roads. Expect heavy traffic on weekends.

In Ashland travelers can expect summer temperatures averaging from the 80s to the high 90s with peaks near 100 degrees. Winters fall to lows averaging thirty-two degrees and highs of fifty-two. In the mountains, snow accumulates above 3,000 feet with temperatures starting near zero and rising into the mid-thirties. Spring and fall brings balmy days in the mid-sixties and mid-seventies.

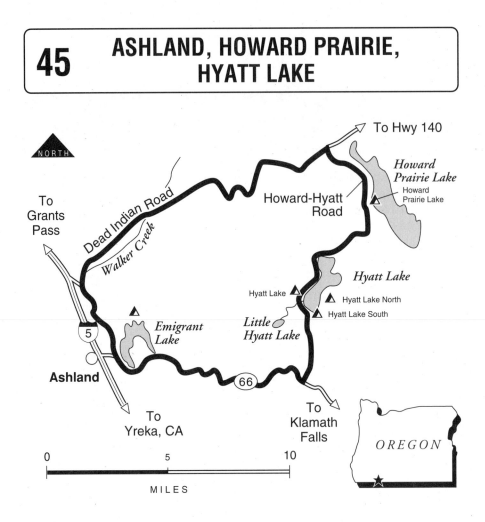

45 ASHLAND, HOWARD PRAIRIE, HYATT LAKE

In its infancy, Ashland consisted of a water-powered flour and sawmill and was named by early settlers with ties to Ashland County, Ohio and Ashland, Kentucky.

The Oregon Shakespearean Festival has brought the town enduring fame. It began as a three-day event in 1935 and has grown to a season which starts in April and ends in November. A Shakespeare Exhibit Center, open on performance days, displays costumes, set pieces, and props. In the Fantasy Gallery you can try on costumes and pose for pictures. Lithia Park, adjacent to the festival grounds, straddles 100 acres of creek banks and offers hiking, nature trails, tennis courts, Japanese and formal rose gardens. Mount Ashland Ski Area is eighteen miles south of town and offers four chair lifts, twenty-three runs, rental shops, cafeteria, and daily snow grooming. Skiing usually starts around Thanksgiving and continues into April.

The drive begins by leaving Ashland and Interstate 5 at exit 14 then briefly follows Oregon Highway 66 east. After 0.5 mile, you turn north onto Dead

Indian Road. The road has been a main access for so long that the origin of its name is uncertain. According to one version, a band of Native Americans were killed and buried somewhere along the route.

At the beginning, you'll travel through the center of flat dry grasslands, low rolling hills, a few steep bluffs, and rocky outcroppings. A creek, shrouded in alders and oak, parallels the south edge and adds color to the buff countryside. The flatlands are composed of sandstone which was deposited about fifty million years ago. It is a land of little water and is used mostly for cattle grazing.

Soon the road snakes up and round ridges in a steep thirteen-mile climb through oak woodlands. Several turnouts afford opportunities to view the brushy, crumpled hills and ravines below. As you ascend, watch for cattle crossing the highway and bicyclists in the roadway, for this is a popular cycling route despite the steep grade. After eight miles, the alders disappear and aspens, laurel, Douglas and white fir, lodgepole pine, and other evergreens begin mixing with oaks.

Near the summit, the road straightens and flattens. Turning south at mile marker 17 onto Hyatt-Howard Prairie Road, you begin traveling across a high-plateau prairie. It was named for local homesteaders who were among the first to settle in the area.

Small meadows hemmed in forests of Douglas fir, ponderosa, black and white pine dot the roadsides, affording easy, short hikes into grassy fields. Watch for wildlife, for the woods are home to deer, elk, squirrels, raccoons, and black bear. Around the lakes, you may see osprey, bald eagles, pelicans, cormorants, and a variety of other waterfowl.

Plentiful game, a good water supply, easy access, and mild winters made this area a Native American trading center. Although it is illegal to collect them, you may find arrowheads and other artifacts along lakeshores, meadows, and trails.

Grizzly Campground, at mile marker 2, is a Medford Parks Department facility with primitive sites, day-use areas, and boat access. A hiking trail begins at the campground and joins the Pacific Crest Trail east of the lakes. From 5,000 feet at Dead Indian Road Summit you descend to 4,500 at Howard Prairie Lake and Resort.

The six-mile-long lake is dependent on snow for water and fluctuates dramatically from year to year. When it is full, you can boat to several islands, and take advantage of its reputation as an outstanding early season wild and stocked rainbow trout fishery. By mid-June, it becomes a recreation area for sailboating, swimming and waterskiing, which is limited to the southern end. As a prime summer-sailing lake, it is the home base of a local yacht club.

The resort overlooks the lake, marina, swimming beaches, and boat ramp. In addition to groceries, gas and a restaurant, it operates a forty-unit campground. RV trailers with kitchens occupy half the sites and serve as cabin rentals. Boat and jet ski rentals are also available.

The highway climbs 300 feet in the five miles to Hyatt Lake. Along the way small meadows surrounded by stands of thick forest, provide grass for deer and elk, and serve as informal summer campsites and winter snow-play areas. This section, which also includes a small store with a cafe, sometimes closes due to heavy snow. East Hyatt Lake Road, about midway, loops around Hyatt Lake's eastern shore on seven miles of winding paved blacktop, and passes three BLM campgrounds with seventy-two sites, lakeside day-use areas, and a section of summer homes.

A short drive off the main road leads to Hyatt Lake and a small resort with a restaurant, boat, canoe, and cabin rentals, a campground with tent and full hookups, and a boat launch. Groceries, daily fishing licenses, bait, and tackle are available at the store, which is a drop-mailing site for hikers and horsemen using the Pacific Crest Trail. The resort operates seven days a week, beginning with the opening of fishing season in April and continues through September then serves cross country skiers on winter weekends.

Nestled in a forest of tall ponderosa, Douglas fir and lodgepole pine, Hyatt Lake is smaller, more secluded than Howard Prairie. Usually, you will find excellent fishing for bass and stocked rainbow trout. Fish from over twelve to twenty inches are often taken from the lake by trolling and still fishing.

From Hyatt Lake, you continue south through the thick roadside forest for four miles to Highway 66. En route you'll pass a gravel side road to Little Hyatt Lake, which offers scenic camping and hiking, and the southern entrance to the Hyatt Lake Recreation Area loop road.

A rustic restaurant is situated at the Highway 66 junction. The section of Highway 66, which you take west eighteen miles to Ashland, has been designated an Oregon Historic Highway. It dates to the 1846 Applegate Trail, which was the major pioneer route into southwestern Oregon.

One mile west of the junction, you begin the descent from Green Springs Mountain summit, elevation 4,551 feet. A trail near the summit extends through forest to sweeping views of the countryside.

During the next eight miles, you'll descend more than 2,000 feet. With the road swirling around ridges and hugging cliffs, take advantage of several strategically placed turnouts, for this section offers superlative views of the Bear Creek valley to the west and deep canyons to the east. In morning and evening, deer are often seen along the highway. The dark gray basalt is only a few million years old and covers thin layers of light gray and greenish-white volcanic ash.

Near the bottom, you enter a canyon filled with willows, scrub oak, and cedar. On the valley floor, the road passes Songer Wayside, which offers a pleasant picnic spot overlooking Emigrant Lake.

After following the lake's intermittent shoreline for 5.5 miles, you enter the Emigrant Lake Recreation Area. The man-made lake is a favorite local fishing spot for bass, trout, blue gill, crappies and catfish. Mid-afternoon winds bring sailboarders, boaters, water, and jet skiers. In summer lake shores serve as outdoor theaters for music festivals, some of which feature name entertainers.

A forty-one-site campground with water and restrooms is sheltered in scrub oak and madrone. You can also enjoy a waterslide, group camps, day-use areas, swimming beaches, and rent jetboats. A KOA campground is situated near the entrance.

Ashland Vineyard Winery, near the freeway, offers a last stop before the drive concludes at Interstate 5 and exit 14.

46 UPPER KLAMATH LAKE LOOP

General description: A ninety-mile loop drive around Upper Klamath Lake and Wildlife Refuge, into the eastern Cascade foothills and Klamath basin farmlands.

Special attractions: Three museums, Upper Klamath Lake and Wildlife Refuge, fishing, canoe trails, historic sites, Winema National Forest, resorts, Collier Memorial State Park.

Location: South Central Oregon between Klamath Falls and Chiloquin.

Drive route names and numbers: U.S. Highway 97, Oregon Highway 140, West Side Road, Seven Mile Road, Sun Mountain Road.

Travel season: Route is open all year with prime travel season from April through October.

Camping: Two state park campgrounds, one with full hookups and one with primitive sites; Three forest service campgrounds with tables, fire rings, flush or vault toilets.

Services: All services in Klamath Falls, Fort Klamath and Chiloquin.

Nearby attractions: Crater Lake National Park, Lake of the Woods, Fish Lake, Lava Beds National Monument, Lower Klamath Lake National Wildlife Refuge. Klamath Forest National Wildlife Refuge, Ashland-Klamath Falls Loop Scenic Drive, Lake County-Klamath County Loop Scenic Drive.

For more information: Klamath County Department of Tourism, Klamath County Museum Building, 1451 Main St., P.O. Box 1867, Klamath Falls, OR 97601, (541) 884-0666, (800) 445-6728 (USA and Canada). Winema National Forest, 2819 Dahlia, Klamath Falls, OR 97601, (541) 883-6714.

The drive: The loop begins in Klamath Falls, at elevation 4,107 feet ,and rises to 4,766 feet in the Cascade foothills. After traveling by three museums in downtown, it moves to Upper Klamath Lake's western shore, climbs through Winema National Forest to a resort area, turns east, and levels off into farmlands. The return begins in a forest then passes through open sagebrush country and onto the east shore of Upper Klamath Lake.

Klamath County's high dry climate produces about 300 days of sunshine per year. In summer highs average eighty-four degrees and lows 51.7 degrees. Winter temperatures range from twenty-one to thirty-eight degrees. Spring days span sixty-four to seventy-two degrees, and autumn falls between sixty-nine and eighty-three degrees.

Native Americans inhabited the Klamath basin for at least 5,000 years before the arrival of fur trappers in 1825. Kit Carson and John C. Fremont camped on Upper Klamath Lake in 1843 while searching for a pass through the Cascades. Klamath Falls began in 1867 as a ferry and bridge crossing on

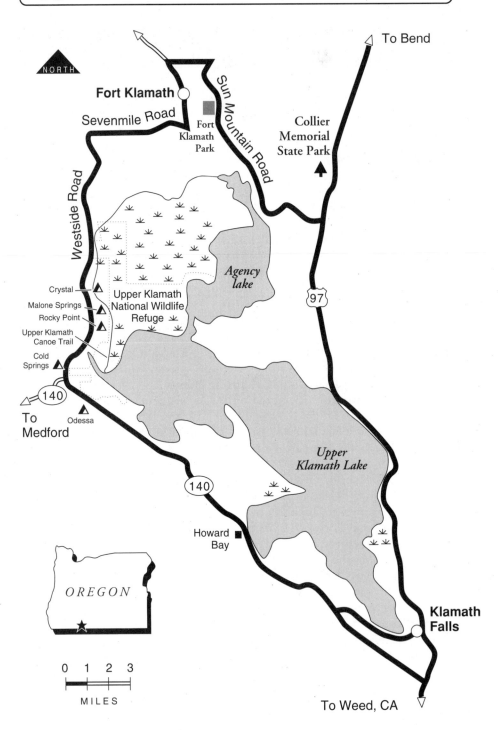

46 UPPER KLAMATH LAKE LOOP

NORTH

To Bend

Fort Klamath

Sevenmile Road

Sun Mountain Road

Fort Klamath Park

Collier Memorial State Park

Westside Road

Agency lake

Crystal

Malone Springs

Rocky Point

Upper Klamath National Wildlife Refuge

Upper Klamath Canoe Trail

Cold Springs

97

140

To Medford

Odessa

Upper Klamath Lake

Howard Bay

Klamath Falls

OREGON

To Weed, CA

0 1 2 3
MILES

the Link River. Originally called Linksville, the name was changed to capitalize on a small falls, which has since been submerged by power dam backwaters.

Klamath County Museum, housed in a former armory of Classical Revival design, offers an excellent introduction to Native American and pioneer history, wildlife, and regional geology. The town sits on an area of very young volcanic rocks and on top of natural steam and hot water.

After fire destroyed the original town in 1889, George Baldwin began rebuilding by constructing the hotel that bears his name. A state and national landmark, the four-story Baldwin Hotel Museum retains its original furnishings along with foundation stairs carved from solid rocks and bricks manufactured from Yreka, California, gold mine tailings.

The Favell Museum, situated two blocks west of the Baldwin Hotel on the banks of the Link River, features Indian artifacts from throughout the western United States, British Columbia, and Mexico. Collections include 60,000 arrowheads, stone, bone, shell, quill work, pottery, miniature firearms, and extensive exhibits of western art, bronzes, and taxidermy. The Link River Nature Trail starts near the museum. On the easy walk along the river bank, you may see white pelicans, great blue herons, and some of the other species of waterfowl that migrate in and out of the area.

An exit mid-way between the two museums takes you north on U.S. Highway 97 and west along Lakeshore Drive. The route passes marinas, a residential area, small farms on or overlooking Upper Klamath Lake, and then opens into fields as it reaches Oregon Highway 140. At 435-acre Moore Park, you can picnic on the lake shore with the Cascades as a backdrop and take a short scenic drive into hills overlooking playgrounds, tennis courts, and a boat launch.

Upper Klamath Lake, at 133 square miles and about 90,000 acres, is Oregon's largest body of fresh water. The lake fills a basin created sometime during the last million years when the earth's crust dropped along fault lines which can be seen along both the east and west shorelines. Situated in the heart of the Pacific Flyway, it attracts more than 250 species of birds and an estimated seventy to ninety percent of the waterfowl that migrate along the route. If you're a fisherman, you stand a good chance of catching rainbow trout, catfish, yellow perch, and mullet. Several boat launches, rentals, and tackle shops are situated along the shore. The lake serves as a natural reservoir for the Klamath Reclamation Project, logging operations, and Klamath River power plants. Its upper shores yield abundant algae, which is harvested commercially.

As you approach Highway 140, watch for bald eagles, for they are present all year. At Howard Bay, a few miles north, you may see nesting pelicans, Canada honkers, blue herons, and snow geese. On clear days, as you drive north, you'll see the cylindrical cone of Mount McLoughlin on the western horizon. At 9,495 feet, it is southern Oregon's tallest mountain.

After climbing a rim overlooking the lake, the highway reaches the summit of 4,766-foot Doak Mountain. Two miles further, a good dirt road leads four miles east to shoreline picnicking in a ponderosa pine forest at

Collier Memorial State Park features an exhibit of historic logging equipment, full hook-up campgrounds, and river and creek fishing.

Eagle Ridge Park. Four miles north of the turnoff, you enter the 1.1-million acre Winema National Forest. The 4.4-mile Varney Creek Trail, near the border, starts at 5,600 feet and is a moderately difficult hike to sweeping views of Upper Klamath Lake and wilderness peaks. Odessa Creek and Malone Springs campgrounds contain a total of seven sites. The first forest service timber sale took place at Odessa Point in 1905, and the event was immortalized by placing the site on the National Register of Historic Places.

Two miles north, Highway 140 turns west, and the drive continues north on West Side Road to Harriman Springs Resort, which also has a marina and RV park. Next door, the lodge at Rocky Point Resort was originally a 1930s lumber camp. In addition to four cabins and twenty-eight RV spaces, facilities include dock space for twenty-eight boats.

A 3.5- and six-mile canoe trail, through a portion of Upper Klamath Wildlife Refuge's 14,376 acres of marsh grass, bullrushes, cattails and water lilies, begins at the resort and winds into two creeks and Pelican Bay. The routes, which follow ancient Native American trails, are open from April through November. This section also produces trophy-sized trout. Guide services for fly and drift fishing and duck hunting are available at the resort along with boat and canoe rentals.

West Side Road continues north as a high mountain avenue lined with trees. From pullouts, you can see the dark blue canoe trails meandering through the yellow and green marsh grass. Cherry Creek Trail, off Forest Service Road 3450, provides a strenuous 5.3-mile trek through the Cherry Creek Natural Research Area and a mixed conifer forest into terrain carved by glacial action and the magnificent scenery of the Sky Lakes Basin. Nanny Creek Trail, accessible by turning west for 4.5 miles on Forest Service Road

3438, rewards a difficult climb through 4.3 miles of rocky contours and heavily forested slopes of 6,917-foot Lather Mountain by weaving around the shorelines of several mountain lakes.

The road exits the forest through a corridor of willows, cottonwoods, dogwoods, alders, and ponderosa pine. Following Seven Mile Road east for approximately seven miles, you travel by pastoral farms with picturesque older and modern barns and large herds of cattle grazing in meadows framed by the steel gray of the Cascade's eastern slopes. Fort Klamath's quaint church, stores, motels, and restaurants line the highway as you travel north to Fort Dixon Road, turn east and reenter the Winema National Forest. At Jackson F. Kimball State Park, north of the junction with Sun Mountain Road, you can pitch your tent on six primitive sites, hike in a ponderosa pine forest, fish the headwaters of the Wood River for trout, and watch for deer and other wildlife.

Sun Mountain Road offers several attractions as it heads south for twelve miles to join U.S. Highway 97. Sun Mountain Campground, tucked away in the forest, features hookups and showers. During summer, Fort Klamath Park and Museum is open to the public. It was established in 1863 to protect settlers and wagon trains from Native American attacks. Prior to its abandonment in 1889, Fort Klamath's troops had been major participants in the Modoc War of 1872-73. Artifacts on display date to the 1800s. At the park , you can picnic in a gazebo built over the fort's original dance platform, see a replica of the guardhouse, and visit the graves of the Modoc's leader, Captain Jack, and three other Native Americans.

Approximately 1.4 miles south, Fort Creek Resort is nestled among large ponderosa and scrub pines. Oregon State Fish Hatchery, nearby, conducts guided tours and ponds display hatchlings and trophy-sized trout. Next, you drive by the original agency headquarters of the Klamath Indian Tribe and the reservation's school, hospital, and administrative offices. By following a side road a few miles south, you can take a side trip to picturesque Agency Lake, relax in Henzel Park, and enjoy water-related activities at Williamson River Recreation Area.

A turn north on U.S. Highway 97 takes you through five miles of thick forest to Collier Memorial State Park at Chiloquin. It features a large collection of steam driven logging equipment, a fifty-unit full-hookup campground on the banks of the Williamson River, and good trout fishing on an adjacent creek.

During the thirty-seven-mile return to Klamath Falls, U.S. Highway 97 hugs the eastern shoreline of Upper Klamath Lake, while sagebrush, desert buttes, and bands of sedimentary rock provide the scenery on the east side of the highway. Modoc Point offers great east side views of the lake with Mount McLoughlin visible across the Klamath Basin. En route you'll pass two forest service ranger stations and a junction to Highway 62, which extends to Crater Lake National Park and the Fort Klamath Recreation Area. The Williamson River, which you also cross, is a major trout and mullet stream. Hagelstein Park, about midway to Klamath Falls, offers a final high vista view of the Lake, basin and mountains.

47 ROGUE UMPQUA SCENIC BYWAY

General description: A 180-mile drive on a National Forest Service Scenic Byway through the Rogue and Umpqua River valleys, past lakes and waterfalls into the southern Oregon Cascade Mountains.

Special attractions: Umpqua and Rogue Wild and Scenic Rivers, waterfalls, mountain lakes, narrow rugged canyons, wilderness, Crater Lake National Park, State Parks, historic inns, camping, fishing, winter recreation.

Location: Southern Oregon east of Roseburg and north of Gold Hill.

Drive route names and numbers: Oregon Highways 138, 230, 62 and 234.

Travel season: All year, although the Crater Lake North Entrance and rim drives close in winter.

Camping: One state park with electricity, two National Park Service, five Bureau of Land Management, and approximately twenty forest service campgrounds with tables, fire rings, flush or vault toilets. Some with drinking water. Two county parks with hookups, plus several private RV parks.

Services: All services at Roseburg, Gold Hill and Shady Cove. Limited services along the route.

Nearby attractions: Roseburg-Lower Umpqua River-Reedsport Scenic Drive, Umpqua Valley Wine Tour, Sky Lakes Wilderness, Oregon Vortex, Grants Pass-Jacksonville Loop, Redwood Highway-Oregon Caves Scenic Drive, Ashland-Klamath Falls Loop, Applegate Lake, Mount Ashland Ski Area.

For more information: Roseburg Information Center/Visitor's and Convention Bureau, 410 S.E. Spruce, P.O. Box 1262, Roseburg, OR 97470, (541) 672-9731, (800) 444-9584 (USA). Umpqua National Forest, 2900 Stewart Parkway, P.O. Box 1008, Roseburg, OR 97470. (541) 672-6601. Rogue River National Forest, 333 West Eighth St., P.O. Box 520, Medford, OR 97501, (541) 858-2200.

The drive: From Roseburg, the drive heads east through the Umpqua River's spectacular narrow canyon, climbs into the Cascades, and reaches a high point of 5,820 feet. A side trip to Crater Lake National Park increases the elevation to 7,100 feet. The southern section descends through thick forest along the Rogue River Gorge and a reservoir lake, and concludes in orchards and farmland. The drive can be joined from either exit 124 at Roseburg, or exit 40 at Gold Hill.

In the Rogue and Umpqua valleys, travelers can expect summer temperatures in the 80s and 90s with peaks near 100 degrees. Winters usually fall between forty-four and fifty-seven degrees. In the mountains, summers bring sunny seventy-degree days while winters range from near zero to the mid-thirties. At Crater Lake, snow has fallen at least once on every day of the year. Spring days reach highs of seventy-two degrees and lows around sixty-four, while autumn peaks at eighty-three and drops to sixty-nine degrees.

From Roseburg, Highway 138 starts east through eighteen miles of grassy,

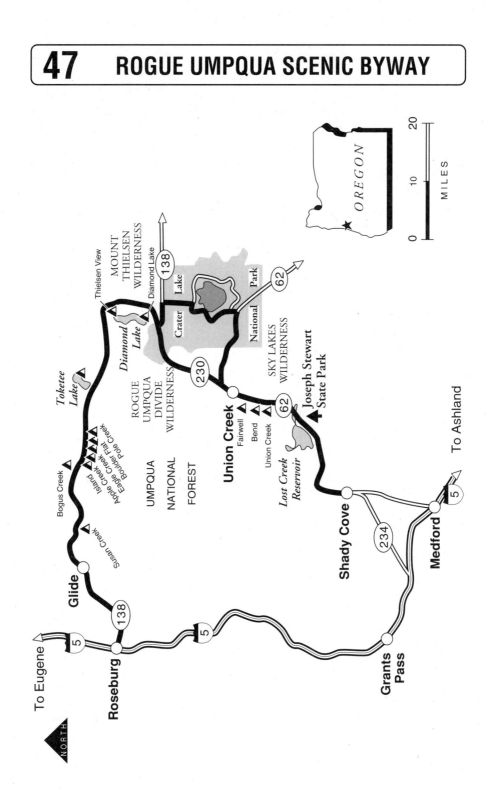

The North Umpqua and Little rivers meet and collide at the roadside community of Slide on Oregon Highway 138.

flat-topped hills, broken by patches of scrub brush, oaks, and pines. Whistler's Bend County Park, at mile marker 15, has twenty-four campsites.

The North Umpqua and Little rivers collide at the community of Glide, and the rare phenomena can be seen from a small park across the street from the North Umpqua Ranger Station. Little River Road follows its namesake southeast for twenty-four miles to seven waterfalls and six campgrounds. Cavitt Creek Covered Bridge (World Guide Number 37-10-06) is also located near Little River Road.

The Umpqua River, which begins in the Cascade Mountains and empties into the Pacific Ocean, parallels the highway as you continue east through the Umpqua National Forest. A thirty-mile section along the drive is limited to fly fishing. While summer steelhead fly fishing has made it famous, the Umpqua also attracts anglers for winter steelhead, spring and fall salmon, trout, small mouth bass, shad, and striped bass. The 984,880-acre Umpqua National Forest spreads into three counties and includes the Mount Thielsen, Rogue-Umpqua Divide and Boulder Creek wildernesses.

Ten miles east of Glide, you leave open country and enter the towering basalt cliffs and thick forest of the North Umpqua River Canyon. The drive incorporates virtually every kind of scenery: waterfalls; forests that start at the road's edge and flow in waves up hills, ridges, and mountains; rock palisades; rushing rivers; quiet lakes; a variety of spring wildflowers; and patches of brilliant fall foliage.

Several waysides with viewpoints provide access to the river. At Susan Creek Recreation Area, you can enjoy the rugged scenery from thirty-three campsites or the picnic area, and follow a winding one-mile trail through a rain forest setting to fifty-foot Susan Creek Falls where piles of stones remain from a Native American spiritual site.

If you are a whitewater rafter or a steelhead fishermen, you can launch into the river at Bogus Creek Campground, six miles east. The campground offers fifteen sites with tables, eleven tent/auto/trailer sites, and four combination multi-family spaces. Fall Creek Falls and Job's Garden Geological Area are within three miles, and a segment of the North Umpqua National Recreation Trail is about two miles away.

A narrow 7.5-mile-long canyon of sheer, tree-covered cliffs and a deep channel of surging rapids signals your arrival at The Narrows, which has been a popular salmon and steelhead fishing spot since the days of the Molalla Indians. Swiftwater Park, near the western end, marks the boundary for bait and fly fishing.

Near The Narrows eastern end, a side road leads to 100-foot Canton Creek Falls, set in steep canyon walls surrounded by large Douglas fir and western redcedar. Steamboat Creek Road takes you six miles east into a magnificent canyon to turbulent Steamboat Falls, which drops twenty to thirty feet. Several campgrounds are located on the side roads or near the junction. They include Scared Man, Steamboat Falls, Island, and Canton Creek.

During the next twenty miles, the road bends southeast, passes three closely-grouped falls at Jack Falls, parallels the Wild and Scenic portion of the North Umpqua River, and begins steadily climbing. The magnificent scenery continues with sheer cliffs marked by columnar basalt, and thick forest. Your camping options in secluded forests include Apple Creek, Horseshoe Bend, Eagle Rock and Boulder Flat campgrounds.

In the Toketee area, you can obtain hiking, snow-park, and wilderness permits at the ranger station, land small planes on the air strip, hike to beautiful Toketee Falls, and 272 foot-high Watson Falls. Toketee Reservoir, nearby, offers boating, a thirty-three-site year-round campground, and fishing for brown, rainbow, and brook trout.

Approximately ten miles east, you may savor the scent of pine from the viewpoint overlooking the ten- to fifteen-foot punchbowl of Whitehorse Falls or from its campground. Clearwater Falls, 3.5 miles east, is a beautiful thirty-foot cascade, which you can see on a short walk to an overlook or from its campground. This area is also a hotbed of cross-country skiing and hiking with several routes starting at the highway.

A few miles further, a side road takes you to five miles north to Lemolo Lake Recreation Area. The lake is one of the few places in Oregon where you can catch wild, trophy-sized brown trout, along with rainbow, brook trout, and kokanee salmon. At 4,142 feet, it also offers frigid water skiing, three boat launches, and four campgrounds around its rim. A resort rents tackle and boats, and has food, gas, and lodging.

Six miles east, you'll see Diamond Lake through the trees. Situated at 5,182 feet, and bordered by 9,200-foot Mount Thielsen and 8,363-foot Mount Bailey, Diamond Lake is one of the Cascade's scenic jewels. During summer and fall, you stand an excellent chance of catching some of the annual stock of 400,000 rainbow trout. Boating, canoeing, swimming, sailboarding, hiking and hunting for deer, elk and bear are popular pastimes. In winter when ice usually covers the lake from January to mid-April, you can take snowmobile tours around its rim and to Crater Lake National Park. Snowcats will transport you to Mount Bailey for downhill skiing, and there are 300 miles of cross-country ski routes to explore.

Rustic Diamond Lake Resort rents ninety-two motel rooms and cabins with a capacity for 520 people. It has a grocery store, service station, full service marina, and horse stables. You can also rent motor boats, canoes, paddle boats, mountain bikes, and horses. Three forest service campgrounds contain 450 tent and RV sites.

A few miles east, Highway 138 leaves the Umpqua National Forest, offers access to the Mount Thielsen Wilderness, meets Highway 230, and passes the north entrance to Crater Lake National Park. Highway 230, part of the scenic byway, climbs to 5,320 feet. En route to a junction with Highway 62 at Union Creek, it offers twenty-four miles of forested mountain scenery and access to the Wild and Scenic Upper Rogue River, Mount Bailey Trails, and the Rogue-Umpqua Divide Wilderness.

Crater Lake is Oregon's scenic icon, and virtually everything pales by comparison. The giant caldera was formed some 7,000 years ago when Mount Mazama collapsed in the aftermath of volcanic eruptions. The depth of 1,932 feet and the clarity of the water create its famous sapphire blue color.

You can see the lake from viewpoints at Rim Village. A nine-mile western drive, a twenty-three-mile drive along the eastern rim, and the north entrance road usually open by early July and closes around mid-October. At 7,100 feet, they offer spectacular views of the lake and Cascade peaks. Trails branch off the loops to surrounding mountains and the Pacific Crest Trail. The Cleetwood Trail begins on the northeastern rim and concludes inside the caldera at the water's edge. Narrated one-hour-and-forty-five-minute boat cruises of the lake start from the eastern drive. Rangers present amphitheater programs and special activities for children during summer.

The 183,180-acre park encompasses a historic lodge, Rim Village Visitor Center with a restaurant and gift shop, and an extensive network of trails to remote attractions such as sandstone pinnacles and the Rogue River headwaters. Mazama Campground features 193 sites and Lost Creek Campground has sixteen. In winter, you can cross-country ski and play in the snow on unplowed roads.

Exiting Crater Lake by Highway 62, you'll enter the 630,000-acre Rogue River National Forest. This section of predominantly Douglas fir and ponderosa pine passes Huckleberry Mountain and a campground that bears its name. The area was a berry-picking site for the Klamath Indians.

The community of Union Creek, twenty-two miles west of Rim Village, was built in the 1930s by the U.S. Civilian Conservation Corps. It is on the National Registry of Historic Places.

About five miles south, a turn west will take you to the brink of the Rogue River Canyon and Natural Bridge, where the river thunders through a deep, extremely narrow chasm in a spectacular display of white water. In summer,

Scenic Diamond Lake is a center for year-round recreation with a resort motel, several campgrounds, and other facilities.

it disappears into Natural Bridge lava tube. During high water, it overflows and buries the tube. A 2.5-mile hiking trail connects the gorge and bridge.

Several forest service campgrounds with a total of 178 tent/trailer spaces and fourteen tent sites are situated along the fifteen miles to Prospect junction. They include Rogue River Farewell Bend, Union Creek, Abbott Creek, Natural Bridge, River Bridge, and Mill Creek.

If you're traveling north, Prospect represents the last gas for forty-three miles and signals the beginning of the tree-lined corridor, which extends beyond Diamond Lake. The Prospect Ranger Station issues backcountry permits, maps, and trail information. Mammoth Pines, five miles north of town, offers a pleasant walk on a marked nature trail identifying trees and plants of the Rogue River National Forest. To see more spectacular waterfalls surrounded by forest scenery and volcanic rock take Mill Creek Drive to the Avenue of the Boulders, Mill Creek, and Barrfalls.

South of Prospect, with the highway paralleling the Rogue River and descending a high plateau, you leave the snow zone and travel by llama farms, horse, cattle, and sheep ranches. After about six miles, triangular Lost Creek Reservoir fills a forested canyon. It is an idyllic spot for boating, trout and steelhead fishing. Casey State Park offers picnicking, boating and lake fishing. At Joseph P. Steward State Park, you'll find 151 electrical and fifty tent sites, plus a restaurant, marina, and a six mile bike trail. More than five miles of hiking paths include connections to the Pacific Crest Trail.

At Shady Cove, population 1,418, Rogue Elk County Park also provides tent and trailer camping. It is a popular departure point for river rafters, boaters, and anglers anxious to try the Rogue's renowned trout and steelhead fishing. Nearby, the historic Rogue Elk hotel was built in 1916, and its guests included luminaries such as Zane Grey and Herbert Hoover.

South of town, the drive concludes on Highway 234. On the eighteen miles to Gold Hill, you cross Sams Valley and pass near Tou Velle State Park, which is a day use facility with fishing and a boat ramp on the banks of the Rogue River. During the last few miles, the flat topped mesas of the Table Rocks frame the western horizon.

48 ONTARIO, LAKE OWYHEE, VALE LOOP

General description: A 102-mile-round trip through a variety of agri-business fields along an Oregon Trail route to a rugged canyon and scenic lake.

Special attractions: Oregon Trail route, ruts, and campsites; Colorful rock formations; Lake Owyhee, rock hounding water skiing, boating, fishing.

Location: Eastern Oregon between Ontario, Lake Owyhee and Vale.

Drive route names and numbers: Oregon Highway 201, U.S. highways 26/20, Lyle Boulevard.

Travel season: Routes are open all year. Lake Owyhee Resort usually closes between mid-December through mid-March.

Camping: One state park campground with full hookups and primitive sites.

Services: All services in Ontario. Limited services in Nyssa and Vale.

Nearby attractions: Wild and Scenic Lake Owyhee River, Succor Creek Canyon, Leslie Gulch, Bully Creek Reservoir, Farewell Bend State Park.

For more information: Ontario Chamber of Commerce/Visitor and Convention Bureau, 88 S.W. 3rd Ave., Ontario, OR 97914, (541) 889-8012. Nyssa Chamber of Commerce and Agriculture, 14 S 3rd St., Nyssa, OR 97913, (541) 372-3091. Vale Chamber of Commerce, P.O. Box 661, 275 N. Main St., Vale, OR 97918. (541) 473-3800.

The drive: Starting in Ontario, the drive begins by traveling through rich agricultural lands then weaves through a rocky canyon and climbs a bit as it approaches Lake Owyhee. A rim drive around the lake's eastern shore offers spectacular views of the lake surrounded by steep, colorful cliffs. Returning through the canyon, the drive follows the route of the Oregon Trail north into dry rolling hills described by a pioneer as "a barren, God forsaken country, fit for nothing but to receive the foot prints of the savage and his universal associate the coyote." From Vale back to Ontario, the route cuts through more of the 300,000 acres of desert that have been transformed by irrigation into fields producing seventy-eight diversified crops.

Summer temperatures average from 74 to 84 degrees, but can reach into the 100s. Winters range from the low teens to an average between thirty-seven and forty-seven degrees. Spring days are in the pleasant low sixties and autumn averages between sixty-two and seventy-four degrees. Ontario is situated near the confluence of five rivers. All major highways entering Oregon from the east, north, and south, converge in or near Ontario. An abundant water supply and strategic location have made it Oregon's second largest agricultural area and an important transportation center.

Highway 201 extends south from Ontario for about three miles, then becomes U.S. highways 26/20. On the seven miles to Nyssa, you'll receive a quick course in crop identification as roadside signs identify fields of wheat, sugar beets, onions, tomatoes, cabbage, sweet corn, potatoes, and bean seed. The varied crops attract wildlife, and you also have a good chance of seeing

48 ONTARIO, LAKE OWYHEE, VALE LOOP

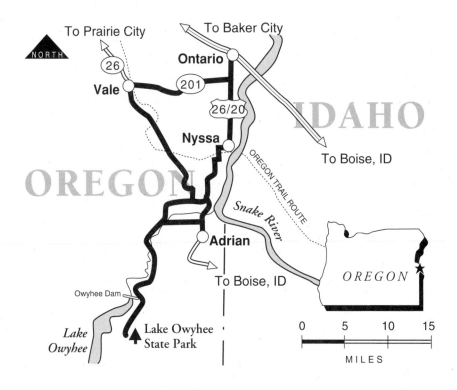

deer, pheasant, and other animals enjoying a quick snack.

Many of the underlying rocks in this area were laid down as sediments between fifteen and twenty million years ago when basalt flows dammed streams and created a large lake which extended as far east as Boise. The sediments make excellent soil for growing a variety of vegetables.

Nyssa is an agricultural community with a White Satin Sugar processing plant. From Nyssa you take Highway 201 southwest through fields of clover seed, potatoes, onions, flax, and coreopisis flowers.

At mile marker 5, the route crosses the Oregon Trail. Look east from the historical marker, and you will see the point where wagon trains forded the Snake River and entered Oregon. A grange hall, near the marker, sits on the trail, which parallels the highway for a few miles before angling northwest.

Nine miles west, the route leaves the flat farm lands and weaves between steep, multi-hued cliffs and the narrow Owyhee River. Green poplars and cottonwoods and lush marsh grasses, sometimes frequented by geese, herons and cranes, offer a pleasant, peaceful contrast to the brilliant reds and twisted, rolling hills, and mountains.

During the next ten miles, panoramas of rocks sitting precariously atop ridges, hills, and bluffs spread out in front of you and converge at the

Colorful rock formations surround the highway to and from Lake Owyhee.

canyon's base. Small meadows of silvery sagebrush, and dry washes fan out from cliff palisades, and brush-covered buttes. Rocks and bluffs, pale yellow near the canyon's beginning, change to russet, bright red, chocolate brown, mauve, and pink.

The striking colors are a combination of volcanic basalts and sedimentary rocks. Although basalts are usually black, ironoxides released as the stone weathers and erodes have turned many in this area to rust and browns. The colors indicate to geologists that the climate was very hot and wet when the lava flowed into the area about twelve million years ago.

A narrow rock tunnel opens into a wide field framed by red and pink cliffs. The highway climbs a grade overlooking the river, crosses Owyhee Dam and hugs cliffs midway between the lake below and the ridge tops above.

The mountains, lake, river, and dam were named after two Hawaiians who were killed by Indians in 1819. An intricate system of tunnels, ditches, and pipes delivers water from the dam to more than 118,000 acres of crop, livestock, and dairy lands. When full, the 525-foot-high structure holds back 1.12 million-acre feet of water, forming a fifty-three-mile long lake with 310 miles of shoreline.

Although considered one of the most overstocked and underfished lakes in America, it attracts largemouth and smallmouth bass tournaments throughout the summer. You'll also find it a reliable fishery for crappie, perch, and catfish. With waters reaching eighty-five degrees in summer, this is a favorite spot for sunbathing, water skiing, and boating.

The canyon surrounding the lake contains virtually every color of the rainbow. Along the shore are pinnacles and spires, steep cliffs, and alluvial fans coming down to the water's edge, outcroppings hundreds of feet high extending into the lake and natural caves carved in cliff sides. While the steep, rocky terrain makes hiking difficult, rockhounds searching for thunder eggs and agates are often rewarded for their efforts.

Virtually all of the lake's fifty-three miles can be explored by boat. The wild and scenic section of the river, which feeds the lake, has a reputation for providing white water river running thrills. In fall, this region is open to hunting for ducks, geese, chukar, quail, mule deer, antelope, and bighorn sheep.

The pavement ends five miles south of the dam at Lake Owyhee Resort. It rents seven cabins and eleven motel rooms. The marina accommodates boats up to twenty-eight feet. Other facilities include a lounge, bar, fishing supplies, and boat rentals.

Lake Owyhee State Park, two miles from the entrance, features ten sites with electricity, and thirty tent sites. They are arranged on terraced levels, so every camper has an unobstructed view of the lake.

From Lake Owyhee, you retrace the last twenty-four miles through the magnificent canyon. Because of the jumbled land scape and winding road, the views traveling east are significantly different than what you saw coming into the canyon. You may wish to take advantage of numerous wide spots and pullouts for photographs.

Turning north on Lyle Boulevard, the route follows the Oregon Trail fifteen miles into Vale. Most of the rolling hills covered with brown grass, sage and scrub brush, are administered by the Bureau of Land Management and leased to local ranchers for grazing. About six miles south of town, you cross Keeney Pass, a gently rolling hill which did not pose a challenge even for wagon trains. BLM information boards highlight Indian conflicts along the trail, costs, and amounts of clothing needed for the journey, types of wagons, and the role of mules and oxen. You can see the original trail ruts from the information center; a short trail leads to the ruts and over the hill.

Vale, with about 1,700 people, is an agri-business center with fertilizer blending plants, a grain elevator, several feedlots, and Oregon's top-volume livestock sales barn. Sites linked to the Oregon Trail include an emigrant grave and a marker on the courthouse lawn placed by Ezra Meeker, who led a wagon train west in 1845 and retraced the route in 1906. A stone house, used as a trail way station and shelter during conflicts with Native Americans, is on the National Register of Historic Places.

Malheur Crossing, situated on U.S. highways 26/20 on the eastern edge of town, was a major Oregon Trail campsite. From the river banks on cool days, you can see steam rising as hot springs empty into the stream. Most wagon trains spent their first night in Oregon here and used the hot water for bathing and washing clothes.

The crossing was also the departure point for a famous lost wagon train and one of Oregon's most enduring legends. In 1845, a train of 200 people, led by Steven Meek, left the main trail and headed west through the Oregon desert to the Willamette Valley. Several died from lack of food and water when they became lost and wandered for several months through a maze of canyons, dry washes, and mountains. Surviving members claimed to have discovered a gold mine, which they named the Blue Bucket. Although the mine has never been found, the story precipitated a gold rush and the ultimate settling of Malheur County.

About six miles east of Vale, Malheur Butte rises above the mint and seed fields. A dirt side road extends from U.S. highways 26/20 to its base; undeveloped trails lead to the summit. The butte is the neck of an extinct volcano and was used as a lookout by Native Americans who scouted wagon trains passing by to the west. The rich soils in surrounding fields were deposited as lake sediments between three and ten million years ago. Fossil leaves found in underlying rocks include avocado and other plants that grow only in a very wet, humid climate, indications that this was once a tropical setting.

South of the highway, approximately three miles east of the Butte, you'll see Oregon State University's Malheur Experiment Station. It researches weed control and an assortment of locally produced vegetables to increase yields and improve crop strains.

After turning north on Highway 201, the drive concludes back in Ontario.

49 LAKE COUNTY-KLAMATH COUNTY LOOP

General description: A 245-mile signed loop through forested mountains, high desert, and rimrock hills.

Special attractions: Klamath Forest National Wildlife Refuge, Fort Rock, Summer Lake Wildlife Area, Abert Rim, Reservoir Lakes, two national forests, Collier Memorial State Park, Winter recreation, fishing, hunting, hang gliding.

Location: Southeastern Oregon between La Pine, Chiloquin, and Lakeview.

Drive route names and numbers: U.S. Highway 97, Silver Lake Highway (County Road 676), Oregon Highway 31, U.S. Highway 395, Oregon Highway 140, Sprague River Highway (County Road 402).

Travel season: Routes are open all year. Some side roads are not plowed in winter.

Camping: One state park campground with full hookups; One national forest service campground along route and several within five to fifteen miles of route with tables, fire rings, flush and vault toilets. Some with drinking water. Several private RV parks along the route.

Services: All services in Chiloquin and Lakeview. Limited services in Silver Lake, Summer Lake, Paisley, Bly, Beatty, Sprague River.

Nearby attractions: Christmas Valley, Hole-In-The-Ground, Crack-In-The-Ground, Lost Forest, Warner Ski Area, Goose Lake Recreation Area, Gearhart Mountain Wilderness, Upper Klamath Lake, Crater Lake National Park.

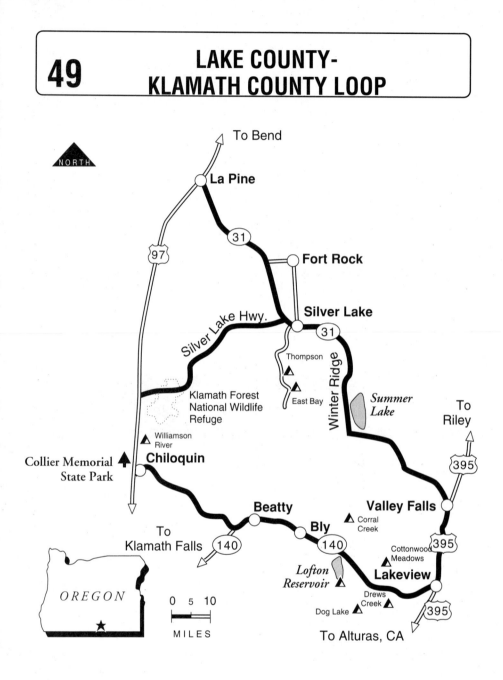

For more information: Central Oregon Visitors Association, 63085 N. Hwy. 97, No.104, Bend, OR 97701, (541) 328-8334, (800) 800-8334. Lake County Chamber of Commerce, 126 North E St., Lakeview OR 97630, (541) 947-6040. Fremont National Forest, 524 North G St., Lakeview, OR 97630, (541) 947-2151. Bly Ranger District, Box 25, Bly OR 97622, (541) 353-2427; Paisley Ranger District, P.O. Box 67, Paisley, OR 97636, (541) 943-3114; Silver Lake Ranger District, P.O. Box 129, Silver Lake, OR 97638, (541) 576-2107. Winema

Fort Rock, a giant natural amphitheater, is the rim of a volcano that formed under an ancient lake bed.

National Forest, 2519 Dahlia, Klamath Falls, OR 97601, (541) 883-6714. Chiloquin District Ranger, 38500 Hwy, 97 N., Chiloquin, OR 97624. (541) 783-4001.

The drive: From U.S. Highway 97, the drive can be joined in Chiloquin or about twenty miles north at the Silver Lake Highway. If you are driving from Bend, take Oregon Highway 31 one mile south of La Pine and start the route at Silver Lake. This adds sixty miles to the tour but takes you through the Deschutes National Forest and within eight miles of Fort Rock and Hole-In-The-Ground. You can also start from U.S. Highway 395 at Valley Falls or Lakeview.

While elevations range from 4,000 to over 5,500 feet, most roads are flat and straight, with gradual climbs and long curves. From its beginnings on the Silver Lake Highway, the route travels through farmland and marshes, into forested mountains and by buttes, then descends to sagebrush and grasslands near Silver Lake. Between Silver Lake and Valley Falls, it roughly follows John C. Fremont's route by staying on lowlands in the shadow of Winter Rim while traveling by desert, dead lakes, and huge corporate cattle ranches. The return west from Lakeview is through sparse forests in high mountain passes, pasturelands, and thick forest near Chiloquin.

In 1843, John C. Fremont noted the extremes in temperature and topography when he wrote that his expedition was snowbound on a ridge while the desert below was bathed in summer sunshine. He named the ridge Winter Rim and the area below Summer Lake. Generally, the high altitude brings warm but not unbearably hot summers, ranging from an average sixty-seven degrees in Lakeview to the mid-eighties for the region. Winters average in the high thirties but often fall below freezing. Average temperatures in spring are about sixty degrees and sixty-seven in autumn.

Traveling east from U.S. Highway 97 on the forty-one-mile long Silver

Lake Highway, the drive begins with the mashes and bullrushes of Klamath Forest National Wildlife Refuge, which is an important nesting area for ducks and geese. Continuing east, the road climbs into the mountains and the 1,100,000-acre Winema National Forest while passing cinder pits, buttes, and meadows.

Numerous unpaved forest service roads branch off the main highway for access to fishing, mountain hiking, and snowmobiling. Jackson Creek Campground, fifteen miles east of the refuge and five miles southeast on Forest Road 49, offers twelve tent trailer sites in a secluded forested setting at 4,500 feet. Watch for antelope, elk, and mule deer as the highway crosses into the 1.2-million-acre Fremont National Forest and descends from high ridges to Bear and Antelope meadows.

After joining Highway 31, the route moves south to Silver Lake. The "lake" is a dry basin that fills with water about once every thirty years.

A gravel road connects Silver Lake with Fort Rock State Park, seventeen miles north, where an ancient volcano wall rises 325 feet above the plain. It formed when molten rock burst through a prehistoric lake bed and solidified into a giant circular rim. Over time, the south face was eroded away leaving a giant horseshoe-shaped amphitheater. Trails lead into it.

Other sites nearby include: Fort Rock Cave, an important archaeological site, where excavated artifacts indicated this area was inhabited at least 9,000 years ago; Hole-In-The-Ground, a volcanic crater one mile across and 300 feet deep; and Crack-in-the-Ground, a narrow two-mile-long, seventy-foot-deep chasm.

Duncan Reservoir, five miles south of Silver Lake, generally produces good stocked rainbow trout fishing. April and May are the best fishing months at Thompson Reservoir, eighteen miles south, as it usually runs dry during summer. Silver Creek flows out of the reservoir and is a redband wild trout fishery. The forest service's Thompson and East Bay campgrounds total thirty-two sites with drinking water and boat ramps. Check with Silver Lake Ranger Station for road conditions, fishing, and wildlife areas.

The fifty miles south to Paisley begins with vast expanses of sage and juniper desert framed by buttes and ridges. After thirteen miles, the road makes a gentle climb over Picture Rock Pass. At the 4,830-foot summit, a short trail takes you west from the pullout to a rock wall decorated with ancient Indian petroglyphs. The viewpoint affords a sweeping view of Ana Reservoir and Summer Lake in the desert below with Winter Rim (also called Winter Ridge) fault block towering 3,000 feet above them. Ana Reservoir, fed by large freshwater springs, is one of the area's better rainbow trout lakes. White-striped hybrid bass grow fat feeding on tui chubs; the bass were introduced to control the chubs. An informal campground includes vault toilets and drinking water.

Summer Lake, with a store, cafe, RV park, cabin rentals, and a bed and breakfast, sits between its namesake and Winter Ridge. A wayside with restrooms commemorates the Fremont Expedition, which camped here on December 16, 1843, and included Kit Carson and Tom Fitzpatrick as scouts and guides. Their reports encouraged others to migrate to the Oregon Country.

Spring Creek at Collier Memorial State Park is a productive trout stream in a picturesque setting.

At Summer Lake Wildlife Area, near the wayside, 18,000 acres of marsh, pot holes, and dry brush land provide breeding and resting areas for Pacific flyway birds. You may see Lewis Woodpeckers, larks, black terns, Franklin gulls, trumpeter swans, owls, kingfishers, tundra swans, curlews, and cranes. In autumn, parts of the refuge open for duck and geese hunting.

The road continues south between Winter Ridge and twenty-mile-long Summer Lake. With a high alkali content and a depth of four to five feet, Summer Lake is too shallow for boating, contains no fish, and sometimes dries up completely during summer. A picturesque, classic one-room schoolhouse is situated west of the highway about four miles south of town. Slide Mountain Geologic Area, at Winter Rim's southern end, is a remnant of a dome-shaped volcano. Thousands of years ago, the entire north face collapsed, exposing the interior, and leaving a huge pile of debris at its base.

Summer Lake Hot Springs, 5.7 miles north of Paisley, overlooks the lake and caters to campers with nine no-hookup sites and a 15x30-foot enclosed pool fed by hot springs. Day use is not encouraged, and there is a one-hour limit on swimming.

At Paisley the route makes the first of several crossings of the rainbow trout-stocked Chewaucan River. The community includes a trailer park, motel, air strip, and public shooting range. Ten buildings in the Paisley Ranger Station compound were built by the Civilian Conservation Corps in 1938-39 and are on the National Register of Historic Places.

Continuing southeast, you'll cross land owned or leased by the ZX Ranch. It is the Northwest's largest ranch and includes more than 1.4 million acres of private and government permit land. On the twenty-two miles to Valley Falls, the highway cuts through sagebrush-covered rolling hills and mesas that change during the day from browns to a variety of blues and dark yellows.

Highway 31 ends at Valley Falls where you'll find a general store and RV park. Looking east from the store, you can see Abert Rim, named by Fremont for one of his party. The thirty-mile long fault escarpment rises 2,000 feet above the desert floor and is topped with a sheer 800-foot lava cover. Forest service and Bureau of Land Management personnel have installed facilities at the southern end to accommodate increasing numbers of hang gliders who use it for launchings.

Taking U.S. Highway 395 south, the route passes Chandler Station Ranch, which is preserved with turn-of-the-century furnishings. Nearby, Chandler Wayside State Park provides a refreshing break with picnic tables by a small stream.

Reaching a junction with Highway 140, which heads east to Warner Mountain Ski Area and Hart Mountain National Antelope Refuge, U.S. Highway 395 merges with Highway 140 West. They remain a joint route for the six miles to Lakeview.

Oregon's only geyser sits alongside the highway one mile north of town and across the road from Fremont National Forest Ranger Station. Part of a resort complex with a motel and two hot spring-fed pools, Old Perpetual traditionally shot sixty feet into the air every ninety seconds. By the 1990s, watchers were sometimes waiting more than half an hour as droughts and drilling had altered the schedule.

At 4,800 feet, Lakeview bills itself as Oregon's tallest town. The buttes, mountains, and faults surrounding flatlands, and often perfect wind conditions attract hang glider flyers from throughout the nation.

As Highway 140 leaves Lakeview by climbing Tunnel Hill summit at 4,863 feet, side roads lead five and eighteen miles south to Little Cottonwood and Drews Reservoir. Cottonwood is home to a variety of fish, including eastern brook and rainbow trout. Two forest service campgrounds offer twenty-one sites near hiking trails and boat ramps. Cast your line in Drews Reservoir and the rewards are uncertain. You may land bullheads, crappie, and trout, or a ten-pound channel catfish. Drews Creek Campground features four family units and two group sites.

During the next twenty miles, the drive dips into the Drews Valley, reenters Fremont National Forest, climbs Drews Gap at 5,306 feet, then reaches its highest point of 5,504 feet at Quartz Mountain Pass. A network of cross-country ski and snowmobile trails that range from three to twenty-one miles in length start near the summit. Other popular snowmobile routes begin at Cottonwood Meadows, twenty-four miles west of Lakeview, and end in Drews Valley. Cottonwood Meadows, eight miles north of Highway 140, via Forest Road 3870, includes a twenty-four-unit family campground, boating facilities, fishing for stocked rainbows, and three trailheads into the surrounding area.

Other side roads head south nine miles to Lofton Reservoir Recreation

Area, and north seventeen miles to Corral Campground and the Gearhart Mountain Wilderness.

In addition to a seventeen-unit forest service campground in a scenic lake and woodland setting, Lofton features fishing for stocked rainbow trout, electric motor boating, and a good chance of seeing deer, elk, muskrat, and bald eagles. As the name implies, horses are allowed at Corral Creek where you camp in five tent-trailer sites. Fishing the Sprague River, photographing deer and elk, and hiking into the 22,823-acre Gearhart Mountain Wilderness are camp-based activities.

The wilderness centerpiece is Gearhart Mountain, a broad sloping network of ridges, glaciers, and streams topped by craggy cliffs. Elevations range from 5,900 feet at Corral Creek to 8,364 feet at the summit. The Chewaucan and north and south forks of the Sprague River originate in the wilderness.

After Quartz Mountain, the scenery opens to plateau meadows, ringed with ponderosa and lodgepole pines, isolated islands of trees, and distant high, round dry-grass-covered mountains. Fremont Forest Sprague River Picnic Area, eight miles west, provides a perfect spot for enjoying the scenery while swimming and fishing the Sprague River for German brown and rainbow trout.

Bly Ranger Station, four miles west, exhibits Civilian Conservation Corps stonework and rustic architecture. Eight structures, built between 1936 and 1942, are on the National Register of Historic Places.

West of Bly, the drive continues on top of the plateau as it follows the Sprague River thirteen miles to Beatty. Turning northwest onto Sprague River Road, the scene changes from sparse forest with a sagebrush and dry grass ground cover to nine miles of farmlands with grazing cattle ringed by distant low mountain slopes. After the community of Sprague River, the route follows the river through a picturesque gorge, and reenters the Winema National Forest. At Chiloquin, it turns north onto U.S. Highway 97.

Five miles north, Collier Memorial State Park straddles the highway. A campground with fifty full hookups and eighteen tent sites sits on the bank of the Williamson River. The west side day-use area in a tall ponderosa forest offers relocated pioneer cabins with artifacts and an extensive collection of historic logging equipment ranging from high wheel skidders to locomotives. A 0.5-mile nature trail winds through the village and along rippling Spring Creek, which is known for its trout fishing.

Watch for deer as U.S. Highway 97 heads north through the thick forest. Thunder Beast Park, ten miles north of Collier, delights children with its display of twelve life-sized prehistoric animals. A few miles beyond, the drive reaches its conclusion as it passes the entrance to the Silver Lake Highway.

General description: A 161-mile loop through Malheur Wildlife Refuge and the Diamond Craters Outstanding Natural Area.

Special attractions: Malheur National Wildlife Refuge, Diamond Craters Outstanding Natural Area, Frenchglen Hotel, Peter French P Ranch and Round Barns, Harney Lake, Malheur Lake, wildlife, rock formations, historic sites.

Location: Eastern Oregon between Burns and Frenchglen.

Drive route names and numbers: Oregon Highway 78, Oregon Highway 205, Center Patrol Road, Harney County Roads.

Travel season: Routes are open all year. Flooding often necessitates detours and gravel road route changes. Check with Wildlife headquarters on road conditions. While there is wildlife at Malheur all year, migrations are greatest in late March, September, and October.

Camping: No campgrounds on the route. Bureau of Land Management maintains three campgrounds from four to eighteen miles southeast of Frenchglen on the Steens Mountain access road.

Services: All services in Burns. Limited services at Malheur Field Station, Frenchglen, Diamond, Princeton, Crane, Lawen.

Nearby attractions: Steens Mountain, Kiger Gorge, Wild and Scenic Donner Und Blitzen River, Alvord Desert.

For more information: Harney County Chamber of Commerce, 18 West D St., Burns, OR 97720, (541) 573-2636. Malheur National Wildlife Refuge, HC-72, Box 245, Princeton, OR 97721, (541) 493-2612. Malheur Field Station, HC-72, Box 260, Princeton, OR 97721, (541) 493-2629. Frenchglen Hotel, Frenchglen, OR 97736, (541) 575-2773. U.S. Bureau of Land Management, HC-74, 12533 Highway 20 West, Hines, OR 97738. (541) 573-4400.

The drive: Malheur Wildlife Refuge is situated in southeastern Oregon's high desert country. Although the elevation is 4,100 feet, the roads are flat and straight. Throughout the drive, the scenery is a mixture of alkali flats, rimrocks, and sagebrush covered hills, with the distant Steens Mountain on the southern horizon. Along the roadside you'll see extensive marshes, meadows, and riparian areas. While Highway 205, Diamond Lane, and Highway 78 are paved, prime wildlife viewing areas are on long stretches of gravel; side roads into Diamond Craters are dirt.

Be prepared for extremes in temperatures. Freezing is common from September through May. Summers zoom into the 90s and over 100 degrees. If you visit during summer, bring mosquito repellent and drinking water. In autumn temperatures average about sixty-seven degrees.

From Burns, the route heads southeast for two miles on Oregon Highway 78 then turns south on Oregon Highway 205. After cutting through nine miles of flat hay fields, it climbs a ridge rimmed with columnar basalt and enters 185,000-acre Malheur National Wildlife Refuge. Established in 1908 by president Theodore Roosevelt, the refuge extends south for more than forty miles and preserves several lakes, marshes, numerous ponds, and hills as a migratory bird sanctuary. A total of 287 species of birds and fifty-eight mammals have been seen here.

From a summit viewpoint on the ridge, which fans out like a tilted table top, your panoramic view encompasses vast expanses of flat desert sagebrush and bunch grass, the thin line of highway, and gently rolling hills. The land and rimrocks were formed about 2.9 million years ago, when a volcanic vent erupted near what is now the town of Burns. Pumice and volcanic ash covered approximately 7,000 square miles in a layer thirty to 130 feet thick.

About twelve miles south, you cross the Narrows, a thin strip of land that separates Malheur Lake, east of the highway, and Harney and Mud lakes on the west. A side road leads west seven miles to Harney Lake. During the early 1980s, three years of heavy snow packs flooded the basin, turning the lakes into one huge inland sea, covering 180,000 acres, and creating Oregon's largest natural lake. Dry years followed, and the waters returned to their original basins. The rising and ebbing waters created new islands and uncovered ancient Indian burial grounds, campsites, artifacts, and gem-quality agates. But collecting organic materials and artifacts is prohibited.

A side trip to Malheur Wildlife Headquarters, six miles east of the highway on a partially paved and rough gravel road, is virtually a must. The refuge issues birding hot-spot tip sheets and checklists. A museum displays approximately 200 mounted local birds, and a 0.4-mile trail to an overlook presents a good view of the Blitzen River Valley, Malheur Lake, and distant Steens Mountain. Various trees and shrubs attract warblers and other birds.

If you decide to continue on paved Highway 205 during the next fifteen miles, you will climb more low ridges—some framed by columñar basalt and rimrocks—pass cattle grazing areas, and possibly see cranes, ducks, and scattered wildlife in roadside marshes.

Graveled Center Patrol Road, which begins at the mid-point of the headquarter's access road and parallels Highway 205 and the Donner und Blitzen River, offers a slower pace and a better chance of seeing wildlife. The river was named by an 1864 calvary company. After enduring a thunderstorm here, they named one channel Dunder and another Blitzen, German for thunder and lightning. Later the name was Anglicized to Donner. The river is often simply called Blitzen.

Center Patrol Road, starts with Malheur Field Station, which provides hostel and dormitory facilities to individuals and educational groups, and Wright's Pond, a Canada geese and redhead duck nesting area. Topping a low hill, the road continues south through hay fields and marshlands. Beaver dams, which sometimes interfere with water flow and must be removed, may be seen near stands of riverbank willows. Rattlesnake Butte, a lava-shaped cinder cone, east of the highway, was a major Native American campsite. The area south of it was homesteaded in the 1880s. You may see deer and ducks feeding on hay and seeds in this area.

50 MALHEUR WILDLIFE REFUGE, DIAMOND CRATERS

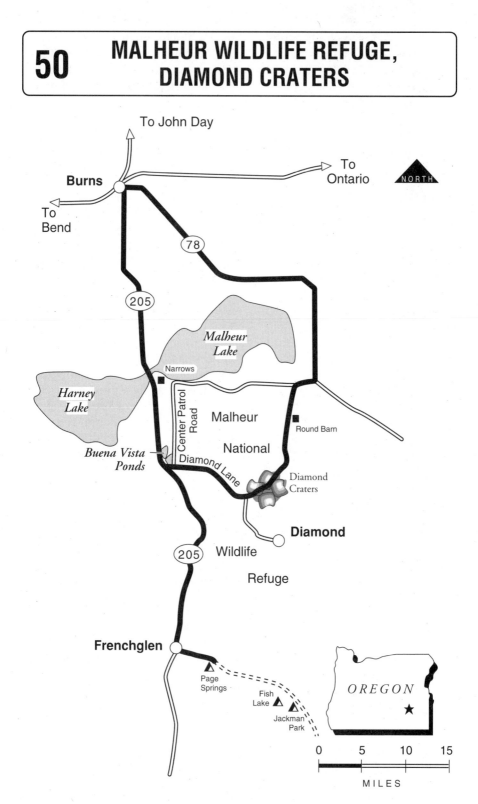

To John Day

Burns

To Ontario

NORTH

To Bend

78

205

Malheur Lake

Narrows

Harney Lake

Center Patrol Road

Malheur

Round Barn

National

Buena Vista Ponds

Diamond Lane

Diamond Craters

Diamond

205

Wildlife

Refuge

Frenchglen

Page Springs

Fish Lake

Jackman Park

OREGON

0   5   10   15

MILES

The Frenchglen Hotel, built in 1914, is administered by Oregon State Parks and has rooms and food available during the summer travel season.

Buena Vista Ponds, accessible by a connecting road to Highway 205, are spring and summer nesting areas for Trumpeter Swans, a summer stop for white pelicans, great blue herons, and egrets, and a staging site for mid-November migrating waterfowl. A dike separates the ponds and divides the area into nesting and feeding sections for cranes, ducks, geese, blackbirds, and other birds that also use the ponds. A viewpoint on a lichen-covered, steep bluff offers an overview of the ponds with Steens Mountain in the background.

Rejoining Highway 205, the route passes through grazing land with horse corrals, juniper and sage-covered hills, and a canyon with striking columnar basalt walls. At roadside pullouts, take time to scan the columns slowly. You may see mud swallow nests, wood rats, and the threatened prairie falcon. Golden eagles and bobcats, which usually prowl under cover of darkness, also inhabit the rimrocks.

On the four miles of dirt road east to Krumbo Reservoir, take time to search out fading Indian petroglyphs, or rock carvings, made centuries ago. At the lake, surrounded by juniper-covered hills, you can fish from boat or shore for trout, warm-water bass, and crappie.

At Benson Pond, a mile south of Krumbo's access road, cottonwood trees shade mirror smooth water. The area offers a good chance of seeing mule deer, coyotes, great-horned owls, orioles, and an assortment of ducks.

Frenchglen, ten miles south, has gas, a general store, and private campground. The Frenchglen Hotel, built in 1914, is an Oregon State Parks site. Operated by a concessionaire, it offers eight rooms and meals.

From Frenchglen a rough dirt road heads east up and around Steens Mountain, a rugged thirty-mile long fault block with glacier carved, hanging valleys, spectacular gorges, and alpine lakes. It should not be attempted with long trailers or low-clearance vehicles. Heavy duty, four-wheel drives are best for this route.

The first four miles to BLM's Page Springs Campground, are easily passable by any vehicle. The campground has thirty sites with water and pit toilets. P Ranch Barn, two miles east of Frenchglen on this road, represents the last remnants of the cattle empire of Peter French. Before he was killed by a competitor in 1897, French's land totaled 132,000 acres and included most of the wildlife refuge. The site contains the chimney of his ranch house, several willow fences, and the barn, which was built in 1876. Sandhill cranes, Canada geese, red-tailed hawks and roosting wild turkeys are often seen here.

From the Ranch at the refuge's southern boundary, you can return by a gravel road along the Donner und Blitzen Canal and several ponds, or retrace Highway 205 north seventeen miles to Diamond Lane.

Diamond Lane (Harney County Road 409) crosses the Blitzen River, and meanders east to Diamond Junction through six miles of hay fields, alkali flats, and sage-covered flatlands sandwiched between graceful sloping buttes. The community of Diamond, six miles east on a dirt loop road, dates to the 1870s, and at its peak, had a population of about fifty people. Services include a store and a hotel, built in 1898.

Turning north on Harney County Road 404 (Lava Beds Road), the route enters the Diamond Craters Outstudy Natural Area. The black craters were formed sometime during the last 25,000 years when molten basalt surfaced through cracks in the earth and spread in a thin layer over a dry lake bed. Before the first layer cooled, more molten rock was interjected beneath the hardening but pliable surface, forcing the crust upward and creating six structural domes. The area, 4,150 to 4,700 feet above sea level, has been described by geologists as "a museum of basaltic volcanism" containing the "best and most diverse basaltic volcanic features in the United States."

During the next fifteen miles as the route passes through lava flows, you'll see pressure ridges, shield volcanos, lava tubes, trenches, collapsed craters and calderas, natural bridges, spatter cones, ramparts and ridges, driblet spires, small box- shaped grabens, and volcanic maars, which have filled with water and become small ponds and lakes. If you decide to hike into the lava fields, proceed carefully, for the rock texture varies from smooth to wrinkled, ropy and billowy. Rocks, from pebbles to room-sized boulders that were hurled into the air during eruptions, are everywhere. Park your vehicle only on hard-packed road surfaces, or you may become stuck in lose cinder, volcanic ash, and clay.

Three miles north of Diamond Craters, Peter French's Round Barn sits in grand isolation on a flat plain of sagebrush. It was built around 1880 and used for breaking and exercising horses in winter. The conical roof is supported by juniper centerposts, braces, and poles. It encloses a stone corral sixty feet in diameter and a track between the corral and outside wall.

The fifty-mile return to Burns passes through farmlands covered with hay and roadside marshes where you can sometimes see deer foraging in the tall grass. After exiting the Wildlife Refuge, the route takes Highway 78 through Princeton, Crane and Lawen—small communities, each with a store, gas, and a few residences. Crystal Crane Hot Springs, about midway, is a health resort with six hot tubs, a naturally heated outdoor swimming pool, and space for RVs and camping. Low hills on distant horizons frame the flat fields leading northwest to Burns.

ABOUT THE AUTHOR

Tom Barr grew up in Grants Pass, Oregon. While attending college, he spent several summers on the Oregon Coast working at radio stations and newspapers. After graduating from the University of Oregon, he lived in Portland where he wrote and edited guidebooks for a tour wholesaler who operated transcontinental motor coach tours throughout the continental United States, Canada, and Alaska.

He has traveled extensively throughout Oregon on assignments for Reader's Digest Books *(Off the Beaten Path, On The Road USA)*, Fodor's Travel Guides, Northwest Mileposts, and Rotarian Magazine. He is also the author of *Unique Arizona, Unique Georgia,* and *Unique Washington: A Guide To The State's Quirks, Charisma, and Character*, and has written the text for two photo books titled *Portrait of Oregon* and *Portrait of Washington*.

Tom Barr lives in Marysville, Washington.

get FALCON GUIDED

FALCON GUIDES ® are available for where-to-go hiking, mountain biking, rock climbing, walking, scenic driving, fishing, rockhounding, paddling, birding, wildlife viewing, and camping. We also have FalconGuides on essential outdoor skills and subjects and field identification. The following titles are currently available, but this list grows every year. For a free catalog with a complete list of titles, call FALCON toll-free at 1-800-582-2665.

SCENIC DRIVING GUIDES

Scenic Driving Alaska and the Yukon
Scenic Driving Arizona
Scenic Driving the Beartooth Highway
Scenic Driving California
Scenic Driving Colorado
Scenic Driving Florida
Scenic Driving Georgia
Scenic Driving Hawaii
Scenic Driving Idaho
Scenic Driving Michigan
Scenic Driving Minnesota
Scenic Driving Montana
Scenic Driving New England
Scenic Driving New Mexico
Scenic Driving North Carolina
Scenic Driving Oregon
Scenic Driving the Ozarks including the
 Ouchita Mountains
Scenic Driving Texas
Scenic Driving Utah
Scenic Driving Washington
Scenic Driving Wisconsin
Scenic Driving Wyoming
Back Country Byways
National Forest Scenic Byways
National Forest Scenic Byways II

HISTORIC TRAIL GUIDES

Traveling California's Gold Rush Country
Traveler's Guide to the Lewis & Clark Trail
Traveling the Oregon Trail
Traveler's Guide to the Pony Express Trail

WILDLIFE VIEWING GUIDES

Alaska Wildlife Viewing Guide
Arizona Wildlife Viewing Guide
California Wildlife Viewing Guide
Colorado Wildlife Viewing Guide
Florida Wildlife Viewing Guide
Idaho Wildlife Viewing Guide
Indiana Wildlife Vewing Guide
Iowa Wildlife Viewing Guide
Kentucky Wildlife Viewing Guide
Massachusetts Wildlife Viewing Guide
Montana Wildlife Viewing Guide
Nebraska Wildlife Viewing Guide
Nevada Wildlife Viewing Guide
New Hampshire Wildlife Viewing Guide
New Jersey Wildlife Viewing Guide
New Mexico Wildlife Viewing Guide
New York Wildlife Viewing Guide
North Carolina Wildlife Viewing Guide
North Dakota Wildlife Viewing Guide
Ohio Wildlife Viewing Guide
Oregon Wildlife Viewing Guide
Tennessee Wildlife Viewing Guide
Texas Wildlife Viewing Guide
Utah Wildlife Viewing Guide
Vermont Wildlife Viewing Guide
Virginia Wildlife Viewing Guide
Washington Wildlife Viewing Guide
West Virginia Wildlife Viewing Guide
Wisconsin Wildlife Viewing Guide

■ *To order any of these books, check with your local bookseller
or call FALCON® at **1-800-582-2665**.*

Visit us on the world wide web at:
www.falconguide.com

FALCON®